College Football and American Culture in the Cold War Era

SPORT AND SOCIETY

Series Editors
Benjamin G. Rader
Randy Roberts

A list of books in the series appears at the end of this book.

College Football and American Culture in the Cold War Era

Kurt Edward Kemper

University of Illinois Press
Urbana, Chicago, and Springfield

C 5 4 3 2 1
∞ This book is printed on acid-free paper.

Library of Congress Cataloging-in-Publication Data
Kemper, Kurt Edward.
College football and American culture in the
Cold War era / Kurt Edward Kemper.
p. cm.
Includes bibliographical references and index.
ISBN 978-0-252-03466-4 (cloth : alk. paper)
1. Football—United States—History—20th century.
2. College sports—United States—History—20th century.
3. Sports in popular culture—History—20th century.
4. Cold War.
5. United States—Politics and government—20th century.
6. United States—Social life and customs—20th century.
I. Title.
GV951.K46 2009
796.332'630973—dc22 2008047505

In memory of Wilma Poplawski,
a season ticket-holder to the end;

and

For my parents,
Letha and Don,
who made me a "fanatical and articulate apostle"
for public education, social justice, and college football;

and for Robin,
who made me everything else decent

Contents

Acknowledgments

Charles Phillips, who gave me one of my first jobs as a writer, once wrote that "books too, have stories." This one began a long time ago as a graduate paper in Bob Sutton's seminar on Western history at George Mason University. From there it morphed into a conference paper at the 1996 annual meeting of the Western Historical Association. With the exception of a brief cameo in my dissertation, it lay dormant for several years before evolving yet again into an article in the *Journal of Sport History*, before it finally flowered into the work before you. Throughout those years, I have incurred incalculable debts, for which the brief mention that follows is damn poor compensation but will have to suffice until I can come up with something more substantive. Any scholarly work that has, in any way, a connection to south Louisiana usually makes the obligatory *Streetcar* reference; and I too, like Blanche Dubois, have relied upon the kindness of strangers.

My first level of research was always the university archives on the campuses of the schools that lay at the heart of my narrative. At UCLA, Charlotte Brown and Kathy Lo helped me track down missing footnotes, wayward documents, and back issues of the student newspaper. Dennis Bitterlich, although no longer at UCLA, seemed to be able to lay his hands on virtually anything regarding the history of that institution and, most importantly, give the researcher the confidence that nothing was being overlooked or forgotten. Without Dennis, this book never would have been started, and at any point in the future when we find ourselves together, he doesn't ever pay for drinks again. Ditto for Tamar Chute at Ohio State, who not only cheerfully filled the usual research requests but also suggested documents I would never have found otherwise, most notably the journals that included the writings of Jack Fullen. In addition to the usual poor compensation offered academic archivists, Tamar must also bear the burden of being a Wolverine behind enemy lines in Columbus, and for that, she is deserving of combat pay. I must also give special thanks to Kevin Leonard at the Northwestern University Archives who, after returning a strange phone call to the local YMCA where I was staying, managed to pull out a small trove of material late on a Friday afternoon in the time it took for me to take the Purple Line out to Evanston. At no time was the maxim "Good things come in small packages" more true than on that Friday afternoon, because the materials that Kevin found for me included Tug Wilson's fantastic 1958 conspiracy memo on the Rose Bowl. I received able assistance at the University of Alabama from Merrily Jensen, who was kind enough to re-pull every single box I had examined when my photocopies did not contain full citation information. I also found valuable material in the files of university archives at LSU.

In addition to the various university archives in which I worked, I also found valuable assistance at other research repositories, both in and out of academia. Laura Lyons McLemore and Teresa Rice offered great help in accessing two crucial paper collections in Special Collections at LSU Shreveport; Karen Carver helped me find what I needed in the David King Papers at the University of Utah; Kevin Cauley tracked down material for me at the Archives of the University of Notre Dame; Laura Koser found material for me at the South Carolina Historical Society; Jenny Mulowney and David Kessler facilitated my research at the Bancroft Library at the University of California; and Wayne Weber aided me at the Billy Graham Archives on the campus of Wheaton College. Taylor Watson virtually gave me the run of the Bear Bryant Museum in Tuscaloosa, not only letting me look though material that had not even been processed yet but also letting me tag along on a lunch date that included Clem Gryska. You have not truly experienced Alabama football until you've had a chance to listen to stories from Coach Gryska. Lian Partlow and Laura Verlak at the Pasadena Historical Society helped me track down material from the Tournament of Roses Association from the period. An often overlooked, underused, and certainly underappreciated resource is community libraries, and I had the pleasure of working in two of the better ones in the Birmingham Public Library and the Pasadena Public Library. I received first-class assistance from Jim Baggett in Birmingham and Denise Mendez, Jean Penn, and Eileen Penson in Pasadena. Ellen Summers at the NCAA Library also helpfully tracked down material for me. Alan Aldrich and Stephen Johnson at the University of South Dakota helped me locate both the classified and unclassified transcripts of the Senate McCarthy hearings.

Deserving of their own paragraph are the interlibrary loan staffs of the two institutions at which I was employed while I wrote this book. Claire Wilson of River Parishes Community College, with no budget or mandate to aid faculty research, managed to get her hands on everything I asked for, including microfilm collections. Likewise, Muriel Schamber and Joan Olson at the I. D. Weeks Library at the University of South Dakota filled countless and, I'm sure at times, strange requests for materials for me. They, too, ably adapted to a situation for which they were not given the resources, filling my requests even though I was on a satellite campus and finding ever inventive ways to get the materials delivered to me.

In so many ways, this book is a culmination of my development as a historian, and I have incurred many intellectual debts along the way as a result. Robert Johnson and Steven R. Ward were early influences who taught me to love the past and find mystery in it. Michael Lanza, who unfortunately did not live to see the publication of this work, was a teacher of the first order and shaped virtually everything I know about the black experience in America. He always reminded me that American history was "a struggle to reconcile what is with what ought to be." His death makes the profession much poorer, and the annual meeting of the Southern Historical Association a hell of a lot less fun. I miss him tremendously. Bill Martin gave me my first academic job, for which I will always be grateful, as well as a much-appreciated teaching reduction that facilitated work on this book. A colleague, a mentor, and a historian, his friendship made my brief teaching experience at the community college level that much more enjoyable. He provided what every writer needs at some point, which is encouragement, and the belief that the project was valuable. Like so many in these pages, his continued support fills me with gratitude and humility.

Several scholars offered me valuable insight, encouragement, and general assistance. First and foremost, Chuck Shindo literally did everything possible to aid this book. Chuck willingly took me in as a grad student refugee with a reputation as damaged goods, for which I will never be able to repay him. From there, he proved to be a mentor of the first tier, offering criticism with encouragement, always challenging me to see "the layers of history." In addition, he also provided occasional employment as an outgrowth of our mutual fascination with old houses, a place to stay when I had occasion to come back to Baton Rouge for additional research, and cold beer on demand. Chuck has read more versions of this manuscript in more forms than anyone except myself, each time patiently prodding me to make it better. Everything you need to know about Chuck's selflessness is that in addition to seemingly always putting my work before his, he willingly directed my dissertation on UCLA even though he went to USC. Fight On, Chuck! Also at LSU, Gaines Foster helped my development as a scholar and a professional historian; he also read versions of chapters 5 (several times) and 4, offering valuable comments on each. Gaines, I hope you finally find in my work "a sense of nuance and subtlety"; if not, it is no fault of yours.

Andy Doyle and Tim Bryant served as valuable sounding boards on the South and southern football particularly. Both also gave me access to some of their own research, and Tim read drafts of chapters 2 through 4. Kevin Allen

Leonard offered valuable comments on chapter 5 and generally served as an able advisor to my queries regarding Western historiography. Charles Martin has never failed to answer patiently my incessant questions regarding the intersection of race and sports, encouraging me since we first met when I was a graduate student attending the Southern Historical Association's annual meeting; John Thelin and Rebecca Lowen allowed me to bounce off of them my impressions of Cold War higher education; Murray Sperber also offered his thoughts on my project at an early stage and helped me locate materials at Notre Dame; David Chappell helped me cherry-pick football references out of collections he had worked in; Greta de Jong graciously provided me with the FBI file of the Southern Gentlemen organization; Richard Armitage offered some much needed clarifications to chapter 2; Christine Riedel, formerly of the *Michigan Daily* and *WashingtonPost.com*, helped me interpret the vagaries of collegiate media.

Robert Hilderbrand, of whom I had the pleasure, fifteen years apart, of being both student and colleague at the University of South Dakota, was one of the first to read the entire manuscript. Bob provided what every unedited manuscript requires: a laserlike eye for bad grammar, poor constructions, and overinflated assertions of excitable assistant professors. His suggestions and corrections made the manuscript much clearer; his enthusiasm and support made the process that much more enjoyable. For both, I am grateful.

Greg Hospodor has been a friend and a colleague since our days as graduate students at LSU. I had the immense good fortune to have Greg assigned to give me my campus tour when I was considering graduate schools, and we slogged through the oftentimes difficult and alienating process of graduate study together, forming our own little two-man dissertation writing group. Greg first heard of this project as we stood in line for student season football tickets outside Tiger Stadium and has remained an enthusiastic supporter ever since, reading several drafts of what became chapter 5. Besides being an outstanding classroom teacher, he constantly took me to school on the basketball court of married student housing in our regular games of H-O-R-S-E whenever we took a break from writing our dissertations. In paraphrasing Sherman's description of his friendship with Grant, Greg stood by me when everyone thought I wasn't any good, and I stood by him when everyone thought he was crazy.

Throughout the years, I have received able assistance outside of an academic setting in learning to think critically about college football and its role in American higher education and American culture. At various points in the past twenty years, I have become indebted to Dave Fehrs, Trent Dlugosh, Andrew McMichael, Steve Black, and Greg Hospodor for their insights, humor, sarcasm, and cynicism regarding college football. The six of us are bound by two unshakable faiths: 1) college football is better than pro football; and 2) Notre Dame is the antichrist. Though I seldom understood the long-term value of our conversations (largely because they often occurred in front of a television and included beer), they too, have shaped this book for the better.

At the University of Illinois Press, Bill Regier was an early and solid supporter of the project, even when the first reviews revealed that the manuscript still had a long way to go. In addition to being a fine editor, he has been immensely patient with me as a first-time author. I am also grateful to the two anonymous readers who forced me to refine and reshape the manuscript (not always in ways that I thought best at the time!). Their suggestions made the manuscript much stronger and more scholarly valuable.

Financially, I have received varied, if limited, monetary assistance. I had the great fortune to be invited to participate in the National Endowment for the Humanities–funded seminar Sport and American Society, cosponsored by the Chicago Historical Society and Northeastern Illinois University, ably directed by Patrick Miller and Steven Riess. Not only did the seminar allow me to live in Chicago for the summer amidst some of the great libraries of American academia, but it also helped sharpen my thinking about the book and think seriously about what my story meant, as opposed merely to what it said. The endowment is vital to funding scholarship across the humanities realm and I am grateful for its financial assistance. I also benefited tremendously from the one-on-one interaction with both Patrick and Steven, brilliant scholars in their own right who willingly set aside their own work to help me refine mine. As a graduate student, the Graduate School at LSU offered some assistance for a trip to California. At the University of South Dakota, I was generously aided by funds from the Office of Graduate Research, which facilitated my trip to Tuscaloosa. I also received monies from the Weaver Fund in the Department of History and general departmental discretionary funds, which helped me get to Columbus and offset other research costs. I would be remiss if I did not also mention Matt Moen, my dean in the College of Arts and Sciences while I was at USD. He helped arrange not only a teaching reduction in consecutive semesters at a crucial stage in my writing but also a shuffling of my teaching responsibilities, allowing me to teach courses with direct bearing on my writing, at a not insignificant consequence to his own budget. Everybody should have a dean like Matt, who makes it his job to allow us to do ours. I am immensely thankful.

Perhaps most importantly, I have had the constant support and assistance of my family. My sister, Kathleen Thompson, and my grandmother,

Wilma Poplawski, paid for my first trip to Los Angeles that allowed me to determine that UCLA students really did threaten to boycott the Rose Bowl. Unfortunately, Wilma died at the age of 91 just as this book was coming to press. Though a college football fan late in life, the week before she died she was in her seat at the Rose Bowl as UCLA upset Tennessee. She was larger than life and her absence leaves an unfillable void. Both of my parents offered me varying combinations of food, lodging, and employment on a second, extended research trip to Los Angeles, and my mother served as an able research assistant, tracking down loose ends for me in both Westwood and Pasadena. More generally, my parents inadvertently bred and cultivated my religious-like devotion to college football at a young age and have continued to nurture it long after I left home. Fall Saturdays at the Los Angeles Memorial Coliseum and the Rose Bowl are some of my favorite memories of growing up. My brother, Scott, whom I refer to as the Rainmaker, has been my constant long-distance phone companion, patiently listening to me recount seemingly every book I read and every document I found in the course of my research. His voracious consumption of online news made him a font of obscure news references and unknown Internet resources relative to the project. He remains my best friend and, along with Robin, my most trusted advisor. My children, Nicholas and Madeleine, were born during the middle stages of this project and most assuredly delayed the publication of this book, but just as assuredly, made it better as well. The time spent fulfilling my parental obligations pushed back the completion of this book, forcing me to think about it in a much more sophisticated way than if I had completed it several years earlier. Anyone who has ever had kids knows that occasions like sleeping with the light off for the first time or learning to ride a bicycle require little more than a parent's comforting presence. I developed whole sections of this book in my head while sitting quietly at the foot of my children's bed, walking around the block behind their tricycle, or rocking them to sleep in the middle of the night. For assistance on the book, I am thankful; for their love and support, I am forever in their debt.

Historians always thank their spouses last in their acknowledgments, which is stupid, but no one has ever accused me of being original or intelligent, so I too will thank the most important person last. My wife, Robin, likes neither historians nor college football, yet somehow managed to end up with me; it's one of many reasons I'm certain I ended up with the better end of the deal. Because of her, not only does the book that you are holding exist, but as I look back on my life with Robin, I am now a reasonably happy person with only a few bad days, instead of the other way around. These are better days.

College Football and American Culture in the Cold War Era

Introduction

On January 1, 1962, the University of Minnesota handily beat UCLA in the forty-sixth Rose Bowl game, a game that was regarded by most everyone who witnessed it as dull. That year's Tournament of Roses marked a few firsts, including the first repeat appearance by a team from the Big Ten Conference, with Minnesota having played the University of Washington the previous year; the first match-up between two black quarterbacks, the Gophers' Sandy Stephens and the Bruins' Bobby Smith; and perhaps the first black woman to appear in the Rose Parade in the form of UCLA student Pearl Robinson.[1] The specific events of that year's Tournament of Roses, however, masked a larger tension within the world of college football and, ultimately, the United States as a whole. Although the game itself says little about America during the postwar years, the selection process that brought Minnesota and UCLA to Pasadena is revelatory of a persistent anxiety within American society that helped shape a distinct postwar culture. The various local controversies sparked by the game's selection process not only revealed the ascendance of football in the American postwar sporting culture but also its role as a primary purveyor of American values and character. Thus, the game's significance had little to do with who played in it or who won it; instead, its importance lay in the process that led up to it and in what it revealed about American culture and society during the Cold War era.

This book attempts to explain the parameters and constructs in which Americans interpreted not merely the events surrounding the selection process of the 1962 Rose Bowl but also the culture of the Cold War period itself. The Cold War era witnessed a host of anxieties on the part of many Americans, including the unending confrontation with the Soviets, the specter of nuclear weapons, changing racial and sexual relations, and a general concern about the consequences of national technical superiority and material abundance. In the face of such anxieties, Americans sought out cultural institutions that reinforced their sense of national identity and held at bay their nagging insecurities. As a result, Americans utilized football as a cultural mechanism to rationalize changes they sometimes found alienating, to magnify American distinctiveness in the face of Soviet gains, and to vilify that which they found to be outside the bounds of respectability. They understood football as a broad, though varied, embodiment of national values. Like the larger Cold War culture of which it was a part, the meaning of football in the postwar years ranged across contemporary issues and in its relationship to regional values. Americans fit their assumptions of community, individualism, masculinity, exceptionalism, and race, among others, alongside—and sometimes apart from—the larger national cultural force of anticommunism and American exceptionalism.

The selection process of the 1962 Rose Bowl serves as a window to a variety of college communities and the ways in which followers of those schools' football teams used the game as a nexus through which they negotiated and interpreted postwar American society. In contrast to the local varieties of football's meaning, the game appeared on a national level as one of many proxies for Americanism. The reactionary nature of Cold War American society witnessed established elites searching for tools to bolster existing institutions and repress iconoclasm and dissent. As a result, in the years following World War II, presidents, congressmen, academics, and popular observers ascribed to football its Cold War–era meaning. These individuals positioned the game as representative of a laudable America, and they found in football a cultural force that not only embodied a national distinctiveness and patriotism but also toughness, discipline, self-deprivation, and other values deemed crucial to confront the Soviet challenge. Football was not alone during this period in its manipulation by others to defend the status quo. What is distinctive, however, is the ability of those forces—throughout the political, social, and cultural spectrum—to put football to their own service. Dissenters, critics, and iconoclasts, too, used football as a common touchstone to illustrate problems in American society, demonstrating football's flexibility to be used as a tool of both reaction and progress.

Accepting such sweeping validations of football, Americans applied the game in broad strokes to define an American way of life. The various schools involved in the selection process for the 1962 Rose Bowl witnessed this elevated cultural prominence of football. Though interested parties at each school utilized the meaning of football differently, they all accepted football as a cultural institution imbued with celebrated American values, illustrative of Americans' need for national validation. At Ohio State, both supporters and opponents of a Rose Bowl invitation placed the issue within the context of Cold War service; at Louisiana State and the University of Alabama, a potential Rose Bowl invitation forced observers to grapple with the consequences of their exclusion from a national sporting culture as a result of segregation; and at UCLA, students used the opportunity of the Rose Bowl to hold up football as an exemplary contrast to un-American restrictions on civil liberties and civil rights. Thus, the events of the 1962 Rose Bowl selection process revealed how Americans used football to determine what was American and what was not.

These events revealed an anxiety over the meaning of national values and lifestyles, over the very meaning of America itself; and it was this anxiety that informed football's postwar cultural meaning. Following World War II, college football mirrored emerging patterns in American society and the economy. As a result, when Americans looked at college football in the postwar years, they found the same trend toward increased costs, decreasing competition, production tied to technological advancement, and an increase in rational efficiency that other aspects of American life witnessed during the period. In this regard, however, the postwar form of big-time college football was only a continuation of processes initiated decades earlier, some as far back as the 1890s. Its distinctiveness during the period came from the manner in which Americans put the game to use as a cultural prism through which to interpret the rapidly changing domestic landscape of Cold War–era America. As a result, the postwar years did not change football so much as Americans used football to explain the changes of America during the period. In this regard, although the interpretation of football varied tremendously during the period, its overall meaning as a cultural touchstone remained consistent.[2]

What allowed football to achieve such standing was the general assumption on the part of so many during the period that football came to represent the essence of America. In the broadest context, Americans waged the Cold War to assert the supremacy of a vague and often changing notion of "the American Way of Life." The American Way of Life, to be sure, included capitalism, democracy, and notions of religious liberty. Just as assuredly, though, it also included more varied manifestations in which Americans felt they saw their own distinctiveness and superiority demonstrated. Without examining such assumptions very deeply, Americans enshrined football as a repository for a broad range of values and regional identities. The clearest statement of the game as a manifestation of a generic American Way of Life came in the late 1950s from Arthur "Tonto" Coleman, former athletic director at Louisiana State University and later commissioner of the Southeastern Conference. In a passage entitled "What Is Football?" Coleman described the game as "a great American tradition," embodying "physical prowess" and team orientation aimed at victory, all of which made it representative of "the

American Way of Life." The game, according to Coleman, was "rugged . . . almost brutal, for men only. . . . It was gallantry personified, the closest thing to gladiatorial combat" allowed in a civilized society like the United States. Representative of a distinctly "American spirit," football "has absolutely no hold on foreigners." Here was the cultural boilerplate of postwar football, full of generally reinforcing and completely inoffensive assumptions that attached to the game a rugged, manly, national exceptionalism at a time when Americans fervently desired such cultural validation.[3]

In this regard, football demonstrated the function of culture during the Cold War for so many Americans. While overt messages of anticommunism overflowed from films like *I Married a Communist* and novels such as those in Mickey Spillane's *Mike Hammer* series, they masked a deeper message that illustrated Americans' need to find something distinctive and reinforcing about American life. It was not enough to oppose communism; a vibrant American culture during the time needed to espouse what was right about America, ultimately to convince Americans in the face of their anxiety that the country would prevail in its struggle with the Soviets, overcome its potentially destructive social heterogeneity, and keep its abundance and superiority from enslaving its people. In this regard, institutions imbued with notions of American distinctiveness and representative of the American Way of Life were undeniably manifestations of Cold War culture. As a result, when Americans used football to interpret and rationalize events of the period, it marked an example of Cold War culture even when events themselves were not an outgrowth of the political, diplomatic, and military struggle of the Cold War. Put more simply, the culture of the Cold War interpreted far more than the Cold War itself.

Few aspects of American life illustrated this better than race. Perhaps no other issue so troubled Americans of every social and political persuasion as that of the struggle for racial equality, in large measure because it was so intertwined with their most fundamental assumptions of the meaning of America. On occasion, race emerged in explicit Cold War political contexts, as when southerners labeled the civil rights movement a communist conspiracy or when the Soviets criticized segregation as evidence of American hypocrisy. More often, however, Americans approached the question of race in a Cold War frame of reference apart from such political connotations. When they interpreted race through the prism of Cold War cultural institutions such as football, the discussion did not reveal Americans' understanding of linkages between race and the Cold War so much as it illustrated race as an issue that challenged Americans' consensual understandings of their own superiority and unity. In this regard, race in the context of football was about how Americans saw themselves more than anything else.

Although scholars have exhaustively examined the Cold War's effects on domestic politics, society, and the economy, less is understood, and with far less agreement, about the culture of the period. The relatively consensual commitment on the part of most Americans to the Cold War accompanied a period of intense anxiety. This anxiety stemmed from numerous factors ranging from fear of nuclear annihilation to realizations that combating communism often led to restrictions of basic American values such as free speech and association. The Cold War also witnessed an intense popular scrutiny of varied social institutions and customs, from marriage to segregation to religion. Indeed, one scholar has argued that the Cold War "infiltrated" the "lives and psyches" of Americans, pointing to the tremendous increase during the period of church attendance, the skyrocketing consumption of an expanding pharmacopeia, and the broad expansion of mental health services.[4] Thus, while most Americans committed themselves to the cause of anticommunism, they maintained nagging insecurities about where such efforts might lead or what changes those efforts imposed upon themselves and American society alike.

The role of sport as a manifestation of Cold War culture has remained largely unexamined by academic scholars. Surveys of the role of sport in American life since 1945 consistently address the major social issues of the period—most notably race, economic change, and social atomization—and see them as evidence of the evolution of the commercialized sporting spectacle.[5] Such works generally see games and sports historically serving as an escapist cultural form. Following World War II, however, in the words of one such interpretation, "Sports had become a national obsession."[6] Seldom are such conclusions identified as the result of any specific historical circumstances, implying that such a development was an inevitable outgrowth of a postmodern consumer-oriented society. Though this scholarship examines the Olympics and international sport, a Cold War context is largely absent in these works as a force upon the domestic American sporting culture. Sport, according to these works, is at best a benign cultural institution and at worst a decaying institution stripped of its joy and socially contributory roles.[7] As a result, sports scholars of the period have resisted interpreting sport as a cultural manifestation of the anxieties of the Cold War era. Thus, the development of sports during the period following World War II appears detached from other cultural forms and is thus minimized in significance. For these authors, sport as a cultural force is little more than commercialized escapism that, while certainly shaped by larger forces such as desegregation and economic growth, is independent of an American culture that girded itself in the face of a host of national insecurities.

If sports scholars have largely ignored the culture of the Cold War, scholars of Cold War culture have largely ignored sports. Traditional cultural interpretations of the Cold War, particularly those that attempt to explain the social upheaval of the 1960s, see the preceding period as conformist, repressive, and monolithic. More sophisticated interpretations have seen greater nuance in the period but still identify Cold War culture as a singular phenomena.[8] The more astute of such works generally accept an America beset with anxiety from both within and without, creating reflexive assumptions that, consciously or not, shaped much of American cultural life. They focus overwhelmingly on cultural texts, which is to say, they interpret the Cold War themes of films, books, television, and even arcade games, while too often ignoring the cultural values that caused Americans to embrace such cultural forms in the first place. In this regard, scholars fail to see in sport specific historical circumstances unique to the Cold War experience that might allow them to interpret sports as a form of Cold War culture. Thus, existing literature universally accepts the increasing competitiveness of postwar American life and the unparalleled appeal of commercialized sports while also acknowledging the pervasive role of the Cold War in American culture—but fails to suggest any interrelationship between the two.

This book claims that Americans crafted and embraced a culture during the Cold War era aimed at convincing themselves of their own distinctiveness based on values and characteristics associated with football. To understand the origins of postwar football's meaning, however, one has to start long before the selection process of the 1962 Rose Bowl, or even the Cold War itself. You have to go all the way back to World War II and the role of service football in first linking the values of football with the defense of the Republic. It is there that the story of postwar football begins.

Prologue: The Game the War Made

On November 29, 1941, virtually all of official Washington journeyed north to Philadelphia to watch the annual football contest between the U.S. Military Academy at West Point and the U.S. Naval Academy in Annapolis. No national championships hung in the balance, yet the game had been sold out for months and another two thousand unanswered requests for tickets piled up on the floor of Philadelphia's Municipal Stadium. Fans from out of town arrived on one of forty-two special locomotives that the Pennsylvania Railroad scheduled for the event, while those left without tickets could still pay two dollars to watch the game at remote pay-per-view locations in the city. Among the almost 100,000 fans enjoying the game and the unusually mild weather sat the First Lady and almost the entire cabinet. Only President Roosevelt and Secretary of State Cordell Hull stayed away, the former on his way to Warm Springs, Georgia, while the latter remained in Washington attending to urgent diplomacy with the Japanese. The Army-Navy game always maintained a big-game feel, particularly on the East Coast, but this game came at a time when the world faced a crisis of global proportions. On the day of the game, the *Philadelphia Sun* noted, "There probably never was a time when interest in the game was greater than it is today, the international situation being as it is, the eyes of the nation being on its young men in the military and naval academies." The players that day, almost to a man, would surely soon be engaged in pursuits with far deadlier consequences. This game, more than its predecessors, entailed a sense of tragic, yet inevitable, significance. When Army and Navy played each other in November 1941, almost everyone in attendance understood they were watching more than a game. It would be one of the last college football games before America's entry into World War II, and the cultural significance of football would never be the same.[1]

The Military and Naval academies embraced football at the end of the nineteenth century like most other colleges and universities then in existence. Ironically, while most supporters of athletics in the United States at the end of the nineteenth century identified sports with ideological constructs, it was not until the fitness run-up to World War I and its aftermath that the academies placed special emphasis on competitive athletics. Following the war, the Army appointed General Douglas MacArthur as the superintendent at West Point, and he began a concerted effort to integrate the role of sports into the academy's tactical training. MacArthur was convinced that competitive athletics bred good combat officers, and no sport served that function better than football. To cement the message, he ordered inscribed on the campus's athletic building one of his own maxims: "On the fields of friendly strife are sown the seeds that on other days and other fields will bear the fruits of victory." Far more than fitness, competitive team sports—and football in particular—taught lessons of sacrifice, self-denial, and unit cohesion. For MacArthur and many others within the American military establishment, the values of football not only made for victorious warriors but also for virtuous Americans.[2]

The arrival of World War II provided an opportunity to demonstrate such a relationship, and both the military and society in general largely accepted the connection. Not only did the war strengthen existing cultural assumptions about the benefits of football, it also provided a set of circumstances that changed the direction of the game and elevated its cultural significance.

The Japanese attack on Pearl Harbor conveniently came at the end of the 1941 season, allowing the stewards of college football nine months to reconcile prewar assumptions of the game with the wartime realities of male enlistments, draft call-ups, travel restrictions, and, at least on the West Coast, fears that a large crowd sitting in a stadium offered easy bombing targets to the enemy. Many observers, both within and without the sport, viewed the continuation of college football during the war as crucial. President Roosevelt declared that the continuation of such civilian diversions was good for home-front morale and reminded the troops of what they were fighting for. As such, enterprises like major league baseball and college football appeared patriotic by continuing operations. More directly, many argued that football, unlike baseball, actively aided the war effort because of the values and conditions of the game. University of Wisconsin head coach Harry Stuhldreher, one of Notre Dame's famed Four Horsemen, claimed that by continuing to play the game, college football assisted the training process and eventually the war effort itself. The "stamina, teamwork, and coordination football men are getting on the gridiron will help make them better soldiers."[3] Perhaps the most explicit link between the values and lessons of football and the process of war came from professional coach Jimmy Conzelman about the change in thinking forced by the war. College football players found a different world upon graduation in 1942, according to Conzelman.

"They have been taught to build. Now they must learn to destroy." He noted the "reprehensible" nature of war and the difficulty of "inculcating a will to destroy. . . . Democracy makes us a pacific people. The young man must be toughened not only physically but mentally. He must be accustomed to violence. Football . . .," according to Conzelman, "teaches that after all there isn't anything so terrifying about a punch in the puss."[4]

By the start of the 1942 season, the NCAA approved two crucial, and supposedly temporary, rules changes to address the problem of fewer players and, in particular, skilled players. For the first time in the modern era, the NCAA allowed freshmen to play with the varsity, and it abandoned substitution rules that barred a player from returning to the game after his removal in favor of far more relaxed substitution rules, known as two-platoon football. These rules, however, could do little to affect the reality of wartime manpower needs, and by 1943 many college programs suspended their football operations.[5] For defenders of the game and those charged with maintaining the war effort, suspension of play was simply unacceptable. Even before the start of the 1942 season, General Robert Eichelberger, commander of the Army's First Corps, wrote to Colonel Earl "Red" Blaik, head coach at West Point, to stress the tremendous importance the game played in the war effort. "I want to emphasize that competitive athletics in our schools and colleges simply cannot be allowed to fall by the wayside if we are to go through to a win against the Axis."[6] Viewing the decline of civilian wartime football with alarm, *New Orleans Item* editor Fred Digby labeled those who claimed football could not continue under wartime circumstances as "softies who would kill football and competitive sports" in exchange for a less expensive, and less competitively valuable, program of intramurals. Digby did not equivocate on the meaning of such circumstances, labeling an intramural program stressing fitness akin to the nineteenth-century nationalist German Turnverein, implying that opposition to football was treasonous.[7] Near the war's end, naval Commander William R. Kane, echoing Stuhldreher's prewar comments, wrote an article for the 1945 NCAA *Official Football Guide* titled "Football Pays Off," in which he declared that the same qualities that made excellent football players—namely, toughness, aggressiveness, coordination, and discipline—also made outstanding naval aviators.[8] Even the advertising industry recycled this message, as in a 1943 ad for Chesterfield cigarettes with a football player and airman positioned under MacArthur's "friendly strife" quote.[9] As the United States found itself embroiled in combat on two fronts, prevailing popular assumptions argued that football was crucial to military victory.

Quite apart from concerns arising from the decline of civilian wartime football, the military had already begun developing a program that would inadvertently give the game a tremendous boost both during and after the war. As early as October 1941, military planners proposed utilizing "the average American's interest in sport as a means of aiding in the development of an efficient fighting force."[10] The military embraced sports in World War II just as it had in the previous European conflict. Unlike its reliance on civilian aid agencies in World War I, however, the military took full and complete responsibility for the provision of equipment, facilities, and qualified personnel. Army and Navy Special Service Officers (SSO) developed a broad-based, multipurposed sporting program for the troops to provide diversionary activities, overall fitness, an avenue for teaching competitive instincts, and a culture of masculinity that enabled men to go into combat assured of their manly capacities. Service football, in varying forms, sprang up virtually everywhere as part of the SSO programs. When equipment and personnel allowed, the military provided full-scale tackle football; in locales where lack of manpower prohibited the full-scale game, the troops played six- and seven-man football; in countless other postings lacking equipment or formal structure, they played a rough-and-tumble version of touch football. In every form, though, authorities sanctioned the game as a purveyor of manliness, competence, and deprivation required of military personnel. One service coach during the war declared, "Football is not a game for sissies and any man who is afraid of getting hurt or going through some vigorous training periods need not come out for the team."[11]

By 1943, SSOs developed a series of "bowl games" on American bases throughout the world designed to replicate all the trappings of the collegiate spectacle. These games featured bands, cheerleaders, pregame parades, and, in at least one instance, a bowl queen. Following tradition, they were held during the holiday season, mostly on New Year's Day, though at least one was scheduled for Christmas. These games took a cue from their commercial home-front predecessors by taking their names from local identifying characteristics. Thus, a base in Hawai'i hosted the January 1, 1945, Poi Bowl, while the troops played the Lily Bowl in Bermuda; the Spaghetti Bowl in Florence, Italy; the Mustard Bowl in Dijon, France; and the Champagne Bowl in French wine country. Fans, servicemen, and military leaders made sure these games were competitive and well received. More than 25,000 paid to watch the Poi Bowl, and Notre Dame was invited to play a service all-star team in the January 1944 Arab Bowl in Oran, Algeria. Even critics of big-time service football who complained that placing such importance on the game took away from more direct combat training acknowledged that "football is an excellent conditioner and one of the best competitive sports in any physical training program."[12] Thus, at every level, service football enjoyed tremendous support; but played at its highest level, wartime football was intended to have great meaning, so that the participants and observers felt "that they were engaged in an important and necessary demonstration of American life."[13]

Military planners designed this broad-based sports program to build upon the participatory, fitness model that the military utilized during World War I. However, at least some within the United States saw sports, especially football, as an effective training regimen as well. Jack Kelly, special assistant to President Roosevelt, noted that "we need battleships and planes and guns to win this war but above all we need strong tough men to operate them." Both the Navy and the Marine Corps felt those tough men could come from the ranks of football. One commentator noted that recruiters found future tough aggressive Marine officers when they "combed college football squads to find 'combative types.'"[14] The belief that football bred such traits informed a naval advisory committee charged with crafting a training regimen for the Navy's fighter pilots. The committee itself had a distinctive college flavor to it: six of the nine committee members came from the ranks of intercollegiate athletics, including a conference commissioner, four athletic directors, and a head football coach. With the precedent of popular support from World War I and the legacy of football as a bulwark against the enemies of the Republic, this group recommended that football serve as the cornerstone of the Navy Aeronautic V-5 Preflight Schools, commonly referred to as V-5. As such, the Navy named Lt. Cmdr. Thomas J. Hamilton, himself a former college football player and recently head coach at the Naval Academy, to create the training regimen for V-5. Hamilton's program abandoned traditional methods of drill that required rigid responses to standard circumstances, stressing instead the individual's reliance on initiative and innovation. Specifically, Hamilton's program believed that sports like football helped pilots "develop characteristics in stimulus and response that were transferable to combat conditions." By keeping the men together in combat units after training, V-5 used football "to generate desirable psychological attitudes and group loyalties." Every trainee was required to learn the fundamentals of the game and play it on a daily basis. Though the program used as many as nine different sports, football remained the program's cornerstone. In an effort to teach trainees that there was "no substitute for victory" and that "gracious defeat [should] be forgotten," V-5 games were designed for maximum aggression and contact, with rules being tweaked not only to allow but also to encourage those outlets.[15]

Hamilton's proposal was not met without criticism, however. Former heavyweight boxing champion Gene Tunney, who served during the war as director of physical training for the Navy, rejected the notion that playing football somehow prepared American men for combat: "If professional athleticism could win a war, we would have won this one by now." Tunney instead argued for the importance of general fitness for war service. Army Air Corps generals Henry "Hap" Arnold and Ira Eaker agreed with Tunney, rejecting the notion that "a football player is more likely to possess the flying requisites than the tennis player or the track man." The generals argued that "no definite set of physical characteristics can be tabbed" as indicative of combat success. Tunney, Arnold, and Eaker dismissed claims that football experience correlated to combat success. Hamilton's proposal, however, argued that such criticisms did not account for the toughness engendered by the game.[16]

Beginning in May 1942, Hamilton created five preflight training centers scattered throughout the country, with each center containing a varsity squad. Amazingly, though they were unregulated by the NCAA, the NCAA allowed V-5 programs to compete against college teams, and by the end of the war, virtually every major college program played, and usually lost to, a V-5 team. In bolstering scheduling and enjoying its exemption from military travel restrictions, V-5 teams tremendously aided, albeit on a small scale, the continuation of civilian college football.[17] The program in effect subsidized college football and led many to claim that it "saved college football" during the war. This perception, as well as the value of the V-5 program to the war effort, led the Association of Football Writers of America to name Hamilton its "Man of the Year" in 1942. For years afterward, defenders of the game and sportswriters would laud Hamilton as the man who "saved football" during the war.[18] But the influence of V-5 went much deeper in affecting the future of football. In addition to the more than 80,000 trainees who went through the program, it also caused the instructors who put the program into place to redefine standards of coaching. After the war, many of these instructors, such as Woodrow "Woody" Hayes at Ohio State; Paul "Bear" Bryant at Alabama; Paul Brown at Ohio; Don Faurot at Missouri; Madison "Matty" Bell at SMU; Jim Tatum at Maryland; Bud Wilkinson at Oklahoma; and George Halas in the professional ranks crafted Hall of Fame careers using V-5 methodologies. As a result, coaches who attempted to emulate these legendary figures after the war unknowingly embraced V-5 methodologies. The influences of V-5 even extended into the high school ranks when the program published and distributed its instructional manuals to high school coaches and initiated a series of coaching clinics for high school coaches.[19]

At war's end, V-5 personnel formed the V-Five Association of America to bring the training regimen and ethic of wartime sacrifice to postwar sports. To that end, the association published annual directories "to foster and directly support" the promotion of football and other V-5 activities.[20] Thus, by the end of the war, military elites imbued the game with a high-minded ideological justification, a justification that many felt was validated with victory over the Axis powers in 1945. One scholar of the period has gone so far as to suggest that the unconditional surrender won in the war carried over to winning attitudes of football.[21] Such assumptions allowed football to enjoy an unprecedented postwar boom. In 1945, 220 schools fielded college football teams, and the following year, the number jumped to almost 650.[22] The termination of the war did not end its effects on college football, however, which the game continued to feel for years. Two totally unrelated decisions helped facilitate college football's postwar boom, solidify the game's popular support, and accelerate some of its greatest abuses.

The first decision came when the NCAA decided to suspend all transfer rules and penalties on account of the disruption of the war. Thus, students who had their playing career interrupted by the war could transfer upon their return from the military to another school without losing the customary year of eligibility. This option appeared particularly attractive for many veterans who had traveled extensively as part of their military training and service and could now envision themselves going to college other than at the nearest state school. Additionally, those who played during the war in service programs like the V-5 teams did not have to count those years against their eligibility because technically it was part of their military training and commitment to Uncle Sam, even though they played most of their games against college teams. As a result, Bear Bryant lured almost his entire V-5 team from North Carolina Preflight with him to his first head coaching job at the University of Maryland. The years immediately following the war witnessed a recruiting free-for-all that many observers termed a "meat market," while still others suggested a darker side to this phenomenon by referring to it as a "black market" in players. Schools around the country attempted to lure the best players with fabulous financial inducements and many players simply held out for "the highest bidder." Allegations circulated rumoring college payrolls in excess of $100,000, even $200,000 in one place.[23]

The second decision that affected postwar football came in 1944 when Congress passed the Serviceman's Readjustment Act, popularly known as the GI Bill of Rights, or just the GI Bill. The GI Bill contained several provisions aimed at aiding the transition of demobilized veterans back into the civilian economy, one of which included complete reimbursement for tuition, fees, and books, plus a living stipend, for those who wished to pursue higher education. The GI Bill inadvertently facilitated the postwar recruiting orgy on two fronts. The wartime sports programs identified talent of untold numbers of athletes who, now with the government's aid, could attend college. As A. W. Hobbs, dean at the University of North Carolina, noted, "There are hundreds of good athletes in the armed forces who were not in college before the war, but who will be sought after with great vigor when it is over."[24] Additionally, with the federal government paying a veteran-player's educational expenses, schools used their recruiting budgets to lure nonveterans, allowing them to sign twice the number of players for the same amount of money. In other instances, some schools funneled that money directly to the player in the form of cash inducements. One coach promised his players he would "see that each got a full scholarship in addition to the GI Bill benefits."[25] In either case, the new transfer rules combined with GI Bill funds allowed schools to stockpile the most talented players. As one coach at the time observed, "The mistake the NCAA made after the war was to let boys go anywhere to college on the GI Bill, rather than back to where they'd [played before the war]. The rich got richer and the poor got poorer."[26]

Other components of the GI Bill facilitated that trend. Those who took advantage of the higher education provisions of the GI Bill overwhelmingly saw it as a route to upward mobility, professional independence, and social respectability. As a result, veterans gravitated to the large state schools and their professional programs rather than to private liberal arts colleges. Thus, 40 percent of the 2.2 million individuals who went to college on the GI Bill went to just thirty-eight schools, overwhelmingly large public universities with emerging or established football programs. As Donald Andrews noted, "quite accidentally, the GI Bill considerably transformed the quality" of college football.[27] Veterans returned to campus and pursued both the playing and the watching of college sports with gusto. Consider that "the magical era of [the University of] Kentucky basketball was created via a basketball version of the GI Bill" with at least four veterans returning to teams that won consecutive national championships in the 1940s.[28] According to Milton Greenberg, 70 percent of the University of Michigan's 1947 Rose Bowl team went to college on the GI Bill, including Bob Chappius, who appeared on the cover of *Time* magazine as part of an article on the GI Bill. Chappius finished second in that year's Heisman Trophy balloting, losing to fellow veteran and GI Bill recipient Johnny Lujack of Notre Dame.[29] The expansion of higher education through programs like the GI Bill also benefited college football by creating a perceived need to integrate these new students into the college and university experience. University administrators increasingly saw college football as a way to create community and instant loyalty to schools, particularly for older students and those forced to commute by postwar campus housing shortages. When distance or circumstance separated veterans from the traditional campus experience, many educators argued that college football would reconnect them. Notre Dame literally used football as a way to pitch the university by creating the practice of inserting into its college football broadcasts promotional messages for the university's academic programs. University president Father Theodore Hesburgh argued that college football acted as a "public service" to bring the uninitiated into the university fold.[30]

Just as the war created measures like the GI Bill, it also led to the Cold War struggle with the Soviets. And as World War II directly affected college football, so too did its by-product, the Cold War. To combat growing Soviet technological capacity, in both military and nonmilitary realms, the federal government began funneling unprecedented amounts of money into American universities and colleges. The 1950s witnessed more than a 100 percent increase in federal research and development expenditures, the single largest increase in history. By 1960, higher education received more than 10 percent of federal research funds.[31] However, this rising tide of grant and contract money did not lift all boats. Just twenty schools received 79 percent of all federal monies, with the overwhelming majority of these programs and their accompanying funds ending up in the now exploding public universities. This dramatic rise in federal support to public education provided "a generous state subsidy to public colleges and universities, which allowed them to keep the price of tuition artificially low."[32] This subsidy of public education indirectly aided college football by allowing public school athletic departments to keep their scholarship budgets disproportionately lower than those of private schools and other public schools not at the federal trough. Additionally, this tuition imbalance allowed much larger numbers of nonscholarship players, who paid their own way, to attend public schools in hopes of "walking on," thus providing huge talent pools. Finally, Cold War federal funding provided the potential for a shift in university resources to many outlets, including the athletic department. Rebecca Lowen has demonstrated how research contracts not only brought in to the university additional revenue but in fact paid for entire departments, including operating costs as well as salaries of professors, clerical staff, and graduate students.[33] Most of these funds came as "soft money," allegedly for a short determined, but frequently renewable, period of time. This contrasted with "hard money," defined as specific, long-term revenue budgeted in the university's annual available funds. The frequency of soft money renewal during the Cold War, however, created the question among university administrators, "After how many years of renewed funding did soft money became indistinguishable from hard money?" When that event occurred, schools shifted funds freed up by self-supporting units to other divisions on campus. With athletic departments' voracious appetites for money to fund postwar football's spiraling costs, schools better positioned themselves to "absorb athletic deficits as part of their educational program."[34] It is no surprise that from 1950 to 1962, only one private school won the national championship, and only three have won it since World War II.

By the end of the 1940s, college football found itself the unwitting beneficiary of several unrelated circumstances that exaggerated the game's prominence and diffusion. Wartime policies, postwar programs, and Cold War necessities all conspired to give college football an expanded prominence. In the years that followed, Americans accepted without challenge the assumption borne from this period that football represented the values and lessons that had served the Republic in her hour of need. As the Republic faced new challenges in the form of the Cold War abroad and social and cultural upheaval at home, those assumptions only intensified, allowing college football to achieve distinctive cultural standing.

ONE

Pasadena: The Terms of Postwar Football

"So long as there is a Rose Bowl . . . there will be a free United States."
—Edwin Server

In November 1946, the sports sections of virtually every major newspaper in the United States howled with criticism over the announcement of a secretly negotiated contract between the Pacific Coast Conference (PCC) and the Big Ten Conference to match teams from those two organizations in the storied Rose Bowl game on New Year's Day. Only the southern California media largely approved of the arrangement, with one paper revealing its opinion of the story's significance by putting it in a bannered front-page headline. Not all locals were as supportive, however; some officials of the Tournament of Roses Association decried the exclusion of teams from around the country. The East Coast media criticized the inability to invite Army to the upcoming game, while the *New York Times* revealed the antilabor sentiment of the period by derisively referring to the Rose Bowl in the wake of the new arrangement as "a closed shop." Southern comment was even more hostile, declaring the contract "the biggest mistake the Rose Bowl ever made." The intense passion and scrutiny that the decision received prodded *Pasadena Star News* editor Rube Samuelson to declare that "the State Department has its Russian problem, the Rose Bowl has its Big [Ten]."[1] Far from serving as yet another exaggerated example of sportswriter melodrama, Samuelson's comment revealed the increasing ease with which Americans used the rhetoric of larger national events to explain college football and vice versa. The process by which Americans came to explain college football and the crises of the post–World War II period in the language of each other came from the intense anxiety of the period and concerns over national fitness, character development, and moral rectitude. The willingness of so many Americans to find these attributes as natural outgrowths of football and thus to see the game as a bulwark against communism nurtured the cultural institution of football in the postwar years.

By the early 1950s, Americans slowly understood that the doctrine of containment formulated to restrain Soviet influence required a tremendous investment in money and resources for an indefinite period of time. Under those circumstances, the policy of containment bred frustration among many Americans because it ran contrary to the basic tenet of the American military tradition: to immediately confront an aggressive enemy with massive firepower and pursue the war to the point of unconditional surrender. Containment required a patient, passive response that ran counter to the wishes of many Americans. As a result, containment, and the absence of a shooting war that would bring unqualified victory, created a malaise that could not easily be resolved. Additionally, nuclear proliferation magnified the potential consequences of such a shooting war, meaning that containment created the need for Americans to see progress and victory in other, more immediate and satisfying areas. Thus, sports evolved as a natural outlet for Cold War tensions, and American "athletic excellence" illustrated a priori evidence of the superiority "of our free system of government and vast educational network."[2] Though sport enjoyed a prominent place in American society by the middle of the twentieth century, Americans could not take for granted athletic superiority over the Soviets. Several indicators in the early 1950s suggested that the United States was falling behind the Soviets in both mental and physical fitness.

Throughout the 1950s, popular assumptions of an America grown "soft" took root amid the material affluence of the postwar period. Such concerns were not unique to the period; national apprehension over softness has recurred in waves since the onset of industrialization. Americans put their postwar anxieties over softness, however, explicitly within the interrelated contexts of the Cold War and the pitfalls of prosperity. Many were stunned to learn during the Korean War that captured American POWs faced brutal physical and mental deprivation at the hands of their communist captors. Under such strain, perhaps as many as 70 percent of American POWs collapsed under interrogation, bringing about a "wholesale breakdown in morale" both at home and on the front. The specter of mental weakness appeared for the entire world to see when communist forces displayed twenty-three captured American soldiers, the so-called "Lost Sheep," who claimed they wished to defect to North Korea.[3] Concerns over the mental fitness of adults during the period occurred alongside existing anxiety about the mental fitness of youth, particularly in the matter of juvenile delinquency. By the mid-1950s, popular paranoia reached a fever pitch on the subject of juvenile delinquency. The FBI announced in 1953 that half of all car thefts and burglaries were committed by those under the age of eighteen, and J. Edgar Hoover projected that by 1965, one in five American boys would have a police record by the age of twenty. By 1954, Congress established a standing Subcommittee on Juvenile Delinquency, and the following year the issue achieved pop culture status with the release of *Blackboard Jungle*, a film featuring out-of-control high school students to the soundtrack of Bill Haley's "Rock Around the Clock."[4]

Concerns over physical fitness soon paralleled American anxieties over mental fitness. An international study published in 1956 revealed that the fitness and dexterity skills of American youths lagged far behind European youths. The military made plain the consequences of physical and mental softness when it estimated that by the end of the decade, such issues would disqualify five of every seven candidates for military service. Such pronouncements made for easy linkages to the Cold War, suggesting that such physical and emotional softness portended dire consequences for national security. Like so many quantitative points of comparison during the early Cold War, perceptions of Americans losing ground were magnified when compared to Soviet gains. Senator Hubert Humphrey ominously warned that communist dominance came from their superior sports and fitness programs. "One thing is certain—each day, each week, each year—the Soviet Union and its captive nations are increasing their efforts for the physical fitness of their populations."[5] Humphrey's rhetoric both reflected and helped create the growing American paranoia of communist bogeymen everywhere. Just as the American public heard of a Soviet economy outdistancing their own in terms of gross national product and a Soviet military producing a growing missile gap, they now saw themselves on the losing end of a "muscle gap" as well.

Responding to such fears, leaders in the military, the civilian government, and the private sector consciously began crafting what historian Donald Mrozek has labeled "the cult and ritual of toughness." According to Mrozek, leaders believed that mere physical fitness, though still necessary, was no longer enough to combat the growing Soviet menace. In addition to fit bodies, Americans needed to cultivate mental toughness by inuring themselves to pain and deprivation, and by accepting such conditions as necessary for the assurance of victory, either on the playing field or the battlefield. This required confronting the consequences of the material abundance that marked the postwar American experience.[6] Dartmouth president Ernest Martin Hopkins noted his concerns during the period with the feminizing influence of material abundance in American society. "I believe quite definitely that in a generation like ours where nothing in the way of physical hazard, to say nothing of physical effort, is demanded under ordinary circumstances . . . [physically demanding] games have a merit and that up to the limit of personal injury it is advantageous to a man to have some knowledge of the fact even of what physical pain is."[7] No less an authority than the American Medical Association endorsed the exposure of American youth to painful and dangerous play in a 1959 pamphlet on the importance of youth fitness. "A fractured ankle may leave less of a scar than a personality frustrated by reason of parental timidity over participation in contact sports."[8] The new cult of toughness extended even to the spiritual realm. The evangelist Billy Graham criticized depictions of Christ that would show him as "effeminate." Instead, Graham described Christ as a prototypical linebacker, strong, virile, manly, "he would have been a star athlete on any team." For Graham, the depiction of Christ as a tough, manly athlete also served as an antidote to the growing concern over juvenile delinquency. At a revival in North Carolina, Graham recited Hoover's juvenile delinquency statistics but claimed that tough, manly sports countered the causes of juvenile delinquency, "insecurity, bad environment, [and] too much leisure," among other things.[9] For these observers, embracing the cult of toughness was necessary to arrest the American slide into dissipation.

The cult of toughness hinted at the hard road ahead for American claims of global supremacy. Only a resolute toughness could develop "the vigor and determination necessary to satisfy the awakening aspirations for progress and the elimination of poverty and want," both at home and abroad. Thus, the elevation of toughness as a cultural value established its primacy not only in defeating the Soviets but also in enabling America to overcome the barriers to progress everywhere and assume the mantle of world leadership. In his inaugural address, President John F. Kennedy linked these themes in declaring the United States summoned by the "trumpet" of a world historical moment, "not as a call to bear arms, though arms we need—not as a call to battle, though embattled we are—but a call to bear the burden of a long twilight struggle . . . against the common enemies of man: tyranny, poverty, disease, and war itself." Americans must "be willing to work for the physical toughness on which the courage and intelligence and skill of man so largely depend."[10] The stakes of the Cold War demanded that Americans simultaneously search for material progress while developing a national character of toughness and self-denial. Thus, Americans needed the greatness to create material comfort and the fortitude to keep it from corrupting them.

No team sport better represented the route to the new cult of toughness than football, a sport that evoked manliness, technological superiority, and material affluence. The generation of coaches and their disciples bred by Tom Hamilton's V-5 program viewed football not so much as a game but as a "gut check," an exercise in toughness, self-deprivation, and the willingness to endure pain. Most coaches at the time denied water to players during practices as a way to teach such lessons, and the question most coaches asked when discussing a player's injury was not "Is he hurt?" but "Can he play?" The most legendary stories came when players overcame seemingly debilitating injuries not just to play but to affect the outcome of a game. Thus, just as Kennedy challenged Americans to "pay any price, bear any burden" in their quest for world leadership, Paul "Bear" Bryant told his players that winning football was only achieved by those willing to "pay the price."[11] In these constructs, football during the Cold War era emerged not so much as a game decided by skill and talent but as a contest of want, will, and self-denial.

Throughout the period, Americans linked football with the pillars of domestic society, implying the game's role in shaping a national identity. When the National Football Foundation and Hall of Fame held its annual awards dinner in 1958, attended by industrialists, theologians, military figures such as Douglas MacArthur, and politicians, including the president of the United States, *New York Times* columnist Joseph Sheehan commented on the attraction of football. "What sport—or, in fact, what avocational activity of any type—could have mustered a turnout comparable" to the awards dinner?[12] Football, according to its supporters, was a game that bred leadership at a time when Americans thirsted for that quality. One university faculty member noted the postgraduate careers of his school's recent football heroes and found among them decorated military veterans, religious leaders (including the founder of Campus Crusade for Christ), and successful businessmen. Such assessments argued that individuals identified with college football represented the values and characteristics that differentiated the United States from the Soviet Union: military supremacy, capitalism, Christianity, and democracy.[13]

At a time when Americans were increasingly concerned with differentiating themselves from the Soviets, football emerged in the eyes of many as representative of a distinct American exceptionalism. When Soviet premier Nikita Khrushchev visited the United States in 1959, many fans and writers in

Ohio suggested he see an Ohio State football game. "A Big Ten game would give him a good impression of the real spirit of America." Indeed, four years previously, American hosts ensured that Soviet housing officials attended the Maryland-South Carolina game as an insight into American culture.[14] Football, like American life itself, was rigidly codified and highly structured, with the complexity of the game growing as gamesmanship forced annual rules changes. The game also represented the nation's technical sophistication with the rapid improvement in equipment, particularly shoulder pads and helmets made of the latest plastics and plexis. In the words of Jeffrey Meikle, "Plastic became an integral element of an expansive era, one of its most revealing elements."[15] Finally, the game represented the affluence of American society; few sports contested anywhere in the world matched the expense of football equipment, particularly as the technology rapidly accelerated. The continued evolution of the new plastic football helmets provided a good case in point. While their sophistication drastically increased their safety value, by 1950 their cost exceeded that of an entire uniform from the 1920s.[16] Thus, football was associated with modernity, American technology, and economic abundance, all assisting Americans in identifying it as distinctly American.

Few individuals more prominently advocated football as a game of Cold War toughness than the thirty-third and thirty-fourth presidents of the United States, Dwight D. Eisenhower and John F. Kennedy. Both presidents made the elevation of toughness and fitness a component of their national agendas and seldom missed an opportunity to connect those efforts with football. Eisenhower, himself a former college football player, frequently harkened back to his playing days at West Point. In reviewing his wartime service, he once remarked that he was constantly on the lookout for the "natural leaders" created by football and acknowledged that the outstanding men on his entire staff were ex-football players. Eisenhower believed "that football, almost more than any other sport, tends to instill in men the feeling that victory comes through hard—almost slavish—work." Although Eisenhower's own career came to an end with a savage knee injury, he felt that such occurrences, and by extension the possibility of injury to all players, were acceptable costs of a game that taught its players the necessary character and values the Republic needed in its time of crisis. One of Eisenhower's disappointments was that his two terms as president coincided with the downturn of Army football fortunes while the Naval Academy witnessed renewed success during the period. When Eisenhower appointed General William Westmoreland as commandant of the academy in 1960 shortly before he left office, the president informed the general, "The only thing I charge you to do Westmoreland is to buck up that football team."[17]

Eisenhower firmly believed that football embodied uniquely American values while it simultaneously demanded the toughness necessary to counter Soviet advances. In his 1958 acceptance speech as the first recipient of the National Football Foundation and Hall of Fame's Gold Medal, the president noted that "wherever human liberty is respected, competition is the animator of progress. In football, in business, in politics . . . the normal urge to excel provides one of the most hopeful assurances that our kind of society will continue to advance and prosper." Eisenhower declared that "morale—the will to win, the fighting heart—are the honored hallmarks" of the game, and that such competitive values were crucially applicable in the defense of the Republic. "For there is another kind of competition which America must meet—ponderous, persistent, deadly. It is clever and powerful and it is out to win by whatever means and at whatever cost." The benefit of football, in Eisenhower's view, was that it so successfully married the physical with the mental. The struggle with the Soviets "require[d] fitness—fitness in its deepest and broadest sense. We know that fitness is far more than a healthy body. It is more than an alert, disciplined, mind. Fitness is the sum of all values which enable a man to act effectively in his nation's behalf in this great contest. In this environment, fitness is man's maximum development to make all of us a stronger nation."[18]

Associating football with values crucial to American Cold War success, Eisenhower directly linked the game to the country's Cold War efforts. Backed by a Joint Resolution of Congress, Eisenhower announced a National Olympic Day in October 1954 to generate popular support for the American effort two years hence. In selecting a time to address the nation on the subject, he chose the halftime of ABC's *College Football Game of the Week*. Soviet Olympic successes in 1956 led Eisenhower to create the U.S. Olympic Development Committee (USODC) as a way of maximizing the nation's Olympic resources. Ignoring prominent figures within the U.S. Olympic Committee and even the federations of sports contested at the Olympics, Eisenhower chose Tom Hamilton, the wartime savior of the decidedly un-Olympic sport of college football, to head the USODC.[19]

Eisenhower's embrace of football and those associated with it gave the game a cultural prominence and significance that went far beyond the field. Eisenhower's linkages to the game, though, paled in comparison to the support football received from John F. Kennedy. Commenting forty years after Kennedy's death on the importance that football played in the president's mind-set, Charles Pierce wrote, "Football was what they played on the New Frontier . . . there was a tyranny of the new at work, stretching from outer space to Southeast Asia. Football was a part of all that."[20] Kennedy, like Eisenhower, made the curious decision to address the significance of the Olympics through the venue of college football. In 1961, the president announced a major reshuffling of amateur sports, which included a massive commitment on the part of the federal government to combat declining American success and prestige in the Olympic arena. Although such governmental subsidization in the name of combating Soviet Olympic gains marked a formal abandonment of amateurism as national policy, the president was unwilling to concede to the Soviets the cultural cachet that Olympic success entailed. Explicitly rejecting the opportunity to offer such a major Cold War policy speech to the annual meeting of the U.S. Olympic Committee, Kennedy instead chose to deliver it at the annual banquet of the National Football Foundation and Hall of Fame.[21]

Kennedy seldom passed up a chance to connect with voters over the issue of college football, particularly in the South as confrontations over civil rights created southern white hostility toward his administration. When the University of Alabama won the 1961 National Championship, the president met with the team when they journeyed to New York to be honored by the National Football Foundation. Similarly, he called Tuscaloosa to offer encouragement to the team during a pep rally before the team's Sugar Bowl game against Arkansas. Kennedy frequently referred to football as a cultural touchstone common to all Americans. During the 1962 crisis at the University of Mississippi surrounding the enrollment of James Meredith, the university's first black student, the president urged Mississippians to avoid violence. Hoping to appeal to a common source of pride, he reminded them, "You have a great tradition to uphold, a tradition of honor and courage, won on the field of battle and on the gridiron."[22] Perhaps no moment best symbolized Kennedy's belief in the values and meanings of football than his speech announcing the United States' entry into the space race. Declaring in 1962 in his finest New Frontier rhetoric that America would put a man on the moon by the end of the decade, Kennedy staked the prestige of the nation—and by extension, the free enterprise system—to success in space. The president gave his address in Houston, Texas, the future home of the space program, on the campus of Rice University, a school distinguished in academics but with limited football success, particularly against the nationally prominent University of Texas. Kennedy acknowledged that space travel would be difficult and the struggle would be marked by those who would say success was unobtainable. Kennedy asserted that Americans, however, did things "not because they are easy, but because they are hard." Such efforts marked the best of the American spirit, and success under those circumstances illustrated the leadership, progress, and "peaceful cooperation" America had to offer the world in its hour of peril. "Why choose the moon?" the president asked rhetorically, "Why climb the highest mountain? Why, thirty five years ago, fly the Atlantic?" And then, to thunderous applause, "Why does Rice play Texas?"[23] In Kennedy's equation, America would go to the moon, demonstrating its greatness in the face of overwhelming obstacles in the same way that tiny Rice University struggled against the mighty Texas Longhorns on the gridiron. The magnitude of the obstacle glorified the nobility of the effort and amplified the satisfaction of success.

Kennedy was not alone in his administration in elevating the prominence and meaning of football. Robert Kennedy, attorney general in his brother's administration and himself a former player at Harvard, similarly elevated the game's social and cultural significance. The attorney general, like his brother, linked physical fitness and mental toughness. In his address to the American Football Coaches Association's 1961 Coach of the Year dinner, Robert Kennedy claimed that such qualities helped deliver American victory in World War II but that the nation had abandoned both fitness and toughness in the years since. The individuals best suited to reverse such a decline, according to Kennedy, sat before him in that very room. Football coaches could "exert a tremendous influence for good in this country. . . . You who participate in football, who have played well and trained others to play well, symbolize the needs of the nation." Kennedy, like his brother and Eisenhower before them and American elites like Oliver Wendell Holmes and Henry Cabot Lodge dating back to the nineteenth century, continued to see football as the peacetime crucible in which national character was forged. "Except for war, there is nothing in American life which trains a boy better for life than football. There can be no substitute for football."[24]

The Kennedy administration seemed to overflow with individuals associated with the game, and the administration made sure the public knew it. In providing the keynote address at the 1962 Heisman Memorial Trophy awards banquet, Robert Kennedy claimed he was there not as attorney general but as a former college football player. The president also placed Tom Hamilton in charge of the restructured Olympic program, once again noting him as the man who "saved football" during World War II. Kennedy restructured Eisenhower's fitness program into the Presidential Council on Physical Fitness, imbuing it with all the significance of a vital Cold War defense initiative, and promptly named Charles "Bud" Wilkinson, head coach the Oklahoma Sooners, to head the venture. Wilkinson's appointment illustrated that football even trumped party loyalty in the president's eyes, as Wilkinson was soon to run for the Senate as a Republican. Another prominent head coach with Republican ties, Earl "Red" Blaik, seemingly served as minister without portfolio in the Kennedy administration. First nominated to adjudicate the dispute between the Amateur Athletic Union and the National Collegiate Athletic Association (NCAA) over control of amateur sports, Blaik also served as the president's personal observer of the negotiations in Birmingham, Alabama, following that city's massive civil rights campaign. Nicholas Rodis, a former teammate of Robert Kennedy at Harvard and former head coach at the University of Connecticut, served as the director for all athletic and sports programs run by the State Department. And Kennedy nominated Byron "Whizzer" White to the Supreme Court in 1962, noting White's football career at the University of Colorado and his second-place finish in the 1937 Heisman Trophy balloting.[25] Although each of these men maintained qualifications far in excess of their football experience, the trumpeting of their associations with the game strengthened existing assumptions about football's role as a purveyor of toughness and leadership.

Eisenhower and Kennedy were only the most prominent supporters of football who placed the game at the center of the emerging postwar culture of toughness. Verne Freeman, an associate dean at Purdue University, strongly supported the national fitness and sports agenda of the two presidents, declaring them "*absolutely essential* to the ongoing life of our nation. . . . Weaklings don't get anywhere in this world and they won't in the next world."[26] Commentators during the period increasingly focused on football as a distinctive purveyor of the fitness and toughness that Eisenhower and Kennedy encouraged. Republican senator from Kentucky John Sherman Cooper noted on the floor of the Senate that the game's "emphasis on discipline, competitive spirit, physical fitness, teamwork and courage contributes to the vigor and moral and physical fiber of our country."[27] Popular assumptions that football represented values crucial to American Cold War success allowed many observers to link the game to an explicit American exceptionalism. Michigan State's head coach Clarence "Biggie" Munn declared that "I would rather my son be a football player than a Phi Beta Kappa [because] . . . you learn democracy and Americanism in the game of football."[28] Similarly, an Ivy League coach was so blunt as to suggest that "football is our best defense against communism," a sentiment echoed almost exactly by Army head coach Red Blaik, who described "football as a disciplinary force, and as the antithesis of communism."[29] If football itself was essential to the preservation of the Republic, the Rose Bowl posited itself as a bastion against the encroaching communist foe. "In these times of international tensions, with the spectre of war and attempted domination casting shadows on a free United States . . . the Tournament of Roses lightens the dark corners of fear. . . . So long as there is a Tournament of Roses, so long as there is a Rose Bowl Game . . . there will there be a free United States."[30]

Among the most vocal purveyors of the notion that the culture of football was vital to national security was the National Football Foundation and Hall of Fame. Established in 1947 by former coaches, players, and benefactors of the game to build a college football hall of fame, the foundation emerged during the Cold War era as the game's most ardent defender, cloaking football in the rhetoric of national defense and the cult of toughness. In an official credo that echoed both the preamble of the U.S. Constitution and Abraham Lincoln's Gettysburg Address, the group declared "A Noble Cause Is at Stake." Asserting the need for a permanent hall of fame, the credo began, "We hold these things important," among them the need to honor "the heroes of the past," so that their sacrifices and efforts shall not perish from memory, "that there shall be no softening of our fibre as we face the task of world leadership." The fear of Americans gone soft played a prominent role in the foundation's message, claiming that the game "will serve as an inspiration so that our youth, unlike the ancient Greeks and Romans, will not 'grow soft.'" The group viewed with alarm the potential by-products of America's postwar affluence but saw football as the antidote. "In an age where there has been considerable tendency to softness and the relaxing of our standards of fortitude and physical preparedness, the foundation believes that football will continue to be a significant and vital factor in helping to strengthen and prepare the physical and moral fiber of the Nation for our defense in the years to come." The foundation frequently placed the game in explicit Cold War contexts. Football was "a vital force in the life of the nation, developing the rugged virtues and tough leadership qualities indispensable for the survival of a free world menaced by a ruthless and conspiratorial tyranny." Similarly, the foundation viewed the game "as an incubator of 'competitive fibre,'" claiming it turned out men capable of directing an "economy toward defeating Russia in its avowed aim to destroy us." The benefits of football, according to the foundation, would accrue not just to its players but to the nation they represented, claiming the game's "important role in the advancement of our way of life." Indeed, striking a tone of Kennedy-esque global citizenship, football promised "a better life for all mankind."[31]

In equating football with the defense of the Republic, the foundation also looked with hostility upon individuals who challenged or criticized the game. The group included as a formal program initiative its place "to combat . . . the unwarranted attacks made on football in the public press by those who are uninformed or prejudiced." Chester LaRoche, the foundation's president in the late 1950s and early 1960s, took every opportunity to attack "the negative influences which have inveighed against the game," arguing that critics of the game were in fact "enemies" who threatened national security and the future of the Republic. When noted academics James B. Conant and Henry Steele Commager published remarks critical of the state of the game, LaRoche lamented that the foundation "had not gone far enough" in rebutting these men and their "negative influences." He attempted to co-opt Sidney James, editor of *Sport Illustrated,* in an effort to get the magazine to rebut such criticisms. LaRoche focused his most acidic rhetoric on those who had dropped football altogether, particularly the University of Chicago. "We should dig into the facts concerning Chicago. It is probable that the character of their student body has dropped off badly, and they are now overloaded with beatniks, leftists, and undesirables. It could be proved that dropping football was a disaster." On another occasion, LaRoche asserted that Chicago "suffered" so extensively from dropping football that the university might now be receptive to its return.[32]

LaRoche and the foundation were not the only ones to view attempts to de-emphasize the game as threats to national security and the national character. Bill Stern, the lead broadcaster for Mutual's college football telecasts, asserted on the air in October 1958 that schools which dropped or minimized football, such as Chicago, Harvard, City College of New York, and New York University, were "hotbeds of communism." In the absence of big-time football, according to Stern, the wholesome energies of college youth that could have gone to constructive character-building exercises found no outlet. "In many cases, too many of them have turned to Communism."[33] Individuals who publicly voiced opposition to football faced the harshest reprisals. In 1959, Wade Thompson, a faculty member of the English Department at Brown University, proposed the abolition of intercollegiate football at Brown. The responses to Thompson's proposal brought, among others, allegations of treason, homosexuality, and communism.[34] Similarly, Gary Althern, undergraduate student editor of the University of Colorado's *Colorado Daily,* editorialized in September 1962 his desire to see the Buffaloes lose of all their games that season so as to make it easier to abandon big-time football in Boulder. When Althern followed his football editorial with one harshly critical of strident anticommunist Senator Barry Goldwater, many observers linked the two pieces as intertwined evidence of Althern's subversiveness. Responding to such critics, the university president subsequently removed Althern as editor.[35] Thus, by directing the code words for subversion and deviance at football's critics, defenders of the game helped craft a culture that simultaneously elevated football to national importance while placing those critics beyond the respectable pale of that culture.

Americans viewed football during the Cold War era as evocative of a distinct national exceptionalism that embodied values of universal acclaim. To reject the game, then, was to reject these values and this sense of American distinctiveness. Thus, critics such as Thompson and Althern found themselves linked with communism, homosexuality, and a host of alleged character flaws that existed outside the bounds of the American way of life. The suggestion that anything less than a lusty embrace of football during the period could be linked to all manner of deficiencies emerged most often in popular discussion of the newly created Ivy League. Formally created in 1956, the Ivy League sought to distance itself "from the toxins of big-time" football, in the words of John Watterson, by restricting or abolishing many of the game's accepted practices.[36] The move away from big-time football earned the game's founders a barrage of criticism. George Preston Marshall, owner of the professional Washington Redskins, declared, "The Ivy League is destroying the game it created." One Big Ten alumnus simply stated that "Ivy League football stinks," while a UCLA partisan dismissed the eastern brand of the game relative to big-time football, "We play football, not potsy." Descriptions of Ivy League football as "potsy" suggested that its critics saw it as unmanly, effeminate. One critic of Ivy League football restrictions feared that it marked a surrender to "over-stimulated introverts and pinkish weaklings."[37]

The notion of effeteness soon dominated descriptions of Ivy League football. An electronic keyword search of the *New York Times* historical database reveals that the description of football at Ivy League schools as "effete" did not appear in the pages of that paper prior to the creation of the formal Ivy League. After the consummation of the Ivy Group Agreement in 1954, however, the phrase appeared with increasing frequency. In discussing a slate of upcoming games in October 1959, one writer noted that the best "the effete East" could offer was a game involving Penn. The same month, a discussion of the college kicking game noted that "the effete East" eschewed the point after touchdown for the two-point conversion. In May 1961, another scribe noted Navy's dissatisfaction with having to share the Lambert Trophy, given each year to the best team in the East, with Yale, "regarded as effete in hard-nosed football circles." The following year, Arthur Daley revisited the Ivy League's decision to abandon spring practice, noting that the "activity has borne an unjustified stigma—at least in the effete East." Notions of the Ivy League's effeteness so successfully colored national perceptions of football reform that the Ivy League haunted proponents of big-time football like a specter to be avoided at all costs. When considering Ohio State's decision not to accept the 1962 Rose Bowl invitation, one Buckeye partisan lamented, "I hope our university does not pattern itself or imitate some of the effete Eastern Colleges with the consequent loss of vigor, both in mind and body."[38]

Linking Ivy League football with "effeteness" and "pinkish weaklings" illustrated the ease with which Americans perceived a hostility to football as a proxy for a host of un-American traits. The charge of effeteness in post–World War II America bore distinct implications, suggesting not just a masculine shortcoming but an ideological one as well. To be effete, to be unmanly, was to be soft, weak, both physically and mentally and, thus, to be corruptible. Commentators during the Cold War universally agreed that the defense of the Republic required a fit populace, capable of stoic sacrifice and self-discipline, not just in the personal sense but in an ideological sense as well. It is not coincidental that one of President Kennedy's favorite terms was "vigor." Critics claimed that communism promised easy solutions, offered easy protections, by placing all responsibilities on the state rather than the individual. Success in American society required constant perseverance and striving, a lifetime of struggle unnavigable by individuals too weak to resist the promise of a socialized society. To be effete in postwar America was to be un-American, possibly a threat to national security. This perverse logic informed the intense homophobia of the period, which manifested itself in ways both profane and profound, from popular assumptions to governmental action. Senator Joseph McCarthy once crudely declared that anyone who opposed him "was either a Communist or a cocksucker." With little more subtlety, Congress passed the McCarran Act, which barred homosexuals from becoming U.S. citizens and forbade those already here from traveling abroad, while President Eisenhower issued an executive order barring homosexuals from federal employment. Allegations of Ivy League football as effete were in fact challenges to their loyalty and commitment to waging the Cold War.[39]

The decision by the Ivy League to distance itself from big-time football at the exact moment that many Americans identified the game as so thoroughly evocative of American life not only judged criticisms of Ivy League football as effete but also coincided with increasing criticisms of Ivy League schools for their alleged ambivalence toward moral development in general and communist sympathies specifically. Noted conservative intellectual William F. Buckley Jr. indicted his alma mater, Yale, for its abandonment of Christian and capitalist values that had served as the school's foundation for three centuries, and his criticisms were not the only ones. Similarly, T. Garland Tinsley, in a letter to the *New York Times*, noted that the recent scandals in college athletics marked a wholesale "collapse of conscience in these United States." The culprit, according to Tinsley, resided in the elite halls of American academia, where "a slavish devotion to an entirely false concept of academic freedom is turning our colleges into booby traps for young and impressionable minds." Describing the intellectual discourse that occurred in American higher education in the 1950s as "evil and alien influences," Tinsley placed the blame on professors. "Too often today the American way of life—from a belief in free enterprise to faith in democracy—is belittled by our enlightened professors. These men decry the past, scorn the present and offer various forms of socialism and collectivism as the only hope for the future." The salvation of American higher education could be found, he argued, by "turn[ing] again towards the ideals and simple faith that made us great," including institutions of church, education, and sports as a means of instructing patriotism, "rectitude, and high moral principles." In this fashion, we would avoid not only the scandals of college athletics but also the erosion of the American character. To Tinsley, the distancing of the Ivy League from big-time athletics was an assault, and not even a thinly veiled one, on the future of the Republic.[40]

An editorial in the *Mobile Press-Register* made an even more explicit link between Ivy League sports policies and its supposed unwillingness to challenge the communist menace. The author noted that while the Ivy Group Agreement required all athletes to sign a pledge stating they would abide by the agreement's provisions, particularly disclosing financial assistance, half of the Ivy League schools at the same time opposed loyalty oaths that "Congress thinks would assist our government in stamping out Communism and subversive activities. For it is well-known that the Communist technique is to try to influence members of the faculty as well as the students." According to such logic, the limitations of Ivy League football and sympathy to communism were borne from the same bankrupt values.[41]

Americans' understanding of football as a purveyor of that which marked the best in society during the Cold War enshrined the game as integral to the American way of life. Nothing better illustrated the rarified prominence of college football during the Cold War than the public response to a series of scandals in the 1950s within college athletics. The magnitude of the scandals was such that one scholar declared the period "was the closest that organized college sports came to a collapse of safeguards and standards."[42] Although the scandals all originated from the same kinds of factors that had plagued college sports since the 1890s, the varied public response to them revealed that Americans viewed college football by the 1950s as an exalted cultural form.

In January 1951, college basketball fans almost everywhere were shocked to hear of a massive betting scandal where players either "shaved" points to get the score under the point spread offered by bookies or threw games outright. As the scandal deepened beyond its origins in New York's Madison Square Garden and four New York area colleges to schools in the South and Midwest, observers realized college basketball had a cancer growing on the game. Although New York basketball aficionados had suspected fixed games for years, the scandal did not fully come to light until Manhattan University's Junius Kellogg acknowledged that two of his teammates had offered him money to rig an upcoming game. Soon, more than thirty players from seven different schools faced criminal indictment, and investigators revealed a game infested with gamblers and organized crime figures. Many questioned whether the game could be saved. In the wake of such a challenge to the very existence of the game at the college level, the public nonetheless universally lauded those who exposed the fixes. Arthur Daley, sports columnist emeritus for the *New York Times*, described Kellogg as having "the inherent moral decency, the high moral fiber, and the deep religious scruples" to contact the authorities. Other players who cooperated received similar treatment in the press while the players complicit in the scandal received the harshest public criticism. To a man, they were all banned from the NBA, and when the New Jersey franchise of the upstart American Basketball League signed three of the accused players, the league's other owners agreed to fold the ABL rather than allow the "fixers" to play.[43] As the college sports world digested the basketball cheating scandal, two cheating scandals in college football were exposed the same year.

The drastic expansion of college football following World War II, in both number of schools playing the game and in the expense required to play big-time football, increased the pressures and rewards for cheating everywhere. The recruiting free-for-all allowed many schools to embrace the belief that they too could enjoy the apparent riches and public acclaim associated with big-time college football. At the College of William and Mary, which had not even hired its first full-time head coach until 1933, the board of trustees made the decision in 1946 to embrace big-time football by wading in to the recruiting wars and scheduling nationally known opponents, all with the aim of financial profit. In so doing, however, the board helped initiate one of the period's worst academic scandals. By 1951, with the college president's support, a faculty investigation uncovered numerous violations involving the athletic department in general and the football team in particular, including forged transcripts, cash payments, preferential treatment, pressure on faculty to change grades, and violations of the school's honor code by both students and athletic department officials. The committee recommended the dismissal of culpable individuals, including the athletic director and the football coach, and called for a return to college football on a smaller scale. When apprised of the situation, the board repudiated the faculty findings and initiated its own investigation, noting that such an effort should not have been necessary "if matters had been handled more positively . . . and with greater tact." The board offered a public rebuke to the faculty members involved and a vote of no-confidence in the college president, leading to his immediate resignation. The board declared the importance of big-time college football not only by ignoring its academic consequences, which many felt put the school's accreditation at risk, but by personally hiring a new football coach and athletic director and reasserting its commitment to big-time college football.[44]

The wantonness of the impropriety at William and Mary shocked many, as did the recriminations against those who brought it to light. But what happened there paled in comparison to what emerged the same year at West Point. Beginning at least as early as 1948, football players, with the tacit approval and perhaps the assistance of the coaching staff, developed a network where cadets shared upcoming information about quizzes and exams with cadets in the same subjects but whose classes met on different days. By 1951, cadets had formed a full-blown cheating ring in which participants provided upcoming questions and their answers. While this violated academic integrity at every university in the nation, it also specifically violated the Academy Honor Code whereby cadets agree not to lie, cheat, or steal, or to tolerate those who do. As with the basketball scandal, a student approached to participate exposed the West Point cheating ring. Eventually, the academy expelled more than ninety cadets; more than a third came from the academy football team, including Bob Blaik, the starting quarterback and son of head coach Earl "Red" Blaik. The scandal destroyed one of the most dominant football programs in the nation, one that had won three national championships and two Heisman Trophies in the 1940s. In this instance, however, the whistle-blowers became the victims.[45]

Almost immediately, public and media condemnation centered on those who had "betrayed" their classmates, who, by their own admission, had cheated. One newspaper derisively referred to one of the "informants" as a "judicious little prig," while Robert Daru, a New York lawyer critical of the cadet dismissals, alleged that the dismissals occurred only as a result of "cadet 'stool pigeons.'"[46] One player who had revealed what he knew of the cheating ring acknowledged that his mother never forgave him for such treason: "She lived 45 years after the incident and she never forgave me. Not to her dying day. She would just say, 'Ned, we never raised you to be a snitch.'"[47] Commenting on the scorn these individuals received, Arthur Daley declared in the *Times*, "Americans have adopted the code of the underworld whose First Commandment is: Don't squeal!"[48] In comparison to the players implicated in the basketball scandal who were barred from professional competition, players from West Point enjoyed successful pro careers, with players being drafted and two others serving as referees in the NFL. The scandals of 1951 illustrated that football enjoyed a cultural sanctity identified with the American way of life, and those who diminished it deserved the condemnation befitting anyone who would tear at the social and cultural fabric of the Republic in time of crisis.

The association of football as representative of an exemplary American way of life and the willingness of many Americans to downplay or dismiss entirely the implications of the 1951 scandals fit the existing larger Cold War morality. In 1954, President Eisenhower appointed former president Herbert Hoover to lead a commission charged with making tactical recommendations on the waging of the Cold War. The Hoover Commission famously told the president that "hitherto accepted norms of human conduct do not apply . . . long-standing American concepts of 'fair play' must be reconsidered," leading to constitutional violations of free speech, free press, and due process and to scores of other limitations.[49] The Hoover Commission revealed that in the name of anticommunism, nothing was un-American. Popular cultural understandings during the period of what was American and what was not increasingly took on the trappings of Hobbesian logic. In 1947, *Look* magazine published a domestic national security primer in "How to Spot a Communist," followed in 1954 by a U.S. Army pamphlet of the same name. Both pieces noted that sure signs of "subversive behavior" included "intelligent people," concerned with issues like fair play and equality, using words like "exploitation," and showing a "predisposition [for] civil rights concerns."[50] To criticize the postwar abuses in college football by stressing its academic improprieties and anti-intellectualism, or the vast sums of money made from the labors of supposedly amateur students, or the segregated practices of southern teams and the corrupt values of integrated teams that scheduled them anyway sounded dangerously subversive to many. The Cold War inured Americans to such abuses and they readily accepted them from both their government and their alma mater.

Defenders of college football so easily linked attacks on the game with communism because the game represented one of the most time-honored campus institutions, and any challenge to such tradition appeared un-American. In that regard, college football was not alone. Attempts to democratize the Greek system at the same time by banning restrictive membership clauses, mostly aimed at blacks but also Asians, Jews, and Catholics in some houses, met with similar anticommunist rhetoric. When the California State Assembly considered a 1957 bill that would ban discriminatory membership clauses in Greek letter houses, one opponent of the bill declared that "as American citizens, we cannot tolerate this political invasion of sacred personal social rights guaranteed in our . . . Constitution." The origins of such an action lay at the feet of "minority groups seeking to legislate social privilege and create a 'classless' society. . . . The target is really what we know as the 'American Way of Life.'"[51] Anticommunist defenders of traditional campus institutions found no more prominent spokesmen during the era than U.S. Senators Barry Goldwater and Joseph McCarthy. In addressing the National Interfraternity Council in 1960, Senator Goldwater declared that "where fraternities are not allowed, communism flourishes," referring to the Greek system as "a bastion of American strength." He viewed any attempts to restrict the Greek system as a quick route to domestic subversion, singling out Harvard as a nonfraternity campus that had allowed such subversive ideologies to breed "a faithless generation."[52] Similarly, McCarthy saw criticisms of football as evidence of communist subversion and a repudiation of such institutions as marriage, social conformity, and the American Legion. As part of his infamous hearings into alleged communist subversion in American government, McCarthy investigated the Voice of America (VOA) program, a division of the International Information Agency within the State Department, in February and March 1952. Attempting to link bureaucratic missteps within the VOA to supposed communist sympathizers employed by that agency, McCarthy called Reed Harris to the witness stand. McCarthy spent much of Harris's three days on the witness stand questioning him about the book *King Football*, which Harris wrote in 1932 as an undergraduate at Columbia.

By Harris's own admission, the book was a sophomoric attempt to criticize a host of institutions representing paternalism and authority, one of which was college football. McCarthy focused on Harris's attack of intercollegiate athletics, especially football, with the Wisconsin senator reading into the record a passage that noted, "Russia has barred football from her new athletic program" because the sport appealed "to the least desirable emotions."[53] Thus, McCarthy saw football in the same terms Goldwater viewed fraternities. Opposition to either institution was so easily marginalized and linked with communism because both represented a generic American way of life.

At the height of the Cold War, supporters of football understood the game as a vital cog in the emerging cult of toughness. These individuals interpreted football as a purveyor of desired American values representative of the Cold War mind-set. Some observers at the time also directly linked the game to the waging of the Cold War itself. Joseph Kaplan, a renowned physics professor at UCLA and chair of the U.S. Committee on the International Geophysical Year, offered a series of articles for popular consumption in the 1950s espousing football's Cold War role. Kaplan firmly accepted existing assumptions linking the physical with the mental, refusing to "distinguish between the need and fittingness of scientific activity on one hand and athletic activity on the other. Our nation seriously needs both." Kaplan also embraced the increasing specialization and rationalization of the game, which for so many Americans was disorienting and ambiguous. Kaplan argued that football should not reject the two-platoon system but embrace it as integral not only to the rationalization of college football but also to the rationalization of the Cold War economy that would lead to American supremacy over the Soviets. "If we are to gain any superiority over [the Soviets] in any given essential category, in peace or war, we must do it by concentrating on the development of specialists." In that way, according to Kaplan, the game—and, by extension, society—intensified competition and bred excellence. He explicitly linked the increase of specialization within college football to the similar occurrences in the larger economy, creating better talent. "Since competition fosters growth, it is logical for highly competitive football to grow big—and sometimes rapidly." He pointed to his own academic discipline as a good example by citing the intense competition for scientists among the nation's elite university research labs, a phenomenon known as "Big Science." The most specialized labs, directed by the most talented researchers, would be rewarded with federal grant dollars, allowing the rich to get richer and larger, thereby allowing them to attract more talent and make greater scientific discoveries.[54]

Kaplan argued that specialization created excellence from the crucible of competition, and no better crucible existed than football. Not surprisingly, the National Football Foundation echoed Kaplan's assumptions on the relationship between the game and competition, claiming football offered "a unique training ground for leadership in our competitive economy."[55] Like so many others during the time, Kaplan understood football to be indicative of a kind of American exceptionalism. "Football is the most competitive of sports. Its teamwork, its ruggedness, its Spartan spirit, a throwback to our pioneering ancestry, all have tremendous appeal to our basic American characteristics."[56] A uniquely American game, football thus appealed to a uniquely American experience, creating, in Kaplan's world, a culture of uniquely American values. Having linked football to an American past of frontier individualism, however, he also viewed the game as analogous to a bureaucratized American experience necessary to conquer the final frontier, space. Noting the prominence of space as a Cold War battleground, Kaplan argued that the acceptance of specialization was a necessary evolution of American culture in order to achieve Cold War victory. "The Space Age is geared to specialization, and there's no room for amateurism. Amateurs cannot make the 20,000 moving parts of a Vanguard rocket function. It is also a fact that amateurs cannot participate smoothly in a complicated football play."[57] Kaplan was not the only academic who embraced sports as a purveyor of competition. James B. Conant, former president of Harvard, argued that "The spirit of competition . . . is a healthy aspect of our American emphasis on sports. There is no reason why the same type of motivation could not be utilized in the study of mathematics, and foreign languages, provided, as in athletics, selection of the naturally talented is accepted as a matter of course."[58] Thus, the culture of football during the Cold War era represented not merely toughness and fitness but competition and national exceptionalism as well, all of which Americans easily fit into existing assumptions about their way of life.

If football helped illuminate America's Cold War path to the moon, Kaplan also envisioned the Cold War as a means to reform college football. The intertwined national priorities of space and the Cold War, according to Kaplan, created ever greater demands on intellectual talent. Such demands would rapidly intensify the academic performance of capable individuals while leaving behind those left unprepared for such competition. "The athlete in the Space Age will face an even stiffer fight to justify a classroom seat." Kaplan argued that the values of football, however, helped players maintain that seat. As a result, football not only provided competitors fit and tough enough to compete with the Soviets, but the intellectual demands of the Space Age would banish the academic abuses identified with college football. Because "academic curves tend upward," Kaplan argued, and that "improvement will be intensified in the Space Age," only those who mastered football specialization in addition to academic excellence would prosper. He predicted "that in the next ten years, the player who barely gets by" would become obsolete.[59] In Kaplan's views, the postwar abuses of college football, particularly the search for football talent based on the going rate rather than academic potential, would solve itself, allowing for a natural return to some fictional day when legitimate amateurism prevailed and "real" students played college football. Thus, college football would deliver Cold War victory and Cold War necessities would deliver college football reform, allowing the game to return to its allegedly pristine bygone era; the future would deliver the past.

Moreover, Kaplan's argument that Cold War necessity would deliver both academic and athletic achievement fit within the prevailing post–World War II ethos of abundance and assumptions of a society without limits. Lyndon Johnson promised Americans that they could have a Great Society at home and Cold War victory abroad by proclaiming, "We can do it all." Proponents of the game said much the same thing in declaring that big-time football and scholastic excellence were not mutually exclusive but, in fact, both means to the same end—the defeat of the Soviets. Concurrent with the idea of the liberal consensus that dominated American politics in the decades following World War II that promised domestic abundance at home and global security abroad, the vision of Kaplan, LaRoche, Kennedy, and others proposed that the culture of football in the postwar years did not require Americans to choose athletics over academics; they could have both.[60]

Kaplan's insistence on seeing academic reform and intellectual development emerge from the ultracompetitive world of big-time college football illustrated not merely the optimism of the period but also the insistence that the culture of abundance would deliver not merely "more" but "better." If the specialization of two-platoon football created a more rational game merely for the aggrandizement of spectators and coaches but came with long-term negative consequences, then it was little more than opulent luxury, serving no purpose but to appease insatiable consumerist desires. Americans raised the specter of luxury throughout the period by frequently warning that American abundance could lead to the valueless decadence of ancient Rome. Here, again, was the dilemma of the postwar culture of abundance: to create wealth and leisure while keeping its corrupting influences at bay. Kaplan's claim that the postwar version of the game would make both football and America better deftly linked football with the larger American cultural imperative of the Cold War to use progress for the benefit of all.

The culture of material abundance that marked the postwar period, however, emerged alongside limitations to existing assumptions of individuality and masculinity. Such broader cultural shifts also colored Americans' understandings of the transformation of college football. The dominance of the corporation more clearly defined both economic and cultural change during this period than any other facet. William H. Whyte, C. Wright Mills, Arthur Miller, and most successfully, David Riesman, all wrote caustic descriptions, for both academic and popular audiences, of the corporation's effect on the American scene.[61] According to Whyte's interpretation, corporate America created the Organization Man in American society, a personality devoted entirely to the corporate structure that employed him, devoid of all individual characteristics and identifying personalities. The intense competition of market capitalism and the attendant accumulation of wealth by fewer and fewer corporations that had been a part of the American economy since the onset of industrialization drastically accelerated in the years following World War II. At the onset of Cold War defense spending, just 100 companies landed 70 percent of all defense contracts and controlled half of all American corporate wealth. In the fifteen years following the end of World War II, the number of American firms was reduced by half, while corporations such as Dow Chemical grew 750 percent by 1958. As the number of companies in the marketplace decreased, the profits of those remaining increased dramatically. In the 1950s General Motors and American Telephone and Telegraph (AT&T) became the first corporations in history with profits in excess of $1 billion. By the early 1960s, only fifty companies controlled half of all corporate wealth in the United States. Corporations of such size were run by immense, impersonal bureaucracies, with workforces in the thousands and tens of thousands. In 1890, historian Frederick Jackson Turner declared the American frontier officially closed, based on census data, symbolically terminating the independence of the individual in America. In reality, that moment came in 1956 when, for the first time, more Americans worked for somebody else than for themselves.[62] Whyte, Mills, and Miller all commented on the consequences of these events on individuals: the loss of identity, the challenge to traditional notions of masculinity, the complete subjugation to corporate authority, and the disappearance of independent initiative.

The alienation of the individual and the cultural criticisms that followed found their way to college football as well, allowing many to see the larger postwar economy as an analogy to the changes affecting the game. Sociologists David Riesman and Reuel Denney declared that changes in the economics of the game during the period so closely resembled the larger American economy that the game could be spoken of as "industrial football."[63] The postwar recruiting frenzy and the attendant arms race of facilities, equipment, and salaries drove the operating expenses of college football into the stratosphere. At a time when faculty salaries ranged from $3,000 to $10,000 annually, one article estimated that at minimum, college football programs required operating budgets of $275,000, a figure that did not include player scholarships or additional, extralegal, or illegal inducements.[64] The ever-increasing costs of college football soon imposed the same Darwinian consequences faced by smaller companies in the larger national economy. Just as American companies disappeared in the face of oligopolistic competition, so too did college football teams. The expansion of major college football after World War II began to subside rapidly by the 1950s. The 1950–51 academic year witnessed more than fifty schools abandon football because of cost, a number that would exceed 150 by the end of the 1960s, many of them private parochial schools excluded from the postwar gravy train of the GI Bill and federal research contracts. Alleging that "football is pricing itself out of business," one article claimed that "the little fellows are being squeezed out and the bigger ones are getting bigger."[65] Riesman and Denney declared in starker economic terms that "football was now so mechanized that [some schools] could no longer afford the necessary entry fee for machinery and personnel." At the height of the Cold War era, "football had come to resemble other industries or mechanized farms, into which a new firm could not move . . . [without] large corporate investment. The production of a team involves the heavy overhead and staff personnel characteristic of high-capital, functionally rationalized industries."[66]

The larger postwar economy not only provided context for the changed economic imperative of the game but also allowed Americans to accept, or at least interpret, the rise of two-platoon football. Supporters of the two-platoon system inevitably framed their comments in the context of rational market terms. The new system of player specialization marked only the latest rationalization of the game, creating "much faster football," delivering "a superior product" that ultimately marked an "improvement in the quality of the game."[67] Two-platoon football made the game far more specialized and team oriented, while individual players enjoyed greater and greater responsibilities in smaller and smaller aspects of the game. Thus, while the individual declined in importance, his role as a cog in the larger team machinery increased. In his examination of the use of sport to mold Cold War–era youth, Russell Crawford notes the ubiquity of team identity as a traditional literary theme and a media vehicle. Articles in popular magazines such as *Life* and the *Saturday Evening Post* noted that star players did not truly achieve greatness until they learned to accept the primacy of team accomplishments. In the adolescent fiction anthology, *Teenage Football Stories*, Leo Margulies described the game as "above all, a team game. . . . It is a game where ability pays off—ability to fit into the team even more than as an individual." According to Crawford, when athletes, both real and fictional, "finally accept[ed] that they must conform to the group, they [made] decisions . . . little different, at their root," than those made by noted anticommunists "Whittaker Chambers or Harry Truman."[68]

Not everyone found two-platoon football an addition to the game, however, leaving many Americans to wonder if two-platoon football was "real" football. As chair of the NCAA rules committee, legendary Tennessee head coach Robert Neyland simply adjourned one committee meeting rather than endorse the two-platoon changes the committee was prepared to enact, famously describing it as "chicken shit football."[69] Most telling was that critics described two-platoon football with the same rhetoric as that used by Mills, Whyte, and Miller to describe the malaise of American culture produced by the corporatization and emasculation of the postwar economy. The mass exchanges of on-field personnel proved disorienting to many observers. One writer noted that "Factors such as [substitution] rules changes and subsidization . . . have helped bring about player anonymity."[70] More strident critics decried the two-platoon system because it limited to the offense the glory of "getting away on long runs or throwing touchdown passes." Defensive players might "finish [their] college career without ever carrying the ball." Delaware head coach William D. Murray declared the two-platoon provision "the worst thing to enter college football . . . stars on offense will no longer have to take the knocks that come from playing on defense. Soon there will be no such thing as an all-around football player."[71] Another coach, Larry Mullins at Kansas, argued that such changes denigrated the game itself: "Why should we develop boys to be just half football players. . . . There are some quarterbacks in particular who haven't made a dozen tackles during their collegiate careers. This is not football."[72] Denied the opportunity to share the spotlight, these players endured "the dirty work and someone who's never made a tackle will get his picture in the paper."[73] Another writer saw the new rules as providing "less opportunity for one man to emerge as an individual star, however heroic his performances." The decline of the player as individual marked the full bureaucratization of the game. In addition to separate offensive and defensive units, coaches also created "separate kickoff and receiving units. Some will go so far as to insert a special place-kick crew for the point-after-touchdown attempt."[74] In the words of one observer, "the triple threat star of yesterday has become a faceless employee."[75] Just as the corporatization of the postwar economy required the Organization Man to subsume his identity and accomplishments to the group, the rationalization of college football in the form of the two-platoon system bureaucratized the defense, limited the individual's contribution, and elevated the corporate identity of the team.

The cultural understanding of players as employees in the corporatized world of college football also allowed many to acknowledge and accept the pseudoprofessionalism that had marked the game since the 1890s. Such expression frequently took the form of explicit market terms. Undergraduates at the University of Michigan did not begrudge the special privileges Wolverine players received on campus, including special dorms and meal plans, in light of the amount of "work" they put in to the game. Sportswriter Roger Kahn, acknowledging his hypocrisy of criticizing the NCAA for its own hypocritical insistence on amateurism while he himself still enjoyed watching college football, noted, "I don't approve of intercollegiate hypocrisy, but it is senseless to begrudge the quarterback his living." Similarly, one Colorado coed rejected the insistence of amateur terms in describing the football team on her campus, "They're earning a living just like everyone else. Who am I to knock capitalism?"[76]

The willingness of observers to compare components of college football to the Cold War illustrates the level of cultural dominance that Americans ascribed to the Cold War itself during this period. It also, however, illustrates the elevated significance of college football in the minds of many Americans when they linked the game with the intense upheavals and anxieties of the period. In that regard, Americans utilized football as a way to come to terms with the changes of the postwar period every bit as much as they used the language of the Cold War and the postwar economy to understand the changes in college football. The willingness to interpret the rules changes and specialization during the period as creating college football's own version of the Organization Man, complete with the loss of identity, the sublimation of the individual, and the importance of the corporate structure reveals such utilization. Additionally, scholars like Kaplan, Conant, and others explicitly understood football as a means to allay American anxieties regarding the loss of small-producer competition and the fear that the Cold War period marked some fundamental departure from the American past. Thus, football in the postwar period emerged as a cultural mechanism for many Americans to interpret and accept the changes of postwar American society.

If Rube Samuelson's correlation of the Cold War and college football suggested the game's elevated cultural significance in the postwar years, it also hinted at the intense contestation over the Rose Bowl in college football. Although independent of the Cold War, the 1946 decision of the Big Ten and PCC to exclude other conferences from the Rose Bowl resulted from drastic differences over the meaning of intercollegiate athletics. Historian John Watterson has argued that no issue loomed larger within college football from the 1920s to the 1940s than the question of player subsidies. The tremendous growth in popularity of college football during the period drastically increased the pressures to win, prompting many schools to expand—and in some cases, legitimate—the various inducements given to college football players. No area of the country so willingly and openly accepted the new practices as the South.[77]

In 1929, the nonprofit Carnegie Foundation undertook a study of college athletics, revealing the most detailed, explicit evidence to date of violations of college football's amateur principles, citing southern schools as some of the most egregious violators. Little had changed a decade later when sportswriter John R. Tunis published a series of articles discussing the pervasiveness of player subsidies. In breaking down which schools engaged in which practices, Tunis created a whole separate category for the southern schools, led by the Southeastern Conference (SEC), whose members gave outright scholarships.[78] The open embrace by some schools of player subsidies by the late 1930s marked only the first shot in the spiraling arms race within college football that accelerated rapidly after World War II. The by-products of the GI Bill and the more liberal substitution rules, which now remained in place after the war, marked another plateau of the arms race, soon followed by new stadiums, training rooms, football-only dorms, and the pseudo-independent fund-raising arm of athletic departments to pay for it all—the nonprofit, tax-exempt booster association. As one southern athletic director paternalistically noted, "Football is a mighty costly business, son. It's a wide-open, million-dollar big business."[79] As a result, SEC schools roundly ignored criticisms of outright scholarships. "Traditionally," according to Roger Kahn, sports editor of *Newsweek*, writing in *The Nation*, recruiting customs in the South dictated that "anything the NCAA can't prove goes."[80]

Critics from the Pacific Coast Conference and Big Ten also implied that southern schools, who accounted for a disproportionate number of Rose

Bowl opponents by the late 1930s, used their Rose Bowl profits to elevate the recruiting wars. One observer linked the need to recruit players for both offense and defense with the expense, and attendant excesses, of wooing them: "Since more players were required to make [two-platoon football] work, more intense proselytizing is required. Keener competition for talent boosts the 'inducements' given to some very odd, road-show scholars."[81] Far from being a contagion that could be quarantined in the South, the excesses of player subsidies affected the entire country. Kenneth "Tug" Wilson, commissioner of the Big Ten, claimed that such behavior in the South caused reactive cheating in the Big Ten so as to keep players from defecting to the SEC. "Naturally, the result of these raids is a step-up in our own recruiting," including illegal activity "by alumni and coaches to keep our boys home."[82] It was this sequence of events that prompted the Big Ten and the PCC in 1946 to negotiate an exclusive five-year, renewable agreement to match schools from the respective conferences in the Rose Bowl.

Contrary to Wilson's sanctimonious criticisms of the SEC, the Big Ten and the PCC were not entirely above the fray on the question of player subsidies. Though not at the level of the SEC's policies, Tunis's 1939 report identified half the members of the Big Ten and PCC as providing various forms of financial assistance for "good football material."[83] The Big Ten, and to a lesser extent the PCC, roundly criticized athletic scholarships because they offered jobs programs instead. This allowed players to "work" for their tuition and fees while engaged in various make-work tasks both on and off campus. One student at PCC-member University of Southern California was responsible merely for emptying the campus pay phones once a week. Other tasks required even less, with officials fabricating time cards or fabricating the jobs themselves, just funneling money to players without even asking them to engage in the pretext of work. Through these means, the two conferences managed to avoid outright athletic scholarships and self-righteously criticize those who did offer them. One issue allowing the PCC and Big Ten to view themselves as above the fray of the postwar period was their embrace of the notion of faculty control of athletics. Both conferences created faculty athletic councils responsible for intercollegiate athletic governance and mandated that faculty members represent member schools at the conference level. As a result, most of the abuses associated with the PCC came not from within the campuses but from off-campus booster groups. Additionally, in comparison to their competitors around the country, the PCC and the Big Ten made a much better attempt at self-governance by periodically punishing member schools that violated conference rules. Thus, when the two conferences arranged their New Year's Day nuptials in December 1946, they fancied themselves the last two virgins remaining at the college football dance.[84]

Supporters of the new agreement plainly put it in the context of the recruiting and subsidization controversy. University of California head coach Frank Wickhorst argued that the arrangement would reduce "proselytizing" by schools hoping to play their way into the Rose Bowl jackpot. Wilson was even more direct by hoping that the proposed agreement "would prevent Southern schools from cutting into the Rose Bowl melon and perhaps cajole them into altering their views of collegiate amateurism." According to Wilson, Southern recruiting was the demon seed from which all violations of amateurism sprung: "We must set up a policy whereby a boy will choose a school for its educational value rather than the school choosing a boy for his athletic ability." Even ostensibly impartial observers noted the role that the Rose Bowl played in the increasing tensions between the SEC and Big Ten–PCC alliance. The *New York Times* declared "the Southern schools were the main target" of the new agreement. The paper declared the new arrangement was a way to "shut out the Southern colleges, who were generally regarded by the holier than thou boys as football carpetbaggers who need the [Rose] Bowl loot in order to keep their talent-producing machines operating."[85]

Southern schools reacted with indignation over their exclusion from the Rose Bowl. University of Alabama head coach Frank Thomas resented what he perceived as PCC ingratitude towards the South: "The Coast Conference has shown little appreciation for the way in which Southern teams have helped to perpetuate the Rose Bowl game when it was impossible to lure any other teams out." Even officials at the Tournament of Roses Association felt the South had been slighted. George S. Campbell, past tournament president, declared that the agreement "certainly slaps our old friends from the South," a sentiment echoed almost exactly by Robert McCurdy, another past tournament president: "Our good friends at Alabama, Georgia, and Tennessee" must feel as if they've been "kicked in the face."[86] One commentator went so far as to suggest that even the federal government opposed the agreement because prior to its enactment, virtually everyone expected Army to get the bid for the 1947 game. Civilian and military officials felt that Army's appearance on the West Coast in such a prominent game potentially aided Cold War military recruiting.[87]

The 1946 agreement lasted barely a decade before it unraveled in the late 1950s amidst divided Big Ten faculty sentiment and an egregious scandal among the Pacific Coast schools. In the wake of such calamities, stewards of the Rose Bowl embarked on an odyssey in the fall of 1961 aimed at returning the Rose Bowl to a game featuring opponents from across the country. In so doing, they inadvertently laid bare the anxieties, conflicts, and paradoxes of postwar American society. For the better part of a month, and in some instances longer, the sports pages of newspapers from across the country argued over, editorialized upon, and generally dissected the role of higher education in the face of Soviet advances, the place of students in the era of the multiversity, the propriety of sports as a vehicle for social change, the costs and consequences of segregation, and the struggle between national values and regional practices, all in the language and context of college football. Such discussions revealed the intense longing of Americans during the period to embrace and identify with distinctly American values. The explicit political, economic, and social references that elite and popular commentators ascribed to football elevated the game's cultural distinctiveness. Having accepted football as containing such connotations, however, allowed Americans to apply the game in broad strokes to define an American way of life. If football emerged during the period as a cultural mechanism by which Americans interpreted the domestic upheaval of the period, then the 1962 Rose Bowl was perhaps its most explicit manifestation.

TWO

Columbus: Struggling for the Soul of the Cold War University

"Lemmings do not race any more blindly for the sea than Buckeye fans toward Pasadena."
—Jerry Brondfield

By late November 1961, the already abysmal relations of Ohio State University faculty members with the local *Columbus Dispatch* managed to degrade into a virtual blood feud, setting off a near lynch-mob mentality among many Columbus residents and leaving some faculty members wary of opening their doors or answering their phones. Across the country, community enmity and vitriol aimed at university faculty members on countless campuses during the period mounted when faculty invited known or even implied communists to speak on campus, allegedly used their lecture platforms to challenge U.S. foreign policy or suggested that Karl Marx might be worthy of study after all. The Ohio State faculty, however, had done none of these things, at least not in November 1961. Rather, the faculty decided to reject an invitation for the school's football team to participate in the Rose Bowl game, which in the eyes of their critics was every bit as detrimental as if they had done any of those other things. Although many faculty members had been leery for years of commercialized football's prominence on campus, the launching of the Soviet satellite Sputnik in 1957 sharply focused faculty understanding of the relationship between higher education and the Cold War. As a result, faculty and their supporters examined perceptions of undergraduate admission requirements, graduate programs, the university's research reputation, and legislative funding and found them all wanting. At any time, such a conclusion was painful; at the height of the Cold War, the faculty deemed it a threat to national priorities. As a result, faculty members hoped to reorient the priorities of the university and its supporters toward greater earnestness and commitment to issues more pressing than a football game.

In the eyes of the *Dispatch* and football's defenders, however, the faculty emerged not as patriotic Cold Warriors but as stereotypical esoteric intellectuals who looked down upon the locals from their ivory tower, snobbishly dismissing the one vibrant link between citizens and the university: the football team. These individuals countered the Cold War rhetoric of the faculty by deploying some of their own, accepting the relationship between football and toughness that many at the time saw as crucial to national character. For these individuals, football was not a distraction from Cold War priorities, it *was* a Cold War priority. Thus, in the perspective of both the faculty and their opponents, football served as a medium through which the anxieties of the Cold War emerged and could be negotiated. As a result, postwar football revealed itself in Columbus to have broad cultural resonance, marking both its malleability and universality.

While it took the anxieties of the Cold War to coalesce faculty opposition to the Rose Bowl in 1961, many of their concerns had existed for decades. Organized in 1896 as the first of the modern intercollegiate athletic conferences, the Western Conference, as the Big Ten was originally known, described itself as a collection of faculty representatives. The conference operates without a written constitution, governing itself instead "by precedent and the various resolutions passed from time to time" by the member-schools' faculty representatives. The real meaning of faculty control emerged in 1900 when Northwestern University's faculty representative, H. S. White, proposed a measure known as the White Resolution, allowing any member institution's faculty council a thirty-day review period to essentially veto actions of the conference. White Resolution checks became so commonplace that to avoid a veto, conference meetings began sending legislation back to the campuses for faculty approval before enacting them.[1] In few instances was the true meaning of faculty control as demonstrated by the White Resolution more apparent than on the issue of the Rose Bowl. From its inception, the conference declared that all "games shall be played on grounds either owned by or under control of one or both of the colleges participating in the contest, and all intercollegiate games shall be played under student or college management and not under the control of any corporation or association or private individual." The emergence of bowl games, however, soon challenged this policy. Faculty representatives met to discuss the Rose Bowl's invitation for Michigan to play Stanford in the inaugural 1902 contest. Although the meeting minutes describe the game's sponsor as a "floral association," representatives somehow failed to find this in violation of its previous policy.[2] Emerging faculty opposition on the matter, however, ensured that only one more Big Ten team appeared in Pasadena for another 45 years.

As southern acceptance of scholarships and aggressive recruiting tactics created unease both on the West Coast and in the Midwest, many involved saw an alliance between the like-minded Big Ten and the Pacific Coast Conferences (PCC) as a natural resolution to the problem, while simultaneously reserving "the Rose Bowl melon" for themselves. As the *New York Times* put it, a Rose Bowl alliance would "establish the New Year's classic as a 'closed shop' against colleges which do not see eye to eye with the Big [Ten] and Coast conferences on athletic standards."[3] Such an arrangement, however, would have necessitated an open embrace of the corporate commercial interests that bowl games represented. As such, Big Ten faculty consistently rejected such overtures. Though some had sought an alliance much earlier, the first formal attempt at a Rose Bowl alliance came in September 1940. The conference representatives supported the alliance, but after referring the matter via White Resolution to the faculty councils, it was rejected. The conference even prohibited member institutions from participating in the Rose Bowl independent of a formal conference alliance. In 1944, the Rose Bowl solicited Ohio State, but the conference voted with "unfailing consistency of policy" to reject postseason play.[4] The crisis of the postwar years, however, finally pushed the tide of support for an alliance in favor of such an arrangement.

Approached again by the PCC in September 1946, the Big Ten faculty representatives engaged in "extensive discussion" on the matter, agreeing to a tentative contract in November. The final contract, however, maintained several conditions, illustrating the level of opposition to the contract and the ambivalence toward the Rose Bowl itself that many faculty representatives maintained. The first two conditions declared that the contract would last only five years and that no member would be forced to participate. In other words, if the deal went sour, the Big Ten would be rid of it in short order, and if the conference champion turned out to be a school that vehemently opposed the arrangement, it reserved the right to turn down the invitation. Illustrating also the concerns many had for the overt commercialism of the Rose Bowl, the Big Ten insisted that the contracting parties include only the two conferences, excluding the Tournament of Roses. Even with these conditions, the measure met with opposition from Illinois, Minnesota, and Purdue.[5] If supporters of the alliance breathed a sigh of relief at its consummation, they were in for a surprise. The new arrangement, set to take effect the following New Year's Day, occurred so late in the season that media speculation had already identified Army as the favored opponent for the January 1947 game. Five years before the cheating scandal broke and only a year from the end of World War II, it seemed as if everyone wanted to see West Point's unbeaten, untied cadets in the Rose Bowl. When popular opinion and most sportswriters suggested the two conferences put off the alliance for a year to allow Army to come in January, Big Ten faculty representatives acknowledged the tenuousness of their own support. Big Ten representatives rebuffed suggestions of deferral by claiming "they had no authority to make the arrangement effective" beyond the 1947 game. Big Ten commissioner Tug Wilson noted that "Some of us have worked 20 years to get the conferences together" and if faculty representatives tried to defer the pact, they would have had to go back to their campus faculty councils for approval. With that they ran the risk of having the entire alliance overturned: "Frankly, we fear we'll not get another chance if we fail to put the original agreement across."[6]

Big Ten faculty support for the Rose Bowl contract remained divided. When the original five-year contract came up for renewal in 1951, Minnesota, Northwestern, Purdue, and Wisconsin unsuccessfully opposed the measure but succeeded in keeping the length of the new contract to just three years. Discussions over renewal in 1953 for another three-year period met with opposition from Michigan State, Minnesota, Northwestern, and Wisconsin, but the six remaining schools carried the measure for renewal. In 1956, the latter three schools unsuccessfully opposed yet another extension, this one now an "open-ended" contract requiring a two-year notice of termination. Clearly, by the mid-1950s, Big Ten faculty remained wary of the Rose Bowl arrangement.[7] Much of this wariness came from explicit concerns of the commercialization of bowl games and the overemphasis they placed on football. The experience of Ohio State's 1957 team provides a good example. To satisfy the tremendous excitement surrounding the Buckeyes' invitation, the university chartered an entire train to transport the members of the athletic board, members of the athletic department, and the board of trustees, including all of their spouses. A second train, funded by the Oldsmobile division of General Motors, carried the 150-piece marching band, cheerleaders, and chaperones. Twice en route to Pasadena, as the trains stopped to hold impromptu pep rallies for Buckeye boosters along the route, the band struck up "In My Merry

Oldsmobile" in a synergy of sponsorship and advertising that the folks at GM must have appreciated. Oldsmobile also paid for the band to make a sightseeing excursion to San Francisco once they were in California, while the Columbus Chamber of Commerce threw a "Christmas Party away from home" for the players, complete with a full Christmas dinner and gifts for every member of the team. Although such sponsorships allowed commercial entities to pick up many costs, it also increased the commercialization of the whole process, with nothing rankling critics more than the band's provision of what amounted to a free traveling advertisement for Oldsmobile. The unsubsidized extravagance of Ohio State's official traveling party cut deeply into the school's share of the game's profits. The contract allotted Ohio State less than $25,000, but after expenses the school's net amounted to $15,522.[8] Although the kind of commercialization and overemphasis that informed faculty opposition existed long before the Cold War period, several circumstances developed after the 1956 renewal of the Rose Bowl contract that drastically sharpened faculty thinking on the issue.

Many faculty at Ohio State opposed the Rose Bowl contract, yet their school had always voted to affirm the alliance. This occurred because the university's athletic authority rested with an athletic board composed of ten members, including six faculty members appointed by the university president. The other four appointments came from students and alumni. As a result, so-called friendly faculty found their way onto the athletic board, and seldom did Ohio State buck the majority in conference matters. In this manner, faculty control of athletics at Ohio State was never independent of the administration. The absence of vigilant faculty oversight allowed abuses within the athletic department to go unchecked, perhaps the biggest being the jobs program for athletes. In addition to on-campus jobs, the program also included employment through the Columbus Chamber of Commerce, which by 1955 was disbursing roughly $75,000 to $80,000 annually to Buckeye athletes, most of them football players. Many of these jobs did not actually exist, serving as little more than a fictitious cover for cash payments to athletes. As a result, the NCAA and the conference placed Ohio State on probation in April 1956, banning all Buckeye teams from postseason competition for three years. Officials at Ohio State did not deny the allegations, claiming instead that some of the most sanctimonious accusers were themselves just as guilty.[9]

With the abuse of the jobs program at Ohio State and other conference schools, the conference finally scrapped the charade and authorized outright scholarships for athletes, though based on a formula linking financial need

Figure 1. Though no one denied that Ohio State had broken conference rules, this cartoon suggested what most everyone knew: the Buckeyes weren't the only ones. From *The Lantern*, May 2, 1956.

with academic performance.[10] In the midst of the conference investigation of Ohio State and the abolition of the jobs program, the faculty chose to take matters into its own hands. In June 1955, "a restive faculty" appointed a committee under the leadership of English professor James F. Fullington to report on the "role and status of intercollegiate athletics" at Ohio State. The scandal over the jobs program and the probationary status of the athletic department colored the report of the Fullington Committee. While the faculty council charged the committee with broadly investigating athletics in general, the committee correctly identified football as the driving force in the athletic department. With its release in May 1957, the Fullington Report declared that Ohio State lacked faculty control in the truest meaning of the phrase. "The faculty," according to the report, "gradually and perhaps unknowingly relinquished much of its regulatory and policy-making privilege to the university administration and trustees." The report did not limit its condemnation to the faculty for vacating its responsibility but also criticized the athletic department for its stewardship in the face of faculty abandonment. From its earliest actions, the athletic department accepted the commercialization of football as necessary to "carr[y] the financial load for virtually all the other sports," thereby encouraging the kinds of abuses that landed Ohio State on probation.[11]

The Fullington Report recommended the abolition of the president-appointed athletic board and the creation of an athletic council whose faculty members would be elected by the university-wide faculty council. Additionally, the faculty council would elect the conference faculty athletic representative. Finally, the athletic council would be responsible for crafting athletic policy but accountable to the faculty council. In November 1957, with approval of the board of trustees, the faculty council enacted the recommendations of the Fullington Report, with only one revision allowing for the university president to nominate members to the athletic council subject to faculty council approval. This restructuring of athletics policy at Ohio State did not, however, bring immediate peace to the faculty over the role of athletics within the university.[12]

The denouement of the jobs and scholarship issue emerged as yet another source of irritation to the faculty. Having abolished the corrupt jobs program in 1956, the conference then scrapped its hybrid academic performance–financial need scholarship in 1961 for a full-blown athletic scholarship irrespective of need or academic performance. Ohio State's faculty representative Jim McCoy noted that with other conferences such as the SEC providing such benefits to players, the Big Ten needed to match those offers "in order to compete with them in the rat-race recruiting for stars."[13] The stipulations of the new aid program inflamed the faculty because not only did it abolish the reliance on academic performance but it also rewarded academic mediocrity. To be eligible for a Big Ten scholarship, players needed only maintain a 1.7 grade point average (GPA) in their freshman year, increasing to a 1.8 GPA for their sophomore year, a 1.9 GPA in their junior year and a 2.0 their senior year. Although the conference attempted to spin this new program as an attempt to rein in recruiting abuses, the Ohio State student paper put it in its baldest context. "It would be much more noble to discontinue the awarding of athletic grants completely rather than endorse the proposed Big Ten rule. However, abolishing athletic grants would also mean favoring Big Ten athletic competition on the Ivy League model, eliminating any chance" for national championships.[14] Thus, at least in the eyes of the *Lantern*, nobility and winning football were mutually exclusive.

Further explicating the Fullington Report's linkage between revenue and overemphasis, head coach Woody Hayes threw rhetorical gasoline on the fire when he suggested that Ohio State's football players were athletes first and students second (or not at all), exclaiming, "You don't attract the kind of crowds it takes to fill these arenas unless you pay a lot of attention to your job—and the job, to some extent, of these boys is football."[15] Perhaps the greatest paradox arising from the new scholarship program was that it violated existing academic policy. The new conference rules stipulated a player needed to maintain a 1.8 GPA by the end of his sophomore year. However, university policy demanded that students maintain at minimum a 1.9 GPA by their sophomore year, with anything less than a 2.0 warranting academic probation. Thus, a student could enjoy good standing with the conference and the athletic department while on academic probation within the university.[16]

Big Ten faculty concerns over academic integrity and athletics intensified with the scandalous demise of the Pacific Coast Conference. Throughout the 1950s hints of illegal football slush funds at PCC schools cropped up in the media. By 1957, conference investigations revealed extensive violations of conference rules, including cash payments, special treatment for athletes, and academic improprieties. Once these circumstances became public knowledge, the chancellors at Washington and UCLA, two of the worst offenders, stonewalled and misled conference investigators to cover up their schools' complicity. The conference placed four schools—Washington, Cal, UCLA, and USC—on varying forms of probation. Like the earlier Big Ten scandal that landed Ohio State on probation, the guilty parties felt they had been unfairly targeted by the other members of the conference who had engaged in similar activity. As a result, the four guilty schools blamed the other conference members for their predicament and severed all athletic relations with them. In 1958, the PCC formally voted to disband, with representatives from UCLA and Oregon not even speaking to one another.[17]

Big Ten personnel mulled over the PCC catastrophe and its implications. The secretary of the alumni-oriented Ohio State University Association[18] and editor of the alumni magazine *Ohio State University Monthly*, Jack Fullen, wrote to a like-minded faculty member at Northwestern concerning the Rose Bowl agreement between the Big Ten and the PCC. Though Fullen questionably linked the PCC's breakup to the Rose Bowl itself, he nonetheless described the defunct conference as "the malefactors in the worst football scandal in the annals of intercollegiate athletic[s] with whom the [Big Ten] is proposing to deal."[19] Suggesting that a continued Rose Bowl arrangement with this group sullied the Big Ten by association, Fullen ominously implied that the next scandal might be closer to home. Furthermore, the national media found the various scandals and crises of college football salacious copy and seldom avoided an opportunity to expose the seamier side of the game. In a six-month period from December 1956 to June 1957, *Look* magazine alone ran five features with titles like "Inside the West Coast Football Scandal" and "Football Scandal Hits the Big 10."[20] For faculty already concerned about the role football played within the academic process, the linking of academic reputation with scandal now heaped scorn upon indignity.

Under any circumstances, these events would have animated university faculty, but taken in the context of 1950s Cold War America, they carried an importance that exceeded that of college football. The rapid changes witnessed in American higher education following World War II made for an intensely competitive environment. Competition for federal research dollars, funding from state legislatures, and an expanding undergraduate student base made universities and their faculties more aware than ever of academic reputation, research facilities, and scholarly output. At Ohio State, such awareness came with the painful realization that in the postwar years, they increasingly witnessed shortfalls in library acquisitions, student scholarships, and faculty salaries. As a result, many well-regarded faculty, mostly in the humanities, left Ohio State for more distinguished, better funded universities and, according to one former administrator, Ohio State faced difficulties in replacing them. Prior to World War II, the American Association of Universities, a collection of the most distinguished research universities in the nation, undertook a study of the nation's best graduate programs, and Ohio State ranked highly in several fields. After the war, however, those same departments were the ones that witnessed high turnover. The English Department, for example, lost roughly a third of its faculty in six years. As a result, Ohio State's ranking within the AAU took a hit, and some feared its membership was in jeopardy. At the height of the Cold War, according to John Thelin, AAU membership was based almost entirely on a school's reputation in research, scholarship, and doctoral programs. Exclusion from the AAU implied a clear loss of institutional prestige. Additionally, Ohio State faced a crisis of identity over admissions requirements. Alone among Big Ten universities, Ohio State maintained an open admissions policy whereby any student with an Ohio high school diploma could gain admittance. Although faculty from an earlier time looked with pride on this populist provision, it was increasingly seen as a mark of mediocrity during the intensely competitive days of the early Cold War.[21]

Many observers at the time focused on the stinginess of the legislature and its unwillingness to realize that academic excellence cost more than mediocrity. Other issues however, also harmed the university's ability to recruit new faculty—indeed, harmed the reputation of the university itself. One such issue was the notorious Speaker's Rule. Like similar rules limiting free speech on college campuses during the period, the board of trustees enacted Ohio State's Speaker's Rule after legislative allegations that the university harbored communist sympathies. Following the appearance of Columbia professor of education Harold Rugg to speak on campus in 1951, a controversy ensued concerning alleged leftist remarks by Rugg. Although Rugg's exact comments remain in doubt, the board of trustees swiftly responded to ensure that such "un-American propaganda" never again found a platform on the campus of The Ohio State University. The board instructed the president's office to vet all future campus speakers "ten days prior to the extension of the actual invitation" to speak. Opponents quickly dubbed the new policy the "gag rule," and some of the most vociferous opposition came from humanities faculty within the College of Arts and Sciences. The stifling effect on academic freedom was palpable. Faculty members rescinded invitations to avoid subjecting colleagues to the humiliating "security checks," while scholarly groups avoided meeting at Ohio State altogether. In 1952, the American Physical Society moved its annual meeting of more than 800 physicists from Columbus to Chicago. One assistant dean, when explaining the rule to incredulous faculty job candidates, claimed he inevitably received some version of "You mean I have to plan ahead of time and have the Board approve anyone I want to come in here and speak on any subject?"[22]

Anxious over academic reputation and frustrated with restrictions on academic freedom, faculty grew downright exasperated when public opinion concerned itself only with football. On a visit to Columbus in the 1950s, U.S. Senator Leverett Saltonstall inadvertently linked the football issue with faculty anxieties about academic reputation when he proclaimed, "All I knew before coming here was that the University has a great football team."[23] In looking back on the period, Spanish professor and assistant dean Richard Armitage put the faculty's frustration regarding popular opinion in a nutshell when he asked rhetorically, "They know us for football and winning Rose Bowls. But do they know we have a great mechanical engineering group?"[24] Faculty members at Ohio State were not the only ones in the Big Ten who bitterly noted the manner in which the public ignored academic successes in comparison to the football program. At Northwestern University, the dean of the Graduate School, Moody Prior, grew "discouraged at indications that we are not given all the credit which is due to us for our attainments and accomplishments." Noting Northwestern's own opposition to continuing the Rose Bowl alliance, Prior felt it would have been "a terrible calamity" affecting the recognition of Northwestern's academic reputation if the school had supported the Rose Bowl contract.[25]

When considering any potential conflict over football at Ohio State University, one must always contend with the school's larger-than-life head coach, Wayne Woodrow Hayes, known to everyone simply as Woody. Hayes's relationship with the faculty has never been authoritatively defined, but most interpretations of the period saw Hayes's relationship with the faculty as combative. Even before his tenure at Ohio State, Hayes ran into faculty opposition when he coached at Denison University. While his biographer asserts that it came from faculty anxieties over the increasing prominence of football, it may have been merely a reaction to Hayes's profligate profanity.[26] At Ohio State, legendary diplomatic historian William Appleman Williams later claimed that Hayes threatened his job in one 1951 confrontation, the first year on campus for both men. Williams had failed the team's halfback in his Western Civilization course and Hayes attempted to pressure him to change the grade. Hayes allegedly reminded Williams of his untenured status and informed him that the profits of the football program provided for his salary. When Williams refused to change the grade, Hayes informed him, "Well, you better goddam well believe that I'll change your job, *Instructor* Williams."[27]

Hayes certainly did have his defenders within the faculty, Williams's allegation notwithstanding. Virtually all objective observers note that Hayes maintained a respect for the academic mission of the university. He was notorious among his players for evicting academically poor athletes from the dorm, only to move them into his own home where they benefited from the personal tutoring of either Hayes or his wife, Anne. Hayes also maintained a general respect and admiration for the faculty, frequently attending scholarly lectures and programs given by the faculty. He often took his meals at the Faculty Club, engaging faculty members in subjects he enjoyed. Professor Richard Armitage, a critic of big-time football's excesses, admitted that "Woody got along fairly well with the faculty. Better than many. And he admired them." Political scientist Harry Jaffa, a supporter of Hayes, echoed the sentiment in asserting that Woody viewed the faculty "as the lifeblood of the university . . . far more important than the football program."[28] Thus, while Hayes certainly had his detractors in the ranks of the faculty, the origins of a building faculty anxiety over football could not be laid at Hayes's feet.

With academic reputation and academic funding at the heart of faculty concerns over football at Ohio State, it is not surprising the building storm over the Rose Bowl eventually included Jack Fullen, the head of Ohio State's alumni association. Ascending to the position of alumni secretary in 1928, Fullen immediately set out to further the reputation of his alma mater and turn the alumni association into a fund-raising dynamo. In 1939, he personally created the Development Fund as the university's primary source of extralegislative funding. By 1960, the fund contained more than 29,000 donors and included more than $1.4 million in annual contributions. In its twenty-one-year existence, it had raised more than $9 million, with half of that going to faculty research. By 1962, the fund's endowment lagged behind only that of Harvard and Yale. Most faculty members found him a tireless advocate for their concerns, and he often sat in as a nonvoting observer of faculty councils. Acutely aware of the costs of higher education, Fullen used the pages of the *Ohio State University Monthly*, which he edited, to browbeat the legislature, criticize misordered academic priorities, and harangue casual observers of the university who only cared about the football team. It was in this latter capacity that Fullen soon became Buckeye Public Enemy Number One in the eyes of many football partisans.[29]

By the late 1950s, Fullen had criticized in print the jobs scandal that landed Ohio State on probation, the special admissions considerations that athletes received, the scholarship funding available to them unavailable to other students, and the general hypocrisy endemic to American intercollegiate athletics and its notions of amateurism. Before all of that, however, Fullen had refused to pay obeisance to Woody Hayes. Fullen, good-naturedly at first, then with greater bite, took exception to Hayes's imperious ways, his histrionic behavior that bordered on the embarrassing, and his implication in the jobs scandal. What most observers then and later ignore is that Fullen had generally liked Hayes for a time and, in fact, on three different occasions defended him in print. What soured the relationship between the two was not merely Hayes's sometimes outrageous behavior, the most famous of which got him fired in 1978 after he slugged an opposing player in Ohio State's Gator Bowl loss, but their conflict over the increasing role that sports, particularly football, played in defining American higher education at a time of international crisis.[30]

It is not coincidental that the tone of Fullen's anti-football, anti-Hayes rhetoric changed drastically after 1957, when the Soviets launched their Sputnik satellite. For Fullen and many others, that event marked a watershed moment that raised the stakes of the Cold War, demonstrating how far ahead the Soviets were in science, math, and their practical applications. In the wake of such a stunning intellectual setback, American higher education needed to respond with a renewed commitment to intellectual discourse. The faculty, according to Fullen, were "painfully aware that the country is experiencing a conspicuous lag" in the fields of "science, technology and . . . education. And speaking of contests, they believe that the most conspicuous one for us to watch and to be really concerned about is the one being fought in the classrooms of the U.S.A. and the U.S.S.R."[31] In the eyes of Fullen, the future of the Republic and the free world was at stake. As a result, Fullen's editorials increasingly placed the ongoing concern over athletics at Ohio State in the context of the Cold War. While the Soviets were "financing thousands of [their] brightest students clear through the PhD degree . . . our universities are constantly raising fees. Half of the upper fourth of America's brightest students are not going to college, mostly for financial reasons. I am sure that few, if any, of the upper fourth of our most promising football stars are not going on to college."[32] Attempting to goad the legislature into increasing the university's funding in a post-Sputnik world, he noted not only that Soviet support for higher education revealed a greater respect than that demonstrated by the Ohio legislature but also that even neighboring Indiana outspent the Buckeye State in education appropriations. Fullen closed by sarcastically noting, "However, last night OSU beat Indiana in basketball."[33] The fault lay not just with the Ohio legislature but also with a populace willing to equate athletic success with academic accomplishment, an occurrence Fullen lamented in verse:

> While Laos is lost, and Cuba, too,
> This is what we do;
> While Khrushchev rants
> And Kennedy pants,
> This is what we do;
> While brains stay cheap,
> While the backfield's deep,
> Maybe we *are* "through."[34]

When criticisms of faculty opposition to football's prominence appeared, in particular one that claimed that "all university professors are oddballs," readers of the *Monthly* leapt to their defense using rhetoric similar to Fullen's. Deploring the lack of respect shown esteemed faculty members, one reader noted, "In Russia, the university professor is the most respected, highly paid member of the society."[35]

The backdrop of the Cold War also placed renewed focus on the role of the student. For many commentators, the challenges of the Cold War required a "great educational awakening" among college students "to safeguard the future of the United States" against the scholarly and educational advances of the Soviets. Although defenders of the game argued that the values and lessons of football were critical to ensuring Cold War victory, the game's critics also linked football to the Cold War by suggesting that its overemphasis distracted American society from the larger task at hand. "American higher education has permitted its intellectual pilings to become . . . barnacled with a host of secondary functions" such as "undue emphasis on football." The Cold War thus demanded that students devote themselves to the "one great cause—learning" if they were to defeat "the Ivans." Doing so would require them to reject traditional campus distractions such as football in favor of studious earnestness.[36] At least some popular commentators suggested that such an awakening was inverting the traditional campus social order. An October 1959 cover of the *Saturday Evening Post* featured two comely coeds ignoring the star football player in favor of a bookworm absorbed in an aerospace text. Though the image suggested that football players had been completely supplanted on campus by aspiring engineers, the accompanying text reminded the reader that football players were not so one dimensional. "Don't sell Big M short. There's no law against a football star's becoming another kind of star, too, and lots of them have done so." One national writer, in an article entitled, "Sad News from the Campus, Nobody Loves the Football Hero Anymore," suggested, perhaps a little disingenuously, that fellow undergraduates looked critically at football players because of their inability to "discuss earth satellites." At a time when "intellectualism is in fashion," the writer found football's anti-intellectualism misplaced.[37]

The glorification of football at the university level during such critical times was also criticized for its ripple effects. Richard Armitage noted that "overemphasis in a large university leads the way to overemphasis in secondary schools at a time when national leaders are attempting to pump more substance into the schooling of our young people."[38] The American preoccupation with sports at a time of such crisis proved particularly disturbing to Fullen because it contained such dark historical portends. While the United States was "bleeding for scientists, engineers, teachers, and brains," the Big Ten instituted its new scholarship policy requiring only a 1.7 GPA for athletes and providing them with more financial aid than regular students. The willingness to accept such "low standards" was a national disgrace. "At a time when the real long range battle with the Communists is being fought in the classroom[s] of the two societies, this double standard is a mockery of the supposed 'higher' education." Fullen, suggested that if the United States did not get its educational house in order, the American Republic would soon go the way of the Roman's. The willingness to embrace sports at such a cost to national security brought to Fullen's mind "the old Roman bread and circuses all over again." With so much at stake, the emphasis on football at the expense of academic funding marked "a corruption of values" that blinded many Americans to the real challenge at hand. "On the way to the Coliseum, they are passing laboratories where underpaid scientists are timing experiments which will secure the country's freedom and prosperity."[39] Fullen was not the only observer at the time to see the analogy of the Romans. Moody Prior, dean of the Graduate School at Northwestern University, felt that few Americans "sufficiently realized" the stakes in this "new era of education. American higher education must become the finest anywhere in the world, not only because we must look well in the eyes of the world in everything we do" as the leader of the free world, "but because second best in education is no longer good enough for survival." In Prior's eyes, Americans faced a time of decision. "If we tell the world that we are willing to devote our efforts and to channel the enthusiasm of our youth in the direction of a Roman circus, we have clearly indicated that we may not be among" those willing to offer service to the Republic in her hour of need.[40]

With renewed authority resulting from the reorganization recommended in the 1957 Fullington Report and an intensified sense of national crisis spawned by the launching of Sputnik the same year, faculty at Ohio State attempted to reassert the intellectual priorities of the university while also placing football in proper perspective. It was in this environment that the Rose Bowl contract came up for renewal in 1959, and faculty opinion across the Big Ten had decidedly shifted on the matter. The most obvious concern was the scandalous dissolution of the PCC. The corporate entity with which the Big Ten had contracted no longer existed; as a result, the PCC officially notified the Big Ten in October 1959 of the termination of the Rose Bowl contract that had been in force since November 1946. Ohio State president Novice G. Fawcett disingenuously claimed, "We had no one with whom to contract."[41] In reality, any discussion of a new arrangement had to consider that the rump Athletic Association of Western Universities (AAWU), which had assumed the responsibility of providing a West Coast opponent, included the worst offenders in the PCC slush-fund scandal. Additionally, the structure of the AAWU left many wondering if the new conference provided for true faculty control with its loose organizational lines and "reli[ance] primarily on . . . informal agreements to govern financial aid policies, recruiting practices, etc."[42] This last point was of particular sensitivity considering that throughout the fall of 1959, particularly at the November meeting, the Big Ten faculty council witnessed contentious debate on whether the expansion and costs of college football had "lessened faculty control." As a result, the council appointed a committee in 1959 consisting of athletic directors and faculty members to examine the issues surrounding any possible renewal of a Rose Bowl agreement.[43]

The proposals put forth by the Rose Bowl Committee demonstrated a desire to preempt much of the existing faculty opposition. The report proposed limiting appearances to no more than once every three years, scheduling of practice and travel time so as not to interfere with academic schedules, and an equitable distribution of game tickets and financial proceeds, thereby elevating the conference from "invited guests" of the West Coast schools to equal contracting partner. The committee's report also praised the Tournament of Roses Association for "preserving the standards of dignity appropriate to educational institutions, which must be our cardinal consideration at all times."[44] The existence, operation, and rhetoric of the Rose Bowl Committee suggested that the Big Ten Conference still deferred to its member faculties and accepted the ideal of faculty control as superior to any competitive or financial considerations. In fact, nothing could have been further from the truth.

As far back as the summer of 1958, conference commissioner Tug Wilson began plotting to subvert faculty control and continue a Rose Bowl arrangement with the West Coast schools. In a confidential memo outlining such a strategy, Wilson acknowledged the shifting faculty opinions on the matter and surveyed existing faculty positions. He identified Minnesota, Northwestern, and Wisconsin as consistently opposed to the Rose Bowl, with Michigan's support listed as "touch and go" and Ohio State likely to oppose. Wilson specifically noted that the conference could no longer count on Ohio State's approval due to the administrative restructuring in the wake of the Fullington Report and that "the matter would have to be submitted to the full faculty . . . which was not the case in past years." Those five schools could force a 5-5 deadlock, killing any votes to renegotiate. Revealing his feelings on the matter, Wilson also noted that the situation would be hopeless "should any other institution defect" to the opposition. In his eyes, those who opposed the Rose Bowl were enemies. Fully acknowledging "the possibility of a negative action by our faculties," Wilson, joined by the rump schools now making up the AAWU, attempted to maintain a

Rose Bowl relationship "without the necessity of referring the matter to our faculties under the White Resolution." Seeking to develop such a strategy, he secretly met with the AAWU athletic directors in August 1958, a meeting that included Ohio State's athletic director Richard Larkins "because of Ohio State's crucial position" in any future votes. Wilson baldly announced that all present shared "a mutual desire" to "[avoid] a White Resolution action" on the Rose Bowl matter. To that end, the Big Ten group suggested a rather fantastic legalistic maneuver on the part of the West Coast schools. The PCC schools were to reconvene, rescind their earlier termination of the Rose Bowl contract, and "seek a substitute resolution which would convey to the [AAWU] as original parties on interest the rights and responsibilities held by the Pacific Coast Conference in the Rose Bowl contracts, in order to preserve the continuity of those contracts." This would keep the original contract in force, precluding the need for Big Ten faculties to approve a new arrangement and preventing the faculties from asserting its statutory authority over athletic policy. "Legally . . . this would not require[,] and in fact would not permit[,] the Big Ten Conference to act except to void the contract on its own part," an unlikely possibility. After consulting with its lawyers, the West Coast schools rejected the plan, also acknowledging that it would require enemies to convene once more, an entirely unpleasant prospect considering some representatives were not even speaking to one another. The rejection of a PCC/AAWU legal maneuver prompted Wilson to suggest one on the part of the Big Ten. He suggested that the athletic directors reword future proposals "in the negative, i.e. 'to disapprove further Rose Bowl participation,'" requiring a majority to overturn, as opposed to requiring a majority to enact, future Rose Bowl participation. "This is a technical hedge against a 5-5 division," a maneuver that even Wilson admitted was "a dangerous procedure."[45] By any definition of the term, what Tug Wilson proposed in August 1958 was nothing less than a conspiracy to erode faculty control in the oldest, most prestigious intercollegiate athletic conference in the United States.

What is even more astounding about Wilson's suggestions is that having thus proposed to undermine the premise of faculty control upon which the conference was founded, he continued to view the Big Ten and the West Coast conferences, both of whom having just emerged from notorious recruiting scandals, as morally above the rabble of college athletics. Just as Barry Goldwater would defend anticommunist violations of civil liberties with the phrase, "Extremism in defense of liberty is no vice," Wilson felt that strong-armed tactics were justified in the face of grave threats. For Wilson, the future of college athletics was at stake. Continued Rose Bowl participation would position the two conferences to determine that future or at least insulate them from the excesses of those who would destroy amateurism as Wilson defined it. "In particular, it would be desirable to use the Rose Bowl game as an incident to a closer bond" between the two conferences and their like-minded policies.[46] The conference's Rose Bowl Committee agreed, stating that West Coast schools enjoyed a "similar . . . educational standing" to the Big Ten schools and that continuing the Rose Bowl was only a first step to "enlarging our athletic competition with them in other sports." Noting that such exceptionalism was "by no means confined to athletics," the committee referenced the "'Big Ten–California Study of Educational Costs' as an instance of the broad areas of common interest which have been symbolized by our participation in the Rose Bowl." Thus, Wilson envisioned the Rose Bowl as only the first step in creating a semipermanent relationship between the two groups. When AAWU schools proposed a Christmas basketball tournament to be played in the newly built Los Angeles Sports Arena, Wilson jumped at the invitation to provide three Big Ten representatives, envisioning that such "arrangements, on a long range basis, might be set up on a formal" contract similar to the Rose Bowl agreement. If it remained impossible to exclude faculty involvement and a White Resolution action, Wilson urged that "the Rose Bowl relationship be re-cast into an incident to the establishment of closer bonds between [the two conferences], so that any negative aspects of the Rose Bowl can be sublimated in a broader meaning and a broader program." The cementing of these athletic ties would provide an escape hatch for the two conferences should NCAA policies continue to violate Wilson's notions of amateurism. The existence of such "postseason meetings" like the Rose Bowl and a basketball tournament in the mold of the proposed Christmas event could serve "as a substitute for NCAA championship participation, with the group of schools which more nearly resembles our own than any other."[47] If faculty control provided for Wilson's version of amateurism but the insistence of faculty control would hamper his ability to counter the renegade tactics of the SEC, then in Wilson's vision, he had to destroy faculty control in order to save it.

Though Wilson's maneuverings were reprehensible, he had reason to fear an invocation of the White Resolution on the Rose Bowl matter. Wilson's shenanigans failed to persuade a majority of faculty representatives in 1959 to maintain the existing arrangement, and the contract formally lapsed following the January 1, 1960, game. Wilson and the Rose Bowl supporters scrambled to cobble together a six-school coalition that could withstand a White Resolution referral to the faculty councils. At Ohio State, the athletic council voted to support renewal of the Rose Bowl arrangement. When that resolution came before the full faculty council, however, it met with strong opposition. Faculty concerns over the Rose Bowl arrangement echoed earlier criticisms of misplaced priorities, overemphasis, and financial lunacy. Professor Carl Fulda deplored Ohio State's reputation as a "football school," specifically citing Senator Saltonstall's comment that he knew nothing of the school other than its football program. Richard Armitage noted that in every other instance, postseason play determined championships: "The Rose Bowl game determined nothing." Additionally, according to Armitage, overemphasis of football caused "students and their parents to select colleges on a basis other than educational."[48] Not surprisingly, the faculty council overturned the recommendation of the athletic council and instructed its conference representative to vote against any new Rose Bowl arrangement. When the conference met in May 1959 to consider honoring the remainder of old PCC contract with the AAWU, the vote deadlocked 5-5, with Illinois, Minnesota Northwestern, Ohio State, and Wisconsin opposing the AAWU invitation.[49]

Holding out hope that faculty opposition merely came from the legal issue that the PCC no longer existed, Wilson encouraged Tom Hamilton to approach the Big Ten with a new contract "under the same provisions as contained in our previous contract," formally identifying the AAWU schools as the new contracting party. When Hamilton offered the new contract in January 1960, the conference accepted it by a vote of 8-2, with only Minnesota and Ohio State dissenting, but automatically referred the matter to the individual schools under the White Resolution. When the conference reconvened in March, it once again divided 5-5 on the new Rose Bowl contract.[50]

While the deadlocked vote now freed the Big Ten from contractually sending a Rose Bowl opponent, a single sentence tacked on to an obscure conference rule still allowed for a Big Ten school to play in Pasadena. Following Ohio State's 1921 Rose Bowl appearance, the conference at its June 1921 meeting had passed a rule stating, "Post-season competition in all sports is prohibited. Seasons in all sports, unless otherwise limited in these Regulations, shall close with the NCAA championship meet in each sport." The conference invoked the rule that December to deny Iowa a trip to Pasadena. However, when the conference negotiated the 1946 Rose Bowl contract, it added the sentence, "Nothing herein shall apply to the Rose Bowl game." Some opponents of the Rose Bowl attempted to strike the addendum permanently, but that measure was defeated, suggesting that it was contractual issues rather than the Rose Bowl that troubled some faculty opponents.[51] Thus, while the conference was not obligated to send a team to Pasadena in January 1961, an individual team could still accept an AAWU invitation if it was offered. By coincidence, Minnesota, a consistent opponent of the Rose Bowl contract throughout the 1950s, won the conference championship in 1960. Minnesota faculty had opposed the Rose Bowl contract not because they found football overemphasized or misplacing academic priorities but because of the provision that mandated the appearance of the conference champion. As a result, a legal contract, not the Minnesota faculty, determined if the Golden Gophers would go to the Rose Bowl, in their minds, abrogating faculty control. Thus, Minnesota saw no hypocrisy in opposing the arrangement in both 1959 and 1960 but appearing in the game itself in 1961.

Attempting to force the issue, in March 1960, the conference athletic directors, who began meeting as a body for the first time that year, proposed a blatantly coercive measure. Since faculty opposed the postseason Rose Bowl, the athletic directors proposed a prohibition on all postseason competition, including NCAA-sponsored championships. Such a measure would have brought widespread condemnation upon any faculty member who supported it and was interpreted by one observer as a way to "exert influence upon faculty athletic committees to reconsider an action taken concerning football."[52] Another faculty member was even more blunt, labeling it a "pitifully transparent attempt at blackmail" by the athletic directors.[53] Such a coercive effort suggests that the athletic directors were aligned with Wilson's determination to renew the Rose Bowl arrangement at all costs. It also suggests Wilson's willingness to consider abandoning the NCAA, a move that would have only further cemented ties between the Coast schools and the Big Ten. Finally, the move illustrated a growing difference between those identified with the athletic department and the faculty as a whole. This rift appeared at Ohio State in the 1959 vote when the athletic council recommended 9-1 that the faculty council approve the Rose Bowl renewal. The faculty council, believing "that the Athletic Council was trying to pull a fast one," instructed that body to reconsider its recommendation, which the latter body did, reaffirming its original recommendation, only to have it soundly rejected when the faculty council met a month later. When the faculty council in June 1960 recommended nonparticipation in any postseason football game, including accepting Ohio State's share of the conference's Rose Bowl profits from the previous year, the athletic council responded by declaring that "there was no occasion for such action."[54] After the faculty council again recommended their reconsideration, the athletic council released a report in forceful, yet restrained, tones that reminded faculty members that whether they approved or not, Ohio State was engaged in big-time football. As a conference member, Ohio State was bound to abide by the decisions of the conference, even the ones they voted against. Because the conference decided that Rose Bowl receipts should be split evenly, "refusal to receive our share of any receipts might create the impression that this University is not willing to abide by a majority decision of the Conference." The athletic council recommended that the faculty council specifically earmark Rose Bowl profits "to the reduction of the bonded indebtedness" on the stadium. Such an action, the athletic council argued, would "hasten the arrival of the day when all such indebtedness is removed and the Athletic Department will be free to solve some of its pressing problems." In other words, the pursuit of big-time football would allow the athletic department to pay off the debt, thereby freeing the university from having to pursue big-time football. It is little wonder the faculty council once again rejected the athletic council's recommendation supporting the Rose Bowl arrangement.[55]

Had Ohio State's football team not intervened, these kinds of university turf battles might have continued in the abstract indefinitely. However, after a shaky 7-7 tie to underdog Texas Christian University to open the 1961 season, the Buckeyes reeled off eight consecutive victories, needing only to defeat hated archrival Michigan for an outright conference championship. Media observers continued to reject any possibility that the Big Ten might be excluded from the Rose Bowl, although news reports mounted that the Rose Bowl was considering schools from other conferences, most notably the SEC. Writing from Chicago, one West Coast reporter noted that the general feeling among the locals dismissed such speculations as wildly exaggerated. Ignoring the question of southern segregation entirely, midwestern opinion ruled out the SEC largely due to scheduling shortcomings. Quite simply, the SEC, according to Big Ten partisans, played far too many "soft" teams to be considered worthy of a Rose Bowl bid. The *Chicago Tribune* echoed such sentiments, insisting throughout November 1961 that a Big Ten team would go the Rose Bowl based on scheduling.[56] Prior to the Michigan game, OSU's athletic director Richard Larkins asked the athletic council what he should do if the Buckeyes defeated the Wolverines and were offered an invitation to Pasadena. The council told Larkins to inform the president of an offer immediately, but having gone down this road before, also to remind him that "a policy of non-participation has already been established by the Faculty Council."[57] When Ohio State beat Michigan on November 25, the outcome set the stage for a confrontation at least six years in the making.

The day after the Michigan game, Tom Hamilton called to offer a preliminary Rose Bowl invitation, wanting to confirm Ohio State's willingness to accept before proffering the formal invite. The athletic council hurriedly met on Monday, voting 6-4 to recommend acceptance to the faculty council. Hoping to forestall potential faculty opposition by addressing many of the concerns occasioned by the 1957 trip, commercial sponsorship of the marching band would be prohibited on this trip, there would no interruption of the academic calendar, and no students would be excused from classes.[58] Upon receipt of the athletic council's recommendation, the faculty council scheduled a meeting for the following afternoon, with the Rose Bowl the sole agenda item. When council members arrived at the Faculty Club for the three o'clock meeting, they found a complete circus. Demonstrators marched outside the building carrying signs, curious onlookers from both on and off campus filled the club lounge, and the Columbus media, which had been tipped off to the meeting, assembled with television cameras from every Columbus station, print reporters, and a radio station using a news reporter to provide live updates—all for a faculty meeting.[59] As the faculty began to debate the issue, the frustrations and anxieties over the crises, scandals, and confrontations of the previous six years poured forth in a rhetorical bloodletting that took a mere ninety minutes.

Supporters of the Rose Bowl invitation generally saw the issue in terms of the totality of the university's reputation and of fairness toward the football players. Athletic director Richard Larkins rejected arguments that a reputation for football excellence diminished the academic standing of the university by noting that "gaining 'excellence' in any area was not achieved by destroying another," and that "the 'image' of academic achievements of any institution was not distorted by athletic success." Dean Roy Kottman argued along similar lines by stating, "There is no close relationship between the achievement of excellence in academic affairs and the fact of participating in the Rose Bowl." To deny the players "the Rose Bowl contest for which they have worked so hard and in which they so richly deserve an opportunity to participate" was patently unfair, according to Kottman. Dean Walter Krill also put the matter in the context of the players by arguing that it was disingenuous of the university to participate in big-time football, with all the attendant demands and expectations that such participation involved, without providing the attendant reward to the players. "To me," he stated, "this is not a moral issue but a matter of integrity. Are we going to be honest with the student body?" It did not bode well for the position of these men, however, that as administrators, none of them had a vote on the matter.

In fact, the minutes of that day's meeting and other accounts identify only one voting faculty member who spoke in favor of the measure.[60]

Opponents of the measure were not persuaded, however, and rose time and again to elaborate their opposition in lengthy rebuttals, generally citing personal experiences in support of their arguments. At the core of the issue, according to one observer, was the question, "Do we have faculty control or don't we?" Professor Salvatore Marco saw the matter entirely in the context of the change in the university's governance of athletic policy following the Fullington Report. Since gaining true faculty control of athletics, the faculty council had "considered the Rose Bowl question several times and has on those occasions expressed itself as being opposed" to participation. Expressing a certain annoyance that the athletic council continued to press the faculty in hopes of a different answer to a question that in his mind was settled, Marco declared, "In my naïve way, I had assumed we had made our decision." Professor Arthur Cullman, after noting yet again the Saltonstall comment, highlighted the commercialized and exhibitionistic nature of the Rose Bowl, charging that the game decided nothing competitively. "It is not a championship; it is a commercial venture." Spanish professor Richard Armitage also criticized the commercialization of the venture, noting that the Tournament of Roses Association received 11,000 complimentary tickets to be distributed at their discretion while also receiving $150,000 in stadium rental fees. Following up on Cullman's comments, Professor Marvin Fox asked, "If there are no advantages of any sort to be gained, then why participate? There are, moreover, distinct disadvantages that will result from participation." He noted the "carnival atmosphere" that surrounded the Rose Bowl and its attendant interruption of the academic process. In reality, according to Fox, "there is a distinct advantage to non-participation. It is a way of affirming to the entire academic world" that Ohio State is "first and last, an institution of higher education, and that athletics are restricted to their properly subordinate place within the academic structure of the University." Finally, hoping to appeal to concerns about the university's reputation within the world of academia and sensitivity to Ohio State's status within the AAU, Fox concluded, "We would gain prestige among the great universities of America by such a decision and would prove concretely that we belong in their company."[61]

Arguing against the measure in much the same vein as Fox, Professor Anthony Nemetz challenged claims that going to the Rose Bowl would enhance the university's standing with alumni and friends. Accepting that logic meant playing to the wrong audience, Nemetz argued. "I feel certain that by going our prestige will be enhanced in certain quarters, but how will other universities react?" Playing again to faculty concerns over Ohio State's AAU status, Nemetz asked, "How will this aid our prestige among the Foundations, in government quarters, and generally in places which we esteem?" In the Cold War struggle with the Soviets, it would be federal contracts and nonprofit grants and research consortiums, not those who identified with football, Nemetz suggested, who would fund and wage the battle for the Republic. Vice President Frederic Heimberger, a nonvoting participant, viewed the issue as directly related to the funding challenge facing American higher education amidst the crisis of the Cold War. "Night after night through the bitter cold of last winter, several of us were driving out to every county in this state, trying our best to tell the story of this University . . . the extreme urgency of teaching and research at the highest levels in this time of national peril. We had something to say about the cost of running this University . . . that Ohio was not keeping pace with states in its support of higher education." In making these fund-raising pleas, Heimberger spoke of the quality of the faculty and "the seriousness of purpose" of the students. "Repeatedly, I told old grads that times have changed, that Joe College had vanished from this campus, that Ohio State had become a place of hard and serious study." For Heimberger, the matter before the council lay in direct contradiction to both the message and effort of those fund-raising pleas. "Should we now go back to the people of Ohio and tell them that we were only kidding; that the day-to-day work of this University is really not that important; that, tough as things are on this campus, in the nation and throughout the world, we can still afford the luxury of seriously impeding the efforts" of students, faculty, and staff, "all in order to [play] a football game? . . . If so, then I think that we have no choice but to abandon all pretense of being a major center for advanced education in a time of serious national need and, for that matter, great national peril." In what may have been the most memorable comment that afternoon, Armitage compared the resources and misplaced priorities devoted to football with other academic pursuits. "Give me eighty $1300 scholarships and I'll recruit the best Spanish students from Ohio high schools. Provide me with unlimited facilities and I'll deliver a Spanish team that will beat the University of Buenos Aires, the University of Mexico, and the University of Madrid in four years."[62]

After the assembled faculty had spent itself on the matter, President Fawcett asked them, "Are you sure you've said all you want?" Hearing no other comment, he called for the vote. It was at that time that faculty members became conscious of the intimidating presence of the local media. A motion was made, quickly seconded, and overwhelmingly passed to vote by secret ballot, a measure that visibly disappointed the assembled media outlets. Hoping still to determine the votes of individual faculty members, one enterprising photographer positioned himself behind those charged with tallying votes in an attempt to photograph the ballots and their contents, an effort that brought a verbal rebuke from President Fawcett. When the votes were tallied, the recommendation to send the team to the Rose Bowl was defeated 25-28.[63] If events at the faculty meeting itself seemed surreal, they paled in comparison to what followed over the next several hours.

Spurred by media broadcasts, students and partisans were instantly aware of the faculty decision, and within two hours, crowds, mostly coming from the Greek houses, began assembling at the main intersection of 15th Avenue and High Street. Gathering numbers, the group marched on the president's home and then, after discovering his absence, moved to the Faculty Club, where they broke windows, littered the lobby with straw-filled effigies and antifaculty signs such as "Damn the Faculty" and "Never Were So Many Saved by So Few," before burning effigies of Fawcett, Heimberger, and alumni secretary Jack Fullen, who was out of town and had not even been at the meeting. From there, they marched on the state capitol, gathering supporters and torches from the drinking establishments on High Street. After a brief protest at the capitol, the marchers again returned to campus for another visit to the president's house, which included the burning of another Fullen effigy from the main flagpole at the campus gates. Fawcett, perhaps in slight exaggeration, later recalled that "you had to have security protection to even exist." At its peak, the protesting crowd numbered from two thousand to five thousand, with most of them apparently students. After rumors circulated that the board of trustees might overrule the faculty, Fawcett issued a press release stating that such action would violate Big Ten rules of faculty control and would mean the expulsion of Ohio State from the conference. The decision of the faculty was final. The following evening, students again gathered on the Long Walk for a protest meeting and moved from building to building attempting to get faculty signatures on a petition requiring the convocation of the entire faculty for purposes of a referendum on the issue. After stern warnings from Fawcett following the second day's activities that university disciplinary policies would be enforced, the student demonstrations largely played themselves out.[64]

To his credit, Hayes played no role in agitating the students, and he and the football team attempted to end the demonstrations. Hayes was out of town when the faculty vote occurred, speaking at an alumni function in Cleveland, and the multiple versions of his response have since been elevated into the pantheon of Hayes lore. Informed of the faculty's vote, he reportedly "turned grey" and took a walk through the streets of Cleveland "for maybe an hour" (or more, depending on who is doing the retelling). He later claimed, "I didn't want to go before an audience and say some things I might later regret." When he finally spoke to the gathering, he announced the faculty's decision, reportedly eliciting an audible gasp from the alumni. Hayes, however, quelled any insurrectionary sentiments by claiming, "The faculty make the rules, and the football team must abide by the rules off the field as well as on." Hayes could not resist taking a backhanded swipe at the faculty by noting, "I don't agree with those twenty-eight 'no' votes, but I respect the integrity of the men who cast them, if not their intelligence." Seeing the Rose Bowl issue as potentially damaging to the long-term interests of the university, Hayes declared, "I've thought this thing over and decided that it would be a real shame if this would cause a cleavage in the University. No football team is worth that." In the days following the demonstrations, Hayes called for an end to student demonstrations and a halt to recriminations against the faculty. He was proud to learn that team captain Mike Ingram had waded into the demonstrations, demanding that students return to their dorms.[65]

Hayes's pleas notwithstanding, the condemnation of the faculty, which began immediately following the vote, continued for several days in the form of hostile editorials and letters to the editor. Former Buckeye player and 1944 Heisman Trophy winner Les Horvath called the Ohio State faculty "a hypocritical bunch of jerks." Suggesting the pervasiveness of the myth that football provided untold riches, nineteen signatories of a telegram to the board of trustees asked, "How many of these men who voted no are living on salaries from football revenue?" Fawcett's telephone rang throughout the night with calls that ranged from the hostile to the obscene. In the days that followed, he received letters and telegrams "by the hundreds and hundreds . . . with language of the kind I had never read before." Some of the tamer ones wondered "what Dwight Eisenhower and Jack Kennedy, two fine football players, would think of your most hypocritical decision." Margaret Guiler declared, "God pity America when we no longer play to win." Callers subjected the family of Richard Armitage, who had not even arrived home from the faculty meeting before the phone began ringing, to hostility and vitriol. Upon his arrival, Armitage began answering the phone, attempting to engage the callers, but was met instead with obscenities and accusations before callers hung up. One noted Armitage's research at the University of

Mexico before accusingly asking him, "Is that where you became a Communist?" By far, the most hateful attacks on the faculty linked them with communism. Telegrams to Fawcett declared the faculty's actions as "communistic rule," labeling them as "traitors." Byron Scribner demanded the board of trustees identify those who voted against the measure so that they could "be censured (or even dismissed) for their narrow-minded decision." Labeled as threats to national security, the faculty, in the eyes of Dorothy Melick, should be rooted out of the university with the termination of their teaching contracts. One anonymous letter declared "it [was] time for a shake-up of a faculty which permits known Commies to invade the campus," while still another demanded the trustees "launch a crusade against" the faculty. Glen and Claire Thomas claimed that faculty charges that football was overemphasized resulted in the state and the university being "smeared by the 'hate campaign' tactics by a few narrow-minded individuals," and declared the faculty nothing more than "a secondary group" in the life of the university, while still another letter asked, "Cannot something be done to see to it these 'little' people cannot" hinder the football team in the future?[66]

Even those who avoided leveling baseless allegations against the faculty saw the matter within the context of the Cold War and the domestic anxieties it created. One alumnus declared that postseason spectacles like the Rose Bowl "stand our nation in better stead as a relief valve for our ever increasing tensions." James R. Kidd suggested that faculty preoccupation with academic excellence would leave the United States unprepared to combat the Soviets in other equally important venues of the Cold War. "I realize that Russia has made a big progress in science in the last few years, but I also noticed that Russia won the Winter Olympics very easily." W. E. Slabaugh, under the false assumption that football paid the bills for many other programs, saw the Rose Bowl as a crucial source of income allowing the university to provide a broad fitness program in accordance with President Eisenhower's directive. For these individuals, football represented a clear means to confront the bewildering successes of the Soviets.[67]

The intensity of opposition to the faculty's actions struck many observers at the time as hypocritical. Many wondered where the student demonstrations, media outrage, and alumni mobilization had been when detrimental funding decisions or embarrassing revelations had been made concerning the university's athletic and academic reputations. One newspaper in Troy, Ohio, wondered, "What for instance, if these students had thrown dirt inside buildings and climbed atop [statues] because they didn't like to see . . . faculty salaries standing in the second division of the Big Ten? What if they had made their march to the statehouse to protest the less-than-adequate funds for higher education? . . . Now here might be something worthy of protest and indignation." Another paper asked the same question of the alumni, wondering "how many alumni associations bombarded the Ohio Legislature with telegrams last spring demanding that the financial support of Ohio State be brought up to somewhere near the average for state universities elsewhere?" The *Akron Beacon-Journal* similarly noted that "Ohioans by the hundreds of thousands run a temperature over whether the football team should be sent to the Rose Bowl, but hardly anybody seems to care whether the university's educational program is being adequately supported." Following the student demonstrations, Fullen noted that "had the students demonstrated and marched on the capitol when the General Assembly went home leaving their university with appropriations far less than those honestly requested, it might have been a more constructive type of demonstration."[68]

Illustrating the intense anxiety felt by many Americans at the time, supporters of the faculty also saw the matter within the context of the Cold War. Even before the vote took place, W. S. Judy wrote to Richard Armitage applauding his attempts to put football in perspective during a time of national crisis. "I believe you and [Jack] Fullen have designed the rocket that will put us in space with better purpose than [the Russians]." Students at Ohio State also saw the measure through the prism of the Cold War. The *Lantern* editorialized that "the nation is in a tight fix as regards the world situation. Many things are needed for survival. One of the greatest needs is better education." Condemning the faculty over the Rose Bowl vote, according to the paper, only hindered such a vital need. "Such shameful goings-on are a dis-service to the future, especially [those] who are being educated for the important jobs and the difficult citizenship required of the future." Even students at other campuses saw the faculty's decision to rein in football as having Cold War implications. The student paper at John Carroll University noted simply, "Who knows, Johnny may catch Ivan yet."[69]

In addition to exposing Cold War anxieties on the part of both supporters and opponents, the Rose Bowl episode at Ohio State revealed the reprehensible actions of the Columbus media. Various media outlets inflamed—and, in some instances, created—much of the unrest and agitation that followed the faculty vote. The *Columbus Dispatch* openly favored Rose Bowl participation and categorized faculty opposition in the harshest terms, often resorting to egregious contextualization and blatant mistruths. The paper ran seven editorials, all negative on the question and all unsigned, the factual inaccuracy of which "would have made [Soviet state newspaper] *Pravda* blush with envy," according to Jack Fullen.[70] Some of the paper's news items even lacked a byline. Paul Hornung, the paper's sports editor and such an impassioned Buckeye rooter that he attended OSU games as working press dressed in "head-to-toe Ohio State scarlet and gray outfits" openly cheering in the press box, charged the faculty with conspiratorial behavior and autocratic abuses of power. Hayes had for years openly cultivated Hornung as a friendly journalist, "deftly using him to [Hayes's] own benefit." Hayes could demand what would appear, or not appear, in Hornung's articles and the writer would in turn "defend Hayes at every turn with effusive praise." According to one author, "Hornung wrote as if he were a part of the team."[71] Hornung alleged that faculty had been purposely secretive in its Rose Bowl deliberations, intentionally suppressing information to prohibit a fair airing of public opinion. The Rose Bowl invitation "was kept a closely-guarded secret and the Council's meeting wasn't revealed until hours before the body assembled." The paper referred to the faculty's attitudes toward the Rose Bowl as "un-American," describing its actions as "catastrophic," suggesting that the faculty wielded a tyranny of the minority by "a few narrow, overly-sensitive minds."[72]

The *Dispatch* was not alone in vilifying the faculty. The Columbus *Citizen-Journal* categorized Richard Armitage's comments at the faculty meeting as "the most vicious" and declared that the faculty were instituting "a hate campaign" against the people of Ohio.[73] The electronic media also fueled much of the response to the Rose Bowl vote. Sports reporter Marty Victor aired a piece on local television telling of a bonfire and student demonstrations on the Oval before either of those events had taken place, while a reporter from the *Lantern* witnessed a television cameraman urging a group of students milling about to "sing or chant a little—stir up a disturbance so that I can take some pictures." A day after the demonstrations finally ended, Woody Hayes used his Friday night coach's show on local station WBNS to call for the removal of Jack Fullen as alumni secretary. Fullen labeled Hayes's allegations as "downright slander," demanding equal air time to rebut Hayes's comments. Similarly, Jimmy Crum on station WLWC displayed on his show a letter he had written demanding Fullen's removal from his alumni position, admitting, however, that he himself was not a member of the alumni association because he was not an Ohio State graduate.[74]

In contrast to the commercial media, the student media distinguished itself in covering not just the results of the faculty vote but the circumstances that led up to it as well. The *Lantern* ran editorials that both supported and criticized the faculty position, providing cogent arguments with blunt and direct criticisms without crossing the boundary into personal attacks. In stark contrast to its commercial counterparts, many, though not all, of the *Lantern* pieces were signed, establishing a level of credibility that the *Dispatch* never enjoyed. Perhaps most impressively, the *Lantern* ran several news articles detailing the media's role and at least two editorials that explicitly criticized certain media outlets by name, describing their activities as "offensive." Much of the unrest following the Rose Bowl vote, according to the *Lantern*, "was the direct result of irresponsible radio and television broadcasts, publicizing the demonstrations before they even took place." Considering that many of those same students would likely be looking for jobs upon graduation in the Columbus media market, the paper's stand was an admirable assertion of principle over self-interest.[75]

The role played by the media in creating the unrest was also evident in their coverage of the street demonstrations. Student demonstrations did not have a proud recent history at Ohio State and had historically brought swift and universal media condemnation. In the early 1950s, many midwestern campuses witnessed disturbances as a result of spring weather in the form of water balloon fights and panty raids. Ohio State experienced an unusually riotous and destructive such incident in 1953, resulting in the expulsion or suspension of twenty-seven students. For the next several years, when the university mailed grades home to students, it included a reminder of the incident and the punitive consequences that such activity entailed, citing "risk of personal injury and property damage." The local papers made critical references to the disturbances and approved the administrative responses. The so-called Rose Bowl riots, however, were seen in an entirely different light. Richard Armitage noted that "for the first time in the history of the University, supposedly responsible and peace-loving citizens outside the University actually encouraged the rioting and considered it justifiable." Indeed, the *Dispatch* described the demonstrations as "high-spirited but orderly" and noted approvingly their burning in effigy of Fullen. Many student demonstrators, aware of the potential consequences of their actions, covered their faces, in the words of one anonymous female student, "so we won't be identified and thrown out of school." One letter to the *Dispatch* suggested that "all true Ohioans" should join the students in the streets to oppose the faculty. The public and media response of central Ohioans to the Rose Bowl unrest was in marked contrast to the condemnation that students received eight and half years later at Kent State University, where four student demonstrators were murdered. The general popular response was, in the words of one local resident, "They should have shot more."[76]

It was the *Dispatch*, however, that continued to use the Rose Bowl vote as fodder in its blood feud against the faculty. Following the faculty vote refusing the Rose Bowl invitation, the paper attempted to find out which faculty voted against the measure under the headline "Faculty Bowl Opponents Shield Their Identity." Through a process of elimination and aided by some faculty members who acknowledged their affirmative votes, the paper largely identified individuals who voted against the measure and printed their home addresses and phone numbers. The following day, the paper also ran an article on faculty travel expenses, identifying faculty members who voted no, their home addresses, and any trips and expenditures they took as state employees, comparing this expenditure of "taxpayers' money" to the Rose Bowl trip that would have been "paid from funds derived from football receipts and not taxpayers' money." The subject was even discussed in the state legislature by state senator William H. Deddens, R-Cincinnati, who noted that "Ohio State is sending professors all around the country at taxpayers' expense while the Faculty Council refused to permit the Ohio State team to participate in the Rose Bowl at no expense to the taxpayers." Two days after that, the paper ran an article on the feud between Hayes and Fullen following Hayes's television appearance, explaining that only the alumni board could remove Fullen from his position and printing the names and addresses of every member of the board, obviously hoping to prompt enough pressure to force Fullen's removal. The paper's behavior did not go unnoticed on campus, with many of the offending articles filed in the president's papers. It also resulted in a response to the paper by at least one faculty member. English professor Andrew Wright bluntly informed a representative of the *Dispatch* that the paper "played a direct part in the harassment of the faculty in the latest sorry chapter of *Dispatch* relations to the university" with the intention of "torment[ing] the members of the Faculty Council who dared to vote no." Wright termed such activity "yellow journalism" and viewed "the attack as yet another effort to drive a wedge between the university and the community." So successful had *Dispatch* efforts been in poisoning the town-gown relationship, according to Wright, that he had "never seen in any other university such a complete split between the academic community and the town."[77]

Finally, the issue over the Rose Bowl at Ohio State revealed the changing nature of university governance as a result of the Cold War. Americans were continually reminded of supposed Soviet advances, particularly in its system of education. After the 1957 launching of Sputnik, popular concerns over Soviet advances centered on the fields of math, physics, chemistry, aeronautics, and engineering. Federal patronage of university research during this period overwhelmingly went to applied research in these and related fields. For academics at publicly supported research universities such as Ohio State, this created not only a tremendous social responsibility to help fight the Cold War but also a change in their workload. The laboratory in an academic research context was not merely a physical location, "but a small community of graduate students, post-doctoral fellows, and technical workers" engaged in various stages of research, all requiring senior faculty coordination. Thus, these activities consumed the energies and attentions of faculty members in the sciences, "the privilege of debating the academic calendar or degree requirements for undergraduates [or football participation] is left willingly to the humanists in the faculty senate."[78]

It is not coincidental that the most vocal opponents of football's role at Ohio State came from the humanities faculty. Beginning with James Fullington, and later Anthony Wright in the English Department, Richard Armitage in the Romance Languages Department, and Marvin Fox and Anthony Nemetz in the Philosophy Department, humanities faculty consistently took the lead in seeing nonacademic pursuits such as football as harmful to the university's academic standing and ultimately, its Cold War responsibilities. Even faculty supporters of Hayes and football agreed that "liberal arts professors" lay at the center of the opposition. It was not that math and science faculty were more supportive of football—many joined their humanities colleagues in voting against the Rose Bowl—but that many had pressing concerns that left humanities faculty to take the lead in academic committee work like the athletic and faculty councils. Additionally, humanities departments witnessed the greatest faculty turnover in the postwar years and were thus more acutely aware of the relationship between the school's academic standing and its ability to replace faculty of distinction. Finally, the humanities' lack of immediate application to the struggle with the Soviets made them oppose the distraction of football. While their colleagues in math and science made tangible contributions to America's Cold War efforts, the humanities faculty were left with serving as the university's conscience, attempting to set and maintain priorities on what they regarded as a higher level. As one observer of the entire affair noted, it was "the liberal arts faculty," more than other colleges within the university, who felt that the conscientious stand against the Rose Bowl "vastly improved the university's reputation as an academic institution" fit for service in a Cold War political economy.[79]

Critics of the faculty's actions who wondered how denying the Buckeyes a trip to the Rose Bowl would aid the university's academic reputation missed the point. The Rose Bowl vote was an attempt to reassert priorities amidst limitations and distractions that hindered the academic process at a time of perceived national emergency. No one in Columbus claimed that keeping the football team out of the Rose Bowl was going to win the Cold War or magically make Ohio State a better school, but it was intended to establish a culture of studious earnestness and national urgency about the Cold War peril. Denying the Buckeyes the Rose Bowl was like depriving a child of its favorite toy so as to impose upon him a new consciousness and sense of responsibility. In this regard, faculty opponents of the Rose Bowl implicitly understood the role of postwar football. If the culture of postwar football caused many to use the game as a mechanism by which to interpret the period, then faculty hoped to speak in the cultural *lingua franca* in hopes of gaining the attention of those whose primary connection to the university was through the football team.

Ohio State's refusal to play in the 1962 Rose Bowl created problems for Tom Hamilton and the selection committee for that year's game. Although the committee stated that Ohio State had been their first choice, in reality, they had begun considering other teams weeks before Ohio State's faculty voted against the invitation, an invitation that had already been extended to and rejected by another school. The search for a Rose Bowl opponent thus did not begin and certainly did not end with Ohio State. What remained constant, however, was the consideration of larger Cold War cultural values by decision makers on succeeding campuses as they weighed the bounty of the Rose Bowl against a rapidly changing domestic landscape. In this regard, though the specific issues varied across both community and region, the role of postwar football remained consistent throughout. As a result, when the issue of segregation emerged alongside the Rose Bowl hopes of both Louisiana State University and the University of Alabama, observers understood the episode as a conflict of values integral to the American identity. Thus, while race and segregation emerged as the animating issues, undeniably they occurred amidst the backdrop of Cold War anxiety.

THREE

Baton Rouge: Postwar Football and a Fate Worse Than Integration

"I'm all for segregation until it interferes with something important[,] like football."
—LSU football fan, 1956

In the third week of November 1961, most of the leading daily newspapers in the state of Louisiana, many with well-burnished segregationist credentials, lauded Louisiana State University for its decision to play in a bowl game against an integrated opponent. They did so not in any act of contrition for their earlier segregationist stands or as a statement of surrender to the oncoming tide of integration. What drove the segregationist media in the Pelican State to endorse such a move was instead the cultural force of football during the period and its identification with distinctive American values. The cultural prominence of football during the postwar years allowed these newspapers largely to ignore the question of integration and instead focus on the decision as a triumph of manliness, competitive excellence, and national distinction. The Baton Rouge *State-Times* noted that it allowed LSU "to play all comers" in a democratic pursuit of personal validation and national esteem. Its sister paper, the *Morning Advocate,* noted that universities "should either have teams that meet their competitors on equal terms or find new competitors," and a few days later located the issue in a national context by noting it allowed LSU to demonstrate "the best football played in the United States." Perhaps most strikingly, the *Shreveport Times*, the leading segregationist paper in the state, offered its support for LSU's decision by declaring that it had nothing to do with maintaining segregation but rather in creating a national commonality between "the schools of the Southeast, Southwest, Big Ten, Big Eight, and Pacific Coast Conferences," noting that college football's real "value" was in weaving these institutions—and, by extension, the regions they represented—into the larger national culture of competition and excellence. Otherwise, the paper intoned, LSU "will find themselves . . . with no one to play on prestige fields and no one giving a hoot about them."[1]

The editorial stands of these papers and others revealed the widespread acceptance of college football in the post–World War II South, even when such an acceptance challenged a cherished institution in segregation. White southerners had, since at least the 1920s, if not earlier, interpreted college football in terms of cultural values and regional distinctiveness, validating a southern identity and white supremacy. The postwar years, however, forced white southerners to reconcile their traditional regional interpretations of the game with the emerging view of football as an unqualified expression of national values. As critics from both within the South and outside the United States increasingly challenged segregation, white southerners found themselves faced with competing estimable cultural institutions in the form of white supremacy and integrated college football. Those who sought to resolve this conflict in favor of integrated competition often attempted to separate college football from race by embracing instead the game's postwar terms of American exceptionalism, cultural distinctiveness, and market forces. As a result, without ever renouncing segregation, they hoped to preclude the exclusion of segregated college football from the national sporting culture, thus subtly distancing the game's southern meaning from its previous regional expressions.

The circumstances that brought LSU to the brink of a Rose Bowl invitation in 1961 began well before Ohio State's celebrated faculty meeting. With the formal lapse of the Rose Bowl contract and OSU faculty's increasing opposition to postseason play, Rose Bowl officials knew that the Buckeyes' chances of making it to Pasadena were mixed at best. As a result, Tom Hamilton initiated one of the strangest odysseys in postwar college football. Though many affiliated with the AAWU still desired an arrangement with the Big Ten, the lapse of the Rose Bowl contract that occurred in 1960 theoretically allowed the West Coast conference to invite any team, a possibility made even stronger with the faculty opposition at Ohio State. As bowl representatives from around the country began the process of crafting their annual holiday season match-ups, Hamilton announced that, for the first time since 1946, the Rose Bowl was considering teams from every section of the country. On November 8, 1961, Georgia Tech head coach Bobby Dodd revealed that the Ramblin' Wreck had been contacted as a potential opponent for the Rose Bowl. In confirming the Tech contact, Hamilton noted that he and others on the West Coast had been impressed with Tech's early season victory in Los Angeles over USC, which suggested that Hamilton had been considering other teams for several months. Hamilton informed reporters of the Rose Bowl's new selection policy, stating, "Our policy is to choose an outstanding team from any part of the nation, and Georgia Tech . . . certainly qualif[ies]." Hamilton also acknowledged an interest in Alabama, Mississippi, and Louisiana State, and to demonstrate his earnestness in the matter, he traveled to Birmingham to watch the Georgia Tech–Alabama game.[2]

The possibility of a Rose Bowl invitation caused almost every southern school mentioned to jockey for position in hopes of landing the coveted invitation. When the PCC and Big Ten announced their 1946 Rose Bowl arrangement, southern teams, which had so lustily embraced the Rose Bowl previously, without irony dismissively referred to it as "strictly a sectional affair." With Hamilton's announcement, however, southern schools suddenly clamored for a Rose Bowl invitation like a scorned lover once again enjoying favor. One southern paper referred to the Rose Bowl as "the most favored of all bowl games."[3] The reaction of the South illustrated the transparency of southerners' previously disdainful rhetoric as well as the preeminence of the Rose Bowl, whose "new courtship with the SEC" had "shoved into an unenviable spot" other bowl games that were now forced to select from the Rose Bowl's leftovers. Much to the chagrin of the Orange Bowl, which had designs of its own on Georgia Tech, Bobby Dodd immediately responded to Hamilton's inquiry by stating that he preferred the Rose Bowl over any other contest.[4]

The social changes unleashed by World War II and the Cold War, however, had changed much in the United States since the last time a southern school had appeared in Pasadena. Any attempts to bring a southern school to the Rose Bowl would have to contend with segregation, both in terms of the attitudes of those outside the South as well as of the varying local laws and practices within the South regarding segregation—a veritable minefield of popular passion, local custom, and high-stakes politics. The issue appeared immediately when an Atlanta paper commented on the variety of racial policies involved. Although Georgia Tech had no black players, the school itself was integrated; Alabama, which had successfully fought desegregation, was willing to play teams with black players, but only on the road; and LSU and Ole Miss "traditionally opposed" any match-ups "against teams having Negro players."[5] Unlike the hard-core segregationists next door in Mississippi, LSU's athletic policy varied during the period, and the process by which the school finally arrived at soliciting integrated bowl games revealed the tremendous cultural role football played during the period.

World War II forever altered race relations in Louisiana, as it did everywhere in the United States. Though "white opposition . . . hardly abated at all," according to Greta de Jong, a combination of war-induced militancy at the local level, regional organization on the part of the National Association for the Advancement of Colored People (NAACP), and a belated willingness of the federal court system to begin upholding the Fourteenth Amendment initiated a period of modest gains on the part of black Louisianans. Voter registration witnessed modest increases, and some Jim Crow policies, such as union exclusion, were infrequently abandoned.[6] Traditional interpretations see the Supreme Court's 1954 *Brown vs. Board of Education* decision, which struck down school segregation, as bringing such moderate gains in race relations to a screeching halt. In response, the South initiated massive resistance in its futile attempt to maintain segregation. While the flurry of southern segregationist activity after 1954 is unmistakable, and perhaps nowhere more so than in Louisiana, in reality, white southern concerns over "creeping integration" predated the *Brown* decision. And few institutions illustrated that better than sports.

The desegregation of major league baseball in 1947 initiated a period of trickle-down integration in the minor leagues that reached even the Deep South. In 1952, the independent Texas League, which had a team in Shreveport, Louisiana, announced its intention to lift its informal ban on black players. Such actions were not motivated by any commitment to social justice but by more pragmatic concerns of competitive advantage and the attraction of black patrons to the paying gate. In response, Louisiana state senator William H. Rogers introduced a bill to ban all integrated athletic activity in the state. In a classic bit of southern demagoguery, one of the bill's supporters claimed such a prohibition was necessary for the protection of decent white folk because "the dark-skinned people had taken over up there at a recent ball game." A hasty attempt by the Shreveport senator, Charles Tooke Jr., to table the measure failed 13-19, and the bill quickly moved out of committee. It was a short-lived victory, however, as Tooke engaged in a bit of legislative chicanery to kill the bill. Counting his supporters on the floor in an early morning session, four days later Tooke moved again to table before Rogers could bring the measure up for a vote. Under Louisiana law, motions to table cannot be debated, only approved or rejected. With only twelve votes on the floor and no way to bide time through discussion to wait for additional supporters to arrive, Rogers watched with dismay as his bill was sent to the refuse bin.[7]

Louisiana was not alone in attempting to ban integrated sports prior to the *Brown* decision; indeed, similar attempts were made in both Alabama and Mississippi with far more success. As far back as September 1950, the city of Birmingham, Alabama, enacted a municipal ordinance criminalizing integrated play, which ended the city's tradition of hosting a preseason exhibition professional football game to benefit local charities. In 1953, a resident of Pascagoula, Mississippi, protested an interracial boxing match to the state attorney general, J. P. Coleman. Coleman subsequently ruled all statewide integrated play contrary to "public policy," and thus illegal. Though the attorney general was bound by no court order and acknowledged that no such statute existed, he claimed such a ruling could be reasonably inferred from the 1890 state constitution, a notoriously racist document that mandated segregation and criminalized such practices as interracial marriage. And after the *Brown* decision, but before the Court's 1955 implementation decree, Georgia also attempted to ban integrated sports in February 1955, but the bill, which was introduced in both houses of the Georgia assembly, died without a vote. One of the bill's sponsors, however, vowed to revisit the issue in a later session.[8]

If opposition to integrated play existed prior to *Brown*, a willingness to tolerate it, or at least a failure to stop it, continued after *Brown*. When the New Orleans–based Sugar Bowl invited the Naval Academy to participate in 1954, the school insisted on selling its ticket allotment in segregated Tulane Stadium on an integrated basis.[9] The following season, New Orleans's Xavier University played Keesler Air Force Base in Louisiana's first integrated college football game.[10] Additionally, Loyola University of New Orleans completed a new 6,500-seat field house in 1954 and announced that segregation would be banned at the new facility. Because Loyola hosted the annual Sugar Bowl Basketball Tournament, it meant the integration of that esteemed event as well.[11] Even in Mississippi, segregationist orthodoxy wavered in the face of sporting opportunities when the Junior Rose Bowl, a charity fund-raiser played at the Rose Bowl and popularly perceived as the junior college national championship, invited Jones County Junior College to play an integrated Compton (California) College team. Though segregationists foretold all sorts of dire consequences and some called for the legislature to limit the school's funding, little concerted effort was made to keep the team from playing. Even the newly elected governor, J. P. Coleman, the former attorney general who had outlawed integrated sports by fiat only two years earlier, refused to intervene, declaring, "I don't think there is any question of Mississippi law involved."[12]

Perhaps the biggest erosion of segregationist policies occurred following the 1955 season, when the Sugar Bowl invited the University of Pittsburgh, a team that included Bobby Grier, the first black player to appear in the game. However, the integrated 1956 Sugar Bowl may well have been the drop of integration that overflowed the cup of segregationist extremism, shifting the debate on integrated sports temporarily in favor of massive resistance. The Sugar Bowl's initial decision to invite an integrated University of Pittsburgh was made without much controversy, while Pitt's opponent, Georgia Tech, still a segregated institution at the time, accepted with ambivalence for the racial precedent. A crisis developed, however, when Georgia governor Marvin Griffin announced he was requesting a policy that would prohibit such integrated contests and sought to bar Tech from playing in the Sugar Bowl. Telling Georgians of a coming apocalypse, Griffin declared, "The South stands at Armageddon." Suggesting that an integrated football game would lead to integrated schools and a host of other frightening unmentionable scenarios (read: interracial sex and mixed marriage), Griffin intoned, "One break in the dike and the relentless seas will rush in and destroy us." Segregationists in Louisiana attempted to pressure Governor Robert Kennon to use his executive authority "to prevent race mixing" by canceling the game, which he resisted, claiming the business of the Sugar Bowl was a private matter. Perhaps most tellingly, the event also witnessed mass demonstrations by Georgia Tech students in favor of playing the integrated game, and public comment mildly favored playing the game. Though Georgia Tech eventually played in the Sugar Bowl, the controversy surrounding the game renewed segregationist efforts to ban integrated sports.[13]

The Georgia Assembly, having failed in both 1955 and 1956 to ban integrated athletics, took up the measure again in February 1957. The bill passed the Senate unanimously, and having gained the public support of the governor, advocates felt sure of its passage on the assembly's final day. The bill's defeat came only, as it did in Louisiana in 1952, through political maneuvering. Opponents cited an obscure rule requiring the printing of all bills before final consideration and managed to control floor discussion until adjournment ended the session.[14] The Montgomery, Alabama, city council was more successful, however, joining Birmingham in barring interracial athletics anywhere within the city limits.[15] No part of the South, however, would take the matter as seriously as the state of Louisiana.

Shortly after the 1956 Sugar Bowl, representatives from the Evangeline League, a minor league baseball circuit that included only Louisiana cities, met to discuss ways to stave off integration. Included in their discussions was a proposed amendment to the state constitution requiring segregation in all recreational and sporting activities. Shortly thereafter, Norman David, of the East Baton Rouge Parish Recreation and Parks Commission, declared that blacks were prohibited from Goldsby Park, which contained the parish's minor league baseball stadium. Likewise, the city of New Orleans denied the use of the municipal Pelican Stadium for an integrated baseball game between the universities of Loyola and Xavier, forcing its cancellation.[16] The backlash also extended to college football when Louisiana Tech president R. L. Ropp unilaterally cancelled a game scheduled for November against the Air Force Academy. Ropp cancelled the game when the academy demanded that the game contract include the statement "no player of the U.S. Air Force Academy will be barred from participating in this game because of creed or race." Though the level of political coercion involved is unclear, Ropp was in contact with the leading segregationist in the Louisiana legislature, who commended him for his actions.[17] The sequence of events initiated by the Sugar Bowl culminated six months later when the state legislature succeeded where W. H. Rogers had failed in 1952, by banning all integrated sports outright.

The southern segregationist response to court-ordered integration was immediate and overwhelming, but clumsy. All but three of the South's twenty-two U.S. senators and most of the region's U.S. congressmen publicly signed the so-called Southern Manifesto, decrying the *Brown* decision, refusing to abide by it, and vowing to work for its reversal. At the local level, segregationists, beginning with Mississippi but then spreading throughout the South, formed the White Citizens' Council, aimed at putting a respectable face on organized opposition to integration. The Louisiana legislature was in session in May 1954, when the Court handed down its initial ruling, and declared the *Brown* decision "intolerable, impractical, and unenforceable," before censuring the highest court in the land. The legislature promptly established the Joint Legislative Committee to Maintain Segregation, known as the JCS, which served, in the words of Neil McMillen, "as the official voice of evasion, defiance, and delay in Louisiana."[18] The rise of bureaucratic resistance was soon joined by grassroots and pseudo-grassroots organizations. Baton Rouge businessman John B. Easterly Sr. formed the Southern Gentlemen, a secretive, though allegedly nonviolent, segregationist group that, by November 1954, claimed fourteen chapters across south Louisiana. In January

1956, state senator William R. Rainach, who also conveniently chaired the JCS, incorporated the Louisiana White Citizens' Council, claiming 8,000 members and, within a year of its founding, chapters in a third of the state's parishes. Rainach's dual role as president of the Citizens' Council and chairman of the JCS gave the council a semigovernmental legitimacy. As historian Adam Fairclough has argued, the intensity of the response in Louisiana was not so much opposition to *Brown* but a "counterattack" against the gains that blacks had made since the end of World War II.[19]

Rainach and the JCS immediately set out to craft a legislative response to the threat of integration, which, by 1964, included 131 bills and resolutions, more than double any other southern state. Though it would eventually become one of the better-known pieces of segregationist legislation, the sports ban was not Rainach's idea, nor did it even enjoy his early attention or support. Not all segregationist groups were unconcerned about the question, however. The Southern Gentlemen had included as an "exclusive" purpose for its founding the promotion and defense of segregated "athletics, sports, and all indoor and outdoor games." Throughout its existence, the group maintained a singular vigilance in opposing integrated athletics.[20] The initial bill, sponsored by Lawrence Gibbs, originated in the House, a rarity for segregationist legislation at the time; it proposed outlawing all interracial athletic activity, as well as interracial dancing, games of chance and pastime such as cards, dice, and checkers, and mandated that public attendance at any such events also include segregated seating. Sent to the Senate, it was assigned to Rainach's JCS, where it promptly stalled. Preoccupied with proposed legislation aimed at school segregation and wary of running out of time in the legislative session, Rainach "personally . . . sat on this bill until we got our program out of the way." After the idea generated popular support, however, Rainach acknowledged that he "ran into greater demand on this than anything else in our program put together," and he moved it out of committee in late June.[21]

Sporting interests around the state attempted to derail the bill but were steamrolled. Texas League president Dick Butler claimed that the bill would destroy the minor league circuit but was unable to persuade any Shreveport-area legislator to support a compromise measure that would aid the local franchise. College sports received little better hearing when Senator J. D. DeBlieux from Baton Rouge, though acknowledging his "principled support of segregation," opposed the measure because of its deleterious effects on LSU sports. In a rare concession to local authority on the part of a segregationist legislator, DeBlieux claimed, "They can handle [segregation] better themselves," and he proposed an amendment that would have exempted athletics and athletic training. Segregationists both on the floor and in the gallery derided the compromise. W. H. Rogers, having been outflanked by Charles Tooke in 1952, now attacked DeBlieux from the floor by asking him, "Are you up here representing the people of the state of Louisiana or [the football interests] of LSU?" In reply, DeBlieux noted the members of the White Citizens' Council, who had lined the railing to intimidate potential opponents of the bill: "Even if I don't come back to this Senate, I hope to serve . . . as an honorable and courageous senator. We should have enough courage to stand here and do what you know ought to be done." Few of his colleagues agreed with him, however; he could muster only one additional vote, and the compromise failed. Acknowledging defeat and attempting to restore his segregationist credentials, DeBlieux supported the final measure, which passed unanimously. True to his fears, DeBlieux's constituents did not return him to the Senate. Such was the price of violating racial orthodoxy in segregationist Louisiana.[22]

Having failed to defeat the bill in the legislature, opponents now hoped to pressure Governor Earl K. Long to veto the measure. Long, acknowledging, "It's a hard decision," claimed to be undecided on the bill and asked for guidance from the voters. Individual senators contacted Long off the record and acknowledged the pressure they felt to vote for the bill, telling him to "use [his] own judgement." The Midwinter Sports Association, which put on the annual Sugar Bowl festivities in New Orleans, took out full-page advertisements in newspapers across the state calling on Long to veto the measure and called a special session of its executive committee, which passed a unanimous resolution asking for Long's veto. Paul DeBlanc, the group's president, skirted the issue of segregation, asking the governor to consider instead "the ideals of American sportsmanship," and the prestige and reputation of the state of Louisiana. Whatever lobbying LSU might have done occurred off the record, but they likely urged the governor to reconsider the bill. Nonetheless, claiming public comment on the matter ran about four to one in support of the bill, Long signed it in mid-July. The Sugar Bowl then applied to the legislature for an exemption from the law, but were turned back 67–15 and derided by Rainach for "placing the dollar sign above the color line." The legislature did, however, make two concessions to the dollar sign, or at least to pragmatism, when it amended the final bill so that it would not take effect until Monday, October 15, 1956, allowing for the completion of the Texas League season the previous day and for Navy to play Tulane in New Orleans on Saturday, October 13.[23]

Archsegregationists demonstrated their concerns over integrated sports even prior to *Brown*, but their mixed record on enacting sweeping prohibitions and public opposition when they did illustrated the complicated and transcendent role of sports in postwar American culture. Historians for quite some time have demonstrated that widespread southern commitment to segregation never ran very deep when it meant a direct trade-off with something else. As far back as 1959, historian Howard Zinn noted, "white Southerners are not in effect for segregation when it means losing something they value even more than separation of the races." As a result, campaigns to close public schools rather than integrate or calls to refuse black patronage that also harmed white economic interests inevitably failed in the long run, because whites were unwilling to make tangible economic and social sacrifices for segregation. What has been little examined, however, is the effort of white southerners to avoid identifying such trade-offs as a blow to the segregationist cause. To be sure, few white southerners actively called for integrated sporting events or publicly professed a desire to participate alongside blacks, just as few claimed they wanted their children to attend integrated schools. But to actively suppress integrated play often meant the loss of sporting opportunities for both spectators and participants. Using the Georgia Tech incident as an example, Zinn declared at the time, "Many Southerners will not cling to segregation if it means giving up popular sports." To do so demanded that southerners deny themselves the cultural satisfaction and validation that such contests often provided. The loss of such high-profile competitive sporting opportunities was, according to Zinn, "a fate worse than integration."[24] It was also something that segregationists at the time openly admitted.

The mildly segregationist Baton Rouge *Morning Advocate*, which had labeled Rainach's segregation program "commendable because of its moderation and reason," actually decried the efforts of the Recreation and Parks Commission to exclude black players from the Evangeline League, noting that conditions in Baton Rouge were no different than other Louisiana cities where "Negro players appear regularly without causing any comment."[25] As a result, standing on segregationist principal did little more than threaten the profitability of minor league baseball and thus possibly deny residents the chance to root for the hometown team. Likewise, Gene Nelson, chairman of the commission and originally a supporter of the attempt to drive black players from the league, recognized that popular opinion on the matter was not entirely in agreement with him. Though Nelson resigned himself to the realization that "colored baseball players in professional baseball" was now a fact of life, he was even more frustrated over public acceptance of it. "If we must allow it, and I feel that we must . . . we should make it clear there can be no [other] integrated activities on our parks and playgrounds. We must not allow a change of policy in regard to the ball club to be used as a lever by integration to move into other activities."[26] Another writer agreed, noting that politicians, in passing such sports bans, "try to peddle the spurious bill of goods that all white Southerners think alike and are willing to voluntarily surrender their decency, dignity, and freedom so as the Negro is deprived of his liberties."[27]

True to the fears of critics, the sports ban initiated the marginalization of big-time sports in Louisiana. Black patrons throughout the state now stayed away from minor league baseball parks, with attendance drops in excess of 30 percent in some places. Within two years, both minor league circuits that included Louisiana teams folded.[28] The Sugar Bowl, too, feared for its existence as a result of the ban. Black attendance at the game plummeted to fewer than fifty for the 1957 and 1958 games, such that the segregated section sat virtually empty. In addition to the loss of black patrons, the Sugar Bowl also faced diminishing white interest because of the inability to invite teams of national reputation from beyond the South due to their integrated rosters. Both local and national opponents of the sports ban put the matter in language that starkly illustrated the kinds of national cultural isolation and exclusion brought about by the ban. *Washington Post* columnist Shirley Povich declared the "Louisiana Legislature has legislated the Sugar Bowl right out of importance," relegating the game to "merely a sectional contest to settle some kind of Dixie championship only."[29] The Midwinter Sports Association agreed, noting that the game "would be limited to competition only between local and near local universities and would, in the main, almost eliminate contests which would include the great universities of the East, North and West."[30] Of particular concern for so many Louisianans was the exclusion of the service academy football teams. The military enjoyed a tremendous prominence as a result of the Cold War, and popular interest in and support of the service academies was a part of that. To exclude the service academies from games in and with Louisiana teams not only appeared woefully unpatriotic but also deeply troubled both critics and supporters of the ban. When Governor Earl Long weighed whether to sign the bill, he admitted his misgivings that it would "hold a lot of big league teams like . . . Army out of Louisiana." Playing on such sentiment in their public pressure to urge Long to veto the measure, the Midwinter Sports Association noted on several occasions that Army and Navy would no longer be able to play

Louisiana teams.[31] Thus, both sides of the issue understood the sports ban as contrary to football's postwar role as a cog in the "American way of life." As was soon apparent, though, the realization did not concern ultrasegregationists in the slightest.

The issue of service academy football erupted into a full-blown controversy in 1957. Following the cancellation of the Air Force–Louisiana Tech game the previous year, the secretary of the Air Force issued an order banning the academy from participating in any segregated sporting event, forcing the cancellation of its scheduled 1958 game with Tulane. The Naval Academy announced it would no longer consider invitations to the Sugar Bowl, and by inference, refused to play schools from the state. The actions of both academies brought attention to Army's scheduled game with Tulane in New Orleans that November. With the cadets facing a segregated visitors section, Congressman James Fuller (R-Pa.) demanded in September that President Eisenhower issue an executive order barring all the service academies from participating in segregated events. Desperate to avoid directly involving the White House, secretary of the Army Wilber Brucker ordered the game moved to West Point. Not everyone was placated by the compromise, however. Congressman F. Edward Hebert (D-La.), whose district included New Orleans, was furious at this federal repudiation of segregation, as well as the financial loss faced by his constituents in the hospitality industries. Criticizing Army for moving the game, he publicly ruminated on appointing no more of his constituents from New Orleans to West Point and suggested that so long as the Army maintained such a policy, Louisiana should consider refusing to furnish men for the draft.[32] Although no one took up the congressman's suggestion that the state of Louisiana violate federal law by abetting draft evasion, clearly service academy football contained significant cachet during the period.

Perhaps no Louisiana school suffered as much from the sports ban as LSU. Certainly their athletic aspirations and expectations faced a harsh competitive reality in the ban's varying prohibitions. On a much more complex and destructive level, however, the issue rapidly emerged as a proxy fight in the venomous confrontation between the university and the state legislature. The university's athletic policies and aspirations allowed the segregationist forces in the legislature to unleash virtually all of their power in an attempt to impose a harsh racial orthodoxy on the school and the state. The legislature's failure to succeed within the realm of the school's athletic policy occurred largely because so many Louisianans, even segregationists, understood the cultural significance of football in the postwar years.

The ban's sweeping prohibition on any interracial participation potentially imposed upon LSU athletics what amounted to little more than a deep southern intramural circuit. It also all but guaranteed that LSU could no longer contend for NCAA championships because of the likelihood of playing tournament games against integrated schools. Both the absurdity and cost of the ban appeared when it also meant no LSU athlete could appear in the Olympics. In 1957, Jack West, the school record-holder in the 100 meters, painfully decided to transfer to the University of Kansas because as a college athlete whose amateur status was defined by his academic institution, he was barred from participating in the Olympic trials and even the Olympic Games themselves by the sports ban. As troubling as the exclusion was from such a culturally and politically laden institution as the Olympics, nothing proved as wrenching as the ban's effect on college football.

The postwar interpretation of football as a game laden with national distinctiveness and identified with the development of national character exaggerated the prevailing importance of intersectional games. Intersectional games strengthened the culture of football as a cohesive national force; and southerners, cognizant that intersectional victories provided a manner of satisfaction in the face of rising criticism of segregation, embraced such logic more than others. As a result, LSU fans during the period "clamored for the Bengals to meet some of the top elevens in the Big Ten or the top teams on the Pacific Coast."[33] The sports ban, however, crushed those aspirations. The University of Wisconsin cancelled a two-game, home-and-home football series with LSU just three days after Long signed the bill. The following year, the Colorado State College Board of Athletic Control banned Colorado State from participating in athletic events involving "any team barring athletes because of race." Other schools, such as Marquette, UCLA, and Syracuse followed similar, though less formal, policies.[34] Athletically isolated from the rest of the country due to its racial policies, some foresaw a day when "football in the South will have dropped in caliber to something little more than junior standards," completely excluding the South from a national sporting culture.[35]

These concerns for the effects on LSU sports found little sympathy in the legislature, however, which grew increasingly critical of the university during the period. The hostility and animosity resulted in the two institutions "carrying on what sometimes seemed a cold war," according to Numan Bartley.[36] The legislature imposed itself on a host of university issues, such as admissions policies, student and faculty behavior, and ideological homogeneity, all limiting university autonomy. Thus, while only a single piece of the larger segregationist quilt that the legislature attempted to patch together, the sports ban's restrictions on university athletic policy served as yet another violation of university independence. Louisiana State University admitted its first black graduate student, to the law school, in 1950, and its first undergraduate in 1956, though both came only at the behest of a federal court order. However, both the board of supervisors and LSU administrators staunchly opposed the legislature's desire to maintain segregation through legislation rather than board or university policy. Nonetheless, in 1956, the legislature mandated new admissions policies aimed at making it increasingly difficult, if not impossible, for qualified black students to attend LSU. Qualified applicants now had to submit with their applications certificates "attesting to his or her eligibility and good moral character," signed by the superintendent of the applicant's high school district. Because a previous bill had outlawed the advocacy or abetment of integration by any public employee, any superintendent who signed a certificate for a black applicant could be fired and thrown in jail. Thus, Rainach felt he had devised a way to "cure the complete integration situation at Louisiana State University."[37]

The actions of the legislature, while failing in the long run to appease the federal judiciary, in the short run severely hampered admissions at LSU for *white* students. The hastily written legislation demanding certificates of eligibility from Louisiana public school superintendents made no provisions for those coming from out-of-state schools, private schools, or parochial schools, none of whom were governed by Louisiana public school superintendents. The new admissions law immediately began to wreak havoc in the admissions office, with LSU president Troy Middleton admitting "several difficult cases [are] presented daily." By far the most embarrassing rejection involved Anne Brooks, daughter of U.S. Congressman Overton Brooks, a staunch segregationist and Rainach ally. Anne had graduated from an exclusive private high school in Washington, D.C., and thus had no properly signed certificate. Though her father personally intervened, appealing directly to both Rainach and Middleton, she was denied admission.[38] In addition to embarrassing situations such as the Anne Brooks affair, the new admissions law also had the incidental effect of curtailing football recruiting, making it difficult to land out-of-state players as well as those coming from private and parochial schools. In the years following the war, LSU's reliance on out-of-state football talent, like all big-time programs, increased dramatically. By 1950, out-of-state players accounted for 65 percent of the letter winners that year, and with the exception of 1953, out-of-state players continued to win roughly a third to almost half of the letters through the mid-1950s. Those numbers changed radically following the imposition of the new admissions laws. From 1956, the last year players were recruited and admitted prior to the law, to 1957, the first full year of the new law, the percentage of out-of-state letter winners plunged from 41 percent to 26 percent, and by 1961, the year LSU hoped to earn a Rose Bowl invitation, just 15 percent of the letter winners came from out of state.[39]

Rainach, however, was in no mood to be charitable toward the university or its president. In his estimation, neither was doing enough to combat integration, and the school was little more than a refuge for communists, race-mixers, and all kinds of nefarious traitors to the Republic. The relationship had not always been this strained, however. In 1954, Middleton personally lobbied the legislature for a massive financial upgrade of LSU, bombarding lawmakers with statistics of both the school's needs as well as its past successes. His efforts paid off when the legislature not only gave Middleton everything he was asking for but also increased LSU's funding by $4 million. "The legislature's confidence in Middleton" and their optimism over the university had never been higher.[40] By 1958, things had changed dramatically. On the eve of that year's legislative budget session, Middleton sent Rainach a detailed breakdown of LSU's budget request and mentioned his concerns over reports that LSU would suffer a cut in funding. Middleton also wrote an impassioned declaration of the high stakes of American higher education at the height of the Cold War, declaring that "we must make an all-out effort to upgrade higher education . . . the cost will be high, but as I see it, we have no other choice." Rainach sent only a cursory reply, completely ignoring Middleton's concerns while tersely thanking him for his correspondence and asking Middleton to contact him if he wished to discuss anything further.[41] What had changed in the intervening four years was, of course, the subject of race.

Middleton, though himself a segregationist, had staunchly opposed Rainach's push for the new admissions law and actually attempted to ignore it for a time. Likewise, Middleton found little in the sports ban to applaud. Himself a former college baseball player and service football player and who, as a youth, played integrated pickup games, Middleton likely grasped the implications of the ban on LSU's scheduling.[42] More than that, he also perceived it as a direct rebuke of the university's recent athletic policies, overseen by changes he had initiated. Following the 1954 hiring of both a new football coach, Paul Dietzel, and a new athletic director, Jim Corbett, Middleton then proceeded to restructure the composition of the Athletic Advisory Council, engendering bitter opposition. The council had previously been charged with the development and execution of university athletic policy and had been made up of an even distribution of faculty, students, and alumni. Middleton reduced the student and alumni presence to little more than a token and limited faculty service to those who had tenure, while investing almost all authority in Corbett. The recomposition of the council brought immediate protest from both students and powerful alumni groups furious at being excluded. The head of the New Orleans–area alumni group was "shocked" to hear of the proposed exclusion of alumni participation in such "important and vital" athletic matters. Though Middleton attempted to deflect such concerns by vaguely assuring alumni that Corbett would continue to seek their input, many were bitter over what they perceived as a palace coup.[43]

Firmly backed by Middleton and now free to operate independently, Corbett promptly initiated talks with several "top-flight" schools and began lining up "attractive [intersectional] games" with the likes of Michigan, Ohio State, Air Force, and Pittsburgh. In 1955, LSU scheduled a future series with the integrated University of Wisconsin in boxing and football. Though the exact contractual stipulations with Wisconsin are unclear, when the Badgers' boxing team came to Baton Rouge in January 1956, they left behind one of their best fighters, eventual NCAA champion Orville Pitts, who was black. While it is possible, though highly unlikely, that the football series included a stipulation prohibiting black players for the game scheduled in Baton Rouge, Wisconsin certainly would not have agreed to such a stipulation for the game scheduled for Madison.[44] Alumni grumbling over the new athletic policy and questions over what Pitts's exclusion might mean for the football game to be played in Tiger Stadium prompted the board of supervisors to take up the matter in February 1956. Firmly in Middleton's corner, the board adopted a policy calling for the university to "continue to schedule varsity athletic contests with major institutions of this and other sections of the country. The contract with Wisconsin does not conflict with this policy. The game will be played." Thus, the board, too, embraced football during the time as a means of cohering the different regions of the country irrespective of segregation. Furthermore, the board proceeded to endorse the handling of athletic policy by both Middleton and Corbett by approving Middleton's request to grant Corbett a raise and contract extension.[45] As the LSU Board of Supervisors proceeded to ensure an integrated athletic policy and provide a vote of confidence to the men responsible, a seething William Rainach sat in the front row.

Publicly, Rainach expressed his "disappointment" by the board's actions. Privately, however, he began leveraging political pressure on schools that attempted to schedule games in accordance with board policy. It was at this time that Louisiana Tech canceled its game with Air Force and Rainach sent a personal note of congratulations to the Tech president. Rainach then crafted a message critical of the board and its actions, and released it to the "Citizens Councils to use."[46] Rainach was not alone in condemning the board. The executive committee of the Southern Gentlemen passed a resolution demanding the resignation of all ten supervisors who voted in favor of the statement of athletic policy, declaring their actions had "betrayed the citizens" of Louisiana and suggesting the board had been co-opted by integrationist sports writers and the NAACP.[47]

In the face of such criticism, Middleton decided to go on the offensive. At the following board meeting in April, he delivered a lengthy statement, intended for public release, regarding "the Negro situation at LSU." Middleton emphatically stated that since the university had begun admitting blacks in 1950, it did so "reluctantly, under court order" and that "the historic policy of the University is not to admit Negroes. It is unlikely that there will be a change in this policy." Attempting to counter Rainach's smear tactics, Middleton noted that LSU had vigorously opposed every black applicant and had "been in the courts almost continuously since 1946" toward that end. The responsibility for the breakdown of segregation lay not at the feet of LSU but at those of the legislature, who continued in its failure to vote the appropriations necessary for a truly separate but equal educational system in the state. He noted that LSU still had the only graduate program in education in the state, and as a result, the vast majority of black students at LSU were graduate students in education. Creating a new program at nearby Southern University would have the benefit not only of creating a separate program that Middleton somehow believed would be acceptable to the federal courts but would also be desirable to Louisiana blacks. "It would be safe to assume that if professional and graduate work in other fields, particularly Education, were being offered today at Southern at least some of the 117 Negroes attending LSU would be seeking their advanced degrees at Southern. Likewise, it is reasonable to predict that with Southern University and LSU being in the same city the number of Negroes seeking admission to LSU's undergraduate divisions will never be larger." Here, then, was the classic white supremacist canard: when given the choice, southern blacks desired segregation and would choose it just as southern whites would. Middleton deftly, if not incorrectly, put the whole matter back in the legislature's lap by noting, "Late as the hour is, it is still possible to preserve the practical effects of segregation almost completely at LSU," if the legislature was willing to spend the money on "facilities for Negroes."[48]

Middleton then attempted to rebut Rainach by turning his attention to criticisms of the athletic policy affirmed at the February board meeting. He emphatically noted that the policy was not "an open invitation to Negroes to apply for admission," nor should it be read as an abandonment of the conviction that "segregation in education is desirable." Nor did it imply that the university was going to engage in wanton athletic scheduling against integrated teams. "Changing conditions elsewhere have made it inevitable that Negro students representing other institutions will compete infrequently in athletic contests with LSU students if a strong athletic program is to be maintained." Thus, LSU would schedule integrated opponents only when it was unavoidable, and do so without pleasure. What the decisions did indicate was "that the Board does not propose to delegate to persons outside the University the responsibility" of running the university. Thus, Middleton not only managed to tell his critics to keep their hands off the running of the university but also turned the tables on those who criticized him for navigating a course they had charted.[49]

Following Middleton's statement, ultrasegregationist board member J. Stewart Slack, a Rainach confidant and officer in the White Citizens' Council, offered a resolution to ban all integrated athletics at LSU. The motion was ruled out of order when board members objected to the consideration of such a matter without previous notice. Slack was not to be deterred, however, "serv[ing] notice that I will bring it up again." True to his word, Slack reintroduced the measure at his final meeting as a supervisor in May. The meeting included intense and "considerable discussion," including the reading of 224 pieces of mass-produced correspondence critical of the university's handling of the segregation question, likely provided by Rainach's Citizens' Council. Segregationist member Thomas Dutton declared the university's policy "indefensible and untenable." Taking a swipe at Middleton, he noted, "We have shouted from the housetops that we are against integration . . . that everything we do has been by order of some federal court. But now we go and do something that a federal court never will tell us to do—play against Negroes." Board chair Lewis Gottlieb countered that "we have been playing colleges that have Negroes for more than 20 years. We play colleges, not Negroes." Gottlieb also attempted to reframe the debate in the terms of football's postwar role as purveyor of national identity by once again raising the specter of the service academies' exclusion: "I'm not willing to say that the Military Academy or the Naval Academy cannot associate with us because we do not approve of their actions." According to Gottlieb, to engage in such policies was to wall themselves off from a cultural institution that united and defined Americans, while the prohibition of the service academies dramatically demonstrated the consequences.[50]

Following Gottlieb's comments, Middleton shrewdly informed the board that if it was going to pass the measure, he would expect it to provide him with explicit instructions on its implementation. Specifically, he asked the board to demand that all game contracts explicitly state a prohibition against integrated play; a prohibition against university participation in all events open to integrated teams, such as tournaments and NCAA championship events; the striking of university affiliation when individuals participated in integrated events, "including the Olympic Games"; and finally, a general ban on all bowl games "because of the fact that other contestants may have Negro students on their teams." The board deadlocked on the ban, 7-7, and the measure failed.[51]

Middleton's willingness to engage publicly Rainach and his allies only intensified segregationist criticisms of Middleton and the university. After the legislature passed the sports ban but prior to its enactment, LSU allowed for integrated seating in the student section at the annual North-South high school all-star football game held at Tiger Stadium in early August 1956. State Senator John S. Garrett used it as a pretext to excoriate Middleton and LSU, promising a "full legislative investigation of what is going on at Louisiana State University." Garrett demanded the university bring its athletic policy in line with the impending state law and criticized Middleton's attempts to have it both ways in the segregation argument. "Middleton says he has no authority to act, but when public sentiment gets strong enough[,] you'll see him move to get something done."[52]

Aware that Rainach, Garrett, and others were attempting to mobilize public pressure against him, Middleton attempted once again to seize the initiative. Among the numerous segregation laws passed in 1956 were restrictions on university officials with regards to facilitating race-mixing in any way. By federal court order, however, more than one hundred blacks were already enrolled at LSU, meaning that efforts by university officials to comply with the federal injunction would likely run them afoul of state law. As a result, the university was caught in the middle between "existing orders of the Federal courts and of the legislation recently adopted by the Legislature."[53] Hoping to extricate the university from future legal difficulties while simultaneously illustrating the situation the legislature had created, Middleton developed twenty-one questions that he asked the board to answer regarding student interaction in extracurricular activities. The questions addressed almost every potential situation of student interracial activity, such as use of dorm rooms, bathrooms, swimming pools, and dining halls and utensils. Some answers were more tortured than others, however. At commencement exercises, black graduates were seated with the rest of their classmates in an integrated section, but their friends and family were seated in a segregated section. Further complicating some issues was the purpose of certain university events. For example, in the event of campus activities such as "convocations, plays, musical programs, lectures, etc.," the board mandated segregated seating if the function was for entertainment, but integrated seating if the function was educational. On the question of activities held on campus by student religious groups such as the YMCA, integrated meetings and activities were barred if the purpose was social but allowed if the purpose was religious. The sports ban prohibited integrated seating at athletic events, barring black students from the regular student section, but the board mandated that rather than seat black students in the regular Jim Crow section with other black patrons, they should be seated in a separate Jim Crow student section, thus creating segregation within segregation. The board deemed football a social event, and as a result ruled that any of the social functions associated with it should be similarly governed. These numerous activities associated with college football vexed segregationists everywhere. In 1963, Mississippi governor Ross Barnett ruminated on the consequences of his state university playing an integrated team: "Suppose Ole Miss went somewhere and played a team that uses Negroes. We would have to have a return game with them in Oxford or Jackson. After the game, there would be a social event. . . . What would the Negroes do? Would they dance with white girls? Not in Mississippi." Apparently, not in Louisiana either. Question 17 explicitly raised the issue of school dances, and the board not only prohibited interracial dancing but also ruled that blacks were barred from attending at all.[54]

Rainach's criticisms of the university now also included allegations that the school's opposition to such policies revealed the LSU campus to be a hotbed of communist, integrationist sentiment. The actions of Rainach and the legislature did not go unnoticed by the *Daily Reveille*, the LSU student newspaper. Throughout the postwar period, the student media of most college campuses, North or South, while not always liberal, were generally more progressive than local political opinion. As a result, the editors of the *Reveille* took a far more moderate stance on the question of integration and were openly hostile to the infringements of the legislature on university prerogative. After Middleton made his pro-segregation statements to the board in 1956, the paper editorialized that "integration is something that is bound to come, sooner or later." Though largely aimed at refuting the attacks of the Southern Gentlemen and complimentary to Middleton, the piece nonetheless ran contrary to the president's hope that segregation could still be maintained. Two months later, the paper again touched on the issue when it criticized the discordant nature of the political debate in Louisiana on the subject of race. "Certain political elements have discovered the vote-getting potentialities of the issue and we can rest assured they will continue to harass us with legislation on it until the issue dies." Having labeled the likes of Rainach and his supporters as racial demagogues and their actions as harassment, the paper asserted that the South faced two choices: accept integration at the local level or "continually be hamstrung in Congress by having to fight integration laws."[55]

The paper's criticisms intensified with the legislature in session. After the legislature passed laws aimed at hobbling the NAACP's integration activities in the state and banning such "pro-integration" magazines as *Time* and *Newsweek*, the *Reveille* cautioned that "if the people of the South are not extremely cautious, they may awake some morning to find that they have surrendered all of their liberties for the privilege of sending their children to segregated schools." Comparing such legislative actions with "Hitler's Germany or Stalin's Russia," the piece dismissed the paranoia many whites had of integration, declaring it an "enlightened system" and noting that "outside the South, integration is succeeding." The willingness to accept all tactics in the fight to preserve school segregation would eventually result in a far greater loss than anything that might be gained. In the face of such a choice, the authors declared that they would "rather sit behind a Negro in a free land than revel in the white supremacy of a concentration camp." By far the most direct attack on Rainach and the legislature came on July 19, in an editorial entitled "The Rich, the Happy—and the Dumb!" The paper simultaneously criticized Louisiana's "stalwart citizens who have meekly" allowed the JCS bills to become law "without even opening their mouths in protest," as well as the "fanatics" in the legislature and their "idiotic" agenda. Turning to the students, the piece chastised them for their silence "when the segregationists . . . forc[ed] the law through that may cripple LSU athletics. . . . Will you let the segregationists give away your birth-right of freedom for the pottage of white supremacy?"[56] Thus, even the *Reveille* attempted to shift the emphasis away from segregation itself to football's role as representative of American exceptionalism.

Though none of the editorials identified Rainach by name, few doubted he was the intended target, and he kept a file on the *Reveille* and its offending pieces. Following the July 19 editorial, Rainach ordered William M. Shaw, special counsel and lead investigator for the JCS, to investigate the paper and its editor-in-chief, twenty-seven-year-old Korean War veteran Darrel Eiland. Rainach blasted the paper and its editor, claiming that Eiland was just one in a long line of "radicals" who helmed the paper, alleging, "the last six editors of the *Reveille* have been integrationists." One media report had Rainach demanding administrative censorship of the paper, though Rainach claimed he was misquoted and quickly disavowed such desires. Privately, however, Rainach worked to have Eiland expelled, a move Middleton steadfastly rejected. To his credit, Middleton personally informed Eiland that while he disagreed with just about everything Eiland had written, he vowed to resign before he would allow Eiland to be expelled.[57] In Rainach's eyes, the real problem extended beyond Eiland, who had merely been "subjected to brainwashing of the worst sort." The real culprits, according to Rainach, were the faculty, "who have been planted . . . to bring about integration in Louisiana." In Rainach's paranoid rhetoric, they were a "heavily entrenched cabal"; hiding behind the veil of academic freedom and "serving the Communist cause," they wantonly taught and advocated integration in the classroom. "The radical effects of a clique in the LSU faculty" had furthered "integrationist sentiments on the Baton Rouge campus." Rainach saw the *Reveille* episode as an opportunity to expose the situation at LSU. "It is time for the academic curtain to be drawn aside so that the mothers and fathers of this state will know what their children are being subjected to."[58] Students like Eiland, supposedly raised in good, decent segregationist households, had been corrupted inside the university's gates by a communist-oriented faculty who wished to destroy the state's institutions and, by extension, the very fabric of the Republic. By 1958, Rainach felt he had all the evidence he needed to expose the subversive, integrationist sentiment imbedded at LSU, both in the classroom and on the athletic field, and initiated an all-out war with the university.

With many of the anti-integration laws passed in 1956 ruled unconstitutional by the federal court system, by 1958 Rainach began building a legislative web that would trigger the closing of any public school in Louisiana forced to integrate by court order. In opposition to such actions, the Louisiana Civil Liberties Union circulated a petition opposing the closing of the public schools, though not advocating integration. Of the more than six hundred signatures delivered to the legislature on the eve of the 1958 session, sixty-six came from LSU faculty. Using the petition as evidence, Rainach claimed that there "had been an estrangement between the State University and the People" and moved to initiate hearings into the matter, asking, "What's wrong at LSU?" The segregationist *Shreveport Journal* declared that LSU was "due for a house-cleaning," while Rainach attempted to use Shaw to link the signers with communist groups. Shaw argued that the communists were hiding behind the cover of "academic freedom . . . a song familiar to anyone who has studied the Aesopian language of communism." The House voted 70-0 to haul university faculty and employees, beginning with Middleton and the deans, before a committee to answer questions on the "dispensing [of] anti-segregation views" and attempts at "brainwashing" on campus, a move that caused one of the accused, law professor Charles Reynard, to joke that he obviously was not very effective since three members of the JCS had taken his class when they were students at LSU law school. A climate of fear gripped the university community as many assumed that after the committee finished with Middleton and the deans, they would subpoena the sixty-six offending faculty members and any other individuals whose names came up as supporting or abetting integration. They eventually would have gotten to Jim Corbett, architect of LSU's new football scheduling policy.[59]

The testimony of Middleton and the deans, however, turned the tables on the legislature. Middleton articulately laid out the university's historic opposition to integration, pointing out the fervor with which it consistently had gone to court over the matter, as well as his own personal opposition to integration. However, Middleton vowed that he and the university would not stand outside the law by refusing to comply with the mandates of the federal judiciary. Such adherence to law, according to Middleton, was the only way to maintain an orderly society. As for the offending professors, Middleton declared their actions occurred as private citizens and not as university officials and thus were entirely beyond Middleton's purview. To take action against them would violate their First Amendment rights. The deans similarly testified and successfully painted the university as a stalwart defender of law and order and democracy that had bowed to integration only under federal court order. Both those within and without the university overwhelmingly supported Middleton on the issue. One letter writer lauded Middleton for his testimony, telling him that he was "the man for the job . . . [who would] hold the line against 'creeping intergration [*sic*].'" Rainach's public investigation now blew up in his face, as the legislature not only appeared vindictive and restrictive of basic rights but also provided a public forum for its opponents to criticize the JCS. The committee abruptly suspended and ultimately terminated the hearings with no further witnesses called.[60]

Unable to link LSU publicly with communist subversion and integrationist tendencies, Rainach now hoped to smear the university by initiating covert investigations of university personnel. The investigations and harassment, which included leaks to the media of the most salacious rumors, turned up no evidence of communist subversion or fellow-traveling. It did, however, reveal the fabulous hypocrisy and moral compromise of segregation. Rainach's wrath focused on more than the faculty, extending as well to many of the board members who had voted in favor of the school's athletic policy. As a result, Rainach's investigators discovered that George Baillio, chairman of the LSU Board of Supervisors, was having an adulterous affair with a black woman. The problem for Rainach and other members of the JCS was not Baillio's extramarital activities but the fact that they occurred with a black woman. As the special committee's co-counsel Wellborn Jack noted, "If you have a mistress that's white, as far as I'm concerned it should go no further. That's your own business. But if you have a mistress that has colored blood in her, that's what I'm interested in." Thus, at a time when the legislature imposed on the university a moral turpitude clause for admission and good standing, it would have willingly accepted adulterous behavior on the part of the university leadership, just not on an integrated basis. The committee protected Baillio's reputation by allowing him to resign, claiming health reasons, and buried the incident by sealing the records of the investigations and the testimony.[61]

The willingness of the legislature to use such tactics against the university had a chilling effect on LSU's athletic policy. The sports ban barred only integrated play within the state, technically allowing LSU to play integrated games on the road, which some university personnel pushed for. The board deferred to Middleton on the matter, however, and he vetoed the possibility. Fear of the legislature may well have been a motivating factor. Certainly, the evisceration of Baillio must have limited the board's desire to get out in front of any such measure. Rainach, though not a sports fan, was kept abreast of all issues relating to the possibility of integration from sources throughout the state, and nothing would have escaped his notice. Indeed, correspondence to and from Middleton shows up in Rainach's papers, suggesting that the senator had a mole within the university, quite possibly within the office of the president itself. When Jack West transferred from LSU because the sports ban would limit his chances to make the Olympic track team, Rainach misinterpreted the entire event and fired off a condemnatory letter to Middleton. Because West, who was white, criticized the law (and mildly at that) Rainach assumed he was black, and when a news item noted that university officials "attempt[ed] to persuade West to remain at LSU," Rainach exploded. Illustrating his growing fixation on Jim Corbett as crucial to the alleged integrationist conspiracy at LSU, Rainach determined that Corbett was the unnamed official and demanded that Middleton address the matter. Rainach notified Middleton that amidst court battles to preserve segregation, it did not help the state's [read: segregationist's] case for Middleton to harbor a state employee who deviated from segregationist dogma. When informed that West was in fact white and that Corbett thus had only encouraged a Caucasian student to remain, Rainach was unrepentant, shifting his criticisms to West, saying that "this student is certainly entitled to his opinions about mixing the races and attendance at interracial schools," but that his sentiments signified an abandonment of "the people of this state."[62]

West was not the only one who held such sentiments. Middleton received pressure both from within the university as well as from legislators for the Tigers to play integrated teams on the road. The private criticism Middleton received on the matter decried the ban's effects on Tiger football, suggesting that Rainach was losing the battle of public opinion when it came to segregation and LSU football. In responding to such criticisms, however, Middleton avoided explicit references to Rainach or the legislature, making clear his own segregationist sentiments. Middleton repeatedly informed critics that standing policy demanded "that LSU . . . not schedule athletic contests, no matter the location, if the opposing team has one or more Negroes." There was a fundamental hypocrisy as far as he was concerned in opposing integration at home but not on the road. "If it is wrong to engage in a sport with a Negro in Louisiana, how could one justify engaging in an athletic contest with the Negro beyond the border of Louisiana? To me it is hypocritical to play in Omaha against a team on which there were one or more Negroes and refuse to do the same in New Orleans." Thus, it was Middleton, not the board, who insisted on abiding by the ban for road games as well.[63]

The possibility of integrated games, however, returned in 1958 when a federal court overturned the sports ban, a decision that the Supreme Court affirmed the following year without dissent. Assessing the significance of *Dorsey v. Louisiana Athletic Commission*, Irwin Poche, of the Sugar Bowl's Midwinter Sports Association, stated the obvious: "This should help the Sugar Bowl," and speculation immediately swirled around the return of the service academies to Louisiana. Air Force suddenly became a sought-after opponent for the January 1959 game. The academy, however, was coy on the matter, largely because the game would still feature segregated seating. Congressman Hebert avoided suggesting draft evasion this time but did criticize the academy for "discriminating" against the Sugar Bowl by refusing to play based on state laws and pointed out that Navy had played in 1955 under existing laws without any qualms. Hebert ignored the fact that Navy had insisted on integrating its seating section in 1955 and was oblivious to the fact that the racial climate in 1959 was simply not the same as it had been in 1955.[64] While the court's actions provided considerable leeway to the Sugar Bowl, the legislature's continued desire to maintain the sports ban in the face of the courts hamstrung LSU and Jim Corbett's scheduling hopes.

Observers of the struggle between the legislature and LSU noted that "the faculty has been timid about taking a public stand for open schools since the legislature has shown itself quite willing to punish the university."[65] In reality, however, the legislature often rattled its sword, but seldom did so with any coercive results. At no point during the period did the legislature fire a faculty member or expel any students; it was rebuffed in its call for censorship of the student paper and was bested by Middleton in the battle for public opinion at almost every turn. Although Rainach himself acknowledged his defeat on the LSU question, he never accepted it, vowing to renew the battle at a later time. Noting that "so many people in higher education have opposed what we are doing . . . our work in this field" had largely failed. Unwilling to concede the fight, however, he vowed to confront the university again when "we are in the position to do a thorough, but careful and wise job." On the matter of maintaining the sports ban even after its Court reversal, Rainach recognized that he had never enjoyed the upper hand and was losing support rapidly. As historian William McFerrin Stowe noted, Rainach "came to see that confronting LSU would require greater strength than the segregationist forces had."[66] Rainach himself passed from the political scene with his failed run for governor in 1960, marking his retirement. While Neil McMillen correctly notes that Rainach's retirement marked the rapid decline of the Louisiana Citizens' Council, it did not mark any kind of concession on the segregation question in the legislature. Considering that the legislative cycle following Rainach's gubernatorial defeat witnessed five extra sessions and ninety-two pieces of segregationist legislation, "the racial extremists were more securely in control than ever."[67]

Indeed, the following year, two episodes revealed that LSU officials still pursued the policy of segregation in extracurricular activities. In May 1961, LSU's baseball team won the SEC tournament and the automatic bid to the NCAA College World Series. As with all NCAA postseason events, however, the invite contained the possibility that the Tigers might face an integrated team. Jim Corbett informed the media that "the Athletic Department will be consistent in its position of participating against only members of the Caucasian race and will not accept any invitation where even the remotest possibility exists" for integrated play. Middleton concurred by again stating that "it is the policy of the University that LSU does not play against Negroes." At least one news outlet claimed LSU stayed home "because the Legislature controls finances at LSU."[68] Sensitivity to integrated activity within the LSU student body also created problems in November 1961 when Louis Washington, a black student on the New Orleans satellite campus, appeared in the campus production of *The Queen and the Rebels*. Unable to exclude Washington individually, New Orleans chief campus administrator Homer Hitt fell in line with LSU's scorched-earth policy by canceling the production outright. Though publicly claiming the decision came after reasoned concern for "community relations," Hitt privately conceded to Middleton that he made the decision immediately, and it came four days before the university released the matter to the media.[69] Thus, by the fall of 1961, the university held to its consistent policy of avoiding integrated extracurricular activity, even without legislative mandate. None of those decisions involved college football, however, or the Rose Bowl. Less than six months after the disappointment of the baseball team and four days before the humiliation of Louis Washington, LSU embarked on a journey with a very different ending.

Tom Hamilton's announcement that LSU was being considered by the Rose Bowl sent shivers of excitement through Tiger fans everywhere, except perhaps New Orleans. Since the enactment of the sports ban, the Sugar Bowl, "faced with a diminishing number of prospective teams and shackled by local custom growing out of the racial issue," had become increasingly reliant on LSU. The Tigers appeared in both 1958 and 1959 and were expected again in 1961. Indeed, the LSU–Sugar Bowl connection was so strong as a result of the sports ban that NCAA officials assumed the Tigers were bound to go to the Sugar Bowl in any years they were eligible. Just as the reversal of the sports ban now supposedly freed LSU to schedule teams as it wished, so too the Sugar Bowl was free to invite integrated teams. However, both parties understood the will of the legislature on the matter and also feared a public backlash. One anonymous Sugar Bowl official admitted that the game's sponsors feared the threat of an eleventh-hour injunction from a local judge that would stop the game. "We could find ourselves with 82,000 seats sold and only one team on the field." Though any injunction would surely be overturned, it would come too late to play the game as scheduled. Another fear came in the form of possible "economic reprisals" against the "local businessmen" who constituted the Midwinter Sports Association. Hesitant to "buck local customs," the Sugar Bowl, in the words of one columnist, felt "harassed" in its efforts to find racially suitable teams.[70]

If the Sugar Bowl felt obliged to maintain the veneer of segregation, most observers assumed LSU did as well. When the possibility of the Rose Bowl first appeared, the Baton Rouge *Morning Advocate* tempered its excitement by noting that "segregation policies could keep . . . LSU from participating."[71] Likewise, a letter to the *Reveille* cautioned against any Rose Bowl hype by declaring "the chances of the Bengals" accepting the invitation "slim," based on "the fact that the Tigers may have to participate against a team with Negroes." The student noted the recent episode regarding the baseball team and suggested, incorrectly as it turned out, that the football team was no different.[72] Thus, it seemed natural that the once-beaten Tigers would end up playing in the Sugar Bowl, hopefully, in the eyes of Sugar Bowl officials, against undefeated Alabama. A Sugar Bowl official acknowledged their desperation when he declared, "If we can't land that game, we'll be in a real bind." Another noted that "the pickings are slim if we can't match LSU and Alabama." With "political pressure . . . building up for LSU to go to the Sugar Bowl" and the Sugar Bowl "hard put to field a representative game on . . . January 1," Sugar Bowl officials met with Jim Corbett on Monday, November 13, hoping once again to secure the Bayou Bengals.[73]

LSU, however, in a bit of a gamble and a surprise, announced on November 14 that it would not seek to play in the Sugar Bowl that year and would refuse a bid if it were offered. While interests from the Crescent City howled about disloyalty and complained of being left in the lurch, few parties could claim that a 10-1, fourth-ranked LSU team had anything to gain by playing in the Sugar Bowl in what likely would be yet another rematch with Ole Miss. Indeed, having been all but forced to play in the Sugar Bowl in 1959, Paul Dietzel told Corbett in 1961 that "if this team plays in the Sugar Bowl, you're going to have to coach them because I won't."[74] Dietzel's ultimatum was unnecessary, however, as Corbett had no intention of seeking another Sugar Bowl appearance. The politics of race in many states with SEC schools were drastically affecting their ability to embrace a national athletic program and enjoy the esteem that such a program enjoyed. Mississippi State refused invitations to the NCAA basketball tournament in 1959 and 1961, and would do so again in 1962; its in-state rival Ole Miss refused to play in the 1959 NCAA baseball tournament after winning the conference crown. Similarly, LSU, after winning SEC titles in golf, tennis, and track during the period, backed out of all three NCAA championship events. The *Reveille* in 1961 addressed the bewildering process of competing with no hope of contending for championships, noting the "great losses of prestige and respect around the nation" the conference suffered from its absence at postseason events.

"To a conference that prides itself on one of the most-well-rounded athletic programs in the nation," refusing championship invitations "robs the conference of a chance of further top national honors."[75] Thus, the issue of race was isolating SEC schools from a national culture that lauded competition, toughness, and excellence. For LSU fans who found such validation in the culture of college football and the esteem that it provided, such isolation was indeed "a fate worse than integration."

The decision by LSU to reject any Sugar Bowl offer caused many to ponder the Tigers' bowl possibilities, and school officials knew that if they held to the color line, perhaps there were none. One columnist noted that the decision not to play in New Orleans "leaves the Tigers somewhat up in the air." With few options, LSU might be forced "to call it a season and forget the whole thing."[76] Thus, the announcement on November 14 that LSU would not play in the Sugar Bowl meant that without a change in policy, the fourth-ranked team in the nation might be staying home for the holidays. Far from potentially blundering away LSU's postseason, more than one sportswriter suggested LSU officials purposefully shunned the Sugar Bowl as leverage. One Baton Rouge writer suggested that by rejecting the Sugar Bowl, LSU officials had backed into a corner the pro-football board of supervisors, with the aim of getting the board to green-light a bowl invitation that could mean integrated play.[77] Many felt that if the plum of the Rose Bowl could be dangled in front of the board, it would prove enticing enough to reverse the color ban. Bill Keefe, sports editor of the *New Orleans Times-Picayune*, himself no friend to integration, openly speculated on the effect the prestige of the Rose Bowl would have on any decision. The prominence of the Pasadena game was such that, according to Keefe, "it is not beyond the realm of possibility that the LSU board would yield a bit and agree to a Rose Bowl invitation no matter what team it played." With the "schedule-making for Dixie teams . . . becoming more and more difficult because of the segregation issue," a Rose Bowl invitation "could prompt a majority of the [board] to lift the ban."[78]

Indeed, many interpreted LSU's Sugar Bowl announcement as evidence that a decision had already been made approving integrated play. The *Picayune* went so far as to suggest that the entire issue had been orchestrated for the Rose Bowl's benefit, so as to demonstrate LSU's willingness to play integrated teams. The New Orleans paper was not alone in interpreting events in this way. Dick Friedlich of the *San Francisco Chronicle* began working sources in Louisiana, asking many of the same questions and making the same assumptions. Corbett helped feed this speculation when he deflected questions regarding the matter of race by stating, "When and if we receive any such invitation of that nature, our position will be fully clarified." This was a marked departure from the sequence of events regarding the baseball team earlier in the spring. Even prior to LSU's defeat of Auburn and its clinching of the conference championship, both Middleton and Corbett made it clear that racial policy precluded LSU from going to the College World Series. Now Middleton was silent and Corbett was coy on the matter. Like throwing gasoline on the fire, Tom Hamilton told the Associated Press on November 15 that an LSU official, later identified as Corbett, assured him there would be no racial barriers to their acceptance of a Rose Bowl invitation. "I was given the impression [LSU] could handle the situation." The comment brought swift denials, as when one columnist for the hometown *State-Times* claimed he had "been assured that nobody at LSU told Hamilton or anybody else" such a thing. Even though it appeared that Alabama was quickly becoming the Rose Bowl's first choice, excitement continued to build in Baton Rouge when a West Coast conference official acknowledged that if Alabama faltered, "it wouldn't surprise me if LSU got the Rose Bowl nod." Bill Barnes, head coach of UCLA, one of the likely opponents in the Rose Bowl, commented favorably on playing either the Tigers or the Crimson Tide, noting "we would like nothing better."[79]

With the possibility of a Rose Bowl appearance dangled before them, leading segregationists suddenly became giddy in their willingness to countenance what only a few years before had been deemed as "the opening wedge for complete integration." The board of supervisors scheduled a special session to discuss the matter, perhaps not coincidentally a day after the Louisiana Sovereignty Commission was also scheduled to meet. When queried on the matter, Sovereignty Commission chairman Frank Voelker Jr. acknowledged that the football issue might be discussed. Another commission member stated that he had "no qualms" with LSU playing an integrated team, while a member of the board noted, "Personally, I'd like to see them go to the Rose Bowl."[80] Similarly, a member of the JCS offered no objection to LSU participating in the Rose Bowl, while still another segregationist legislator offered the tortured logic that if invited to the Rose Bowl, LSU "can't afford to reject it because . . . the NAACP and the integration radicals can howl that LSU was afraid they might get beat!"[81] Thus, in defense of segregation, LSU would be forced to accept integration. Even Governor Jimmie Davis, who emerged the victor in the virulently racist 1960 gubernatorial election that included Willie Rainach, refused to oppose the possibility of LSU in the Rose Bowl.[82]

Segregationists who refused to oppose LSU's appearance in the Rose Bowl almost always brought up the issue after attempting to assert their segregationist credentials, suggesting their sensitivity on the matter. Additionally, they continued to place the issue within a national sporting culture, implying that in fact race was not the issue. One columnist, claiming himself "a Southerner by birth, beliefs, and everything that goes with it" ridiculed the New Orleans Citizens' Council for its rationale against integrated play for fear that some day the "Negroes . . . might [win]." "One cannot help but wonder if these same people might feel that we should not compete against the Communist athletes in the Olympics because we might get beat."[83] In linking the issue with Olympic confrontations with the Soviets, the author asserted that such confrontations were freighted with cultural meaning about toughness and superiority. To shirk from them was to abandon "southern customs" of honor, manliness, and loyalty.

Similarly, the *Shreveport Times*, the state's leading segregationist newspaper, suggested that supporting LSU's Rose Bowl aspirations was not at all an hypocrisy. The paper separated the issue of athletic segregation from school segregation by claiming "no legal issue and no social-equality issue is involved in the [Rose Bowl issue]. The fight to regain school and other segregation must be continued with increasing vigor and it can be won. But not by making ourselves ridiculous by contending that an athletic team of a legally integrated school cannot play the integrated team of another school." Tortured as it was, the paper accepted such logic because it validated assumptions of football's cultural prominence while suggesting that such validations either did not have to come at segregation's expense or were in fact not at all related to segregation.[84] When a wire-service reporter attempted to gauge the likelihood of LSU going to an integrated bowl, he was surprised at the level of support. He noted the tradition of athletic segregation at LSU and the baseball team's withdrawal from the NCAA tournament less than six months before. "But baseball fever doesn't compare with 'Tiger fever' in Baton Rouge, where even Gov. Davis asked for a jersey and shoulder pads to help beat Ole Miss."[85]

Though one columnist declared it "overwhelmingly clear . . . that the sentiment of the people of Louisiana is solidly behind the Tiger football team and their desire to accept" an integrated bowl invitation, die-hard segregationists offered the predictably militant rhetoric. The New Orleans Citizens' Council expressed its "shock" at the possibility that LSU would forsake its segregationist traditions. The council claimed "it is far better to content itself with its present policy because in future years the teams may not be as good and to undergo defeat by integrated teams would bring about much unfavorable publicity."[86] Others were more virulent, and less reserved, in their comments. William J. Wright and his wife demanded that both Corbett and Dietzel be fired and that Middleton apologize to all Louisiana taxpayers for countenancing such blasphemy. Vice-chairman of the New Orleans Citizens' Council C. E. Vetter prophesied that if LSU lost an integrated game, "integrationists will quickly point out the superiority of Negro athletes."[87] By far the most outrageous communiqué on the matter came from twenty-five signatories from the north-central parishes of the state who declared that LSU officials "cannot compromise the principles of a vast majority of Louisianans to suit sports, sportswriters and race mixers." Focusing their venom on Corbett specifically, the authors advised the LSU athletic director that "if he continues to believe only mixed sports are top sports then give him a permanent ticket to Michigan State." If he remained in Louisiana, however, and continued to push for integrated contests, the telegram chillingly warned him that "death is inevitable."[88] It is revelatory of the times that such individuals could send a signed death threat to a public official without so much as raising an eyebrow or provoking a response.

Clearly, the popular and political sands had shifted; how much they had done so remained unclear. The answer came in the November 18 meeting of the board of supervisors, held solely to discuss the question of integrated extracurricular activities, mostly athletics. If anyone doubted the precipitating issue, displays representing several bowl games greeted board members as they entered the room. A large bouquet of roses dominated the display, with a small sign that read, "Pick one." Ever the shrewd observer of popular and political climate, Middleton came with a prepared statement that simultaneously managed to tell the board what to do while positing himself merely as its humble servant. He started off by stating what all observers of the matter largely accepted as fact: LSU's athletic future "will be increasingly limited" if the school persisted in its refusal to compete against black players. "It will become increasingly difficult to participate . . . outside of the Southeastern Conference and it is already impossible for the University to participate in contests on a national level." While that comment suggested a general concern for the larger athletic program, Middleton left no doubt what sport really animated the discussion by concerning himself only with football and the potential that LSU might find itself without an acceptable bowl invitation that season. He noted that on November 15, two board members had come to his office indicating their desire to see LSU in the Rose Bowl and stated their willingness to abandon the policy of segregated scheduling. It is perhaps not coincidental that it was the same day Tom Hamilton received word that LSU would have "no problem with the racial situation."

Thus, with the board having acknowledged its support, Middleton now felt it appropriate for the board to review the situation once again.[89]

Middleton's comments once again revealed the wily administrator who had managed to best Willie Rainach while all the while espousing segregation himself. Popular and media perception throughout the period consistently identified the board as the stumbling block to integrated play. Yet Middleton's private correspondence revealed that it was his opposition that decided the issue. Though he always maintained that he was merely trying to be consistent with the wishes of the legislature, Middleton emphatically stated on several occasions that the athletics policy was "my decision" and that "until superior authority" forced him to change, he would instruct "our Board to continue the policy." However, the board refused on four different occasions to act on motions to ban integrated play; as a result, its formal policy remained unchanged from its February 1956 statement that LSU would play anyone without regards to race. When Middleton declared that he would advocate to the "Board to continue the policy," then, it was his policy, not theirs. Thus, when Middleton appeared before the board members on November 18, he was not asking them to change their minds, he was telling them he had changed his. As a result, Middleton would be able to have his cake and eat it too. For years he had been able to convince moderates that the prohibition of integrated play had been out of his hands. By getting the board in 1961 to publicly renew its support for its 1956 policy, he could now turn to segregationists too and claim that the matter was out of his hands. For good measure, Middleton also brought Corbett along to the meeting, and he reiterated the difficulties engendered by the ban on his scheduling efforts, noting particularly the impending crisis over that year's bowl possibilities.

Though the segregationists had been beaten, the board offered them the cursory appearance of a fair hearing by calling for the reading of all public correspondence on the matter. No record exists of Corbett's reaction when the death threat was read or whether it later gave him pause, but it certainly did not dissuade his scheduling efforts. The board also revisited its answers to Middleton's twenty-one questions from 1956 regarding integrated participation in extracurricular activities. Though the board now conceded that black students could participate in university dances and even intramural athletics, it pointedly refused to consider the question of allowing blacks to participate in intercollegiate athletics.[90] Thus, LSU was now willing to play against blacks but was a long way from playing with them. They did so because it allowed them to embrace a football culture that connoted national distinctiveness and also because observers had already separated the matter from segregation at home.

Unfortunately for Tiger football fans, Alabama never faltered in 1961, finishing the season undefeated and remaining the Rose Bowl's most desired opponent. Fearful of being left out of the bowl picture altogether, LSU accepted an invitation to play in the Orange Bowl against integrated Colorado, which it beat on New Year's night, 25-7. The epitaph on the whole episode was written well before the Orange Bowl, however. In the wake of the board's decision, William Shaw, former investigator for Willie Rainach and the JCS, wrote a scathingly condemnatory letter to the board's members, many of whom were his personal friends. Shaw interpreted the matter in explicitly cultural terms and was dismayed by the repudiation of southern cultural values such as loyalty, honor, and respectability, resonant with southerners for generations. Nothing troubled Shaw more, however, than the explicit rejection of segregation, which he saw as inextricable from the matter. He opened by noting that the indecorous clamoring for a Rose Bowl bid had meant the abandonment of "the Sugar Bowl, a great Louisiana institution." The whoring about for greener pastures and the unseemly refusal of an unoffered Sugar Bowl bid was "an insult," according to Shaw.[91] Other commentators in November 1961 drew similar conclusions, declaring LSU's behavior towards the Sugar Bowl "a slap in the face to a bowl committee which has invited LSU every time it could."[92] Shaw portrayed the Sugar Bowl as loyally abiding by local custom in its continued refusal to invite integrated teams, even after the reversal of the sports ban. As a result, Shaw and others claimed LSU had an "obligation" to the Sugar Bowl as the home state franchise, claiming that LSU "owed" the Sugar Bowl for past invitations when they might not have been warranted.[93]

Shaw also noted the loss of honor and respectability, particularly visible to those outside the South. Throughout the battle against integration, segregationist ideologues always believed their only route to success lay in their ability to convince non-southerners that the fight against integration was really about states' rights and local values. "To the millions of people throughout the country who have followed the South's fight to maintain State's Rights and separation of the races, the University's action would indicate that we in Louisiana are prepared to sell out these principles for a little notoriety or public acclaim." For Shaw, the decision to pursue the Rose Bowl and ultimately accept the Orange Bowl bid was a blow not just to the honor of Louisiana but to the whole South and the segregationist movement. LSU had faced its moment in the crucible and failed utterly. "It is only when a voluntary choice, such as the one presented to the University in this case, is offered that we can test the depth of our principles. To the neutral observer, ours must seem shallow indeed." Appealing to deeply held southern notions of white supremacy, personal honor, and responsibility to tightly woven social networks, Shaw also intimated that the episode had degraded the individual board members themselves. He sent his letter to each board member and informed them "that I dislike having to write this letter. Many of you are my personal friends for whom I have the warmest regard. . . . I personally waited more than a week for those who are usually so vocal on matters of segregation to come forth on this issue and thereby save me the painful necessity of this letter. I am only undertaking the task because they have not done so." Thus, the board members had not only dishonored the segregationist cause but themselves and their friendships as well. Shaw was merely upholding his honorable, manly responsibility by rhetorically speaking shame to their faces.

Shaw explicitly rejected the efforts of those who attempted to claim that football and segregation were unrelated. He posited football's increasing postwar cultural prominence as antithetical to segregation, and argued that by linking the two, both football and segregation suffered. He noted "the intense public pressure that was on the Board," creating the appearance of "a compelling necessity that the University participate in [a] post-season game." Shaw decried what he perceived to be the false logic of such assumptions. He pointed out that Notre Dame continued to maintain the discretion to select their opponents while refusing to play in bowl games. The entire affair, according to Shaw, marked a shift in cultural values that elevated football to an exalted status that apparently trumped segregation. Such an occurrence would eventually come back to haunt LSU, according to Shaw. Relying on standard doomsday segregationist rhetoric, Shaw prophesied the downfall of LSU football. Just as segregationists declared that integration would lead to miscegenation and the debasement of American society by pointing to the criminality and living conditions of northern ghettoes, Shaw noted that since the University of Oklahoma, holder of the longest winning streak in college football history and the dominant power in the 1950s, had integrated, it had "fallen from the ranks of greatness and become a second rate football power. We would be wise to consider such an object lesson."[94] Thus, just as integration would supposedly make the South look like Harlem, it would also make LSU's football team like Oklahoma's.

The cultural force of football simply overwhelmed die-hard segregationists like Shaw who watched with dismay as Louisianans at every level clamored for LSU to participate in college football's postseason bowl frenzy. By placing the issue in terms of a national sporting culture unrelated to integration, supporters of LSU's bowl adventure carried the day. As Shaw's letter indicates, traditional southern values such as loyalty, honor, and segregation still maintained real currency, but when faced with the choice of regional values that isolated southerners or national values that celebrated American distinctiveness and unity, many southerners willingly embraced the latter because they could tell themselves the two were unrelated.

While LSU and its partisans wrestled with the disparity in values between football and segregation during the period, another Rose Bowl suitor suffered no such angst. At the University of Alabama, supporters accepted playing integrated teams because it served as a means to unify southerners in the defense of segregation and because northerners politely refused to condemn southern football as an extension of a segregated society. When the Rose Bowl came calling in November 1961, however, the Crimson Tide abruptly discovered that the implications of postwar football now prohibited either result.

FOUR

Tuscaloosa: The Pariah of Postwar Football

"It's worse than un-American, its un-human. . . . An all-white team has no business being #1, it's a denial of democracy."
—Jim Murray

By the end of November 1961, Jim Murray might well have been the most hated man in Alabama. Murray was neither a member of the Kennedy administration attempting to provide aid and comfort to integrationist or communist rabble rousers nor a federal judge seeking to destroy the "southern way of life." Murray was, of all things, a sportswriter, in the far-off locale of Los Angeles. As far as most Alabamians were concerned, however, Murray had done nothing less than single-handedly deprive their beloved Crimson Tide of a Rose Bowl invitation while slandering the saintly Bear Bryant in the process. He had the temerity to bring up in the sports pages such unseemly affairs as segregation, the use of federal troops, and the Ku Klux Klan, and somehow, at least in their minds, link them all to Bryant and the football team. By November 1961, Alabamians had turned indignation against the national media into fine art, having already been outraged by the *New York Times*, *Sports Illustrated*, and *Time* magazine, but Murray's transgressions may have been the worst, not only because they came at the expense of Alabama football but also because they appeared, of all places, in the sports section. Murray was in the vanguard of a new generation of sports columnists who chose to see sports through the prism of social commentary. Having cut his teeth at *Sports Illustrated* in the late 1950s, Murray came to the *Los Angeles Times* in 1960 with a very high profile and an acidic wit. The profile came from the fact that the *Times'* new publisher, thirty-year-old Otis Chandler, who was just beginning his revolutionary changes to that paper, personally hired Murray. Chandler recognized in Murray a sharpness and cynicism seldom found in American sports pages at the time and a willingness to debunk the holiest of cows. The fact that Murray had been previously employed by *Sports Illustrated*, a subsidiary of Time, Inc., meant that Chandler, in his mind, was making quite a splash by stealing Murray from one of the bastions of the eastern media establishment.[1] Chandler's move eventually paid off; Murray won a Pulitzer Prize and long before his death in 1997 was universally regarded by his colleagues as the dean of American sportswriters.

Most white Alabamians, however, were unconcerned with Chandler's designs and somehow managed to see in Murray only a serial exaggerator, a profligate liar, and a bully of the first order. The response to Murray's writings revealed the tremendous anxieties and uncertainties of white southerners in general and Alabamians in particular regarding the social and cultural upheaval that marked American society at the height of the postwar years. If Louisianans and some southerners were convinced that the best way to embrace segregation and postwar football was to ignore any interrelationship between the two, Alabamians and a different set of southerners were convinced that the two were in fact symbiotic. Southerners could have their cake and eat it too, by investing in the game the defense of segregation and white supremacy within the South while muting such meanings outside of the South. As a result, what Murray had done was simultaneously threaten southern football *and* segregation, thereby challenging Alabamians' embrace of both a southern and an American way of life.

Cold War anxieties over atomic security, the national character, and basic American values were visited upon the South as they were elsewhere. The South, however, also faced additional sources of instability during the period that shaped their embrace of postwar football as a cultural salve for the anxiety of the period. Even prior to the Cold War period, the South witnessed the onset of revolutionary changes to traditional southern life. The forces of modernity in the form of mechanical cotton pickers and weed-controlling chemicals, which began displacing rural southern agricultural workers by the thousands in the 1930s, reached full flower during the war years. In the decades that followed World War II, the number of southern farms decreased by almost two thirds, the number of tenant farmers dropped from 1.5 million to 136,000, and sharecropping all but disappeared by 1959 from a wartime population of half a million. Though many left the South for other regions, most migrated to existing southern urban areas, creating bustling, often overcrowded, cities. Southern agricultural dislocation played out as World War II and Cold War defense industries provided urban economic opportunity, creating a push-pull force that drastically escalated southern urbanization. It also, however, untethered southerners from traditional community bonds. As Numan Bartley has written, "The demographic upheavals that accompanied . . . the depopulation of the farms cast huge numbers of southerners adrift. Folk cultures declined as uprooted people endeavored to adjust to a market society wherein labor was a free-flowing commodity and social fragmentation replaced community."[2]

No issue, however, loomed as large as that of race, and during the postwar period southern anxiety on the matter sharpened acutely. Demographic and ideological changes in the Democratic Party brought to the fore increasingly vocal and effective critics of southern racial policies. A willingness on the part of the Supreme Court to define more broadly the Fourteenth Amendment assisted southern blacks in their calls for equality. Additionally, national Democratic Party rhetoric increasingly included language hostile to segregation, such that by the 1950s, many southerners felt besieged on the subject. Additionally, beginning in the late 1940s, the federal policies of both parties understood that southern segregation damaged America's international credibility, particularly with Asia, Africa, and Latin America. Such credibility was further tarnished when the Soviets consistently highlighted incidents of American racial violence to rebut American claims of freedom and equality.[3] As a result, the issue of segregation weighed upon southerners as a regional social issue, a national political issue, and an international diplomatic issue.

Racially motivated events in Alabama in the late 1950s and early 1960s placed the state at the center of national attention and condemnation, intensifying local anxiety on the matter. Even after the 1954 *Brown* decision, the trustees at the University of Alabama consistently rejected desegregating the student body and engaged in all manner of coercion, blackmail, and various other illegalities either to deny admission to black applicants or to convince them to withdraw their applications. Nonetheless, after months of delay and subterfuge, the university finally acceded to a federal court order in January 1956 by admitting Autherine Lucy. Lucy's admission sparked a vociferous opposition that included intense personal harassment and mob activity aimed not only at Lucy herself but at the university personnel who assisted her. After less than a week on campus, Lucy's short tenure as a student ended. Whipped up by the basketball team's upset victory over Vanderbilt, Alabama students streamed out of the game and mixed with off-campus elements, soon coalescing into a mob chanting "Hey, Hey, Ho, Ho, Autherine's got to go!" and "Two, four, six, eight, we don't wanna integrate!" Moving off campus, the mob turned riotous, harassing passing black motorists, damaging their vehicles, and blocking traffic. Though university officials suspended the six white students they could identify as leaders of the mob, they also suspended Lucy, who had not even been present, as a source of the disruption. When Lucy's lawyers included mildly defamatory language critical of university officials in her request for readmission to the presiding judge, the university used such "baseless, defenseless, and outrageous" conduct as grounds for her permanent expulsion. In the eyes of the national media, the outrageous logic of holding Lucy responsible for the riot and her subsequent suspension was exceeded only by the petty rationale for her expulsion.[4]

With the stain of Autherine Lucy's humiliation still present, Alabama found additional ways to earn national scorn and condemnation. In April 1960, the *New York Times* dispatched reporter Harrison Salisbury to profile the racial situation in the city of Birmingham. Salisbury's two-part report, running under the lead headline "Fear and Hatred Grip Birmingham," offered up a scathing indictment of the city, detailing racial violence, bombings, and a woeful indifference or outright hostility on the part of the city's white leadership. Salisbury made the infamous comparison to South African apartheid by referring to Birmingham as "the Johannesburg of America." City officials and residents in general vociferously attacked the *Times* and Salisbury's characterization, and the city dispatched a formal demand for retraction from the paper, issuing a rebuttal that the *Times* felt compelled to run on page one.[5]

By far the most egregious mark on Alabama's reputation occurred in the spring of 1961 with the state's response to the Freedom Rides. Attempting to test the enforcement of federal court decrees banning segregation in interstate travel, civil rights activists engaged in integrated bus travel while insisting on integrating the lunchrooms, restrooms, and drinking fountains of bus depots throughout the South. The first sustained violence against the Riders came just inside Alabama, when whites firebombed one of the buses outside Anniston. When the Riders rolled into Birmingham, Klansmen brutally attacked them on Mother's Day 1961, with no police intervention. The head of the Birmingham police, Eugene "Bull" Connor, had secretly arranged ahead of time to give the Klan fifteen minutes to beat the activists before the arrival of police. For all the racial ferocity that fueled the Anniston bombing, the infamous Mother's Day beatings, and the arrangement between the police and the Klan, nothing compared to what the Riders faced when they arrived in Montgomery. There, a mob as large as a thousand angry whites attacked not only the Freedom Riders but also most of the assembled media and an observer from the Department of Justice.[6]

It was in this environment that Alabamians intensified their embrace of college football. In the face of social upheaval and external challenges to the southern way of life, southerners turned to the institution of football as a form of cultural validation. Southerners, as did all Americans at the time, ascribed to football the values of manliness, deprivation, and toughness that served as the game's hallmarks during the Cold War era. They also, however, attached to football complex constructions of white supremacy and southern distinctiveness.

Southerners attached meanings of exceptionalism and racism to college football long before the Cold War. When Alabama managed to upset the University of Washington in the 1926 Rose Bowl, southerners elevated the players to regional heroes. With three more Rose Bowl appearances by the end of the 1930s, including two more wins, one southern writer noted that "for all the last stands, all the lost causes, and sacrificings in vain," the South finally found a tradition of achievement rather than merely one of nobility. "The South had come by way of football to think at last in terms of causes won, not lost."[7] Likewise, following Alabama's second Rose Bowl victory in 1927, university president George Denny declared that he returned to the South "with my head a little higher and my soul a little more inspired to win the battle for this splendid Anglo-Saxon race of the South."[8] The postwar period, however, not only intensified these sentiments but also witnessed a drastic escalation of hostility towards the South, increasing southern anxiety. As a result, southerners intensified their identifications of football with white supremacy and southern distinctiveness, and retreated ever further into the game as a refuge from the criticism.

The inherently violent component of football coupled with the legal exclusion of blacks made it very easy for observers and commentators to interpret the game during the period as a celebration and revelation of white dominance. In addition to excluding blacks from the playing field, southern college football also ascribed to blacks subservient roles on the game's periphery. Southern white college teams often allowed blacks to attach themselves to their athletic programs in varying capacities, ranging from water boys to "rubbers" (masseurs) to general hangers-on. These black retainers were always men; intensely loyal, the most legendary of their number provided long-standing service. In short, they were the male equivalent of the stereotypical antebellum mammy.[9] At the University of Georgia, Clegg Stark, described by one white Georgia partisan as "a flap-mouthed Negro water boy . . . who doesn't know his own age or how long he has been there," faithfully served the Bulldogs for decades in the first half of the twentieth century. As a token of appreciation, Georgia players chipped in to buy Stark a house; he accepted "wearing his red-and-black Georgia sweater . . . with his head bowed in humility." Stark's service of undetermined length and his alleged ignorance of his own age reinforced white assumptions of black docility and their infantile nature. Legendary Athens high school football coach Hokey Jackson even named his loyal hunting dog Clegg "for Georgia's longtime water boy."[10] The University of Mississippi had a similar character named "Blind Jim" Ivy, who arrived in Oxford in 1896 and served as a food vendor on campus and at Rebel sporting events, particularly football games. Blinded by an industrial accident, Ivy scratched out a living for the next half century loosely attached to the university's athletic department. Students loved to hear the blind man joke that he had never seen Ole Miss lose. When Ole Miss students learned that Ivy's "one-room shanty" was to be foreclosed upon, they chipped in and bought it for him in recognition of his role as "a vital part of this institution for many years."[11]

At Alabama, Merrill Collins began working for the university in 1900 as a twelve-year-old, eventually serving as locker room attendant for the football team. As at Georgia and Ole Miss, students at Alabama held a genuine affection for Collins, who lived in the basement boiler room of the athletic complex. They often acquired food for him from the dining hall and pooled their laundry money to help supplement his meager existence. Additionally, players paternalistically viewed Collins as some kind of talisman or mascot by rubbing his head for good luck before the Auburn game. When Collins formally retired in 1958, Bear Bryant arranged for an employee to take Collins to the Social Security Administration to ensure he received his "pennies," and passed along "the appreciation of the Board of Trustees, the University Administration, and the Faculty," for his "many years of service."[12]

Classic southern paternalism ascribed to Stark, Ivy, and Collins a status dependent upon whites and their institutions. Such relationships took on added significance during the postwar period as white southerners increasingly elevated figures like Stark, Ivy, and Collins to repudiate the criticism of the region. White southerners claimed that the provision of housing and other forms of charity illustrated their benevolence toward "their Negroes." In addition, the long and faithful service that such individuals offered to whites illustrated their satisfaction with southern race relations. Finally, the loyalty of these individuals in the era of civil rights activism made them nonthreatening at a time when southern whites interpreted integrationist demands as presumptuous or "uppity." Thus, southern paternalism in college football not only ascribed to blacks a subservient role but also served as a rejection of the civil rights movement.

If white southerners used college football to identify the proper role of blacks in southern society, they also availed themselves of football's ability to call forth shared identity and sacrifice among spectators by putting the trappings of the game to the service of white supremacy. In September 1962, amidst the crisis surrounding the admission of James Meredith to the University of Mississippi, the Mississippi Sovereignty Commission printed 600,000 postcards addressed to President Kennedy decrying federal actions in the Meredith case, to be delivered to college football fans at Alabama, Vanderbilt, LSU, and South Carolina, all of which had home games on the Saturday preceding Meredith's admission.[13] At the Ole Miss game that Saturday, Governor Ross Barnett whipped into a segregationist frenzy a halftime crowd in Jackson's Memorial Stadium described by Taylor Branch as the last respectable lynch mob of the twentieth century. One Ole Miss supporter in attendance later claimed the spectacle "reminded me of the Nazi youth rallies."[14] Thus, as white supremacy found itself under increasing attack, many white southerners found both a response in and validation from college football.

Though white southerners had attached to football the values of southern distinctiveness and white supremacy since at least the 1920s, at no time did those values face such sustained criticism as they did in the years following World War II. As a result, white Alabamians sought to use football as a neutral ground upon which to make common cultural cause with other Americans during the period. To understand their concept of football as a cultural bridge, however, requires an examination of the ways in which they used the game to create cultural cohesiveness and community identity within the South.

In many respects, the mid-1950s marked the nadir for the University of Alabama. The football team slipped into irrelevance, winning only four games in three years under head coach J. B. "Ears" Whitworth. Whitworth's firing following the 1958 season was made all the more uncomfortable when the coach broke down in an unseemly and tearful display of emotion in announcing the decision to his team. Far more destructive and divisive was the trustees' handling of the integration question, resulting in Autherine Lucy's dubious expulsion in 1956. To protest Lucy's treatment, Nobel Laureate Linus Pauling rescinded his acceptance of Alabama's offer to deliver the keynote address at the university's upcoming sesquicentennial celebration. Additionally, several faculty members quietly left for other jobs, and in 1957 the heretofore highly respected Oliver Carmichael resigned as university president, having managed to disappoint both the segregationists and the liberals.[15] Thus, 1958 witnessed the nearly simultaneous arrival of the university's new president, Frank Rose, and its new football coach, Paul "Bear" Bryant. As observers made clear, the timing was not coincidental, nor were the hirings unrelated.

Though Carmichael displeased virtually everyone with his role in the Lucy episode, it was his inability to deliver on larger expectations that ultimately led to his downfall. Arriving with an impressive pedigree, the Oxford-trained Carmichael had built a resume that included a term as chancellor of Vanderbilt University and the presidency of the prestigious Carnegie Foundation for the Advancement of Teaching. When he arrived in Tuscaloosa in 1953, he brought with him the respect of academic endowments and foundations that were rapidly becoming crucial in the environment of Cold War higher education, a reputation as a dynamic fund-raiser, and a sympathy for faculty concerns, most notably salaries and research facilities. His inability to navigate successfully the race question came about largely because he failed to galvanize his supporters behind any other successes. The trustees were wary of his increasing reliance on federal funding for the university's extension center in Huntsville when such grants came with demands for nondiscriminatory clauses in dorms and other facilities built with that money. Faculty grew frustrated with his inability to raise salaries and improve research facilities, a result of shortcomings from Carmichael's fund-raising efforts. Carmichael's failure to excite the university's supporters during fund-raising drives derived from two sources: race and football. Many potential donors saw Carmichael as soft on the race question and, even worse, unconcerned about the direction of the football team.[16] In noting Carmichael's departure, *Time* magazine claimed that it resulted from his refusal "to share the concern of some alumni over the fact that 'Bama's once-great football team has won only two games in the last 23."[17] Indeed, Bryant later claimed that "the only president who's ever been fired at Alabama was against football."[18] When Rose succeeded Carmichael and promptly hired Bryant, trustee John Caddell wrote to the new president that his hiring of Bryant "was the most popular thing that could have happened from your standpoint." Caddell then informed Rose that he could use such leverage "to make them, 'the people of Alabama,' put up the money for adequate salaries for our faculty."[19]

In addition to providing for Rose's arrival, the crisis of race also drastically increased the stakes of restoring the prominence of the football team. When Ernest Williams, chair of the committee charged with hiring a new coach, solicited advice from alumni and close confidants, responses almost unanimously agreed that in the wake of the Lucy episode, the football team needed to restore the reputation of the university. "Whether we like it or not," wrote one alum, the university and the athletic department were inseparable and the failings of one affected the other. If the athletic department were "to do something big, to do the unexpected," however, it might wipe away the criticism of the national media and "electrify the nation" in acclaim for the University of Alabama. In the eyes of most Tide partisans, the hiring of Bear Bryant fit the bill. Another letter noted "the many problems facing the administration of the university," claiming that the hiring of Bryant would be in "the best interest" of Alabama. Even those who opposed Bryant's hiring saw the issue in the context of the Lucy episode. Noting Texas A&M's impending probation for NCAA violations under Bryant, as well as his notorious training camp at Junction, R. R. Miree labeled Bryant "the most controversial man that could be secured," noting that "one of the things we need least is further controversy."[20] Miree's concerns notwithstanding, in the words of E. Culpepper Clark, "the arrival of Bryant and Rose augured well for university morale."[21]

Bryant's role as savior of statewide morale and reputation illustrated the intense cultural attachment to Alabama football in the state. Almost alone among big-time football powers, the University of Alabama played its "home" games scattered across the state in Tuscaloosa, Birmingham, Mobile, and Montgomery. The playing of games throughout the state allowed Alabamians from every section to embrace the Tide as their team and amounted, in the words of one scholar, to a traveling "tent revival."[22] After Tuscaloosa, the most prominent of these locations was Birmingham's Legion Field, largely because the on-campus Denny Stadium seated only 25,000 until 1961 while Legion Field seated 44,000 by the postwar years. While Tuscaloosa merchants obviously watched with a jealous eye as profits from game day services flowed into Birmingham coffers, the question of where the Crimson Tide played became a matter for community discussion. Thomas Clark, writing in 1961, noted that postwar southern embrace of football—and in the upper South, basketball—illustrated an expanding popular consciousness of higher education. Clark claimed that in the past, sports failed to weave a larger, inclusive cultural narrative, but now, "runaway passions for athletics have placed schools in a curious kind of public domain. . . . Today most southern communities have developed a local mania over their athletic teams."[23] Playing games in multiple locations cemented the identity of the team with that of the entire state but also allowed those locales to feel like equal shareholders in the cultural phenomena of Alabama football. As a result, residents in Tuscaloosa and Birmingham linked where the Crimson Tide played its games with what was "in the best interests . . . of the community."[24]

For these two cities, college football in the form of the Crimson Tide was a community possession that certainly marked economic interests but also notions of urban boosterism, collective identity, and popular passion, a fact university personnel were not hesitant to exploit. In 1959, the university began pressuring the city of Birmingham, which actually owned and managed Legion Field, to upgrade that stadium's seating capacity. In a letter to the chair of Birmingham's Parks and Recreation Board, university president Frank Rose bluntly declared, "If Legion Field does not add the required number of seats, we will have to expand our stadium and move the games to Tuscaloosa."[25] Even after Birmingham agreed to expand Legion Field, the university decided to expand Denny Stadium anyway, a move Bryant disingenuously justified by stating, "It would be difficult to meet our budget unless we can provide additional seats."[26] The expansion of Denny Stadium was only partly about money. It also served as a symbol of the Tuscaloosa community's refusal to be outdone by its neighbor to the north and a future form of leverage against Birmingham. Bryant relied on this latter issue in 1961 when engineering deficiencies forced the closure of the new upper deck at Legion Field. In a huff, Bryant considered moving games out of Birmingham entirely, a point he humbly backed away from when Birmingham residents and leaders howled as if Bryant had proposed hijacking a sacred relic.[27] Long before such leveraging of municipal coffers by professional franchises became commonplace, Bryant and Rose managed to pull off the feat with a college team, not because merchants responded to an economic rationale but because residents accepted the shared sense of communal ownership and emotional investment.

The cultural significance of Alabama football appeared in more than just the municipal contestations over where the Tide played. Bryant's contract at Alabama included the rights to all Alabama game films, giving him a monopoly, in the days before cable television and twenty-four-hour sports channels, on game footage, which he broadcast on his Sunday afternoon coach's show. One of the first coaches to have his own television show, Bryant turned fall Sunday afternoons into Alabama's "strictest Sunday ritual." At a time in the South when many communities still observed blue laws (laws prohibiting commerce or public activities on Sunday), the *Bear Bryant Show* held a captive audience. Many Alabama fans enjoyed an autumn Sunday ritual of morning church, a midday family meal, followed by a 12:30 family viewing of the *Bear Bryant Show*. Filled not only with highlights and player interviews, the show featured Bryant operating without a script spouting platitudes, homilies, and paeans to God, country, and family. As Keith Dunnavant has written, "The Bear Bryant show was a near-religious experience for many Alabamians. . . . The program quickly became the most powerful link between Bryant and his fans, fostering a kind of intimacy, making the fans feel closer to the man and more invested in his team. . . . The show connected the coach to the football-crazed state in a profound way."[28] The *Bear Bryant Show* thus packaged a host of widely celebrated cultural values into Alabama football.

In the face of racial upheaval and social dislocation from urbanization, white southerners found in football a means to create community cohesion and cultural stability. Using football to make those same linkages outside the South increasingly ran afoul of the changing racial climate, however. The widespread embrace of intersectional football games beginning in the 1920s dramatically increased the possibility of games between segregated and integrated teams. To address this potential point of conflict, opponents generally engaged in what became known as a Gentlemen's Agreement, sometimes understood and sometimes contractual, which provided for the benching of all black athletes when competing against southern schools. Northern schools generally accepted without question that playing southern teams required benching their black players. Conversely, those same northern schools realized that in scheduling home games with southern teams, they had to abide by the Gentlemen's Agreement or risk southern schools pulling their team from the field at the last minute, leaving the home team with tens of thousands of fans in the seats on a Saturday afternoon with no game to watch, no concessions to buy, and demanding refunds at the gate. These agreements occasionally met with opposition from supporters of the integrated team, and the shifting winds of race in postwar America made them increasingly difficult for white southerners to enforce or expect. As late as 1952, however, Alabama president John Gallalee is said to have ordered head coach Red Drew to threaten to pull the Crimson Tide from the 1953 Sugar Bowl against Syracuse if the Orangemen used black players.[29]

The death knell of such tactics surely came in 1955 when Georgia governor Marvin Griffin threatened to withhold Georgia Tech from the Sugar

Bowl against integrated Pittsburgh. The ensuing street demonstrations and opposition to Griffin's actions demonstrated football's broad cultural appeal, even at the expense of segregation. The demise of the Gentlemen's Agreements marked the inability of southerners to continue exporting segregation, but many segregationist intellectuals across the South also interpreted the Georgia Tech episode as a threat to segregation from within the South. Understanding that the South was going to lose a purely legal argument on the merits of segregation, many southern defenders recognized the region's only hope lay in healing the division within white southern society between racial temporizers on one extreme and disreputable demagogues on the other. In this fashion, the South might hope to delay and forestall the process of integration until the North either lost interest as it had after Reconstruction or came to agree with the South on the race issue. In either case, football could serve as a valuable tool both to unify the South as well as reach out to the North.

L. Nelson Bell, the segregationist editor of the *Southern Presbyterian Journal*, took Griffin to task in the pages of the *Journal*, claiming the governor's "outburst [was] to be deplored." Bell saw Griffin's actions as a disaster to the segregationist cause by highlighting not only the irrational extremists who flocked to Griffin's banner but also the division in southern society as marked by the student demonstrations.[30] A friend of Bell's wrote to oppose his "affront to the fine people of Georgia," and defended Griffin's actions by noting, "If a man is *for* segregation, he is for it today, tomorrow, and as far in the future as he . . . can see." To equivocate in any way, Bell's correspondent charged, is to be essentially an integrationist. Refusing to yield on the matter, Bell responded by again lambasting Griffin's behavior, "I feel he did our cause a great disservice by trying to stop the Georgia Tech game. . . . He made the South look silly. It looked like cheap political demagoguery and it hurt what thinking Southerners are trying to do to stem a desperate situation."[31] In Bell's eyes, an insistence on maintaining the color line in sports eroded the kind of community cohesion that emerged after the war around institutions like Alabama football because it forced white southerners to choose between the esteemed southern institution of segregation and the equally esteemed institution of football. Worse, Griffin's inflexibility and extremism made it that much harder for those outside the South to find any pragmatic commonality upon which to reach a consensus on the matter of race.

Bell was not the only one who saw Griffin's actions within the context of the cultural divide that existed between southerners on the issue of segregation. John Temple Graves, a columnist with the *Birmingham Post-Herald* and himself more than a casual observer of the larger cultural significance of southern football, noted that Griffin's knee-jerk attempt to hold the line against integration at the expense of a football game sparked "a human reaction" in opposition to the governor.[32] Graves, like Bell, understood that the inevitable result was a division among white southerners between those steadfastly loyal to segregation and those who embraced segregation only so long as it did not come at the expense of something else they valued, like football. Thomas R. Waring, editor of the Charleston, South Carolina, *News and Courier* and a correspondent of Graves, agreed with his friend in Birmingham on the cultural contestation that Griffin's actions revealed. The popular backlash against Griffin's attempt to halt the game "is one of the reasons we have not protested The Citadel's playing integrated teams." Waring acknowledged such conditions were a "capitulation," causing him to abandon "total resistance" to integration in hopes of building a popular front. Otherwise, according to Waring, segregationist intellectuals risked alienating large numbers of southerners and further weakening the already tenuous segregationist position. "I see no point in trying to lead a parade in which nobody marches but a couple of worn out drum majors."[33] Thus, to "accept" the cultural role of college football during the period was to "endure" the occasional integrated opponent.[34]

In placing football in service to segregation, Bell, Graves, and Waring also inadvertently located the game in its postwar context. Accepting the cultural hold football enjoyed on so many southerners, these segregationist intellectuals correctly interpreted it as an expression of values and identities that southerners linked with their understanding of what it meant to be southern. As a result, the game spoke to southerners' yearning for a celebration of their way of life when so much of that life was now under attack. Quite simply, many southerners accepted that the defense of segregation might require a little integration because it was the best way to reap the cultural validation derived from football.

Perhaps nowhere was this trade-off more explicit and more readily accepted than at the University of Alabama. At Alabama, the decision to play against integrated teams was interpreted explicitly, both within the state and throughout the South, within the context of the social and political upheaval of the time. As one Mississippi sportswriter noted, "When 'Bama went north and east and west, it wasn't going to play just a football game, it was going on a crusade, and Bear was our Richard the Lion-Hearted. Bear was our best, and our best could and did beat the best of anywhere else, and that was important to all of us below the Mason-Dixon Line." More than simply upholding the honor of the South, Bryant and Alabama football emerged victorious when little else seemed to favor the region. As the national media revealed Alabama to be awash in racial terrorism and political demagoguery, the Crimson Tide went forth and vanquished all who lay before them. "The state might lose every time its lawyers appeared before the Supreme Court, but Bear's warriors hardly ever lost."[35]

Walking the fine line between providing such regional validation and sparking a showdown over segregation required a delicate combination of outsider complicity and scheduling concessions on the part of southern teams. The scheduling of games with integrated teams could occur only under very specific, proscribed circumstances. Most obviously, such contests were played on the road, thereby avoiding any offense to local segregationist sensibilities. When Waring noted his acceptance of integrated play for The Citadel, he noted that such games could occur "only outside the South, however."[36] Additionally, southern teams had to avoid the appearance of too eagerly desiring to engage in games with integrated teams, largely by not initiating such arrangements. In 1958, University of Cincinnati president Walter Langsam proposed a home-and-home football series with Alabama. Recognizing that the Bearcats lacked a national reputation, Langsam attempted to play on his personal relationship with Frank Rose and even offered to forgo Cincinnati's home game by agreeing to "play on your field in successive years" in hopes of scheduling the Tide. Rose eagerly replied that he was amenable to scheduling Cincinnati and noted that, in fact, he had already spoken to Bryant about the matter. Bryant, too, did not oppose scheduling Cincinnati, informing Rose "he would be happy to correspond with" UC officials regarding the matter. Almost as an afterthought, though, Rose gingerly broached "one big problem regarding our playing northern teams." Without explicitly mentioning the subject of race, Rose noted that the issue "embarrassed" the university, "but I am sure you understand some of the difficult problems we are going through these days." In so doing, Rose gently reminded a colleague and friend that such an arrangement would likely create a delicate situation for Cincinnati as well in the form of potential opposition from those resenting the Bearcats' scheduling of a segregated team. Rose wanted to assure Langsam that such "problems" did not inherently kill the deal, however, and that Bryant would address the specifics in his correspondence with Cincinnati's athletic director. The likely circumstance was that Alabama would have to forgo any home games. Nonetheless, Rose closed by hoping "we can work things out on a future basis."[37]

As Rose's correspondence with Langsam reveals, scheduling intersectional games with integrated teams was fraught with complications. Tacitly accepting their pariah status, segregated teams almost never initiated such negotiations, waiting instead, at least publicly, for teams such as Cincinnati to approach them. This allowed southern officials to claim they did not seek out opportunities to breach the color line. Nonetheless, they actively cultivated such contacts, demonstrating that they desired intersectional play and willingly accepted the interracial component. Waiting for integrated schools to initiate such contacts also allowed for a preselection of northern teams willing to accept the consequences of playing a segregated team. One Louisiana commentator noted that even if southern schools wanted to schedule integrated teams, it did not guarantee that they could "go out and grab just any big name team. There will be tremendous pressure at the home of the out-of-state schools playing any school that practices segregation."[38] Thus, games between segregated and integrated opponents in the postwar period required two interlocking pieces: a segregated team that could finesse the issue with local fans, media, and possibly even politicians; and an integrated team willing to ignore the morality of the issue and a resolve to endure the subsequent criticism. Few events revealed these terms better than the 1959 Liberty Bowl in Philadelphia, matching the newly resurgent Alabama Crimson Tide against Penn State and their black fullback, Charles Jenrette.

After finishing 7–1–2 in 1959, Alabama landed a bid to Philadelphia's Liberty Bowl. Initial newspaper coverage focused on Alabama's return to football prominence and its appearance in the postseason for the first time in seven years. Most papers put the announcement on the front page, above the fold. The *Birmingham News* fawned over the Liberty Bowl, calling it "a plum" and an "attractive proposition," enthusing, "It will be exciting again to see Big 'Bama getting such attention." Virtually every paper in the state ran items similar to that of the *News*. All stressed continuity with Alabama's storied past and reveled in the Tide's return to prominence. Media praise was so effusive that the *News*, perhaps getting a little defensive about the excitement over a mediocre opponent in an event only two years old, declared, "Albeit a new bowl, the Liberty affair is of significance. The Penn State team to be met is a stalwart."[39]

Tide supporters were so enthusiastic over the return of football success to Alabama that most overlooked the issue of race. Alone among the major daily papers in Alabama, the *Birmingham Post-Herald* mentioned in its news story that the Penn State offense featured a black player named Charles Jenrette, a reference they buried at the end of the story. A column in the same paper two days later, ignoring the precedent of playing against Jenrette, declared that the "most significant" part of the Liberty Bowl invitation was that Alabama, pioneer for southern football prominence, was "again opening a new bowl frontier." A column in the rival *Birmingham News* mentioned the prominence of Jenrette in the Penn State attack but did not mention his race, though earlier it had run a team photograph of Penn State in which Jenrette appeared. No mention of the issue at all appeared in the news stories of the *Mobile Press-Register*, the *Tuscaloosa News*, the *Montgomery Advertiser*, the Montgomery-based *Alabama Journal*, and other papers. That is not to say that race did not play a role, however. The *Alabama Journal*, which did not mention Jenrette in any way, did note that both Frank Rose and the board of trustees approved the game, suggesting the stakes included more than a simple football game. The *Post-Herald's* story, which did mention Jenrette, quoted one of the game's promoters as saying "there will be no racial problems," a thinly veiled acknowledgment that no Gentlemen's Agreement would be in force.[40] Alabama, then, was prepared to play a game against a team featuring a black player, without a Gentlemen's Agreement, and with the foreknowledge of most Alabamians—and the overwhelming popular response was disinterest.

The unwillingness to stand on segregationist principle regarding the game reached the highest levels of Alabama's governing elite. Many prominent figures who, on other issues, helped stiffen segregationist resolve, opposed the Tide's holiday plans, but did so in muted tones. The political stakes of the time demanded that the decision to accept the Liberty Bowl bid existed beyond the authority of Bryant and even Rose. The matter eventually found its way not just to the attention of the board of trustees but to the governor of the state. The 1958 Alabama gubernatorial election, perhaps most memorable for spawning George Wallace's infamous comment that he had been "out-niggered" by the eventual winner, John Patterson, largely turned on the subject of race. Patterson, who openly aligned himself with the Ku Klux Klan, positioned himself as a staunch defender of segregation.[41] When faced with the opportunity to stand firm on segregation while coincidentally denying the Crimson Tide their first bowl appearance in several years, however, the governor passed. Personally approving of the Tide's acceptance, Patterson issued a press release that said, "I congratulate the Crimson Tide on its invitation to play in the Liberty Bowl, which will bring Alabama back into national prominence." Patterson concluded by claiming, "I am glad to see Alabama back in the bowls," and in fact did so personally, traveling with the team to Philadelphia.[42]

The board of trustees, which at that moment was engaged in vigorous, and often illegal, activity to stave off the integration of the University of Alabama, served as Patterson's handmaiden on the Liberty Bowl issue. Until his retirement shortly before the Liberty Bowl incident, Hill Ferguson served on the board for forty years and most recently had been the leading segregationist in the board's fight against integration. Upon his formal retirement, the board conferred on Ferguson the title "Trustee Emeritus," and he remained, in the words of E. Culpepper Clark, "a nuisance" regarding the question of segregation. In responding to criticism of the board on the Liberty Bowl matter, Ferguson candidly acknowledged he opposed limiting Alabama teams to playing only other segregated teams, claiming that "if we are to compete nationally . . . we must assume that some of our opponents may show up with individual team members whose color we do not like."[43] Following Ferguson's formal retirement, Gessner McCorvey emerged as the leading segregationist on the board. When warned by a fellow trustee that keeping blacks out of the university would require "drastic" action, he once replied, "I cannot possibly imagine any defense that would be too drastic for my hearty concurrence. . . . The more drastic our action, the better I will like it."[44] In a letter to Rose, McCorvey offered disingenuous congratulations on a bowl bid before informing the president that he would not make the trip to Philadelphia. He did, however, suggest that the band play Dixie several times during the contest.[45] Beyond that, he kept his displeasure to himself. Two other trustees, Brewer Dixon and Thomas S. Lawson, were so active in the trustees' attempts to "Keep 'Bama White" that Clark identified them, along with McCorvey, Ferguson, and one other, as having "set the tone for the board and the university" on the matter. Dixon contacted both Rose and Bryant to reiterate earlier sentiments "that I am one hundred percent behind Alabama accepting the Liberty Bowl bid," and, unlike McCorvey, announced his intentions to be in Philadelphia for the game. Lawson was less effusive in his endorsement and joined McCorvey in remaining in Alabama for the game, but he declared a meeting to discuss the trip "a splendid one," noting that "I sincerely hope that all of you have a nice trip and that the team is victorious."[46]

Less deferential opposition came from those outside the university community, but even that criticism was muted. Foremost among the professed defenders of segregation were the various White Citizens' Councils arrayed around the state who made it their responsibility to keep the university informed of all manner and results of integrated activity, not the least of which (in their mind) was the outcome of the 1956 World Series, won by the New York Yankees over the "Brooklyn African Bums."[47] James B. Laseter, chairman of the West Alabama Citizens' Council, wrote to Bryant, and apparently Rose as well, to "strongly oppose our boys playing an integrated team." Rose contacted Laseter requesting that the council not make its objections public, to which Laseter agreed while explaining, "We did not want to hurt the University."[48] The Dallas County Citizens' Council joined its colleagues in also formally opposing the Crimson Tide's integrated holiday plans, "decrying" the actions of the university, the board of trustees, and the governor. It too shied away from publicity, however, noting, "It is not our purpose to engage in public controversy. No press release nor comment will be made by us for publication." Having vacated the segregationist high ground, the council then had the temerity to criticize the board for doing the very same thing. Illustrating the cozy relationship that the council enjoyed with Rose in particular and other members of the university administration in general, Rose replied to the Dallas County resolution by assuring the group "that your resolution will have full discussion among the Trustees at the next meeting of the Board. . . . There is a great deal we would like to tell you, but because of reasons that you as a lawyer should know better than anyone else we are not free to discuss it."[49]

Finally, the esteemed Dixiecrat columnist John Temple Graves of the *Birmingham Post-Herald*, a "wholehearted segregationist," followed his own advice regarding football and popular passions. It had been Graves who noted the damage to the segregationist cause in 1955 by Marvin Griffin's histrionics. In December 1959, Graves wrote a column regarding Alabama's invitation to Philadelphia, avoiding any criticism of the Tide's participation, attempting to place the event in the pantheon of southern history. Noting the game's location and connecting it to another fateful Pennsylvania locale in the Faulknerian lore of the South, Graves declared (while playing with his capitalization), "Ninety-six years after 'The High Tide at Gettysburg,' there's to be a high Tide at Philadelphia."[50] Graves joined the overwhelming chorus of media coverage by reviewing the Tide's bowl history and noting, as he had in the past, that the Tide's football success might create "a victory complex replacing the lost cause one that has blanketed so much of the South." Graves also understood that the game could be put to the white South's advantage. Episodes like the Liberty Bowl were not defeats to the segregationist cause but opportunities to create new bonds uniting white southerners as they girded themselves for the larger struggle against integration at home. In attempting to strengthen segregation by linking it with football, Graves appealed to a common cultural touchstone of southern distinctiveness. Thus, the Tide would carry the banner of a new southern struggle and succeed in Philadelphia where Lee had failed at Gettysburg.

Not all Alabama segregationists embraced Graves's logic, however, and many refused to accept such indifference to a breach of the color line. Rather than look to a future as envisioned by Graves, they focused instead on the recent past and the Autherine Lucy episode. Alabama alumnus B. G. Robinson wrote to Frank Rose noting his concern that he had not seen any evidence that Alabama had insisted on a Gentlemen's Agreement for the game. Robinson thought it "inconceivable" that "with the Autherine Lucy incident yet smoldering," university officials would consent to such a contest. William Kilgore of Birmingham offered much the same sentiment in his letter to Rose opposing the game. With rhetorical incredulity, Kilgore demanded of Rose, "Do you remember the Lucy inciden[t]?" Pursuing such a policy would lead to "a most certain repetition of trouble," according to Kilgore, "and a very probable unhappy return of such trouble to your doorstep." Others, too, connected the issue to Lucy. The Philadelphia branch of the NAACP strenuously opposed the Tide's invitation, passing a resolution noting "the inhumane and barbaric treatment of Autherine Lucy," and "condemn[ed] the promoters of this event for causing glory, prestige, and wealth to be conferred upon this infamous institution."[51]

For southern critics of Alabama's Liberty Bowl invitation willing to link the issue to the Lucy episode, it was a very short leap to link it to the NAACP itself, which had funded Lucy's legal challenge, and which many white southerners identified as the real culprit. After referring to an editorial that noted a suspicious absence of public condemnation of the Tide's acceptance of the Liberty Bowl invitation, J. Y. Brame suggested that the NAACP orchestrated the entire Liberty Bowl incident. Declaring the alleged news blackout "conclusive testimony" of such a conspiracy, Brame interpreted the Tide's acceptance of the bid as "a great triumph for the NAACP and other race-mixing pinks and punks." Interestingly, however, Brame not only absolved Bryant of all responsibility but suggested that only Bryant could rescue Alabama from a pending travesty. Brame held out hope that Bryant "might save the day at the last moment by refusing to take the field with a gorilla in the opposing line-up, by claiming to be unaware of this circumstance."[52] Like Robinson and Kilgore, Brame still pined for the days of the Gentlemen's Agreement, when the South could dictate their racial policies to opponents, regardless of the game's location. With no apparent sense of irony, Brame's letter arrived at the university courtesy of a four-cent stamp bearing the image of Abraham Lincoln. Brame was not alone in seeing the NAACP as the culprit in the Liberty Bowl affair. Ned Morton, in a letter to the *Tuscaloosa News*, fabulously alleged that "friends of the NAACP are televising the Liberty Bowl game to show the world" that Alabama had abandoned the segregationist cause.[53] Thus, the only public voices to be heard opposing the Liberty Bowl match-up appeared from the fringes of respectability.

If Robinson, Kilgore, Brame, and Morton could fairly be assigned to the segregationist extreme, they were at least accurate in their allegation that the university was abandoning the inflexible doctrinaire ground reserved for the likes of Marvin Griffin. Farther from the mark was William J. Mahoney, columnist for the *Montgomery Advertiser*. He, too, opposed the Liberty Bowl invitation, arguing, "If racial segregation is right and the fight to maintain it in the South is wise and proper, then the acceptance of an invitation to match a white Southern football team and an integrated squad is wrong." Considering that white southerners overwhelmingly favored segregation, Mahoney wondered how the Crimson Tide came to accept the invitation in the first place. He implicitly alleged a vague conspiracy of state and university officials to minimize the existence of Jenrette: "Everybody knew it—except the mass of Alabama voters." Those who were aware of Jenrette's race offered "a loud and prolonged 'Sh-h-h-h!'" when the subject came up. "One can only assume," Mahoney concluded, "that people's wishes in the matter bore no weight."[54] Mahoney's charges do bear some credence. A strikingly limited discussion on the subject of race and Jenrette appeared in Alabama papers. However, news pieces, columns, editorials, and letters to the editor mentioned it often enough to make it common knowledge. The extent of the newspaper coverage revealed not a conspiracy to cover up the underlying significance of the episode but an understanding of the cultural significance of Alabama football. Alabamians had no reason to oppose the invitation. It did nothing to undermine the South's real preoccupation at the time—the ongoing struggle to oppose school desegregation—and so long as northerners did not use it as an occasion to vilify the South, football served as a source of pride and cohesion at a time when white southerners yearned for those qualities.

Contrary to Mahoney's assumptions, many in Alabama overwhelmingly supported the decision to go to Philadelphia and saw the issue exactly in the terms described above. University officials, with no small amount of visible relief, reassured each other throughout December 1959 that public sentiment supported Alabama's acceptance of the bowl bid. J. Jefferson Bennett, assistant to Rose, happily reported to his boss, "You will be interested to note that the [Graduate School] Dean [Albert B. Moore] said the reaction to our invitation and acceptance to the Liberty Bowl was very favorable among the people with whom he was working in Montgomery at the time of our announcement." Jeff Coleman, director of alumni affairs, told Bryant that the alumni response had been very favorable, noting, "From all comments which I have heard, I feel that playing in the game and taking the team to Philadelphia was a fine thing for the University of Alabama." Even those off campus hastened to inform university officials of their support. The president of the Montgomery chapter of the alumni association wrote to Bryant congratulating the team on earning not only the Liberty Bowl bid but also the "return of self-respect to our athletic program."[55] Thus, many Alabamians, perhaps even most, willingly accepted an integrated Liberty Bowl because of the cultural esteem they took from football. Noting the contradiction that "Penn State could not play in Montgomery or Birmingham" but that Alabamians readily accepted the Tide playing the integrated Nittany Lions in Pennsylvania, one editorial declared "it is scarcely an unusual contradiction. Southerners contradict themselves frequently on matters of race. Especially is this true in sports."[56]

What the writer failed to note was that such contradictions occurred only when the South did not have the contradiction thrown in its face. Absent any criticisms of southern racial policies, southerners could embrace intersectional football both as a cohesive force to defend segregation as well as a means to participate in a national culture imbued with American exceptionalism. An editorial in the *Anniston Star* noted that "the matter-of-fact attitude apparently taken by Tide fans becomes them. So far there happily has been no agitation in Alabama in the manner of those Georgians who tried to" stop the 1956 Sugar Bowl.[57] Thus, Alabama partisans demonstrated their grace and humility by calmly accepting the terms of the invitation as offered. The *Tuscaloosa News* echoed the point when it, too, commended not only the decision to accept the Liberty Bowl invitation but also the calm behavior of Alabama fans over the race issue. "This year's Alabama team can help the cause of the Tide and the University if it goes to Philadelphia, plays the hard, clean game of which it is capable and demonstrates sportsmanship at its highest level." The paper returned to this theme two weeks later by claiming that "success, in a hard, clean game . . . would not only boost the resurging Tide's fortunes on the gridiron but could help the state's 'public relations' as a whole in that section of the country."[58] Like Graves, Waring, and others, these writers put forth the logic that the Tide would actually aid the cause of segregation by playing an integrated game in Philadelphia. Here, then, was the most explicit white southern understanding of football within the postwar context. Accepting that segregation created division within the South and hostility from without, white southerners embraced the game of football because it represented both southern and American ways of life. Football could do what segregation could not: tie white southerners to a national cultural narrative without forcing them to choose between southern and American values.

Although Penn State beat Alabama 7-0 in the Liberty Bowl, the game's supporters expressed no regrets with the experience, if not the outcome. At a postgame reception, Jenrette approached Bryant to shake hands and congratulate him on the Tide's good sportsmanship, to which Bryant joked that maybe if Alabama had been a little meaner, they might have won.[59] Other than the Philadelphia chapter of the NAACP, Alabama received no criticism about its segregation policies. University partisans accepted the breech of segregationist etiquette in exchange for the cultural validation provided when the Crimson Tide played for high stakes on a national stage; and northerners upheld their end of the bargain by graciously inviting Alabama and keeping their integrationist sentiments to themselves. When Crimson Tide fans grew optimistic about the possibility that they might land a Rose Bowl invitation in the fall of 1961, they operated under the assumption that a similar set of circumstances would surround the invitation. They were shocked, however, to discover that many outside the South were no longer willing to dissociate the Crimson Tide from the crisis of race and the anxieties of the period. As a result, southern convictions that they could continue using football as a bridge to a national cultural narrative while simultaneously attempting to aid segregation came to an abrupt end.

Well before Ohio State's faculty voted to reject the 1962 Rose Bowl invitation, the West Coast football media considered the possibility that a Big Ten team might not play in the upcoming Rose Bowl. During the weekly luncheon of Southern California Football Writers held on November 6, Ken Hooten, director of the Big 10 Club of Southern California, expressed doubts to the assembled writers as to whether the Big Ten would participate in the Rose Bowl the coming New Year. Hooten, an OSU alum, prophetically cautioned the writers that faculty opposition at his alma mater was not some bluff that would dissolve in the face of a legitimate invitation to Pasadena. The other dominant Big Ten team with a chance to win the conference was Minnesota, but the Golden Gophers had just been to the Rose Bowl following the 1960 season and the Big Ten's now-lapsed contract had included a no-repeat clause. Even though that contract was no longer in force, Hooten offered his "personal opinion that Minnesota would not accept. . . . A repeat trip would be contrary to Big Ten thinking." With the leading teams in the Big Ten unwilling or unavailable, Hooten mentioned then second-ranked Alabama as a possible Rose Bowl opponent for the West Coast champion. Following Hooten's comments at the writers' luncheon, the hometown *Pasadena Star News* declared Alabama a very real possibility, and the following day predicted that Alabama would get the bid.[60] And with that, the great Rose Bowl speculation of 1961 was off to the races.

For even the most casual Crimson Tide fans, the Rose Bowl maintained an almost mystical aura. Many considered the 1926 Rose Bowl Alabama's greatest victory; Bear Bryant vividly remembered listening to the game on the radio as a twelve-year-old. When the possibility of a Rose Bowl trip emerged in 1961, Bryant claimed, "We of Alabama would walk all the way out there to play if we were extended a Rose Bowl invitation." After Alabama eviscerated an undermanned University of Richmond team, one write-up of the game led with the line, "Visions of Pasadena on New Year's Day danced in" fans' heads. One columnist declared that "if Alabama had a choice of bowl games, it would be the Rose Bowl," while another predicted that "Bryant probably will jump at the California trip."[61] For all the acclaim Alabamians offered the Rose Bowl, Pasadena authorities appeared equally excited about the Crimson Tide. Tom Hamilton, executive director of the AAWU, granted an interview to a *Birmingham News* columnist and said, "Our policy is to choose an outstanding team of the country to play in the Rose Bowl and certainly Alabama is on the list." When asked about the Big Ten's plans to ratify a new agreement with the AAWU for the following year, Hamilton responded that "whatever the Big 10 does will have no effect on what we do for the game this year." Hamilton went so far as to journey to Birmingham to watch Alabama play another Rose Bowl hopeful, Georgia Tech. The Tide crushed the Ramblin' Wreck, dousing Tech's hopes but significantly elevating Alabama's. Prior to the Tech-'Bama game, Hamilton and Van Kussrow, the chair of the Orange Bowl's scheduling committee, spoke to "clarify their competitive positions in bidding for Alabama." Kussrow admitted that if Alabama won, he would give up hope of bringing the Tide to Miami because he assumed they would be going to Pasadena. A Sugar Bowl official, who had earlier acknowledged that the Sugar Bowl would "be in a real bind" if it could not land Alabama, admitted, "I believe Bear Bryant favors a Rose Bowl trip over all others." So intense was the courting process between Alabama and the Rose Bowl that an Atlanta writer called it a "torrid . . . love match."[62]

If Alabama and the Rose Bowl seemed smitten with the idea of reuniting, many of the West Coast football interests were just as enthused. In a straw poll, the Southern California Football Writers Association favored seeing Alabama in the Rose Bowl over Minnesota, Ohio State, and Purdue, by a vote of 13-6-1-1. Sid Ziff, sports editor of the *Los Angeles Times*, wrote a column openly pining for a southern team to play in the 1962 game, acknowledging that while he preferred a long-term tie-up with the Big Ten, a one-time southern engagement might ease some of the sting from the 1946 agreement. Rube Samuelson, editor of the *Pasadena Star News*, called by one writer "the official editor of the Rose Bowl," agreed with Ziff. Definitively favoring Alabama, Samuelson wrote, "The ayes have it. The votes have swung toward enthusiasm and Southern charm." A week later, the Los Angeles Rotary Club's annual kick-off luncheon, held prior to the USC-UCLA game, overwhelmingly chose Alabama over any Big Ten team, while Lathrop Leishman, chairman of the Tournament of Rose's Football Committee, expressed to one southern writer his desire to "bring back a southern team to the Rose Bowl." Even a Purdue partisan living in California forsook his hometown Boilermakers to announce that he had no problems acceding to Alabama in the Rose Bowl.[63]

If the Tide had won over some of the local media, it also apparently emerged as the favored opponent among the one group that really mattered, the teams of the AAWU. Each of the five schools submitted to Hamilton's office a list of teams they preferred, and Hamilton admitted having sent "feelers" to these schools. Jess Hill, the athletic director at USC, claimed his list "includes the 10 or 12 top teams in the country." An official at the University of Washington was even more direct, openly admitting that Alabama was at the top of its list and agreed with earlier reports that both SC and UCLA also wanted Alabama. Virtually everyone thought that UCLA preferred Alabama, not only because the Bruins had already played Ohio State in the regular season but also because both head coach Bill Barnes and his chief assistant Deke Brackett had played their college career in the South.[64]

In addition to public support in the media and among the AAWU member schools, Alabama's Rose Bowl hopes enjoyed more clandestine support. Alabama alumnus Daniel J. Haughton, president of the influential southern California aerospace firm Lockheed Aircraft, instructed his corporate vice president, John E. Canaday, to champion the Crimson Tide's case on the West Coast. A UCLA graduate and a regent of the University of California system, Canaday enjoyed considerable influence with academic, athletic, and regional power brokers, and he discreetly worked to land Alabama in the Rose Bowl. Both Canaday and Haughton remained in contact with Frank Rose throughout November 1961 regarding the matter.[65] By the middle of

November 1961, seemingly nothing could derail the Crimson Tide from appearing in Pasadena on January 1, 1962.

On November 14, however, a UCLA student group calling itself the Negro College Students of Southern California, which claimed to include football players, announced its intention to lead a boycott of the Rose Bowl if Alabama received the invitation. Using language similar to that of the Philadelphia NAACP two years earlier, the students argued that the invitation "would give financial profit to the university to further its segregation policies."[66] Having interjected the subject of race into the issue, the students could only marvel at what followed. The day following the students' announcement, *Los Angeles Examiner* columnist Melvin Durslag wrote a piece entitled "Alabama an Insult to Bowl," in which he denounced not only the idea of inviting a segregated team but also his colleagues in the Football Writers' Association for their endorsement of such a proposal. Durslag put the matter in the larger context of social change and moral responsibility by noting, "At this stage in the sociological revolution, it would be sheer lunacy for people who believe in integrated athletics to mess with a school whose leaders hold firmly to segregation. For all their peculiarities, Californians still recognize equality of the races." Noting that the state attorney general had recently prohibited the Professional Golfers Association from upholding its whites-only policies at PGA tournaments in the state, Durslag declared, "It would be a scandalous affront to USC or UCLA . . . to invite an opponent which wouldn't permit either on its field for reasons of race." Durslag acknowledged that prohibiting Alabama because of state policies unfairly targeted the players who, he claimed, "would doubtless vote for integrated athletics." According to Durslag, however, the larger issue was essentially a moral one that trumped any unfairness to Alabama's players. "Anything less could not be reconcilable to . . . conscience."[67] Less than a week later, Durslag returned to the issue by again noting that Alabama would "be entirely welcome in Pasadena with one provision—that UCLA . . . would be welcome to play Alabama . . . in Tuscaloosa. The problem is no more complicated than that." Durslag acknowledged critics who suggested that the best way to confront Alabama's undemocratic policies was not to rebuff them but to expose them to an integrated society. In response, he recalled the 1959 Liberty Bowl and noted that it had changed nothing. "How can one be so blissfully naïve, so beautifully ignorant as to believe that the barriers can be dissipated with a football game?" Durslag again framed the matter as a moral issue involving civic responsibility: "It is not the function of Californians to tell Alabamians how to run their state. . . . But those who believe in integrated sports must stand firmly and with resoluteness. . . . And for Californians to take a weak stand on this now . . . would be scandalously inconsistent with their principles."[68]

Had Durslag been the only Los Angeles columnist to address the issue in terms of race, the episode might have turned out differently. However, four days after Durslag's first column on the matter, *Los Angeles Times* columnist Jim Murray weighed in with more volume, more heft, more humor, and more bite. With the announcement that the Rose Bowl was considering both Alabama and Georgia Tech, the *Times* sent Murray to Birmingham to cover the game between the two. Murray immediately saw Alabama's victory and its Rose Bowl consequences in a larger historical context. "The University of Alabama just about wrapped up the all-white championship of the whole cotton-picking world here this weekend" were it not for "a band of Negro students at UCLA. The Uclan students' announcement that under no circumstances would they be willing to waive the Emancipation Proclamation even for a single New Year's afternoon hit this southern city as hard as if Fort Sumter had suddenly returned fire after all these years." Noting that Alabama had "hoped to use this game for a ticket to Pasadena . . . the invitation from the Coast was to stay where they get the front of the bus all to themselves." Murray also noted the Autherine Lucy episode and the harassment she received after her expulsion, which ultimately forced her to relocate to Dallas. "Alabama is an integrated institution—but only in the boiler room. What withered the roses was the fact the only Negro student it ever had didn't dare stop running till she reached Texas."[69]

The next day, Murray returned to the issue in a column provocatively titled "Bedsheets and 'Bama," noting Birmingham's role as "gateway to the Ku Klux Klan," a place where "Evening Dress" means "a bed sheet with eyeholes. And, bring your matches. We're lighting a cross." Noting the incongruity of spending his entire column in the sports section on the issue, he declared, "I came down to Birmingham not to find social injustice but to cover a football game. But the crosscurrents of our time are such that two are interrelated." Murray declared segregation "worse than un-American. It's unhuman." Ranking the Crimson Tide as the number one team in the nation was "a denial of democracy." The embrace of the South's arcane social policies was "a toast to a dead Empire. Lift a glass to a world that no longer exists" except in the South.

Murray did note, however, "another side to Birmingham. The quiet people are stirring." When Murray queried Bryant at a postgame press conference on the proposed student boycott, a local writer called out, "Tell them West

Coast Nigger lovers to go lick your boots, Bear." Murray noted the "instant embarrassment" of the other reporters in the room, and the efforts of many who made it a point to come over and apologize, which led to a discussion that lasted far into the night, convincing Murray that "thoughtful people of the South are concerned." Murray, like Durslag, considered the argument that there might be benefit in "a lot of people [seeing] that colored boy knock an Alabama hero down and then stop and help him up." Murray conceded that it was "a good question. Can you conquer prejudice with prejudice?" Unlike Durslag, Murray seemed far more hesitant to dismiss that question out of hand. "Let's not force them back in those bedsheets. At least not unless we're sure that's the way they want it."[70]

Murray also had a little fun at Bryant's and the South's expense. The vast majority of Murray's first column on the matter addressed Bryant and his effects on the game since returning to his alma mater. Murray noted with a touch of humor the virtual divinity accorded to Bryant in Alabama, retelling many anecdotes linking the coach with either Christ or the Almighty. He also, however, noted Bryant's taskmaster reputation as both a coach and a recruiter and noted the physical punishment Alabama's style of play meted out to opponents. In the Georgia Tech game, Murray noted, "The stretcher crew was as busy as the backfields," and declared, "Alabama's attack is about as subtle as Khrushchev pounding a shoe." Near the end of the column, Murray put the issue in slightly more sinister terms by referring to Alabama's home jerseys as "blood-colored."[71] Murray's third column dealing with Alabama ignored the issue of race altogether and offered a tongue-in-cheek pronunciation guide for a southern drawl. Though hardly libelous or even mean-spirited, the column did note that even the most erudite speaker might be affected after "spend[ing] a weekend down there," as if it were some foreign place or disconnected land.[72]

In his final column on the subject, however, Murray returned to the issue of race and social change in full throat. He acknowledged "an outpouring of abuse" for his columns, including death threats, but noted, "My only surprise was really that there was so little [criticism]." Many took exception not to the subject but to the place of its publication. These letters were motivated "by the unshakable belief that the sports page should be just a kind of adult comic section in prose and should not concern itself with any issue larger than who won the javelin?" The letters included comments such as "get out of the sociology business." Murray defended his columns by humorously suggesting they had really been a public service to potential Alabama visitors. Fans "had better be prepared to put up with a few inconveniences—like they'd have to take pot luck at the drinking fountain, the water was integrated, that the buses were very careless in their seating and let just ANYBODY sit in the front, and that you might even sit next to a you-know-what at the football game. . . . Our kids don't even get to go to school with an escort of paratroopers." Murray again referred to segregation as an "archaic social custom" before signing off by answering his critics from every direction. "Recently, I went down to a state in the South which . . . belongs to the 20th Century. Only, it not only doesn't like it, it doesn't know it. Or won't admit it. A writer—even a sportswriter—is supposed to cover news. The real news of the game I covered had very little to do with the score. It had everything to do with the smell of roses and the color of the players."[73]

Once the students announced their boycott intentions and Durslag and Murray legitimated them by writing about the issue for the next week and half, media outlets from around the country picked up the story within the context of race. Even the *Chicago Tribune* noted that it would not be "logical" for the Rose Bowl to invite southern segregationists to Pasadena. California media outlets bombarded the Alabama governor's office "concerning the state's attitudes" regarding an invitation to an integrated Rose Bowl, inquiring if the governor "would be receptive to such an invitation."[74]

The interjection of race into the issue initiated a reflexive response on the part of white southerners to reject such criticisms from "outside agitators," which not only allowed southerners to dismiss the criticisms but also paint themselves as the aggrieved party. The *Montgomery Advertiser* was the only major paper in the state to carry the Associated Press story of the UCLA students' proposed boycott but diminished the group by claiming that the school had never heard of the organization. No other paper around the country carried that information, suggesting that the *Advertiser* either attempted to dismiss the possibility of a boycott by deriding the students or that *Advertiser* reporters took the boycott seriously enough that it followed up the wire-service story with its own reporting.[75] Prior to this, there had been virtually no discussion of race as a possible limitation on the Tide's playing in the Rose Bowl, just as the media had largely ignored the question in December 1959. The *Birmingham News* hoped to put up a good front by referring to "greatly exaggerated reports of California objections to an Alabama appearance in the Rose Bowl because of the state's segregation policies." Where a day earlier the *Advertiser* claimed no one had ever heard of the UCLA student group, now the *News* attempted to put the group on the other fringe of respectability by reporting that the same students had been responsible for organizing and implementing a picket demonstration during "a recent West Coast visit of the President."[76]

As sustained criticism in the form of Durslag's and Murray's columns continued to mount, however, Alabamians shifted gears. Writers and editors across the state and throughout the South now claimed that irresponsible outsiders would deprive the Crimson Tide of a deserved Rose Bowl invitation. The *Advertiser* now referred to the proposed boycott and the media coverage as "racial rumblings on the West Coast," while the *Tuscaloosa News* asserted that the Tide's Rose Bowl chances "grow dimmer by the day as the racial angle is further injected into the possible invitation of Alabama to the Pasadena classic." The *Birmingham Post-Herald* made the outlandish claim that "powerful racial groups have extracted from Rose Bowl officials a promise that no school which practices segregation will be invited." One Atlanta editor claimed that "just when it appeared that Alabama might be recalled to the Rose Bowl . . . someone winds up and flings a racial spitball." Even if Alabama managed to land the invitation, one columnist warned, "they may expect the clawing of the racial antagonists after they get there."[77]

Far from abstractly referring to "racial rumblings," the southern media covered the writings of Durslag and Murray, fully apprising their readership of how "outsiders" were portraying the state. The *Post-Herald* put an article about Durslag's first column on the front page of the sports section under the headline "Rose Can Do without 'Bama, Says Writer," reprinting almost the entire piece. The *Advertiser* ran an article on Murray's first column under the headline, "Blood-Colored White Supremacists." The *Advertiser* compared Murray to "poor old adle-brained Ezra Pound," declaring his column "murky and incomprehensible," and suggested he was a dupe for "a small Negro protest" that was nonetheless to deny the Crimson Tide the Rose Bowl. Two weeks later, the *Advertiser* again returned to Murray's writings, covering his humorous guide to southern pronunciation under the headline "Western Nitwit Discovers Dixie." The piece noted that Murray's earlier columns were "written as if dispatched from the Congo."[78]

Once these criticisms from outside the South emerged, southern media discussion of the Rose Bowl changed markedly. Various newspapers throughout the state had previously referred to the Rose Bowl as "prestigious," "illustrious," "glorious," and "the greatest of all bowl games." With the onset of criticisms of the state's segregation policies and perceived "cheap shots" at Bryant, however, southern media comment changed drastically around November 18. *Tuscaloosa News* sports editor Charles Land, who had previously written about the Tide's illustrious Rose Bowl past, informed his readers, "You can chalk up the racial situation as keeping the Crimson Tide from a seventh Rose Bowl appearance . . . Couldn't have been anything else, but its funny that most of the pressure on that count apparently came from the West Coast . . . Intolerant tolerance?" [ellipses in the original]. Land finished by noting that it was no big deal not to go to Pasadena: "The Rose Bowl I've seen on television. . . . Most of the time after better shows were over."[79] Having been rejected by something so many Alabama fans desperately wanted, they responded instead by rejecting it in turn.

Alabamians invested great meaning in Crimson Tide football and took immense satisfaction from its successes, celebrating victories over outside teams as a validation of the southern way of life. Understanding football as an expression of regional cultural identity, white southerners then had the temerity to be outraged when "Yankees" identified the uglier side of southern society with their football team. In linking cultural values and regional identity to football, it never occurred to white southerners that those outside the South would also view football as representative of that society, but in a very different way. Thus, outsiders understood football in its postwar context as a distinct expression of American values, of which segregation most decidedly was not included.

Watching the opposition from California mount, university officials took stock of their options. Irrespective of the student and media opposition, Tom Hamilton and the AAWU continued in their vigorous efforts to see the Tide in Pasadena. On November 20, the *Atlanta Journal* still saw Alabama as "a cinch for the Rose Bowl," and the following day Hamilton himself announced that he had narrowed the field down to Alabama, LSU, Ohio State, and another Big Ten team.[80] Indeed, sometime between November 21 and November 25 and prior to Ohio State's November 26 defeat of Michigan, Tom Hamilton offered a verbal invitation for Alabama to participate in the 1962 Rose Bowl.[81] By that time, however, university officials had already made up their minds. There would be no Rose Bowl for Alabama. Four days after UCLA students threatened to boycott an Alabama invitation, Bryant and Rose traveled to New Orleans to inquire about their Sugar Bowl possibilities. Whether they were merely attempting to keep their options open in the event that the Rose Bowl possibility soured or had in fact already decided to spurn the Rose Bowl is unclear. In either case, five days later the Crimson Tide announced they would spend New Year's in New Orleans. It was a decision made at the highest levels of university authority. Though Patterson publicly kept silent on the matter, it seems impossible to believe that his approval was needed in 1959 but not 1961. Bryant referred questions on the matter to Rose and all but acknowledged it was not his decision. An observer in Alabama's locker room later acknowledged to historian Andrew Doyle that a "crestfallen" Rose, who would later claim it was the players' choice to go to New Orleans, personally informed the team of the decision.[82]

The decision to reject the Rose Bowl invitation likely considered a multitude of issues. Though the local media initially derided the UCLA students' boycott threat, in reality, both the media and the university took the students at their word. The *Post-Herald* summed up the situation best when it declared that "criticism of the state's segregation laws and threats by West Coast racial groups to picket the Rose Bowl if Alabama is invited have practically eliminated the Tide. . . . Even if extended a bid, Alabama probably will decline rather than accept and risk the possibility of the state and the University being embarrassed by racial demonstrations." Writing in the *Mobile Press-Register*, one of the more racially moderate papers in the state and the only major daily not to cover any of Durslag's or Murray's columns, Vincent Johnson noted the specific problems Alabama could expect. The number of black migrants from the South who had fled to California in the postwar years would make for a particularly hostile reception. "Segregation is a tender spot with Negroes in Southern California, many of whom have fled from the South to the West Coast." A particular point of friction would be UCLA's black students, according to Johnson. "There is a tremendous Negro population in southern California and quite a few Negroes attend UCLA. . . . [Alabama's] segregation policies, hardly unknown in that sector of the country, could ignite a terrific amount of pressure."[83] Rose, too, knew what the university was in for if it accepted the invitation. Explaining the university's decision to an alumnus, Rose noted, "We have been assured that we would be picketed and that there would be many embarrassing incidents."[84]

Additionally, those within the university community understood that the university's reputation had real currency on certain issues, and the increasing prominence of race was devaluing that currency. University president George H. Denny made a conscious decision in the 1920s to expand the university's reputation through football, and the 1926 Rose Bowl victory was the culmination of that policy. With that plum in his pocket, Denny had the university take out ads in major East Coast papers, extolling the southern winter climate, a championship football team, and low out-of-state tuition. The ads mentioned something else too: "no quotas." At the height of America's nativist anxiety over race and immigration in the 1920s, many eastern colleges and universities enacted admissions policies barring Jews.

Quite ironically, then, the university attempted to lure students with its football team *and* its racial policies. In 1926, four hundred Jewish students enrolled; the number doubled the following year. By 1930, one third of the student body population at the University of Alabama was Jewish and rapidly became self-perpetuating. Sixty years later, it was not uncommon, according to one Alabama professor, to find numerous third-generation Jewish students from Newark and other East Coast cities. Though many of Alabama's Jewish students came from the assimilated Jewish populations of Birmingham, Montgomery, and Atlanta, a sizable number came from the North.[85] In the postwar years, those students and their alumni families became increasingly vocal in their displeasure with the university's policies on race. After Alabama accepted the 1959 Liberty Bowl invitation, a letter to the *Tuscaloosa News* made a thinly veiled reference to this marriage between football and the recruiting of East Coast Jews. The writer declared such a practice "an invitation to the enemies of the South from the Jersey flats to infiltrate the schools and corrupt the morals of the student body. It is a matter of common knowledge that this has gone on since President Denny took charge of the activities of the University of Alabama."[86] Of particular anxiety for segregationist defenders was that the student body's *ancien régime* on the issue of race, the Greek system, lost the ability in the postwar years to control the editorship of the student paper, the *Crimson-White*. As a result, the newspaper, oftentimes with Jewish students at the helm, positioned itself almost as a fifth-column presence in the 1950s and 1960s, running editorials critical of the university as it continually evaded and obfuscated in the face of federal court authority.[87] As America's Jewish population increasingly made common cause with the civil rights movement, allowing the football team to be identified with the state's brutal record on segregation served to provide one more opportunity for northeastern Jews to reconsider their commitment to the university.

In addition to out-of-state enrollment, the university's reliance upon its Huntsville-based Alabama Research Institute steadily increased with the emerging federal space program. Rocket scientists based in Huntsville, led by the famed captured German Wernher von Braun, had attracted $6 million in federal grants by 1961. Although the federal government was already well aware of the university's racial policies, a high profile calamitous trip to California for the Rose Bowl would certainly draw the attention of another academic partner in the space program, California Technical Institute. Based in the heart of southern California's aerospace industry, Caltech emerged as first among equals of the academic research centers then accepting federal space money. With rocket scientists like von Braun doing most of the practical work in the outlying centers, Caltech's Jet Propulsion Lab increasingly addressed the more theoretical and abstract problems of space flight. The University of Alabama's racial policies had already come across Caltech's radar in the actions of Nobel Prize–winning faculty member Linus Pauling. After winning his Nobel Prize, Pauling's wife, Ava, "made it clear that Linus had the visibility to lead" a campaign of social activism, an effort he embraced so successfully that the U.S. State Department eventually revoked his passport in an effort to restrain him.[88] In 1955, he accepted Alabama's invitation to give the keynote address at the school's sesquicentennial celebration the following year but tersely withdrew in protest following Autherine Lucy's expulsion.[89]

Though Caltech did not play big-time football, its campus lay within walking distance of the Rose Bowl, and the institute maintained an active relationship with the Pasadena spectacle. Caltech students viewed the annual Rose Bowl game as a proving ground for some of the greatest college pranks of all time. In the 1961 game, Caltech students managed to rework the halftime card stunts by the University of Washington's spirit group so that they spelled "CALTECH," an event captured on live national television. By 1961, according to Neil Sternberg, "the Rose Bowl became the personal Mt. Everest of Caltech pranksters." The possibility that Caltech students might at any moment derail the carefully planned New Year's celebration kept those within the school constantly aware of the entire Tournament of Roses program.[90] The institute also reserved seating sections along the Rose Parade route for faculty and staff, after which Caltech sponsored an annual luncheon for faculty, staff, and honored guests.[91] With the Huntsville Center as an academic partner in the space program, Alabama officials, likely among them Frank Rose, would have found the event an unpleasant experience with Pauling in attendance and the possibility that Caltech's contrarian student body might prank the event. Such were likely the "embarrassing incidents" that so vexed Frank Rose. Additionally, bringing its segregationist policies into Caltech's backyard earned Alabama no favors in the complex and competitive world of academic research grants.

In addition to the very real possibility of pickets, demonstrations, and social unease, many in the state wearied of their continued portrayal in the national media, reacting with both hostility and resignation to every perceived slight. Amid the Rose Bowl speculation, *Time* magazine ran a small piece on Bryant that mostly noted his success since returning to Alabama but also referred to him as "brutal taskmaster," "arrogant," and "a chronic weeper and a flagrant headline chaser. . . . He drinks Salty Dogs, runs up scores, browbeats sportswriters, curses his players and believes in corporal punishment." The *Time* article was followed shortly thereafter by a similar piece in *Sports Illustrated.* Even though most of what *Time* and *Sports Illustrated* reported was true, Tide fans and those within the university reacted as they had to the Harrison Salisbury piece a year earlier. Frank Rose's assistant, J. Jefferson Bennett, was so incensed that he wrote a sharp letter of condemnation to *Time*'s editor, accusing it of the worst kind of media sensationalism and outright falsehoods while ignoring the benefits of Bryant's tenure in Tuscaloosa. Bennett's anger so informed his writing that he sent a draft of it to a colleague, acknowledging he should probably let the matter go but that he could not ignore the piece. Bennett eventually resigned himself to the matter and sent in a tamer version of his original letter. Not everyone on campus, however, shared Bennett's discretion. The Kappa Kappa Gamma sorority hanged the magazine in effigy at a campus pep rally.[92]

Because the criticism of outsiders now prohibited university officials and supporters from separating the football game from segregation as they had managed in 1959, it was also impossible for the university to distance itself from the racially charged political environment within the state, particularly as it related to Birmingham. In late October 1961, a federal judge ordered the city of Birmingham to desegregate all public facilities, including parks and the city-owned Legion Field. Rather than comply, the city decided to close the parks, with Mayor Art Hanes crudely suggested that "play[ing] dead on this park integration" issue would lead directly to "a nigger mayor or a nigger police chief." Rather than comply with a court-imposed deadline of January 1, 1962, that would have allowed integrated play, the city laid off 140 parks employees, and the police posted "No Trespassing" signs on New Year's Day just at the moment that the Crimson Tide would have been taking the field in Pasadena to play an integrated football game. As such inflexibility increasingly placed Birmingham at the center of the contestation for civil rights, the university's association with the city became a liability. At least one source claims Bryant had to threaten Bull Connor that if he made any attempt to exclude blacks from Legion Field, Alabama would refuse to play in Birmingham and move their games to Tuscaloosa.

The inability of Crimson Tide football to cordon itself off from white Birmingham's pathology reached its nadir in May 1963 when civil rights demonstrations pushed the city to the brink. Having filled the jails and temporary holding pens at the fairgrounds with demonstrators, Connor's next step was to erect barbed wire cages in Legion Field to hold the demonstrators, some as young as eight and nine. Jefferson County sheriff Mel Bailey understood exactly the consequences of using Legion Field in such a way: "It's not going to look pretty on television; its going to look like a concentration camp." If Birmingham was indeed "hell on earth, the Johannesburg of the South," then Legion Field, the Crimson Tide's home away from home, was to become its Robben Island.[93] Though the 1963 demonstrations still lay in the future, for many outsiders these kinds of embarrassments made it impossible to disassociate one representative of the state from another. In the eyes of many Americans, Alabama was a state filled with lawless, violent, raging bigots. Accepting the Rose Bowl invitation would have allowed all of the scorn, rage, and disgust many felt toward the state and region to be directed at the football team. White southern identification of Alabama football as a vehicle for a celebrated, southernized version of the American way of life and a refuge from the anxiety of the period made this simply unacceptable.

To have acknowledged that they could not go to the Rose Bowl because of their own anxieties, however, would have required white Alabamians to repudiate the circumstances under which they had embraced postwar football. Unable or unwilling to do so, they convinced themselves that they had not rejected the Rose Bowl invitation but that it had never been offered in the first place. And just as important, the fault lay not with them but almost entirely with Jim Murray. University officials never publicly admitted they had rejected a Rose Bowl invitation and, with one still-confusing exception, never fully admitted they had even been invited. Indeed, most individuals to this day refuse to acknowledge that the episode happened at all. Instead, most officials and partisans harped on Murray as almost single-handedly demonizing Alabama so that the Rose Bowl backed away from its initial intentions. Before the invitation process had even been completed, one Alabama supporter wrote that Murray "certainly isn't doing us any good and is apt to stir up some trouble we wouldn't have otherwise."[94] An alumnus wrote the president of the *Los Angeles Times'* media corporation to register his extreme displeasure with Murray's columns and his role in the selection process. "Murray has been bitter, partisan, crude, and has displayed, for those of us who grew up in and understand the South, a complete lack of understanding of Alabama. After several days of virtual slandering of Bear Bryant, the university, the state, the people, and the system which this successful coach has used in developing this fine team," Murray refused to accept responsibility for his "part in Alabama's failure to encourage the Rose Bowl Committee to extend an invitation."[95] Another Tide fan wrote to acknowledge his disappointment in the outcome, but "after giving the matter further thought, I think it is probably best that this was not done because of the complications that might have been created that would have given the University unfavorable publicity after the writings of Jim Murray."[96]

Distraught Alabama supporters from all over the country sent letters to Frank Rose that included copies of Murray's columns, all choosing to see Murray as the chief protagonist in the episode's denouement. Rose did nothing to disabuse these correspondents of that notion, and his varied responses to these communications revealed his willingness to place responsibility everywhere but in his own office. In what may have been his most honest assessment of the situation, Rose informed one alumnus that Murray's "unfavorable" columns convinced officials "that it would serve the best interests of the University of Alabama for us to remove our team from any consideration of the Rose Bowl this year" in the face of protests and disruptions.[97] In the rest of his correspondence on the matter, however, Rose seldom approached even that amount of candor and occasionally veered into paranoid conspiracy rantings. In responding to one alumnus, Rose failed to admit that Alabama had been invited by insisting, "There is no doubt in my mind but that we would have received the invitation" had the Rose Bowl been serious about a team from outside the Big Ten. In addition to Murray's complicity, however, Rose also asserted that unnamed "friends in New York who are closely connected with the television" industry informed him that it had been television that had sealed Alabama's fate with its concern for advertising revenue, desiring "a team from up north because of the centralization of population."[98] In making both the print and electronic media complicitous in Alabama's victimization, Rose struck upon a target that resonated with most Alabamians at the time who were still outraged over the Salisbury, *Time*, and *Sports Illustrated* pieces. According to Rose, however, the media was not alone in victimizing Alabama. In responding to another alumnus who registered his displeasure with Murray, Rose agreed, noting, "I have never known anyone to be so vicious and so prejudiced as he was." Rose quickly absolved Murray, however, by suggesting that Tom Hamilton had in fact strung Alabama along for his own purposes, disingenuously claiming "southern teams were never seriously considered. We were used to pressure the Big Ten to continue their contracts with the California institutions." Rose did claim, though, that UCLA, USC, and the others "had nothing to do with this" and "were all anxious" to invite teams from outside the Big Ten.[99] Responding to yet another partisan who mentioned Murray's columns, Rose again denounced the pieces as "the most vicious unfair articles that I have ever read" and claimed that his "columns did us a great deal of damage in California."[100] Within the university community, Rose insisted that Murray remained culpable in the decision process. Writing to Winton Blount, a member of the board of trustees, Rose insisted, "There is no doubt in my mind but that [Murray's] column destroyed all of our chances for the Rose Bowl."[101]

Rose's duplicity allowed him to avoid responsibility for the decision and more deftly orchestrate the assignation of blame upon outside agitators, in particular the liberal media of both the East and West coasts whom many Alabamians, and white southerners in general, were already so willing to hold accountable for the region's troubles. As such, it fit a pattern of his to describe his role in events after the fact to fit his needs. In 1963, when Governor George Wallace made his infamous "Stand in the Schoolhouse Door" as a last-ditch effort to block the integration of the university, Rose's habit of understating or overstating his role depending upon whom he was trying to cultivate became apparent. According to E. Culpepper Clark, "Rose's overbearing style and tendency to misstate facts began to work against him." With the historical validation of the civil rights movement, Rose, who had once been on a first-name basis with the Alabama White Citizens' Council, attempted to locate himself on the right side of history. At the time of Bryant's death in 1983, Rose claimed that "Bear worked very closely with me behind the scenes to bring about integration and to follow the court orders." By 1988, Frank Rose baldly claimed he had single-handedly convinced the administration to pursue the integration of the University of Alabama in spite of segregationist misgivings.[102]

Although Bryant avoided the political maneuverings that soured many on Rose, and his record concerning race was much better, he, too, maintained a creative memory of the period. In his autobiography published thirteen years after the episode, Bryant also held Murray and the media accountable. At one point in the book, Bryant claimed that the response of the Los Angeles media came because of an abrupt remark he made six years earlier when his Texas A&M team lost to UCLA. When asked if he really thought "a team this inexperienced" could "beat a team like UCLA," Bryant shot back, "Hell yes. Why do you think we came out here?" Claiming in his autobiography, "those things turn around on you. Jim Murray came over and saw us play and made a fuss over our being considered for the Rose Bowl. . . . He wrote about segregation and the Alabama Ku Klux Klan and every unrelated scandalous thing he could think of, and we didn't get the invitation." Considering that Murray was not a *Times* employee for another five years, he certainly was not the reporter in question and was almost certainly unaware of the exchange when he wrote his columns in 1961. In fact, it was Melvin Durslag to whom Bryant had made the remark in 1955 and who was the first to raise the issue of segregation in 1961.[103] But by that time, Murray had already been sacrificed as the *bête noire* of Alabama's Rose Bowl hopes.

Later in the book, Bryant again returned to Murray's complicity while acknowledging that Alabama had in fact received the Rose Bowl invitation only to have it rescinded a short time later. "I have no doubt we would have gone to the Rose Bowl in 1961 . . . if the Los Angeles papers hadn't raised the specter of segregation. Tom Hamilton told [University of Washington head coach] Jim Owens that we were in and Jim called from the Los Angeles airport. 'You've got it. They are going to extend you the invitation.' But about six o'clock both Owens and Hamilton called and said if I had anything else on the fire to grab it. Later, I heard the Los Angeles papers were making it out to be an invitation to the Ku Klux Klan. I resented that, but I couldn't do anything." If Owens did in fact call Bryant for any reason from Los Angeles during that time, it would have been on the weekend of November 18 and 19, when the Huskies played UCLA in the Coliseum. Considering that Murray's first column on the issue did not even appear until November 19, it seems highly unlikely a single column that had been on the streets for less than twelve hours would have caused Tom Hamilton to repudiate a month's worth of work that went into the selection process. Even more problematically, when contacted about the matter after the fact, Jim Owens, a "great friend" of Bryant's and a former assistant coach under Bryant at Kentucky, who claimed "a pretty good memory of the time period," twice denied any recollection of either phone call.[104]

As was the case in Columbus, it was the student media that asked some of the most perceptive questions and came closest to revealing the truth of the matter. In a series of rhetorical questions, the *Crimson-White* wondered why the university would prefer the New Orleans game over the Rose Bowl. It was also the only paper in the state to question openly whether a Rose Bowl invitation had, in fact, been extended and thus, whether Frank Rose had been dishonest. Pressing the issue even further, the *Crimson-White* implied duplicity in Rose and Bryant's trip to New Orleans in late November while still publicly claiming to pursue the Rose Bowl. Though they failed to find the answers to some of their questions, the writers at the *Crimson-White* revealed an ongoing unwillingness to defer to the authority of both the university administration and the commercial media.[105]

White southerners embraced college football in the postwar years as a means by which they might unite the white South in defense of segregation while also using the game as a bridge to football's national narrative of American exceptionalism and identity. Because they associated the football team with what was good about the white South, they dissociated it from the national condemnation over race. Outsiders, however, increasingly refused to accept southern football on southerners' terms. As a result, they saw Alabama football as a manifestation of a sick, racist, un-American value system, entirely outside the bounds of the national cultural narrative of postwar football. The resulting furor over the Rose Bowl bid threatened to turn a source of southern unity and accomplishment into a vehicle for the South's embarrassment and humiliation, drastically changing the calculus of the matter. From the perspective of university supporters, it appeared that radical outside agitators would follow the Tide every step of the way to remind all within earshot of its segregationist underpinnings. With race and segregation ever present, the outcome of the game would take on immense proportions, becoming a virtual referendum on the validity of segregation. A loss against black players would be simply too humiliating to accept in the face of certain gloating from the insufferable NAACP, their race-mixing allies, and communist sympathizers.

All evidence emphatically points to a Rose Bowl invitation that was turned down by the University of Alabama on its own volition. The university rejected that invitation because the conditions of its acceptance ran contrary to the cultural tenets of college football in the Cold War era. Americans of every region during the time found in football a repository of values loosely defined as "American," widely believed to be crucial to the national character, and generally understood as evidence of a national cultural consensus. In contrast, Alabama's appearance in the Rose Bowl would have positioned football as a vehicle for conflict and was revelatory of values that too many Americans were in the process of rejecting. As a result, Alabama might have won the football game, but the refusal of those outside the South to esteem them as equals within the culture of football would have deprived Alabama fans of their cultural dividend. Thus, they could no longer rely on football as an expression of both southern and American distinctiveness. The two were now mutually exclusive.

It is unclear exactly how influential the announcement of the UCLA student group to boycott the Rose Bowl was in the events that followed. The student announcement predated all of both Durslag's and Murray's columns, suggesting at least some amount of causation. Additionally, Murray explicitly referred to the group's actions in his first column on the matter, suggesting their role in motivating his columns. Students at UCLA confronted the paradoxes of Cold War society that championed American freedoms but restricted free speech and association on campus and presumed to entice the third world while practicing segregation. When the possibility of a segregated Rose Bowl opponent appeared, students put those issues in the context of football. As a result, their understandings of postwar football as an embodiment of a benevolent American exceptionalism brought into focus distinctly un-American limitations on basic liberties and freedoms.

FIVE

Westwood: College Football and Cold War Dissent

> *"May the people of this country clearly perceive that in these perilous times, nothing is more important than the character, quality and vigor of our system of education. . . . May those who have benefited from this system become fanatical and articulate apostles."*
>
> —Chancellor Franklin D. Murphy

In November 1961, college football emerged as a multifaceted vehicle for student activists at the University of California, Los Angeles (UCLA) to confront a host of cultural and political anxieties. For years, students had chafed under administrative restrictions on campus free speech and association that only intensified during the repressive years of the early Cold War. Changes to these rules in the fall of 1961 brought sustained student criticism and outright opposition resulting from students' increasing involvement in the civil rights movement. Additionally, students since the end of World War II had identified a racial exceptionalism with the university and the West that positioned UCLA as a "racial paradise" that lacked discrimination. This assumption, however inaccurate, was often linked to the school's athletic tradition and created a sharpened sense of awareness when overt discriminatory practices threatened to appear at the university. Finally, students grew increasingly hostile that autumn over the lack of authority they enjoyed on the university campus. Restrictions on speech and on association combined with administrative fiscal paternalism to embitter students who desired to put their institutions to the service of social activism. In short, students at UCLA confronted with increasing frustration the hallmarks of

American higher education in the years following World War II: heavy-handed restrictions on their behavior in the name of keeping the university above the political fray, the corporate-like structure of the "multiversity" that distanced students from the complex governance of higher education's multiple responsibilities, and an idealism that the sacrifices of World War II and the imperatives of the Cold War would create a new social order where equality and merit prevailed.

In the midst of these various strains of student discontent emerged the possibility that UCLA might be asked to play the notoriously segregated University of Alabama in the Rose Bowl. Student activists quickly leapt to the rhetorical barricades in opposition, applying football's postwar cultural meaning to the varied issues concerning them that fall. Motivated by assumptions of a western exceptionalism derived from a tradition of athletic integration, students proposed a boycott of the game as a natural outgrowth of this exceptionalism. Students understood football as an expression of laudable, distinctive American values that put the United States in sharp contrast to the Soviet Union. As a result, their understanding of campus issues that autumn through the lens of football exaggerated how far southern segregation, restrictions on free speech, and university autocracy were from accepted American values as represented by football. Thus, football served as a cultural mechanism by which students asserted their identity as students and dissented from the abuses of the domestic Cold War.

Quite apart from the cultural use of football to interpret Cold War America, Tom Hamilton found himself in November 1961 continuing to deal with the fallout from one of the worst scandals in the annals of college football to that time. The 1958 destruction of the Pacific Coast Conference and the efforts to replace it revealed the chaotic transformations within big-time college athletics during the period. Nothing illustrated the corporatization of college football during the period like the growing importance of conferences and their organizational structure. Prior to World War II, conferences existed solely as a collective arrangement of member schools agreeing to play by a similar set of rules. Most operated without full-time staff in offices located on the campuses of member schools and with limited resources. Conference organization along corporate lines rapidly accelerated following World War II, however. By the late 1950s, the Pacific Coast Conference paid a full-time commissioner and was governed by an elaborate policy manual and code of conduct as well as a mini-bureaucracy that included standing committees and a permanent infrastructure on establishing and maintaining player eligibility.[1] Other conferences evolved along similar organizational lines during the period. National Football Foundation Executive Committee member and former Notre Dame player James G. McGoldrick bluntly related this organizational trend and the expansion of major college football by declaring, "Big-time football will die if conferences do not continue strong."[2] The appearance of the PCC's centralized organization, however, masked a seemingly unlimited willingness on the part of some of its members to violate conference rules and ultimately destroy the conference itself.

During the nationally scandal-ridden year of 1951, the conference discovered illegal recruiting practices at the University of Oregon, and the commissioner, Victor O. Schmidt, insisted that Oregon fire the football coach responsible for the practices. Though they grumbled about it, the Ducks complied—but not before vaguely intimating that other schools, most notably UCLA, followed similar practices. Those intimations proved accurate when media investigations beginning in early 1956 revealed a football recruiting slush fund at the University of Washington. Sour grapes and recriminations from alumni and boosters initiated domino investigations revealing similar slush funds at UCLA, USC, and California. The NCAA levied penalties, but the conference imposed even harsher terms on the two worst offenders, USC and UCLA, barring the teams from the Rose Bowl for a time and stripping each player of a year of eligibility. It did not go unnoticed that the presiding conference officer in the investigatory tribunals was none other than Oregon's faculty athletic representative, law dean Orlando John Hollis. Bitter allegations of betrayal, revenge, and simple regional boosterism, none of which were entirely inaccurate, turned conference members against one another. When UCLA played Oregon the following season, one UCLA coach explicitly put the game in the context of the scandal by writing on the locker room blackboard before the game, "NO VICTORY FOR DEAN HOLLIS!" In the storied history of college football locker room oratory, it may have been the first time a coach tried to fire up his team by having them stick it to the opponent's law school dean. Stanford president J. E. Wallace Sterling, whose school had voted in favor of the conference sanctions, openly doubted the "trustworthiness" of UCLA officials, who responded that Sterling's "assumption of superiority is insufferable." Some regents from the University of California system publicly aired their "disdain for universities from the Pacific Northwest," particularly Oregon, with the result that Cal and UCLA refused to schedule the Ducks (UCLA did not play Oregon again until 1969). The upshot of the affair was that Cal, UCLA, and USC departed from the PCC in a huff in 1957, joined by Washington the following year. The remaining schools dissolved the conference in August 1958, effective the following summer.[3]

The dissolution of the PCC provided the seed of opportunity, however, for the renegade schools. Temporarily reorganizing under the umbrella of the Athletic Association of Western Universities (AAWU), Washington, Cal, UCLA, and USC, soon joined by Stanford, initiated plans for a much larger "airplane conference." The AAWU schools hoped to create a national conference of schools with an equal devotion to big-time football and academic standards, which would prove attractive to television executives and advertisers based on the "broad geographic scheduling" that such a conference would entail. The desire to create such a national conference did not originate with the rump PCC, however. In 1951, Notre Dame president John Cavanaugh envisioned a "Super Conference" to include perhaps more than a dozen schools, including Indiana, Iowa State, Navy, Michigan State, North Carolina, Oklahoma, Penn, Pittsburgh, SMU, Texas, USC, UCLA, Army, and Yale. Though Cavanaugh posited such a group as a vanguard "to reform college athletics on such issues as financial aid to athletes, long-term coaching contracts, and television," it appears the ability to attract television revenue lay at the center of the proposal. Most of Cavanaugh's logic focused on the television-revenue benefits of such a conference, and it seems laughable in retrospect to envision a conference aimed at reforming the finances of college athletics including the University of Oklahoma, then considered to be the highest paid football team in the land. Though Cavanaugh's proposal failed to garner much support, the idea lingered.[4]

It is unclear if supporters of Cavanaugh's proposal bided their time or if like-minded individuals came up with the idea on their own, but the respective directors of athletics of the AAWU, with the approval of their chief campus administrators, lured Thomas Hamilton away from his position as athletic director at the University of Pittsburgh in 1957 to assemble what was to be called the National Conference. The decision to hire Hamilton came from the belief that, as one pundit put it, "no man living . . . has more close connections" in college football.[5] The number of schools linked with the proposed National Conference surely exceeded those under actual consideration, but the candidates cited most often included the five AAWU schools, the three service academies, Pittsburgh, Penn State, Syracuse, and Notre Dame. Once word of the proposed conference leaked, other schools, witnessing the Darwinian changes in college football during the period, began nosing around for invitations as well. The universities of Houston and Miami both inquired about the possibility of their participation, while others suggested that the University of Pennsylvania, Duke University, Georgia Tech, and even some Big Ten schools also entered into the discussion at some point. Hamilton made no attempt at hiding the conference's agenda of "establishing the most prominent conference in the nation." Other associates saw the venture as a way "to create the most important national conference and get Eastern exposure for those Western teams."[6]

At first blush, the proposal won acclaim from almost every quarter. Several sources claimed that President Eisenhower personally endorsed the inclusion of the service academies. The prominence that Army, Navy, and Air Force would enjoy in such a high-profile venture would prove invaluable in military recruiting and securing civilian confidence in the military at the height of the Cold War. One journalist noted during the period, "The teams of both service academies have . . . been considered by Washington as traveling advertisements for the Army and Navy." Navy's assistant athletic director also acknowledged the financial benefit such a conference would accrue when he declared that Navy was "out to make money in big-time college football" and the National Conference was a means to that end.[7] Sports editors from coast to coast universally viewed the proposal with acclaim. One East Coast editor proclaimed "it will mean the beginning of a new era in college football." Harry Stuhldreher, former head coach at the University of Wisconsin and immortalized in his playing days as part of Notre Dame's famed Four Horsemen, saw the coming of the National Conference as "a must." Other supporters declared it "the most outstanding sports idea in [a] lifetime," foreseeing it not only as the inevitable evolution of the corporate rationalization of college football but the subsequent elevation of the individual schools involved.[8]

A conference that included such prominent and geographically diverse schools promised not only to generate television ratings and advertising revenues but also to excite tremendous popular enthusiasm as well. Hamilton envisioned the prize of such a venture to be nothing less than the jewel of college football: the Rose Bowl. The Rose Bowl enjoyed the oldest and largest television contract, a nationwide radio network, and gate receipts befitting the largest stadium in college football. By 1958, collective revenues exceeded a million dollars. Proposals for the National Conference included a Western Division, made up of the five AAWU schools plus the Air Force Academy, and an Eastern Division to include Army, Navy, Pitt, Penn State, Notre Dame and Syracuse, with the two division winners meeting in the Rose Bowl for what many felt would be tantamount to a national championship game. Even those outside the discussions for an airplane conference conceded the stature of the Rose Bowl. Decrying the "paper-made football champions" decided by the national wire-service polls, one southern columnist suggested a play-off type system where the two top-ranked teams would meet every year in the Rose Bowl to decide the national championship.[9]

If Hamilton, the AAWU athletic directors, and the football media had the National Conference already penciled into existence, they had forgotten to check with the faculty councils of the AAWU schools. For several reasons, the National Conference never came into being, but opposition from the core members played a central role in its rejection. For starters, in hiring Hamilton in 1958 for the purpose of creating the National Conference, the AAWU athletic directors took their lead from their respective chief campus administrators, who were decidedly pro-football. By 1960, however, Cal, UCLA, and USC all underwent top-level administrative changes that witnessed the arrival of officials who were less enamored of big-time football. Additionally, faculty representatives at those schools, who always attempted to rein in the overzealous booster activity that had destroyed the PCC, were also wary of aligning themselves with schools they felt did not match their academic rigor. As late as 1960, officials from both UCLA and Cal vigorously opposed the formation of a conference that would not limit its membership to "those institutions which we regard as having academic standards equal to ours."[10] One writer claims that the venture fell apart only because "someone in the Pentagon" opposed the inclusion of the service academies, but this interpretation seems highly unlikely considering Eisenhower's support of football and his reported approval of the venture, and ignores the vast archival material that points out the academic opposition on the West Coast.[11]

The scuttling of the National Conference came hard on the heels of the crisis in the Big Ten that allowed the Rose Bowl contract to lapse. If Hamilton could not create the single largest, dominant conference in college football, he might still be able to match AAWU teams against the best teams in college football by using the Rose Bowl as bait, "the top bowl game on the holiday menu." To do so would once again require dealing with the SEC and its intense commitment to high-priced football. For Hamilton, however, that was a small price to pay for legitimating the mini-conference that was the AAWU and ensuring the status of the Rose Bowl as the preeminent dateline for postseason college football. As all of this played out in the 1950s and early 1960s, however, the cultural significance of college football witnessed its postwar elevation. Thus, at the exact moment Hamilton hoped to invite Alabama to the Rose Bowl, UCLA students linked their newfound social and political consciousness to the culture of football. As was soon apparent, the aspirations of Hamilton and the students were on a collision course in the fall of 1961.

In the decade and a half following World War II, conscientious students at UCLA who embraced an activist agenda often found the issues of student freedom and racial equality intertwined. Few issues animated student activists like the presence of racial discrimination, yet their capacity to challenge it was often proscribed by existing university restrictions on student activity. As a result, student opposition to one almost invariably lent itself to opposition to the other. Though student consciousness on these issues predated the war, specific historical forces deeply embedded in the Cold War California experience accelerated student opposition during the period.

Dating back to the University of California's founding in the nineteenth century, the school charter prohibited all partisan political, religious, or otherwise controversial activity on campus. Known as Rule 17, these restrictions prohibited campus speakers from addressing most current events, campus clubs from affiliating with off-campus agendas, and individual students from supporting any such activity while on campus or using the name of the university in their activities while off campus. The university's application of Rule 17 and student frustration with it grew markedly during the Cold War period. As it did throughout the nation, an irrational fear of communism created various violations of constitutional protections and common decency. One notable example came at the University of California in 1950 where the regents demanded that all faculty sign loyalty oaths professing their rejection of communism and their fealty to the United States. Though the loyalty oaths were aimed only at faculty, students immediately understood them as emanating from the same mind-set that enforced Rule 17. One student pamphlet on the matter declared that "the real issue involved is that of the right to inquire, to think, to speak, and be heard on the campus—in short, the right of academic freedom." Student critics saw the loyalty oath as "part of the national pattern of witch-hunting and anti-communist hysteria which flow from a policy of cold war." Demonstrating the ease with which activists linked free speech with civil rights, students saw Rule 17 and the loyalty oath as silencing "voices demanding an end to discrimination and brutality against the Negro people." The loyalty oath and restrictions on free speech and association were not merely consequences of the Cold War but, in the eyes of students, weapons "deliberately propagated to maintain the Cold War."[12]

While fear of communism existed throughout the United States during this period, specific issues informed the debate within the University of California. Beginning with the arrival of Clark W. Kerr in the 1950s, first as chancellor on the Berkeley campus and then as president of the entire UC system, public higher education in California was increasingly seen as a model to be emulated throughout the United States. Kerr saw the Cold War as creating what he termed the "multiversity," a publicly responsive campus of ever-expanding enrollment with varied responsibilities of teaching, research, and government service. During his tenure, Kerr oversaw the creation of several campus research and development institutes aimed at off-campus constituencies funded by both federal grants and state taxpayers. The culmination of his broad vision emerged in 1960 with his much-copied "Master Plan for Higher Education in California," respect for which earned Kerr the highly prestigious Godkin Lectureship at Harvard University in 1963. His ability to continue to shape the future of higher education in California and beyond, however, required political and financial capital. As Kerr understood the multiversity, its ability to attract government funding, remain in the good graces of the legislature, and serve the public turned on its capacity to avoid offending any of these interests by remaining above partisan or controversial issues. Thus, the so-called Golden Age of higher education in California required both faculty and students to absent themselves from the pressing issues confronting Cold War American society.[13]

Students increasingly viewed these restrictions, along with the paternalistic administrative rhetoric that defended them, as a hypocrisy that undermined American ideals and American claims of superiority to Soviet political prohibitions. After the administration began regulating the content of the campus *Daily Bruin* in 1955, one student declared that "in our headlong flight from Communism, we are falling into precisely the same evils that we decry in it." Noting that campus freedom consisted merely of the freedom to agree with the governor and the regents, while "disagree[ing] is un-American or subversive. . . . These are dangerous times, and we must have access to all ideas if we are to make correct decisions." Suggesting that state and university officials had compromised their moral legitimacy by embracing policies easily confused with Soviet repression, the student noted, "It is in dangerous times that ruling groups make their most strenuous attempts to stifle free speech."[14] An editorial in the *Bruin* opposing the restrictions on speech and association made the same point when it asked, "Does our only defense against the communists consist of using their odious tactics to subvert our freedoms so we won't be exposed to alien propaganda?"[15] Thus, students understood the university restrictions on speech and association as little different from similar restrictions associated with Soviet political repression. Such linkages increasingly alienated and embittered students, clouding their assessment of the differences between "us" and "them." With growing resentment, one student claimed that "we reap the fruit of a 20-

year heritage of incessant Cold War propaganda" that justified otherwise unacceptable abuses and restrictions both at home and abroad.[16]

Wary of running afoul of Rule 17, student government often shied away from any activity that the administration might consider "off campus." In 1952, white opponents bombed the home of a black family who had recently moved into a previously all-white section of the West Adams district, northwest of south-central Los Angeles. In response, the Student Legislative Council (SLC) passed a resolution condemning the bombing. The *Bruin*, while itself condemning the bombing and supporting the spirit of the SLC's resolution, proceeded to challenge the SLC's authority to address the subject at all, declaring it "completely out of its realm of responsibility and duty." Declaring that there were other issues closer to campus for the SLC to address, the editorial felt that the SLC "should limit its action to things which have a direct effect on the student body."[17] In the days that followed, discussion regarding the powers and authorities of the SLC dwarfed that of the original issue. Student representative Marty Rosen noted that students maintained community concerns all the time in the form of Red Cross blood drives, military procurement drives, and local citizenship programs. A year later as student body president, however, Rosen ruled out of order any attempts to bring before the SLC motions regarding the Fair Employment Practices Commission, declaring such topics "beyond the area of competence" of student groups.[18] The issue proved irresolvable throughout the period, as evidenced when the SLC attempted in 1960 to pass a resolution condemning the actions taken against southern students during the sit-ins of that year. The majority of debate over the matter revolved around "whether or not the Council could take a stand on this off-campus issue."[19] Thus, throughout the 1950s, while students increasingly found their concerns over civil rights linked with their own restrictions on campus speech, they often found themselves unable to confront either.

With Kerr's ascension to the presidency of the university in 1958, he began modifying, and eventually replaced entirely, Rule 17 with new restrictions, dubbed the Kerr Directives, the final modifications of which he unveiled just before classes began in the fall of 1961. These new policies removed almost all restrictions on campus speakers but actually tightened restrictions on student speech and association by prohibiting any student group from affiliating in name or activity with any "off-campus" partisan political or religious organization. As Kerr told an alumni gathering, "The name of the University cannot be used as a good housekeeping seal of approval." Thus, even though Kerr claimed he sought to "liberalize" restrictions on free speech, the Kerr Directives clearly maintained the old policy of prohibiting student participation in anything of substance.[20]

Activist students at UCLA immediately saw through Kerr's self-laudatory references to liberalization and criticized both the meaning and intent of the directives. In February 1961, UCLA student Joel Peck sued Kerr in federal district court over the directives' ban on distributing politically oriented literature on campus. Peck's suit forced Kerr to settle out of court by modifying the directives to permit a much freer distribution of literature on campus.[21] The *Daily Bruin* lampooned Kerr's rhetoric by linking him with nineteenth-century archconservative Clemens von Metternich, while other students questioned exactly what defined an "off-campus issue," arguing that "the officials of the University of California still believe that civil liberties must be violated to keep the University free from politics."[22]

Ironically, the increasing number of off-campus speakers provided for under the Kerr Directives helped bring about rising criticism of the directives

Figure 2. "Our speaker tonight on 'The Restriction of Political Activity on the U.C. Campuses' . . . Clemens von Metternich!!" In linking Kerr with Metternich, students saw the Kerr Directives as no less oppressive than Metternich's infamous 1819 Carlsbad Decrees. From *Daily Bruin*, November 16, 1961.

themselves, as increased student awareness of the world beyond the ivory tower blurred the distinction between on-campus and off-campus issues.

Just as student activists' understanding of their own political restrictions came from the specific experience of the Cold War period and the positioning of California as a national model, so too did their understanding of race. World War II and the Cold War reshaped Los Angeles in many ways, but chief among them was the growth of the city's black population. In 1940, fewer than 64,000 blacks resided in all of Los Angeles, but expanded economic opportunity and concurrent federal guarantees of nondiscriminatory hiring by defense contractors facilitated a dramatic increase in the city's black population. By the end of the 1960s, the city had a black population of almost 763,000. Abandoning the intertwined legacy of sharecropping, Jim Crow, and lynching, more than 1.2 million blacks left the South during the war as part of the Second Great Migration, with many ending up in the exploding metropolises of the urban West. In Los Angeles, they formed tight-knit migrant communities evocative of earlier, community-based migration in American history. A steady stream of recent arrivals from the South to newly predominant black neighborhoods in the south-central part of the city continually reinforced the legacy of the South as a benighted, oppressive locale. In the fertile wartime and postwar labor market, they found higher wages, a greater chance of owning a home, and a better chance at a higher quality of education than they had left behind in the South. Though these quality-of-life statistics lagged behind comparable figures for whites, a fact many black migrants painfully noted, this dramatic increase in standard of living and the perception of opportunity for black migrants allowed most whites to accept the myth that the West lacked discrimination and inequality.[23]

Perhaps nowhere was this myth more accepted, and simultaneously responsible for its perpetuation, than at the city's public university. Originally created as a two-year feeder institution for the Berkeley campus, UCLA began offering four-year degrees in 1925 and its first doctoral degrees in 1938. It remained overwhelmingly white, however, with only ninety-one black students in 1940 and never numbering more than a few hundred until the late 1960s. By the dawn of the postwar period, it was a campus of solid repute but with little distinction beyond the immediate region.[24] As the university grew in the postwar years, students at UCLA clearly attached to the school a distinctive exceptionalism derived from their notions of racial equality and their assumptions about the West. Even before the war ended, student activists on campus, like racial progressives around the country, saw the war as an opportunity to remake American race relations. The valorous service of black Americans in the military, the racial ideologies of the Nazi enemy, and federal demands for nondiscriminatory defense hiring all suggested to some that the Republic stood at the dawn of new era. Racial progressives in the West believed that the absence of established patterns of discrimination combined with the region's newly arrived minorities to facilitate social structures distinctly different from other regions. One commentator in the region declared, "The die is cast . . . in the South or in an old city like New York or Chicago, but we here are present for the creation. We're making a society where the die isn't cast." In the minds of such westerners, the changes wrought by the war provided nothing less than a unique opportunity for black Americans to overturn centuries of racial hostility. "What other race in the twentieth century is going to have such a great experience?"[25] The arrival of black migrants to a region with few formal Jim Crow policies, a seemingly unlimited economy, and a luxury of space that allowed the city to grow outward rather than upward appeared to accommodate the social, economic, and residential needs of both old and new residents. These commentators envisioned the West as a land of unlimited promise for blacks. The heady postwar years helped inform the publication of noted California liberal Carey McWilliams's *Southern California Country: An Island on the Land*, in which he exclaimed, "Today, there can be no question that Los Angeles is destined to be one of the great centers of Negro life in America."[26]

Students at UCLA, too, felt the region stood at a liminal moment. In 1944, William Stout wrote an editorial in the student *Daily Bruin* espousing this notion of western exceptionalism, noting that, courtesy of the war, the West was "being offered an opportunity the nature of which has never been seen in any other section of the country. The opportunity comes in the form of a great influx of Negroes to the West Coast." The fruit of the Second Great Migration would deliver a multiracial West, according to Stout, and this new West would serve as a bright, shining city upon a hill to the rest of the nation. "The great cities of the East, bound by custom and fear, could easily be made to see that prejudice and segregation are not necessary for peace between the races." Echoing exceptionalist thinkers dating all the way back to Thomas Paine, Stout wrote that westerners had it in their power to begin the world over again, at least as far as race relations went. The opportunity of the war simultaneously delivered the West to a "crossroads" but also the "responsibility" to create a new model that would determine its "place in the nation for some years to come." With a sense of gravity and obligation, Stout noted that "the nation's minorities look to the West," and the stakes demanded that "we must not make a mistake."[27] Stout was not alone in seeing the West at the entrance to its future. One national publication agreed that Los Angeles was leading by example when it declared that the city "is showing the country what people of different races can do to live side by side in harmony."[28]

Carey McWilliams also took up Stout's argument when he followed up his earlier volume with *California: The Great Exception*. For McWilliams, California exceptionalism came not merely from its "four-dimensional . . . racial pattern [of whites, blacks, Latinos, and Asians]" but also from the residents of the region as a whole. "California's migrants . . . represent a selection rather than a cross-section of the American population." Noting higher levels of education and public service and a younger age cohort than national averages, McWilliams saw in postwar Californians a population predisposed to open-minded social interaction. By the 1950s, such assumptions no longer remained the province of local commentators. In an article entitled, "Los Angeles: A Race Relations Success Story," *Look* magazine asserted that the city "probably leads the nation in enlightened race . . . relations." For these optimistic commentators, circumstance, historical events, climate, and geography all conspired to create an exceptionalist environment of racial progressiveness.[29]

Student activists concerned with race relations on campus took these notions of exceptionalism to heart, frequently justifying their reformist agendas in similar rhetoric. When activists within the student government attempted in 1945 to ban discriminatory membership practices of campus honorary and academic societies, they ascribed to UCLA a surprising level of influence, suggesting that the banning of such groups at their school "might be the jumping off point for similar action by student[s] . . . all over the nation." Noting that "everything has a beginning . . . the beginning of the end of these clauses and practices might as well begin on this campus. . . . It is time for UCLA to step forward to the front as a leader of universities."[30] When the issue arose two years later, proponents used similar language, again revealing the students' presumptions about UCLA's role in higher education. "It is not hard to believe that such an action taken by UCLA would make an important impression" around the country. "While we are just beginning to become a graduate institution . . . we will eventually be very large, and as reputed in the graduate field as we are now in undergraduate study."[31] The university administration also helped legitimate student assumptions about UCLA's racial reputation. Speaking in 1945 to a student committee working to end discriminatory practices, assistant dean of undergraduates Clyde Johnson lauded the students and the campus as a whole by placing

UCLA "among the top 15 or 20 universities in the country" with regards to antidiscriminatory standards. Johnson declared that due to students' attitudes and actions toward minorities, "the University has attracted nationwide attention."[32] Two years later, university officials, along with off-campus religious institutions, organized the "Panel of Americans" tour. Featuring six UCLA students of diverse racial, ethnic, and religious backgrounds, the panel toured ten major cities, espousing tolerance and inclusiveness. One New York high school principal claimed that in one day, the UCLA students "have done as much combating prejudice as we could have done in a year." When the group returned to Los Angeles after the tour, the *Bruin* noted that the panel's efforts were fundamental to an emerging postwar reconsideration of race relations. Urging students to attend the 11:00 A.M. program, the paper linked enlightened race relations with fundamental American ideals. "That 11:00 cup of coffee may seem important, but it can wait; democracy may not, but it can't."[33] Students at UCLA were not alone in ascribing to themselves progressive views on race. *Look*'s national profile of race relations in Los Angeles identified UCLA as central to the city's successful postwar race relations, asserting that the school set "the precedent for integration in higher education institutions."[34]

Following the war, however, assumptions of western exceptionalism rapidly declined into a whites-only phenomenon. Many black migrants had readily accepted an idealized view of western race relations in the four decades prior to World War II, but increasing white hostility and decreasing relative economic opportunity in Los Angeles caused many to see the bitterness in such claims of a land of milk and honey. Although reformist whites embraced the notion of western exceptionalism, Kevin Allen Leonard has illustrated that blacks rejected such notions. Linking oppression and discrimination found in the West with similar practices in the South, many black residents of Los Angeles "considered themselves part of a larger national group," and as a result, felt "they had more in common with blacks in other cities than with any other group in Los Angeles."[35]

As the optimism of the postwar years gave way to the reality of the domestic anxiety of the Cold War and agitation over civil rights, students at UCLA continued to grant themselves an exalted status in the field of race relations. In 1958, *Bruin* editor-in-chief Tom Welch declared that "we at UCLA can be justly proud in the example of racial . . . integration we possess." Declaring that "UCLA stands as potent evidence of the hope for the future," Welch echoed earlier exceptionalist rhetoric in asserting "we are the coming, positive outlook toward racial integration."[36] Once again the future of the Republic lay in the West. Welch's writings aside, student activists knew that the campus and the region witnessed forms of discrimination. Indeed, their campaigns against discriminatory membership clauses in the 1940s and subsequent campaigns against similar clauses in social societies reveal such knowledge. The problem lay in convincing the larger, nonactivist, student population. The absence of formal Jim Crow laws convinced many students that Los Angeles and UCLA lacked the discriminatory practices of the South. "In Southern California[,] where conditions are not conducive to blatant and open prejudice," casual observers deluded themselves into thinking that equality of opportunity reigned.[37] Students at UCLA convinced themselves that blacks enjoyed more than mere opportunity, however, accepting the notion that UCLA was a "racial paradise" where black students enjoyed exceptional successes. The creation of this campus cultural tenet derived almost entirely from the university's integrated athletic tradition.

Alongside campus institutions such as the Greek system and student government, athletics dominated campus life, and the university's athletic teams came to represent its public face off campus. Like most American undergraduates at the time, students at UCLA fervently supported their football team, transposing the identity of the team, and its attendant successes and failures, onto their own. Though examples of this abound, none illustrates the phenomenon better than the students' rivalry with the University of Southern California. The winner of the annual football game between the schools, known as the City Championship, lays claim to the Victory Bell, which the winner keeps for the year. The Victory Bell was originally UCLA's, but students at USC stole it and held it hostage until UCLA agreed that the bell should serve as a trophy for the City Championship. For UCLA students, this narrative helped to assign to USC a nefarious role in the rivalry and was passed on from year to year in the students' oral culture, as it is to the present day. In years when the Bruins defeated the Trojans and reclaimed the bell, an elaborate celebration of repossession ensued. On the Monday following such victories, thousands of students shut down the intersection of Westwood and Wilshire boulevards and proceeded through Westwood Village, ringing the bell as they wound their way onto campus. By the 1950s, the university began tacitly sanctioning the ritual by canceling classes on such occasions, and in 1961, after UCLA clinched not only the City Championship but the Rose Bowl berth as well, the student *Daily Bruin* ran a satirical cartoon suggesting the link many students felt with the football team, at least following a victory over USC. As a result, college football and its attendant components of public spectacle provided a touchstone central to the

Figure 3. Students at UCLA embraced college football, and their rivalry with USC, with a passion that informed their views, if also befuddling their professors. From *Daily Bruin*, November 27, 1961.

traditional undergraduate experience. Football mattered because so many students, and others, placed so much value on it as a campus institution.[38]

Students closely linked the university's athletic teams with their understanding of western exceptionalism. The university's first football team in 1919 was integrated, and by the dawn of the postwar period, the school's national reputation owed at least as much to its distinctive athletic alumni as to its growing academic success. The late 1930s witnessed the first all-black backfield in college football at a predominantly white school in the form of Kenny Washington, Woody Strode, and Jackie Robinson. Immediately following the war, Washington and Strode desegregated the NFL, and the following year, Robinson did the same in major league baseball. A few years later, the NBA invited another Bruin, Don Barksdale, the first black All-American in basketball, to break the color barrier in that league. Though he deferred his entrance into professional basketball, he eventually appeared as the first black player in the NBA All-Star Game. Even those Bruins who went on to nonathletic pursuits in their professional careers were linked by their athletic exploits at UCLA. Ralph Bunche, who served after the war as undersecretary general of the United Nations and won the 1950 Nobel Peace Prize, was a three-sport star at UCLA, which he attended on a basketball scholarship. The list of notable black alumni eventually included Rafer Johnson, winner of the 1956 Olympic decathlon, and Arthur Ashe, the first black man to win the U.S. Open tennis title. When citing the school's unique racial situation, students inevitably looked to its integrated athletic tradition and recited the list of the school's athletic racial pioneers as if they were citing scripture.

Perhaps because his post-UCLA reputation loomed larger than the others, Jackie Robinson (Jack, in his days on campus) stood as the most prominent example of UCLA's racial exceptionalism. When Robinson returned to speak on campus in 1954, the *Bruin* labeled him "one of the most famous men ever to attend UCLA," and Robinson reinforced the students' notions of their own exceptionalism. Recalling the racial environment of his days on campus, he noted, "I've never forgotten the wonderful spirit of UCLA," and urged the students to take the lead in race relations by "showing the way." Such an endeavor by the university and its students would make their most prominent alumnus "the proudest American in the world."[39] Ralph Bunche offered similar sentiments about the racial environment at UCLA. "Possibly no other institution of higher education in the country has as good a record as UCLA over a long period of years on the question of integration of minority groups, and particularly Negroes."[40] Throughout the generation following the war, students at UCLA justified their concern for civil rights by referring to the school's integrated athletic past. A year following Robinson's campus appearance, a campus editorial unfavorably contrasted discrimination by the Greek houses to UCLA's multiracial athletic tradition, "Here at UCLA . . . we are proud of our achievements in sports. . . . The teams list people of the white race, the negro race, and the oriental races."[41] Students at UCLA understood that the school's reputation provided an automatic point of reference, even for those outside of California. At the height of the desegregation crisis at the University of Mississippi over the admission of James Meredith in 1962, one UCLA student wrote an open letter to Ole Miss students. "Should you doubt that a heterogeneous campus exists, you need only to look to" UCLA. As evidence, the letter cited only black athletes: Bunche, Robinson, and Johnson.[42]

By enlisting the high-profile successes of Bunche, Washington, Strode, Robinson, Barksdale, Johnson, and others to represent the public face of the university, students inextricably linked athletics with the entire school. Equality in athletics implied equality on the campus at large. With sports serving as the measure of equality at UCLA, it follows that the students similarly used athletics to define inequality in American life as well. In 1939, Kenny Washington led the nation in total offense, and Jackie Robinson described him as "the greatest football player I've ever seen." Yet sportswriters denied him First Team All-America status, and he received no first-place votes for the Heisman Trophy. Students at UCLA were stunned. The snub, according to one pundit, gave "the West Coast the right to secede from the football union."[43] It was not Washington's only humiliation that year, however. The East-West Shrine game, an annual college football all-star game serving as a fund-raiser for the Shriner's Hospital, refused to select black players through the 1930s and 1940s. As late as 1945, the *Bruin* still condemned the 1939 roster, which had excluded Washington, Strode, and Robinson, all future Hall of Famers at varying levels. The students at UCLA also used athletics to decry discrimination on other campuses as well. When New York University agreed to withhold its black players from a football game against the University of Missouri in 1940, the *Bruin* assailed the decision. Urging "No Missouri Compromise," the paper opposed NYU's sellout and declared race the "fundamental problem" in the nation.[44]

Student comprehension of the university's racial environment in exceptionalist terms and descriptions of its athletic tradition as an accurate reflection of the campus were further facilitated by their understandings of their private, wealthier, whiter cross-town rival, the University of Southern California. Though USC produced several prominent black graduates early in the twentieth century, the opening of UCLA coincided with a time "when USC's environment became increasingly hostile to colored students."[45] Officials within USC's athletic department expounded racialist convictions, such as legendary track coach Dean Cromwell's assertion that blacks excelled at track and field "because he is closer to the primitive than the white man. It was not long ago that his ability to run and jump was a matter of life and death to him."[46] Cromwell was apparently not alone in the USC athletic department in holding such racialist beliefs. In his autobiography, Strode alleged that Howard Jones, USC's legendary football coach at the time, vowed never to play another black player after one Trojan, Bert Richie, was caught with a white woman in 1925.[47] Such assumptions about USC by black athletes were common throughout the period. Ray Bartlett, a childhood friend and teammate of Robinson, noted that he and Robinson attended UCLA because they believed that the school "would give us a better chance as Negroes than we would get at USC."[48] Even some players at USC acknowledged the perception of racial inequality within their athletic department. Former Trojan C. R.

Roberts was warned by black UCLA students not to go to USC, but Roberts insisted on enrolling anyway. On the practice field, however, Trojan coaches, according to Roberts, elevated running back Jon Arnett on the depth chart over Roberts in the mid-1950s simply because Arnett was white. "They [the coaches] wouldn't have accepted the fact that I [was faster]."[49] The perception at UCLA of USC as a bigoted, exclusive institution allowed students at UCLA to intensify their assumptions about their own racial views and practices. As historian Patrick Miller has written, activists "held up instances of exclusion in sports as a mirror to the ideology of equality and opportunity."[50] At UCLA, students prided themselves on what they thought they saw in that mirror.

The notion of Los Angeles, or even UCLA, as a "racial paradise" was a myth, of course. But it proved strong enough to lull the majority of students into accepting it while frustrating the activist minority on campus who sought to confront campus and local discrimination. Almost all residential property ownership around UCLA's Westwood campus remained lily-white through rigid real estate covenants, making it difficult for some nonwhite students to secure housing. Intensifying the problem, the bulk of student housing fell to the Greek system, which overwhelmingly maintained restrictive membership clauses well through the 1950s. Additionally, some merchants in the surrounding Westwood Village refused to serve black students, who also faced proscriptions against mixed social interaction. Through the early 1950s, the campus maintained a social register in which students could advertise for rides, apartments, and other such arrangements. Racial and religious preferences were common in the listings until the frequency of such discriminatory preferences caused such an uproar that the campus eliminated the register altogether. Nothing caused tongues to wag like the prospect of interracial dating. Basketball player Walt Hazard, a sophomore in the fall of 1961, told of the "thousands of unseen eyes when he walked about the campus with white girls."[51] As a result, activists frequently found themselves simultaneously fighting the hostilities of the bigots and the illusions of the liberals. In 1958, the campus NAACP responded to Tom Welch's *Bruin* editorial in which he declared UCLA "the coming, positive outlook toward racial integration." In a letter dripping with sarcasm, chapter president Ferdinand Leon declared that Welch's stirring optimism "made my heart rejoice. Positively." Leon then proceeded to "add a few notes of rippling rhythm to this silly symphony" by noting discriminatory campus practices that appeared in the *Bruin* the same day as Welch's editorial.[52] Two years later, the paper, generally at the forefront of revealing and criticizing campus discrimination, ran an editorial on the myth of UCLA's racial atmosphere. Declaring that "complacent belief in a myth is a dangerous thing," the editorial argued that students' persistent acceptance that "this is the most integrated of campuses" hampered meaningful reform. The piece explicitly refused to challenge the myth of Bruin athletics as a paragon of racial virtue, however, insisting that athletics was the only place on campus the myth was reality.[53] Thus, even the myth breakers fell under its sway.

Even when student attention belatedly shifted to the South and the increasing confrontations fostered by the civil rights movement, students refused to see that discrimination in the South merely reflected some of the same practices closer to home. While supportive of civil rights activity in the South, one letter to the *Bruin* asked students to look closer to home, "Does a Negro own a home in Westwood; does a Negro eat in the Brown Derby; does a Negro hold a council seat in any district of our metropolis?" Suggesting students refocus their attention locally, the letter concluded by asking, "What of the West? Does the West have no problems that you . . . can attack or perhaps even solve?"[54] After yet another letter to the *Bruin* bragging about UCLA's nondiscriminatory record, Letitia Levison responded by noting that in the entire Associated Students UCLA (ASUCLA; the nonprofit organization that operates the bookstores, student union, restaurants, and such within UCLA), only two black students served in the various affiliated agencies, including the class councils, the judicial board, the activities board and others, while no black student to date had ever been elected homecoming queen, and of the eighty students belonging to the campus spirit/hostess organization known as Bruin Belles, only three were black. Levison noted, however, that thirty-five black students participated on the university's athletic teams.[55] Still a third letter was even more caustic in its criticism of self-righteous critics of the South who then engaged in discriminatory attitudes in the West. "Curse the South, will you?" a student writer asked rhetorically. "Curse the South and then go home and curse the landlord who let those awful wetbacks rent an apartment next door. . . . It's not safe to walk Main Street after dark? Damn those Negroes! Who are you to curse the South?"[56] As a result of such sentiments, in the decade and a half following the war, the only victories by student activists came in striking race and religion from the campus social register and limiting the discriminatory clauses of the Greeks. Activists could not convince most students at UCLA of the severity of discrimination because of the relative isolation of these incidents. Issues surrounding access to the Greek system, off-campus housing, or merchant services only appealed to students who wanted to join a fraternity, needed an apartment, or wanted their hair cut in the Village. Most important, activists lacked a touchstone to which most students could relate. Thus, the combination of restrictions on student speech and the success of black student-athletes successfully limited the scope of postwar civil rights consciousness on the campus of UCLA.

Student frustrations over the Kerr Directives and students' inability to assist effectively the civil rights struggle finally collided in 1961. In the spring, James Farmer, national director for the Congress on Racial Equality (CORE), spoke on campus about CORE's ongoing attempt to test federal laws protecting interstate travel. Among those struck by Farmer's passion was Robert Singleton. A graduate student in international economics at UCLA and chair of the campus NAACP chapter, Singleton grew increasingly frustrated over the prohibition of the Kerr Directives and the ambivalence of many UCLA students about the civil rights movement. For years, campus administrators denied recognition to a student NAACP chapter before finally relenting in 1960. Singleton soon became chapter president, but his willingness to lead the group in direct action that year in support of the sit-in movement garnered the ire of NAACP national executive director Roy Wilkins. As a result, much of the group's future direct action occurred under the rubric of the campus CORE chapter, with many members holding dual memberships.[57] Thus, when Farmer spoke at UCLA to recruit potential Freedom Riders, he found in Singleton, and more than a dozen others, students eager to confront Jim Crow while rejecting the isolation imposed by the Kerr Directives.

When the student Riders returned to campus that fall, their experiences horrified fellow students. Steve McNichols, arrested in Houston, Texas, after sitting in at the Union Station Coffee Shop, was thrown into the Harris County jail, which already held 107 other inmates, mostly hardened criminals. Encouraged by the deputies, many of the inmates proceeded to beat and terrorize McNichols and his three companions for the next forty-eight hours.[58] Upon Singleton's arrival in Jackson, Mississippi, he and the rest of his group sat in the "Whites Only" lounge and were quickly arrested. Police soon upgraded an initial charge of trespassing to felonious inciting to riot, and Singleton found himself staring down the deepest, darkest hole in all of American jurisprudence: death row of Mississippi's infamous Parchman Penitentiary. He remained there for thirty-nine anxious days before his release on bail.[59] In addition to these powerful testimonials, one of the student Riders, Al Barouh, died in a plane crash returning to Los Angeles. An intensely popular student leader, Barouh's death weighed heavily on those who knew him, providing both increased attention to the sacrifices of the

Riders and "a catalyst" for the movement at UCLA.[60] When the students returned that fall, they provided a local, tangible example of segregation's brutality. They also ran headlong into the Kerr Directives.

For years, the campus NAACP chapter was named the UCLA NAACP. But Kerr's new fall 1961 regulations on speech and association now dissociated the NAACP, CORE, and similar groups from the school. As a result, the directives forced the group to abandon the name "UCLA NAACP," with the group known thereafter as the Westwood NAACP. The campus CORE chapter combatively attempted to thumb its nose in Kerr's direction by insisting on the mildly associative Bruin CORE.[61] The Kerr Directives' prohibition of off-campus civil rights activities increasingly found itself the target of sustained criticism in the *Daily Bruin*, which hammered the restrictions at every turn in editorial cartoons and columns. What perplexed students most was the undefined nature of off-campus issues. "Unfortunately, we are not at all sure what Dr. Clark Kerr considers off-campus," ruminated one student. To many students, condemning the violence in the South fell into the "on-campus" category when that violence was directed at fellow students. The *Bruin* challenged students to speak out on all issues that involved the "student in his role as a student," even if it meant "stepping upon the feet of the Kerr Directives."[62] One editor went so far as to call for "a formalized protest of the Directives on the part of UCLA students."[63] When faculty sent petitions to President Kennedy and his attorney general condemning the treatment of the Freedom Riders, the Kerr Directives prohibited those individuals as identifying themselves as professors from UCLA. The students, however, were far less circumspect when they sent an open letter to the campus thanking those who signed the petitions. They signed the letter "UCLA Freedom Riders," blatantly violating the Kerr Directives.[64]

In confronting university authority in their efforts to challenge segregation, however, students felt isolated due to a relatively weak citywide civil rights campaign. As far back as 1950, CORE's inability to stimulate much campus activity had caused it to abandon the affluent west side and concentrate its activities upon the central city. CORE's membership woes continued, however, and the group lapsed into inactivity by 1957. Without the vitality that college campuses provided, CORE officer George Houser noted the difficulty in keeping such organizations active.[65] Later in the decade, Joann Love Allen, in appraising CORE's national office of the situation in Los Angeles, noted that the local chapter "has made no effort to recruit college students into CORE." It is unclear if Allen's appraisal was correct, but any on-campus CORE recruitment efforts would have also run afoul of

Figure 4. The über Kerr, effectively expelling all activist groups. Note the group at the top of the list. From *Daily Bruin*, September 18, 1961.

the Kerr Directives.[66] CORE also frequently aligned itself with the NAACP, not so much as an exercise in coalition building but from the more pragmatic realization that "feeling too small and impotent," the group lacked the resources in Los Angeles to accomplish much independently. In 1958, it joined the NAACP in boycott of the local Budweiser brewery due to that company's discriminatory hiring practices, and in January 1960 it joined the NAACP and several labor groups in picketing discriminatory retail outlets. As late as September 1961, another CORE staffer admitted that the inability to maintain a CORE chapter at UCLA meant that much of the group's efforts were "channeled through the NAACP," though that group itself was also declared "off campus" by the Kerr Directives.[67] Even after the Freedom Rides and the extensive media coverage they generated, Los Angeles CORE's annual report in 1961 acknowledged that it "failed to capitalize fully on our opportunities during and since the Freedom Rides."[68]

The backlash of anticommunism also limited civil rights activity in Los Angeles and left UCLA students adrift. Kevin Allen Leonard has demonstrated that differences within the Los Angeles NAACP, though often colored by anticommunist rhetoric, more accurately revealed a conflict "between the established black elite which had long controlled the NAACP in the city and relative newcomers who wanted the organization to be a more aggressive advocate for their interests."[69] However, embracing that more aggressive position increasingly meant aligning itself, willingly or not, with causes espoused by the American Communist Party or organizations popularly associated with it, namely the Civil Rights Congress (CRC). According to Josh Sides, the NAACP "avoided issues or alliances that might" link it with leftist causes, which would have included student activists who operated under constant allegations of fellow traveling throughout the 1950s. When the NAACP not only failed to join the CRC in denouncing the Los Angeles Police Department for its fatal beating of Herman Burns while he was in custody in 1948 but in fact defended the city's position on the issue, its membership plummeted through the early 1950s. The organization rebounded by 1955 but, true to its national policy, largely avoided the direct action that many college students increasingly found so appealing by the dawn of the 1960s, as Singleton's experiences with Wilkins in 1960 demonstrated.[70]

Students at UCLA, too, found allegations of communism a hindrance to civil rights activism. Throughout the 1950s, Milton Hahn, UCLA's dean of students, whose obsession with communism "bridged on paranoia," steadfastly linked all manner of race-related student activism with communism.[71] In response to student efforts aimed against campus discrimination, Hahn alleged a vast communist conspiracy against UCLA, claiming such students had provided "constant pressure for years to get questionable organizations into the University family so they can damage UCLA from the inside."[72] Hahn's irrational fear of communism at UCLA knew no bounds, prompting him to bring the full weight of his administrative authority down upon the students. Within a sixteen-month period in 1955–56, Hahn unilaterally altered the editorial makeup of the *Bruin*, increased the administrative voice in the SLC, called for a rogue election and then billed the students for it, and changed the student constitution by fiat. Most of the *Bruin* editorial staff resigned in protest and formed *The Observer*, an underground paper that criticized the administration for its abuses and its unwillingness to recognize the campus NAACP chapter. In response, Hahn ordered Lt. William Waldman in the UC Police Department to surveil the students with intent to investigate and disrupt their source of funding. Hahn also prohibited

The Observer's distribution on campus, ordering Waldman to confiscate all copies, filing them under "subversive activities."[73] Throughout the 1950s, Hahn refused to recognize the campus NAACP chapter, claiming that he was only following regental directive. The Berkeley campus, however, home of the regents, had recognized their campus NAACP chapter since 1953.[74] According to Willard Johnson, UCLA's second black student-body president in 1956–57, Hahn's actions revealed an administration "overly suspicious of students concerned about race relations, restrictive clauses, the independent authority of student government, and student concern with broader social and political issues."[75]

Milton Hahn's abrupt retirement in 1959 was soon followed by the arrival of Franklin D. Murphy as UCLA's new chancellor the following year.[76] Murphy arrived at what one student activist called "that critical moment" when the coalescence of political issues, student interest, and social conscience created a campus awakening. Immediately, Murphy made it clear that the days of Hahn's ruthless vendettas against student activists had ended when he ordered the campus NAACP chapter officially recognized. Though they were unaware of it at the time, students also benefited from a power struggle between Kerr and Murphy over the prerogative of the chancellor on his own campus. From the inception of independent campuses within the University of California system and the creation of the office of chancellor, both the state regents and officials in Berkeley saw the position of chancellor as chief administrator on the local level, but the UC president expected to maintain final authority. Murphy had other ideas about the role of the chancellor and the autonomy of the individual campuses when he declared of the UC system shortly after his arrival in 1960, "what was once a colonial empire is becoming a commonwealth of institutions."[77] Such conflicting assumptions about their respective roles and authorities all but ensured a confrontation between Murphy and Kerr, with the conferral of degrees at graduation, of all things, precipitating the rupture. Tradition held that the UC president traveled to each campus for commencement, at which each chancellor was to preside but stepped aside for the UC president to confer the actual degrees. Murphy argued that as chief campus administrator, the responsibility and privilege of conferment lay with him. When Murphy refused to yield on the matter, Kerr, wary of yielding a precedent, had his secretary inform Murphy's office every May that "scheduling conflicts" precluded Kerr's presence at commencement and that Murphy needed to "fill in" for the president. This charade continued until 1965 when Kerr finally conceded the point, but revealed Murphy's willingness to clash with the president on matters of policy and prerogative, an issue that soon had bearing on the issue of student free speech and association.[78]

The new chancellor demanded "that the University must be a marketplace of ideas, not a trade school," declaring it "the manifest destiny of education to test the status quo."[79] Firmly committed to the notion of the university as a marketplace of ideas, Murphy believed that "the best way to defeat a bad argument is to let it show itself in the marketplace."[80] As such, he maintained serious, though private, reservations about the Kerr Directives. Murphy, for example, quietly accepted CORE's use of the trademarked "Bruin" name and offered no rebuke to the Freedom Riders for their use in print of "UCLA Freedom Riders." Thus, while he publicly defended the Kerr Directives, Murphy ignored certain violations when they ran counter to his concept of the free marketplace of ideas. In addition to his support of free speech and association, Murphy aided students' nascent civil rights activities. As part of the Chancellor's Advisory Committee on Discrimination, student civil rights groups checked employment and housing listings in the campus Bureau of Occupations and Housing (BurOc). If black students were told a job or apartment was no longer available, white students inquired about the same listing shortly thereafter. If the job or apartment was offered them, the students reported this to Murphy's office, which had the offending listing struck from the BurOc.[81]

With support from the new chancellor, student activists hoped that they might finally gain headway in engaging the student body on civil rights. Specifically, they hoped the blatant discrimination exposed by the Freedom Riders could be used to illustrate the students' own inequality at home in the form of campus free-speech restrictions limiting their support of the struggle in the South. Thus, they needed to make students identify with the cause and defense of the Freedom Riders. Student Nand Hart-Nibbrig urged others not to ignore the efforts of the Freedom Riders, claiming "the moral impetus has been provided by our Freedom Riders, now let us all get on the bus."[82] With ample coverage from the *Bruin*, students read with growing alarm of the treatment civil rights workers received during a voter registration campaign in McComb, Mississippi. In yet another violation of the Kerr Directives, they circulated a petition on campus to be sent to Attorney General Robert Kennedy, urging him to take prompt action in the wake of 113 student arrests in McComb. They also forwarded a statement of solidarity to the jailed students, praising their "efforts to secure freedom and dignity for all Americans."[83] A *Bruin* editorial by Louis Weschler urged students who could not demonstrate personally to provide financial or moral support, arguing that the responsibility to end segregation should no longer rest solely with the Freedom Riders. He demanded students accept their collective "responsibility to help continue the fight against racial discrimination." Weschler's comments illustrated that student activists grasped the importance of convincing others that injustice anywhere allowed for injustice everywhere.[84]

The rhetoric of the activists shrewdly reminded fellow students that they did not have to go to the South to fight discrimination, but that they did have the responsibility to confront it when it appeared locally. As such, when CORE began demonstrations against a local developer who restricted home sales to whites only, a flyer reminded students, "It is just as important for a Negro to be free to buy a house HERE, as it is for a Negro to be able to attend a university in Mississippi!!"[85] Hoping to play upon such notions of student identity, the *Bruin* inundated students with news items from college campuses across the country throughout the fall of 1961 regarding issues of racial discrimination and efforts to combat them.[86] For the majority of the student body, however, the connection between the Kerr Directives and civil rights activity remained abstract. For practical purposes, students needed an opportunity to support the Riders without themselves going to the South or for segregation conveniently to come to them. In the fall of 1961, both options presented themselves.

Students arrested during the Freedom Rides faced the issue of posting bond money for their trials in late spring and early summer of 1962. Student activists, finding a perfect opportunity to draw out the rest of the campus on the civil rights issue, circulated petitions requesting $5,000 from the student incidental fund as a loan to the Riders, to be repaid upon completion of the judicial process. Student body president James Stiven legitimated their actions by stating, "If it is proven a substantial percentage of the student body desires to use its funds for the benefit of the Freedom Riders, the money should be used for that purpose."[87] Immediately, students debated whether the loan would violate the Kerr Directives. Students knew that they had gotten away with small violations of the Kerr Directives in the form of organizational names and on-campus petitions, but a loan from accounts set up in the university's name was another matter entirely. The magnitude of their brazenness, however, potentially worked in their favor; proponents realized it was a sufficiently gray issue as to force Kerr into either backing down or prohibiting the loan and risking a student eruption. Either way, activists felt it was a winnable situation. Noting that CORE and the NAACP had the money if the Riders needed it, one student noted explicitly the real issue surrounding the loan: "It appears that the money is intended primarily as a symbol of endorsement for the Freedom Riders from UCLA." In that, student activists saw the loan as a way to include the wider campus in the civil rights movement while simultaneously testing the Kerr Directives.[88]

By the students' own admission, the Kerr Directive restrictions lay at the heart of the Freedom Riders bail controversy. As such, student government had no intention of deciding the issue on its own and put the matter to a campus-wide referendum. Far from a simple administrative matter, student Steve Weiner referred to the vote not as a decision on the loan but as a "referendum on the Freedom Rides" themselves. A front-page editorial in the *Bruin* urging students to vote for the loan stated that "implicit in any vote is a moral judgment" about the disparity "between the country's ideals and their implementation" and, in an editorial cartoon, gave the moral high ground to the loan supporters by associating the Ku Klux Klan with those opposed to the loan.[89] As such, activist rhetoric continued to argue that segregation and the Kerr Directives were both violations of deeply held American ideals. Student aspirations to accelerate their support of the civil rights movement, however, were soon crushed by the administration.

The student referendum on the loan witnessed the largest voter turnout in campus history up to that time, and students approved the loan by a 2-1 margin. The university moved swiftly, however, to overturn the students' action, referring the matter to the Board of Control (BoC), an administrative oversight committee created in the early 1950s as yet another manifestation of the multiversity. Designed to ensure "responsible oversight" of funds taken in by student enterprises such as the bookstore and food service, the BoC rejected the loan by a vote of 5-3 without comment. Undaunted, students appealed the decision to Murphy. Though he upheld the BoC's decision, Murphy quietly, and personally, interceded with the campus financial aid office to ensure the availability of funds to the student Riders. The evidence is unclear if Murphy rejected the appeal on his own or was instructed on the matter by Kerr's office, but Murphy's behind-the-scenes maneuvering appears remarkably similar to his earlier support of student civil rights activity as an expression of his personal feelings while still publicly upholding the Kerr Directives as his position demanded. Regardless, student activists and the *Bruin* howled with indignation and betrayal at the boardroom reversal of the students' wishes at the ballot box. A spokesman for Platform, UCLA's first student political party, explicitly put the matter into such democratic context: "The Board of Control evidently does not give primary consideration to the wishes of the very people who support the ASUCLA. It is a sad case

"LIBERAL HOT DOGS AT CONSERVATIVE PRICES"

Figure 5. For student civil rights activists, a vote for the loan was a vote for the Rides themselves, linking their efforts with the larger struggle in the South. Note the Klansman in the upper right-hand corner. From *Daily Bruin*, December 13, 1961.

when a small group of individuals disregard the student body in the case of student body funds." The *Bruin*, in a front-page editorial, was even more blunt, declaring that the event demonstrated "the role to which students on this campus have been relegated by an administration whose philosophy can only be described as high school paternalism." The editorial described student government and its notions of autonomy as "a sham."[90]

As these strains of the civil rights movement and campus activism wove themselves together, UCLA's football team found itself one win away from securing the conference championship and the Rose Bowl invitation. Once the University of Alabama appeared as a likely opponent, however, criticism of Alabama's segregationist policies surfaced almost immediately. An ad hoc student group called the Negro College Students of Southern California (NCSSC), claiming membership from students at both UCLA and USC, called for a boycott of the game if the Rose Bowl invited Alabama. The group's executive committee argued that such a game "would give financial profit to the university to further its segregation policies" and mentioned that it enjoyed support from members of the UCLA football team, implying that any boycott discussion included not just attendance but the playing of the game itself. Starting fullback Kermit Alexander agreed to abide by the boycott, and Alexander later admitted that it was openly discussed within the team.[91] Whether the group actually included USC students is unknown, but it seems unlikely. The press release calling for the boycott, covered in the *Bruin*, was not covered in the *Daily Trojan*, suggesting that it was not even sent to the latter paper. In fact, the only reference to the issue came in the form of a brief mention in the *Trojan*, making no connection to students at USC and actually supporting Alabama's bid for the invitation. The piece argued the unfairness of singling out Alabama for its racial practices when all other southern athletic programs embraced segregation as well. Declaring, "This segregation thing is slowly folding up in the South anyway and we know that it will surely sink in the future, so why keep them away because of this?" students at USC demonstrated little concern for Alabama's segregation policies.[92] It is likely that the group existed solely at UCLA but, due to the Kerr Directives, was forced to embrace a more generic name.

The *Daily Trojan* was not the only paper to place the onus upon the South and dismiss the boycott as unnecessary. The logic of placing responsibility for ending segregation entirely on the South generally labeled those outside the South who attempted to raise the issue, such as the students at UCLA, as ill-mannered rabble-rousers. At the height of the debate over whether Alabama or LSU might get the Rose Bowl invitation, the *Pasadena Star-News* ran an editorial examining the question of "Race and the Rose Bowl," in which it not only dismissed calls to use the game as a challenge to segregation but also absolved the West of any responsibility for doing so in the first place. In the process, the paper trotted out the usual temporizing maxims and canards that simultaneously declared the Rose Bowl off-limits as a forum for social justice while attempting to marginalize those who suggested otherwise. The piece noted the "increasingly important" role that blacks had played in college football since the end of World War II and claimed that sport played a "leading role . . . in providing equal opportunity for all races." It also slyly suggested that the city of Pasadena and the Rose Bowl facilitated such a development by noting not only that Jackie Robinson had grown up in Pasadena but that his entrance into major league baseball occurred the same year that the Big Ten initiated its contract with the Rose Bowl, vaguely implying that the two were related. In so arguing, the editorial suggested the unfairness of the claim that inviting LSU or Alabama aided segregation, when sports in general and Pasadena and the Rose Bowl in particular had already done so much to aid integration. The editorial also claimed that southern legal provisions banning interracial play were only "retaliatory measures" that first emerged in the wake of the *Brown* decision, suggesting that prior to 1954 the question of segregated teams playing integrated ones had been of little relevance. Though such a claim clearly ignored the numerous bans that existed prior to 1954, it disingenuously implied that such a hardening of segregationist resolve came only in response to attempts by northerners to force the issue. According to such logic, just as the Supreme Court had provoked the South by attempting to force the issue of school integration, attempts by UCLA's students to boycott the Rose Bowl might similarly enrage the South. Additionally, in suggesting that concerns over integrated play had not existed prior to 1954, the piece neatly absolved northern and western teams from their own complicity in upholding segregation in sports by accepting Gentlemen's Agreements.

The *Star-News* also touched on the benefits to segregated schools of integrated play: "It would do Southern boys some good to exchange a few whacks and thumps with Negro players."[93] Such claims appeared frequently during the episode, cropping up most prominently in the writings of both Jim Murray and Melvin Durslag.[94] In accepting such logic, however, the *Star-News* revealed its own notions of western exceptionalism by positing the West as a savior that would show the South by example the route to interracial harmony. Finally, the editorial closed by claiming the injustice of excluding segregated teams merely because of their racial policies. Although the piece acknowledged that UCLA or USC would not be welcome to play at LSU or Alabama, it cautioned against "replying in kind. . . . It would be a victory for the forces of segregation, we think, if either [LSU or Alabama] were rejected on the basis of retaliation. There is something to the notion of turning the other cheek." As a result, according to the paper's logic, the West held the moral high ground by accepting the presence of segregation rather than challenging it. Thus, the West could show the South the benefits of integration but was completely devoid of any responsibility for ending segregation.[95]

The *Daily Bruin* rejected such logic out of hand, however, openly endorsing the boycott. Soon after the students announced the boycott, the *Bruin* ran an editorial cartoon opposing the invitation of the Crimson Tide. Featuring the UCLA mascot dressed in Civil War attire, the image clearly linked the potential invitation to Alabama not only with the contemporary civil rights movement but also with the South's long tradition of racial discrimination. Underneath the image, the paper also ran a letter on the subject in which the student writer described racial conditions "here in the North." The cartoon and letter revealed the conflicted view of race and region held by many students. In every other instance, students at UCLA distinctly saw themselves as westerners and used that appellation unsparingly. On the issue of race, however, students had a more schizophrenic identity. Since the 1940s, students who commented on race relations in general categorized themselves as westerners, particularly when they suggested race relations in the West existed within a distinctly exceptional context. However, when the subject shifted from western exceptionalism to southern exceptionalism—namely, Jim Crow discrimination—UCLA students tended to see only North and South. As a result, they embraced the illustrative and rhetorical iconography of the historical polarization between the North and South. In letters and editorials such as the one referring to the 1940 NYU episode as a "Missouri Compromise" and illustrations about the Rose Bowl and Freedom Rider issues, students overwhelmingly identified themselves with the North and notions of equality and integration, while defining the South as an "other," representing inequality, discrimination, and violence.[96]

Though the NCSSC was possibly little more than a handful of UCLA students, support for the boycott rapidly spread off campus. Pat Hull, a student at Colorado College, wrote the *Bruin* that many on the Colorado Springs campus had heard of the UCLA students' efforts and were in steadfast agreement. Hull mentioned many of UCLA's black players, noting they had little moral choice but to observe a boycott.[97] Local commercial media also supported the boycott proposal. The *California Eagle*, one of the city's black newspapers, ran an editorial demanding that Cal and UCLA veto any invitation to Alabama, urging readers to send telegrams to both Governor Edmund Brown and university president Kerr. The paper reminded its readers that "the University of California is a state institution. It belongs to the people, all of the people, of California. . . . Tell them you don't want the Jim Crow University of Alabama in the Rose Bowl."[98] Another black paper, the *Los Angeles Sentinel*, ran the headline "Don't Bring Dixiecrats to Rose Bowl" and noted how offensive the consideration of Alabama was to Los Angeles's black community by wryly commenting, "If they're going to recommend Alabama, they might as well go all the way and invite Ole Miss."[99]

Figure 6. In opposing the South and its customs, westerners became rhetorical northerners. From *Daily Bruin*, November 22, 1961.

Both Melvin Durslag in the *Los Angeles Examiner* and Jim Murray in the *Los Angeles Times* supported the UCLA students' boycott suggestion, declaring Alabama's policies "undemocratic" and "un-American." Even the *New York Times* ran a small piece on the episode. Without exception, commercial media outside the South covered the boycott threat in terms similar to the *Bruin*, interpreting Alabama's appearance as an affront to basic American values and ideals.[100]

Thus, in short order the students linked the Rose Bowl to their assumptions of regional exceptionalism that had informed their understandings of race since World War II. Additionally, they, and others off campus, described the episode in the same language of democracy and equality that animated student discussion of the Kerr Directives. Finally, there was yet a third context arousing student response to the Rose Bowl, allowing its linkage to the activist agenda. The multiversity's obligations to varied constituencies and its need to avoid controversy required ever greater management and oversight. As a result, students witnessed their institutions increasingly fall under ever greater administrative authority throughout the 1950s and early 1960s. The creation of the Board of Control and Milton Hahn's changes to the SLC and to the *Daily Bruin* illustrated this. When the administration similarly moved in 1961 to bring student athletics under its control, it inadvertently inflamed a long-standing source of friction between student activists and the administration.

Like many schools at the time bent on maintaining the amateur myth of college athletics, UCLA insisted on anachronistically viewing athletics as a student institution. As a result, the budget of the athletic department fell under the nominal purview of the student body association. This created a situation that legendary Bruin basketball coach John Wooden later claimed "made the student body president my boss."[101] In reality, the ASUCLA enjoyed little managerial oversight of the athletic department, serving as little more than a financial clearinghouse, watching money come and go but unable to direct it, account for it, or restrict it. As a result, student institutions such as the *Daily Bruin* frequently cast a jealous eye toward the lavish budget and loose accounting practices of the athletic office. In 1934, outgoing *Bruin* editor Robert Shelby advised his successor to be aware of the privileged position football enjoyed, especially relative to that of the newspaper. "You will be chagrined beyond words to find out that the student janitor [a subsidized football player] who empties your wastebasket gets more money than you" (brackets in the original). A subsequent editor, Carl Schaeffer, used much of his editorial power to criticize the economics of football and the use of student monies for athletic scholarships. Schaeffer called on the athletic department to simply admit it gave special financial consideration and aid to football players. The paper's historian contends that student government, likely leveraged by the administration, removed Schaeffer after the first semester, making him the first one-term editor at the paper in a decade.[102]

By the 1950s, a rising student consciousness with university governance, and students' exclusion from the process, brought the question of athletic finances into sharper relief. Lewis Leeburg, ASUCLA president in 1953–54, declared "the major problem in the ASUCLA financial structure is the dependence on football revenue." Echoing a claim heard on countless college campuses for decades, Leeburg noted that "this dependence placed undue emphasis upon football" and allowed for all kinds of accounting improprieties. Acutely aware of many of the specifics because, as president, he had to sign the checks, Leeburg was "particularly bothered" by the expense account practices of legendary football coach Henry "Red" Sanders. "Attempts to get more information were usually met with courteous attempts to supply the least information possible."[103] Leeburg was not the only one frustrated with the students' inability to rein in football and control their own finances. In 1959, Platform noted that the "ASUCLA is a $1,750,000 business," but student government seemed powerless to address issues such as student fees or campus programming. In contrast, "our football team costs us about a 1/3 of a million dollars per year to field . . . and 77% of our compulsory student fees goes to covering the loss incurred by our athletic program."[104]

Throughout the 1950s, uncertainty over football revenues often caused the SLC to refuse to commit to projects that activists wanted student government to pursue. In the spring of 1954, the student-based Council for Mexican-American Education proposed a program by which promising high school students from the Chicano barrios be invited to campus as a way to increase minority student enrollment. Though the SLC supported the program, it acknowledged that athletic expenses cut deeply into their available discretionary funds late in the academic year.[105] The financial situation in the athletic department reached its nadir in 1960, when the athletic director began paying current bills with season ticket revenue for the following year. Fed up with the athletic department's accounting practices, the SLC demanded in October 1960 a chancellor's investigation into the matter, which revealed that the ASUCLA's budget deficit of $372,600 was entirely due to football. In the fall of 1961, the administration formally separated the athletic department from the ASUCLA, but much to the students' chagrin, left them holding the financial bag. In an effort to address the budget shortfall, the newly independent athletic department, in addition to receiving 100 percent of all proceeds from athletic privilege cards bought by students, also received 25 percent of all undergraduate student fees.[106] As result, when the students proposed a boycott of the Rose Bowl, officials within the athletic department ignored the question of segregation entirely, seeing the matter only in terms of finances. After the other AAWU schools received their share and UCLA paid various expenses, the Bruins' appearance in the Rose Bowl netted the athletic department $134,415, cutting the deficit by more than a third and pulling the athletic department from the financial brink. When asked years later about the possibility of the administration's embracing the potential boycott, former athletic director Robert Fischer dismissively stated, "I guarantee that never came up."[107] Coming in the same semester as the Freedom Rider loan reversal, it was impossible for Platform and other student activists to avoid seeing the two issues as interrelated examples of the multiversity's paternalism and its dismissal of student concerns.[108]

The actions of the Board of Control and athletic department officials demonstrated to students that administrative agencies exercised final authority over student institutions and were prone to dismiss students' social consciousness in the process. Students were more successful that year, however, in wresting from the administration the ability to define the public meaning of their own institutions. For years students had resented the administration's manipulation of football's cultural meaning as a counterweight to student activism. As far back as 1934, a confrontation over free speech at UCLA resulted in the expulsion of five students merely for disobeying the campus provost, Ernest Carroll Moore. Following the expulsions, thousands of students demonstrated and boycotted classes to call for the reinstatement of the "UCLA 5." In response, Moore issued a radio address in which he urged students to "clean house" of the activists and "purge the Communists," specifically calling on established campus institutions such as the Greek system and the athletic teams. Those groups responded by forming the UCLA Americans, led by football player Remmy Olstead, which included a midnight initiation ceremony that had all the trappings of a Klan rally and prominently featured several football players as a show of force. Even the reactionary *Los Angeles Times* called the group's vigilantism "open to question."[109] The incident initiated an administrative pattern of linking football with strident anticommunism. In 1940, leftist campus groups protested the production of Harriet Beecher Stowe's *Uncle Tom's Cabin*, claiming that it reinforced negative black stereotypes. In response, the SLC named Kenny Washington, who was also a student senator, to head an investigatory committee to look into the matter. Washington's report rejected the student group's claim and the play continued as planned, but the administration attempted to exploit Washington's role in an effort to undermine the respectability and credibility of the activists.[110] Administrative figures trumpeted the "Washington Report" as having particular credence coming from such a prominent black football player. In commenting on the report, one official lauded Washington as "probably one of UCLA's greatest football players ever" and noted he was "liberal-minded and full of common sense," in sharp contrast to those who brought up the issue. Thus, establishing Washington's football credentials legitimated the report as far as the administration was concerned.[111] Dean of undergraduates Earl Miller, who was so vigilant in his suppression of campus dissent that he shared academic and personal files of student activists with the notorious LAPD Red Squad, declared the entire episode a communist plot. Though Miller declared that leftist groups had attempted to "use . . . a few of our colored students to . . . start some trouble," it was the administration that had "used" Washington for its own purposes.[112]

By the early 1950s, the school's administration had become particularly anxious over the perception that student activism made UCLA a haven for communist activity. In responding to a 1953 query from a local reporter, public affairs director Andrew Hamilton, while admitting that perhaps campus activism might have been linked to communism in the past, claimed no such problem currently existed. Then, as if to suggest that the soul of the university remained untouched, Hamilton authoritatively assured the reporter, "No Communist has ever been a member of the football squad."[113] Thus, well into the 1950s, administrators at UCLA successfully seized upon existing appropriations of football as antithetical to communism. In the process, they also lumped together student activists who agitated for reform in the areas of free speech and civil rights as communists or dupes and used football as a weapon by which to marginalize them accordingly. The support both on and off campus of the boycott issue reversed this historical trend, however. By successfully linking football to the cause of the Freedom Riders, students suggested that accepting Alabama's participation in the Rose Bowl was no less a rejection of American values than accepting the beatings Alabama officials doled out to the Freedom Riders. As a result, students placed football in its postwar context as an expression of celebrated American values and in the process seized from the administration the meaning of football and put it to the service of an activist agenda.

The students' successful linkage of football with the civil rights movement, as well as Murphy's refusal to allow the paranoid anticommunist excesses characteristic of Earl Miller and Milton Hahn, bore immediate fruit. Hardly had the threat of a Rose Bowl boycott passed before the UCLA basketball team faced segregated lodging and seating arrangements at a December tournament in Houston. Refusing to wait for administrative action, the SLC passed a resolution asking the chancellor to issue a policy prohibiting UCLA's participation in any sporting event that included segregated facilities or teams, followed by telegrams to President Kerr and Governor Brown asking for similar policies for the entire University of California.[114] In fact, the university already maintained such a policy for regular season match-ups but had publicly suppressed it at the explicit order of Kerr, who did not "see the necessity at this time of publicizing it outside the immediate University family concerned." It is unclear how long Kerr would have ordered the policy suppressed, but the students at UCLA backed him into a corner, forcing the university to issue the policy publicly. When the university announced the policy publicly in January 1962, however, it did so without acknowledging its previous existence, allowing the students to assume that they had forced the issue upon the administration. As a result, students once again interpreted the episode as an extension of the school's integrated athletic tradition that had justified their notions of exceptionalism since World War II. A column in the *Bruin* declared, "It is only fitting that UCLA, the alma mater of Jackie Robinson and Rafer Johnson, should be one of the first major colleges to take a decisive stand in the area of discrimination and segregation in athletics."[115] Equally unclear is why Kerr ordered the policy suppressed in the first place, but the university's exclusion of postseason play suggested that it refused to let morality or social justice impede the quest for Rose Bowl profits and national championships. As late as 1964, Brad Booth, the UCLA faculty athletic representative, explicitly opposed expanding the policy to include postseason games, writing, "I should be opposed . . . to the University adopting any policy which would keep us out of NCAA-sponsored championship events." In another letter, he happily noted the policy "excluded from the stated prohibitions . . . the Rose Bowl game."[116] As such, a public policy prohibiting discrimination in the regular season but not the postseason opened the university up to charges of hypocrisy. Booth's sentiments on the matter also continued to reveal the dismissal by athletic officials of the students' rising social consciousness.

Having clearly lost the ability to control the meaning of the intersection of race and sports, the university quietly conceded another matter as well. With the students successfully raising the issue of segregation in sports, they provided a platform for the *Eagle* and *Sentinel* to address the continued exclusion of their reporters from the press box of the Los Angeles Memorial Coliseum, where UCLA played its home games. Before the Rose Bowl controversy broke, Brad Pye, sports editor of the *Sentinel*, returned his complimentary general admission tickets to UCLA, protesting what he viewed as the Jim Crow section set aside in the stands just below the press box for writers from the *Sentinel* and the *Eagle*. Once the issue of discrimination and athletics became the *cause célèbre*, both papers ran stories about the situation, making it a news item. One column noted that exclusion from the press box seemed a shabby way to treat two papers that went out of their way to offer favorable coverage to UCLA and particularly to steer black athletes to the school. It remains unclear if the policy was in fact discriminatory or, as those involved maintained at the time, an accommodation of the already overcrowded press box and the reality that reporters for the

Eagle and the *Sentinel*, both weeklies, did not write on deadline. Regardless, in the wake of the Rose Bowl controversy and the new athletic department policy on segregation, continuation of the practice appeared compromising at best, overtly discriminatory at worst. "For a whole variety of reasons and in the best interests of UCLA," Murphy ordered full privileges extended to the black press.[117]

In 1961, students at UCLA encountered a host of concentric issues involving student power, civil rights, and free speech. These issues all intersected with the possibility of a Rose Bowl boycott because students accepted the cultural elevation of football. College football in the postwar years invested the game with values universally accepted as central to an American identity, one that sharply contrasted with that of the Soviets. The students' positioning of football in opposition to university autocracy, segregation, and restrictions on free speech magnified the distance of these issues from idealized Cold War cultural norms. As a result, student activists found in the Rose Bowl boycott a stalking horse for all of their concerns. It served to demonstrate to the student body at large the un-American connotations of segregation, heavy-handed university authority, and restrictions on free speech when students earlier had failed to see it in those terms. In that regard, football emerged as a postwar cultural *lingua franca*, universally understood by everyone because of its expression of values and identities linked to the American way of life.

Conclusion

By the end of November 1961, Tom Hamilton faced an almost unbelievable set of circumstances. Alabama and Ohio State had both rejected an invitation, LSU did not even bother to wait for a Rose Bowl invitation before looking elsewhere, and students at UCLA threatened to turn the Bruins' presence in the game into a platform against larger social injustices. From there the process only became stranger. Still shying away from the Big Ten, Tom Hamilton considered for a time the Naval Academy. Navy had crafted a 7-3 record that year, including a victory over Notre Dame, and Hamilton must have relished the thought of bringing his alma mater back to Pasadena. Although Navy had warily eyed bowl games since its 1956 Sugar Bowl appearance, both the Middies' head coach and athletic director had admitted that a Rose Bowl invitation might make them feel differently. It is unclear how seriously Hamilton considered the Midshipmen, but Navy would not have been willing to make any decision prior to its early December finale against Army, putting off the announcement of an opponent still further into the future.[1] Once it became apparent that the Rose Bowl selection process was an absolute free-for-all, some commentators suggested that Hamilton not only consider an opponent from outside the Big Ten but a host team from outside the AAWU as well. Hall Wood, a wire-service reporter based in San Francisco, suggested exactly that, prior to the SC-UCLA showdown that would determine the AAWU representative. He noted that both UCLA and USC were having mediocre years, with UCLA having lost three games and SC losing four and tying one, and neither ranked in the Top Twenty. Wood pointed out that a codicil in the Rose Bowl contract provided for other teams to appear in the game under specific circumstances. "When the Big Five was formed, it was announced it could select some other club if it didn't have a representative team. This is the year to exercise that option." Wood pointed out that both Utah State and Arizona had better records and were more "representative" of football in the West.[2]

Four days later, anyone who might have snickered at the suggestion of Utah State in the Rose Bowl likely sat slack jawed as Representative David

S. King (D-Utah) rose on the floor of the U.S. House of Representatives to implore the Rose Bowl to consider his home state Aggies, announcing his dispatch of telegrams concerning the matter to the governor of California and both of the state's U.S. senators, as well as to Tom Hamilton. King seized upon Wood's logic, claiming that "since the West Coast has not produced an outstanding team this year," the committee should "choose an outstanding team from another Western State." The congressman from Utah argued that the selection of Utah State, with a record of 9-0-1 at the time, would deliver not only "a more deserving representative" but also foster goodwill among western states.[3] While many Utahans no doubt felt the Aggies deserved a bowl bid, King's role as Utah State's benefactor astounded many simply because he graduated from hated archrival Utah. Though King never explained his patronage of Utah State, it seems likely that politics played a not-insignificant role. Three months after rising to the floor of the House in support of Utah State, University of Utah alumnus King announced his candidacy for the Senate, for which he needed votes from both Aggies and Utes.[4] For several days, Utah-area papers tittered over the possibility of Utah State landing in Pasadena on New Year's Day. However, while Tom Hamilton willingly broke with tradition to consider an SEC team, he stopped short of extending that willingness to Utah State. Though agreeing "that Utah State has a good team," he felt confident that the AAWU would field "a good team well qualified to play anyone in the Rose Bowl."[5] In spurning Utah State, Hamilton politely declined to explicate the economics and demographics of postwar big-time football, a discretion not followed by the *Salt Lake Tribune*, which bluntly though sympathetically dismissed the Aggies' Rose Bowl hopes for a number of reasons. Utah's small population meant diminished television ratings, and its location in the sparsely populated Rocky Mountain region also meant limited regional appeal. Finally, big-time college football schools willingly embraced the increased costs and decreasing competition of the period as a way to reserve the spoils of the game for themselves. Tom Hamilton and the AAWU were not about to invite Utah State up to the trough.[6]

With few other options, and the national speculation over an opponent becoming tedious, in December Hamilton and the AAWU, chastened by the experience of the previous month, wearily settled on the Big Ten for an opponent. In retrospect, the decision to invite second-place Minnesota emerged from wide-ranging opposition to Hamilton's Rose Bowl plans. The departure in the late 1950s of the chief campus administrators who had originally supported the idea of the National Conference and Hamilton's hiring removed from the discussion the proposal's most forceful advocates, leaving mostly hostile faculty to oppose the plan. According to Pete Newell, then the athletic director at Cal, AAWU faculties never lost their desire to maintain the arrangement with the Big Ten. "Strong relations between the faculty people of the Big Ten and the Pacific Coast Conference had been formed over the years so Tom had real opposition with these people. The athletic directors knew it wouldn't pass the faculty representatives."[7] In addition to faculty desire to maintain the Big Ten relationship and its concerns over scheduling athletic events with schools of similar academic standards, concerns over nondiscriminatory policies also entered into faculty thinking. Though UC policy exempted the Rose Bowl from scheduling limitations, faculty sentiment generally aligned with that of the students in rejecting segregated athletics. Faculty on AAWU campuses noted with approval that within six months after UC publicized its policy prohibiting participation in segregated athletics, many Big Ten schools had initiated similar policies. "We believe this to be a desirable practice since any question of the suitability and acceptability of an opponent for scheduling from the discrimination standpoint will be determined at the time it is proposed to enter into a contractual relationship."[8] Thus, faculty accepted that segregation was inseparable from football when it included segregationists.

The fervor with which Tom Hamilton courted the University of Alabama suggests that he failed to grasp the depth of faculty consciousness on the issue of race. Even more apparent was Hamilton's lack of support from the Tournament of Roses Association to end the relationship with the Big Ten. According to Newell, "the most serious opposition to Tom's proposal [was] the Rose Bowl Committee people."[9] Whether officials rejected aligning the Tournament of Roses Association with southern segregation or merely desired to maintain historic ties with the Midwest and the Big Ten is unclear. Hamilton's efforts made him no enemies, however. He remained in his position until 1971, healing the deep rifts from the PCC rupture by shepherding the AAWU's transition into the Pac-8 in 1968 (it became the present-day Pac-10 in 1979). Additionally, the Big Ten reconsidered its position on the Rose Bowl. The selection of Minnesota to play in the 1962 Rose Bowl game was appropriate considering the Golden Gophers would cast the deciding vote in early January 1962 to renew the Big Ten's contract with the Rose Bowl. Minnesota's faculty opposition to the Rose Bowl never achieved the same enthusiasm as at Ohio State. Minnesota faculty only opposed the provision mandating that the conference champion appear, thus removing by contractual obligation the right of the faculty to determine if their school should go to Pasadena. Gopher supporters had used exactly that logic in justifying their opposition to the Rose Bowl contract in 1959 and 1960 and their acceptance of an invitation on an individual basis for the 1961 and 1962 games. Thus, when the AAWU offered the Big Ten a new contract in January 1962 that demanded only that the Big Ten send a "representative team" but not necessarily the conference champion, Minnesota quickly abandoned the dissidents, and the measure passed 6-4.[10]

Forty-five years after the renewal of the contract, Ohio State's Dick Armitage good-naturedly declared of Minnesota's faculty, "They betrayed us."[11] As a result, New Year's Day 1962 saw Minnesota appear in the Rose Bowl, soundly defeating UCLA in what was, by all accounts, a boring game. Though the game itself was unmemorable, the issues that emerged in the selection process persisted. They did so because they transcended the game, illustrating football's role as a venue in which Americans could sift and assimilate the pressing issues that defined the Republic. With the end of World War II, American society faced a host of circumstances that helped spawn an age of insecurity and anxiety. Foremost among those circumstances was the Cold War confrontation with the Soviets that constantly colored the period. Collectively accepting that the Soviet Union stalked their every move and threatened their every breath, Americans embraced a national culture that called forth a reflexive anticommunism for the better part of two decades. As a result, social, cultural, and political elites effectively used football to browbeat, harass, and intimidate those who challenged an American status quo merely by invoking its relationship to anticommunism and the Cold War. The culture of the Cold War was defined by more than its anticommunism, however. Oftentimes, it ignored explicit references to communism at all, speaking instead to the American anxiety that was the hallmark of the age. Concerned that their materialism might indeed have made them "soft," wary that segregation was a cancerous lesion upon the body of the Republic, and anxious that policies and practices aimed at ensuring consensus were in fact draining the national soul, Americans thirsted for a culture of validation. They found this validation in cultural forms that represented values and characteristics evocative of the American experience and national distinctiveness. Cold War culture endorsed all that Americans felt separated them from the Soviets, because it served to reassure Americans in the face of their anxiety that the fruits of the democratic free-enterprise system were superior to anything harvested from collective totalitarianism.

College football ably filled this function for many Americans during the Cold War era. The game contained enough components of force, violence, and deprivation to leave no doubts about its masculinity. Only the strongest, bravest, and most courageous could succeed in the manly world of football. Just as important, it was distinctly American, with only the vaguest similarities to its ancestral forebears played elsewhere. Better still, unlike baseball, no one else played the game, let alone mastered it, intensifying its national distinctiveness. The elevation of football as a form of Cold War culture, however, did not ensure a single narrative interpretation of the game. Indeed, the game's flexibility and malleability allowed it to achieve its soaring cultural prominence. Supporters and critics each could attach the most hyperbolic rhetoric to the game, linking it to grave matters of national concern. Attached as it was to the world of academia, college football easily found itself intertwined in the university's ever-complicated role in postwar society.

At Ohio State, football served as a proxy in the debate over the university's Cold War priorities. Faculty critics hoped to magnify the depth of their concerns in focusing on something as culturally resonant as football, while community supporters of the Buckeyes used the language of toughness and character development to champion what they saw as football's rightful place on campus. At Alabama and LSU, explicit connections between football and the Cold War gave way to more subtle linkages between football, race, and cultural values. At LSU, insistence on segregation threatened to exclude southerners from a national sporting culture that esteemed the values of football. If they insisted on segregated play as the rest of the college football world embraced integration, southern teams could hardly enjoy the cultural validation that football conveyed when they chose to absent themselves from the game as it was played by everyone else.

Alabama partisans, too, understood the relationship between football, regional practices, and cultural values. Willing to play integrated teams as a way to create community cohesion and thus embolden segregationist resistance, Alabama fans saw all that was good and right with southern society in their football team. National condemnation over segregation, however, threatened to overshadow Alabama's football success, identifying the football team as a lightening rod for northern hostility. Thus, what had been accepted as a cultural force in the South to bolster segregation was now to be used as a cultural weapon outside the South to condemn segregation. Cold War culture existed as a manifestation of Americans' need for an evocation of shared values and national distinctiveness. At both Alabama and LSU, segregation deprived southerners of translating the regional validation they received from football into the larger national culture.

Finally, at UCLA, football enjoyed a commonality to the undergraduate experience, and students readily accepted the game as a purveyor of laudable national values. As a result, students understood football as a campus cultural touchstone through which to interpret events both on and off campus. Campus activists used the game as a rallying point to oppose restrictions in American life that students increasingly saw as antithetical to the Republic's postwar aspirations and proclamations. Thus, on each campus, faculty, students, administrators, and others used, interpreted, or manipulated football in different ways and often to contrary ends—but in each instance flowed an unchanging, unchallenged assumption about football's role in American culture as a receptacle of values and characteristics that not only were esteemed universally but also deemed essential to a distinct American way of life.

The postwar consensus that created in Americans a reflexive anticommunism and a cultural yearning for distinct American values, however, began to erode by the late 1960s. Opposition to the war in Vietnam and the politics of identity broke down domestic Cold War orthodoxy. This opposition to the conformity and consensus of the Cold War eroded traditional notions of deference, challenged existing institutions, and generally marked an opposition to authority. It also marked the end of postwar football's uncontested cultural standing. Although Americans continued to embrace the game in increasing numbers, so that football soon surpassed baseball as America's sporting obsession, the game lost its universal cultural significance as a purveyor of values crucial to the defense of the Republic. Americans who still attached that significance to the game increasingly were defined by their location on the political right. They viewed football as antithetical not only to the Soviets abroad but to the effete demonstrators, the pinkish college radicals, and the limp-wristed of all shades at home as well. When country musician Merle Haggard recorded his 1969 conservative anthem "Okie from Muskogee," he noted that, at least in Muskogee, Oklahoma, "football's still the roughest thing on campus, and kids here still respect the college dean." Thus, as Americans ceased to battle their postwar anxieties to battle each other instead, football's meaning emerged as part of that contestation.

Few commentators made such linkages between football and the political upheaval of the late 1960s more explicit than Republican Vice President Spiro Agnew. Addressing a 1971 college football awards ceremony, Agnew identified football as a bastion of "the early American ethic" against "the purveyors of a New Morality and a New Politics" who positioned themselves on the left. So dangerous was football to the forces then attempting to destroy the Republic, according to Agnew, "that in the New Left weekly rating of the people's enemies, the institution known as Football Coach ranks high in the top ten—not far behind the Joint Chiefs of Staff, General

Motors, the CIA, the FBI, John Wayne, and yours truly." In linking industry and government officials with football coaches, Agnew explicitly identified football's critics as threats to the existing cultural order. "There are those in the cadre of cultural revolution who consider us simply two peas in a common cultural pod." Agnew laid such a cultural assault on football at the feet of the Ivy League, the favorite whipping boy of football's supporters since the 1950s. Referring to the "Eastern Establishment schools," the vice president claimed that their lusty embrace of "the New Culture" ignored the historic relationship between football and uplifting American cultural values. This inversion of logic, according to Agnew, saw football as a cultural force that did not uplift the American spirit and character but as one that "reflect[ed] the surviving traces of cultural and political atavism."[12]

Agnew was not alone in linking Ivy League opposition to football with political identity and shifting American cultural values. One columnist during the period humorously declared that the only thing more scandalous than Ivy League athletic success was if someone "caught the faculty voting Republican."[13] So thoroughly had football become associated with specific political values, one writer declared in 1969 that "baseball represent[ed] the leftward or liberal tendency . . . and football represent[ed] the rightward or authoritarian tendency," noting that 1968 Democratic presidential candidate Eugene McCarthy embraced the former game while Agnew embraced the latter.[14] Although the notion that the game of football served as an accurate indicator of partisan political identity is an exaggeration, clearly, the universal interpretation of the game as an unmitigated cultural asset had ended. Postwar football's utility was over.

Notes

Introduction

1. John D. McCollum, *Pac-10 Football: The Rose Bowl Conference* (Seattle: Writing Works, 1982), 185–86; "Tan Quarterbacks a First in Bowl," *Los Angeles Sentinel*, December 28, 1961, p. 10A; "Robinson to Ride in Rose Parade," *Los Angeles Sentinel*, December 14, 1961, p. 3A.

2. The notion of football as a mechanism with multiple cultural applications mirrors what Michael Oriard has already persuasively argued about the game's multiple meanings. Noting that observers of the game's "cultural text" read it as both work and play, order and chaos, teamwork and individualism, Oriard labeled such discussions of the game as part of a "multivocal cultural conversation." Oriard limited the game's "multivocality" to the meaning observers took from the game itself, whereas I am arguing that such multivocality extended to the use observers put the game to explain other aspects of life, away from the game; Michael Oriard, *Reading Football: How the Popular Press Created an American Spectacle* (Chapel Hill: University of North Carolina Press, 1993).

3. To the best of my knowledge, no single version of Coleman's statement has survived. The sections that are quoted in the text are pieced together from two sources, "What Is Football?" *Daily Reveille*, October 11, 1961, p. 8; and Willie Morris, *The Courting of Marcus Dupree* (New York: Dell, 1983), 109–10.

4. Peter Filene, "Cold War Culture Doesn't Say It All," in *Rethinking Cold War Culture*, ed. Peter J. Kuznick and James Gilbert, 156–74 (Washington, DC: Smithsonian Institution Press, 2001).

5. Randy Roberts and James Olson, *Winning Is the Only Thing: Sports in America since 1945* (Baltimore, MD: Johns Hopkins University Press, 1989); Richard O. Davies, *America's Obsession: Sports and Society since 1945* (Fort Worth, TX: Harcourt Brace, 1994); Murray Sperber, *Onward to Victory: The Crises That Shaped College Sports* (New York: Henry Holt, 1998). One work that does place sport specifically within the context of the Cold War period is Thomas Domer's dissertation, "Sport in Cold War America, 1953–1963." Though Domer's work is more interested in sports as a political and diplomatic tool, he examines many of the forces that shaped sports as a national cultural form. As a result, he goes farther than any other scholar in illustrating how sport achieved a dominant cultural resonance as a result of the Cold War and reveals how politicians' attempts at using sport as a policy tool implicitly elevated its cultural prominence. Sadly, Domer's work remains unpublished and virtually unknown to scholars of the period; Thomas Michael Domer, "Sport in Cold War America, 1953–1963: The Diplomatic and

Political Use of Sport in the Eisenhower and Kennedy Administrations" (PhD diss., University of Wisconsin-Milwaukee, 1976). Another work that adequately reveals the cultural pressures of the Cold War upon domestic sporting practices but whose focus also lies elsewhere is Joseph Turrini, "'It Was Communism versus the Free World': The USA-USSR Dual Track Meet Series and the Development of Track and Field in the United States, 1958–1985," *Journal of Sport History* 28, no. 3 (2001): 427–71. Recently, younger scholars have begun mining the relationship between sports and postwar culture; see Russell E. Crawford, "Consensus All-American: Sports and the Promotion of the American Way of Life during the Cold War, 1946–1965" (PhD diss., University of Nebraska, 2004).

6. Roberts and Olson, *Winning Is the Only Thing*, xii; a sentiment Davies echoes almost identically by claiming that following the war, sport emerged as "a vital part in the lives of the American people"; Davies, *America's Obsession*, x.

7. Roberts and Olson as well as Sperber argue this point most forcefully. It is also addressed in more complex fashion by Christopher Lasch, *The Culture of Narcissism: American Life in an Age of Diminishing Expectations* (New York: W. W. Norton, 1978), 100–24.

8. Stephen J. Whitfield, *The Culture of the Cold War* (Baltimore, MD: Johns Hopkins University Press, 1991); Tom Engelhardt, *The End of Victory Culture: Cold War America and the Disillusioning of a Generation* (New York: Basic Books, 1995); Andrew Hurley, *Diners, Bowling Alleys, and Trailer Parks: Chasing the American Dream in the Postwar Consumer Culture* (New York: Basic Books, 2001); Kuznick and Gilbert, eds., *Rethinking Cold War Culture*. Both Paul Boyer and Margot Henriksen authoritatively examine the culture of anxiety created by the atomic age; see Paul Boyer, *By the Bomb's Early Light: American Thought and Culture at the Dawn of the Atomic Age* (New York: Knopf, 1985); and Margot Henriksen, *Dr. Strangelove's America: Society and Culture in the Atomic Age* (Berkeley: University of California Press, 1997). Recent scholars of masculinity have also shied away from examining any relationship between sports and the Cold War; E. Anthony Rotundo, *American Manhood: Transformations of Masculinity from the Revolution to the Modern Era* (New York: Basic Books, 1993) fails to carry his discussion of sports into the post–World War II period while James Gilbert, *Men in the Middle: Masculinity in the 1950s* (Chicago: University of Chicago Press, 2005) ignores sports entirely. On the effects of Cold War culture to the 1960s, see Todd Gitlin, *The Sixties: Years of Hope, Days of Rage* (Toronto: Bantam Books, 1987); and Terry Anderson, *The Movement and the Sixties: Protest in American from Greensboro to Wounded Knee* (New York: Oxford University Press, 1995), specifically the introduction, "Spawning Ground: Cold War Culture." Though Hurley explicitly examines a sporting activity in bowling, he identifies it more as a form of commercialized leisure devoid of specific values than as a sporting activity. Its role in American culture speaks more to postwar anxieties over gentrification, the continued search for social respectability, and a socially acceptable locale for female interaction. As a result, while the consumption of bowling is shaped by domestic concerns resulting from the affluence and anxieties of the postwar period, it is not distinct from other forms of postwar consumer culture.

Prologue

1. "Notables Thrill to Gridiron Show," *New York Times*, November 30, 1941, p. S1; Lars Anderson, *The All Americans* (New York: St. Martins' Press, 2004), 99–100, 106–7.

2. Wanda Ellen Wakefield, *Playing to Win: Sports and the American Military, 1898–1945* (New York: SUNY Press, 1997), 36; on MacArthur and Army football specifically, see James Blackwell, *On Brave Army Team: The Cheating Scandal That Rocked the Nation: West Point, 1951* (New York: Ballantine Books, 1996), 100–101.

3. Wakefield, *Playing to Win*, 90.

4. Robert W. Peterson, *Pigskin: The Early Years of Pro Football* (New York: Oxford University Press, 1997), 139.

5. Murray Sperber, *Onward to Victory*, 97, 248; John Sayle Watterson, *College Football: History, Spectacle, Controversy* (Baltimore, MD: Johns Hopkins University Press, 2000), 201–4.

6. Letter from Robert Eichelberger, commanding general, 1st Army Corps, to Colonel Earl Blaik, July 7, 1942, found in Earl H. Blaik, *The Red Blaik Story* (New York: Arlington House, 1974), 180–81.

7. Sperber, *Onward to Victory*, 133.

8. Donald W. Rominger Jr., "From Playing Field to Battleground: The United States Navy V-5 Preflight Program in World War II," *Journal of Sport History* (Winter 1985): 252–64; Sperber, *Onward to Victory*, 133–34.

9. Sperber, *Onward to Victory*, 137.

10. Rominger, "From Playing Field to Battleground."

11. Wakefield, *Playing to Win*, 84, 180 (fn. 39).

12. Wakefield, *Playing to Win*, 89, 100. Notre Dame, citing its long-standing opposition to bowl games during this period, politely declined the military's invitation.

13. Wakefield, *Playing to Win*, 89.

14. Donald J. Mrozek, "The Interplay of Metaphor and Practice in the U.S. Defense Establishment's Use of Sport, 1940–1950," *Journal of American Culture* 7, no. 1–2 (1984): 54–59.

15. Rominger, "From Playing Field to Battleground"; Harry Alexander Scott, *Competitive Sports in Schools and Colleges* (New York: Harper & Bros., 1951), 67–69.

16. Mrozek, "The Interplay of Metaphor and Practice"; Rominger, "From Playing Field to Battleground."

17. Watterson, *College Football*, 202; Rominger, "From Playing Field to Battleground." Wakefield also notes the tweaking of some rules during World War I for the same purposes, see *Playing to Win*, 25–26.

18. Postwar descriptions of Hamilton almost never failed to mention his role in "saving" football. See "Panthers Stepping Up Western Grid Relations," n.d.; "AAWU Off to Flying Start," 7/1/59; "Hamilton's Gambit West May Be Good for College Grid," n.d., all found in Clippings File, TJH. (See list of archival material sources in the bibliography.)

19. Rominger, "From Playing Field to Battleground"; Scott, *Competitive Sports in Schools and Colleges*, 69–70.

20. Scott, *Competitive Sports in Schools and Colleges*, 69–70.

21. Sperber, *Onward to Victory*, 122.

22. Watterson, *College Football*, 202; Sperber, *Onward to Victory*, 122, 170. It is unclear if Watterson's and Sperber's figures include all college programs or only NCAA member programs. Figures from NCAA football guides and member rosters suggest a growth of football slightly less impressive. According to Ellen Summers, the organization's librarian, 156 schools fielded teams in 1945, with 242 schools doing so by 1950; e-mail from Ellen L. Summers to author, March 8, 2005, in the author's possession.

23. Donald S. Andrews, "The GI Bill and College Football," *Journal of Physical Education, Recreation, and Dance* (September 1955): 23–26; Francis Wallace, "Football's Black Market," *Saturday Evening Post* (November 9, 1946): 20–21, 145; Watterson, *College Football*, 202–3; Sperber, *Onward to Victory*, 169; Stanley Frank, "Saturday Afternoon Meat Grinders," *Collier's* (October 1, 1949): 54–59; Allen Barra, *The Last Coach: A Life of Paul "Bear" Bryant* (New York: W. W. Norton, 2005), 95. For an anecdotal account of how players received cash payments at one school, see Jim Dent, *The Undefeated: The Oklahoma Sooners and the Greatest Winning Streak in College Football History* (New York: St. Martin's Press, 2001).

24. Andrews, "The GI Bill and College Football." For the GI Bill and its effect on higher education independent of college football, see Milton Greenberg, *The GI Bill: The Law That Changed America* (New York: Lickle, 1997); Milton Greenberg, "How the GI Bill Changed Higher Education," *The Chronicle for Higher Education*, June 18, 2004, pp. B9–B11; Keith Olson, *The GI Bill, the Veterans and the Colleges* (Lexington: University of Kentucky Press, 1974).

25. Barra, *The Last Coach*, 95.

26. Andrews, "The GI Bill and College Football." Though the Southeastern Conference would later be identified with some of the worst recruiting habits during the period, it actually made one of the few attempts to rein in the frenzy by demanding players return to wherever they played prior to the war. However, public opinion interpreted such a restriction as an unfair imposition on veterans, and the SEC rescinded the rule; Melvin Henry Gruensfelder, "A History of the Origin and Development of the Southeastern Conference" (MS thesis, University of Illinois, 1964), 195–97.

27. Marc Edward Goulden, "From Country Club to Rat Race: A Social History of College Students, 1920–1960" (PhD diss., University of Wisconsin, 1995), 532–39; Greenberg, *GI Bill*, 44; Andrews, "The GI Bill and College Football." Andrews contends that the caliber of play improved such that fans began expecting that level after the veterans left, thus driving the postwar recruiting orgy. However, if that had been the case, fans would have quickly drifted to the professional game with its increased skill level. The fact that the pro game did not rise in popularity until more than a decade later suggests something else was at work.

28. "An Empire Emerges," *Lexington Herald-Leader*, December 12, 2002, http://www.kentucky.com/mld/kentucky/sports/colleges/university_of_kentucky/4725861 (accessed January 27, 2005).

29. Greenberg, *GI Bill*, 50–51.

30. John A. Perkins, *Plain Talk from a Campus* (Newark, NJ: University of Delaware, 1959), 163; Sperber, *Onward to Victory*, 384–85, 388.

31. R. C. Lewontin, "The Cold War and the Transformation of the Academy," in *The Cold War and the University: Toward an Intellectual History of the Postwar Years*, ed. Noam Chomsky et al., 7, 21 (New York: New Press, 1998).

32. John R. Thelin, *A History of American Higher Education* (Baltimore, MD: Johns Hopkins University Press, 2004), 278, 292. Thelin cites Clark Kerr's figures on the distribution of federal monies; Clark Kerr, *The Uses of the University* (Cambridge, MA: Harvard University Press, 1995).

33. Rebecca Lowen, *Creating the Cold War University: The Transformation of Stanford* (Berkeley: University of California Press, 1997), 150–57.

34. Thelin, *A History of American Higher Education*, 278–79; John R. Thelin, *Games Colleges Play: Scandal and Reform in Intercollegiate Athletics* (Baltimore, MD: Johns Hopkins University Press, 1994), 175–76. See also Lowen, *Creating the Cold War University*, on the shell game of academic funds within the university enterprise.

Chapter 1. Pasadena: The Terms of Postwar Football

Comment by Edwin Server from "Tournament of Roses—Rose Bowl Game: Our First 70 Years," 1961 folder (no Box #), TRC.

1. "Big Nine-Coast Rose Bowl Tie-up Results in Widespread Criticism," *New York Times*, November 21, 1946, p. 52;"Sports Editors Comment on Big 9–Rose Bowl Tie," *Pasadena Star News*, November 21, 1946, p. 20; see also Rube Samuelson, *The Rose Bowl Game* (Garden City, NY: Doubleday, 1951), 210–15.

2. Domer, "Sport in Cold War America, 1953–1963," 20.

3. Adam J. Zweiback, "The 21 Turncoat GIs: Nonrepatriates and the Political Culture of the Korean War," *Historian* 60, no. 2 (Winter 1988): 345–62; Tom Engelhardt, *The End of Victory Culture*, 65.

4. James B. Gilbert, *Cycle of Outrage: America's Reaction to the Juvenile Delinquent in the 1950s* (New York: Oxford University Press), 1986; on Haley and *Blackboard Jungle*, see Jim Dawson, *Rock around the Clock: The Record That Started the Rock Revolution* (Milwaukee: Hal Leonard, 2005); and James Miller, *Flowers in the Dustbin: The Rise of Rock and Roll, 1947–1977* (New York: Simon & Schuster, 1999), 87–94.

5. Domer, "Sport in Cold War America," 108–9; Robert L. Griswold, "The 'Flabby American,' the Body, and the Cold War," in *A Shared Experience: Men, Women, and the History of Gender*, ed. Laura McCall and Donald Yacayvone, 323–48 (New York: New York University Press, 1998); Hubert H. Humphrey, "A Five-Point Fitness Program," *Journal of Health, Physical Education, and Recreation* 33 (October 1962): 21–22, 72–74.

6. Donald J. Mrozek, "The Cult and Ritual of Toughness in Cold War America," in *Rituals and Ceremonies in Pop Culture*, ed. Ray B. Browne, 178–91 (Bowling Green, OH: Bowling Green State University Popular Press, 1980).

7. Mark F. Bernstein, *Football: The Ivy League Origins of an American Obsession* (Philadelphia: University of Pennsylvania Press, 2001), 178.

8. Griswold, "The 'Flabby American.'"

9. "View and Preview," *Daily Tar Heel*, October 8, 1958, p. 2; "Graham Heard by 200,000 in Charlotte Drive," *Atlanta Journal-Constitution*, October 8, 1958, p. 6. Graham's effusive praise of Christ's athletic manliness stopped just short of

anticipating one commentator's facetious reference the following year: "I shall not be surprised when someone comes up with the theory that even Christ played football"; Wade Thompson, "My Crusade against Football," *Nation* (April 11, 1959): 313–16.

10. John F. Kennedy, "The Soft American," *Sports Illustrated* (December 26, 1960): 15–17; selected speeches of John Fitzgerald Kennedy, Kennedy Library online archive, www.jfklibrary.org/speeches.htm (accessed October 18, 2008).

11. Keith Dunnavant, *Coach: The Life of Paul Bear Bryant* (New York: Simon & Schuster, 1996), 100. On the violence and deprivation of water, the most notorious example is Bryant's 1954 Texas A&M team and their preseason camp; Jim Dent, *Junction Boys: How Ten Days in Hell with Bear Bryant Forged a Championship Team* (New York: St. Martin's Press, 2000). Bryant also took such tactics to Alabama; see Tom Stoddard, *Turnaround: The Untold Story of Bear Bryant's First Year at Alabama* (Birmingham, AL: Black Belt Press, 1996). For another coach's use of such tactics, see Dent, *The Undefeated.*

12. "An Unsolicited Tribute," *New York Times*, October 30, 1958, p. 38.

13. Joseph Kaplan, "The Case for Big-Time Football," *Look* (December 12, 1956): 111–18.

14. "What Comrade Big SHOULD See," *Ohio State University Monthly* (September 1959): 1; photo essay in *Life* (November 7, 1955): 33. For a discussion of Khrushchev's 1959 visit to the United States and his itinerary, see Stephen J. Whitfield, "The Road to Rapprochement: Khrushchev's 1959 Visit to America," in *The Other Fifties: Interrogations of Midcentury American Icons*, ed. Joel Formann, 307–32 (Champaign: University of Illinois Press, 1997).

15. Jeffrey L. Meikle, *American Plastic: A Cultural History* (New Brunswick, NJ: Rutgers University Press, 1995), 175. On the link between football and American postwar values, see Fermin Diez, "The Popularity of Sports in America: An Analysis of the Values of Sports and the Role of Media," in *Researching American Culture: A Guide for Student Anthropologists*, ed. Conrad Phillip Kottak, 259–65 (Ann Arbor: University of Michigan Press, 1982). On the role of plastics technology during the period, see Allison Clarke, *Tupperware: The Promise of Plastics in 1950s America* (Washington, D.C.: Smithsonian Institution Press, 1999), pp. 36–42.

16. Marshall Smith and Richard Oulahan Jr., "Football Is Pricing Itself Out of Business," *Life* (October 16, 1950): 60–62.

17. Gene Schoor, *100 Years of Army-Navy Football* (New York: Henry Holt, 1989), 48; Wakefield, *Playing to Win*, 61; William Westmoreland, *A Soldier Reports* (Garden City, NJ: Doubleday, 1976), p. 32. An oral interview Westmoreland gave after the publication of his memoirs has the president saying, "Do something about that damned football team," Rick Atkinson, *The Long Gray Line: From West Point to Vietnam and After—The Turbulent Odyssey of the Class of 1966* (New York: Simon & Schuster, 1989), 79.

18. "Eisenhower Receives Award from Football Hall of Fame Here before 2,000," *New York Times*, October 29, 1958, p. 40.

19. Domer, "Sport in Cold War America," 168, 180.

20. Charles P. Pierce, "Black Sunday," *Sports Illustrated* (November 24, 2003): 56–62.

21. Domer, "Sport in Cold War America," 226–27.

22. E. Culpepper Clark, *The Schoolhouse Door: Segregation's Last Stand at the University of Alabama* (New York: Oxford University Press, 1993), 146; William Doyle, *An American Insurrection: James Meredith and the Battle of Oxford, Mississippi, 1962* (New York: Dell, 2003), 154. The president's words fell on deaf ears, as a riot broke out on campus that resulted in two deaths and the wounding of scores of U.S. marshals.

23. Selected Speeches of John Fitzgerald Kennedy, Kennedy Library online archive, www.jfklibrary.org/speeches.htm (accessed October 18, 2008).

24. "Robert Kennedy Calls Coaches Key to Fitness," *New York Times*, January 12, 1961, p. 34; Griswold, "The 'Flabby American.'"

25. Richard Whittingham, *Rites of Autumn: The Story of College Football* (New York: Free Press, 2001), 246–47; Domer, "Sport and the Cold War," 214–15, 232–33, 246–47, 250; "Byron White Gets Whitaker's Seat on Supreme Court," *New York Times*, March 31, 1962, p. 1.

26. James Talbot Powell, "The Development and Influence of Faculty Representation in the Control of Intercollegiate Sport within the Intercollegiate Conference of Faculty Representatives from Its Inception in January 1895 to July 1963" (PhD diss., University of Illinois, 1964), 233.

27. Extension of Remarks of the Honorable John Sherman Cooper of Kentucky, given July 2, 1960, *Congressional Record*, Appendix, July 5, 1960, pp. A5832–5833.

28. Thelin, *Games Colleges Play*, 109.

29. Thompson, "My Crusade against Football"; Meeting Minutes of the National Football Foundation, April 19, 1961, folder 15, Box #79, UASI.

30. "Tournament of Roses—Rose Bowl Game: Our First 70 Years," 1961 folder (no Box #), TRC.

31. "Men with Missions," *New York Times*, February 28, 1958, p. 24; Advertisement for the National Football Foundation, found in 1958 Official Football Program, p. 38, and Advertisement for the National Football Foundation, found in Oklahoma–Notre Dame Football Program, 30 September 1961, PATH; Extension of Remarks of the Honorable John Sherman Cooper of Kentucky, July 2, 1960, *Congressional Record*, Appendix, July 5, 1960, pp. A5832–5833; "The Foundation and the Hall of Fame;" folder 15, Box #79, UASI.

32. "The Foundation and the Hall of Fame"; Meeting Minutes of the National Football Foundation, April 19, 1961; and January 26, 1961, all found in folder 15, Box #79, UASI. It is unclear whether James accepted the proposal, but as early as 1955, James agreed to use the pages of the magazine for the covert interests of the Central Intelligence Agency in combating Soviet athletic gains and at CIA direction used the resources of the magazine to aid the defection of the 1956 Hungarian Olympic water polo team; see Domer, "Sports in the Cold War," 73–76, 90–96.

33. "Lack of Football Cited as Reason for Communism," *Daily Bruin*, November 7, 1958, p. 1. Paul Tillett, in his 1965 study, "The Social Costs of the Loyalty Programs," also noted the Stern comment; see Victor Navasky, *Naming Names: The Social Costs of McCarthyism* (New York: Viking Press, 1980), 335. Not everyone

took Stern's comments seriously, however; *The Nation* editorialized that they allowed Stern to make "a sufficiently grotesque public ass of himself," "Stern's Law," *Nation* (November 15, 1958): 350–51.

34. Thompson, "My Crusade against Football."

35. Lawrence G. Weiss, "Goldwater and Colorado U," *Nation* (December 8, 1962): 402–4.

36. Watterson, *College Football*, 245–55. Besides Watterson, the following portrayal of the Ivy League draws heavily from Bernstein, *Football*; and John R. Thelin, *The Cultivation of Ivy: A Saga of the College in America* (Cambridge, MA: Schenkman, 1976).

37. "Still Ivied Autumn?" *Newsweek* (October 15, 1956): 75–78.

38. "Festooned with Ivy," *New York Times*, October 23, 1959, p. 37; "The Foot in Football," *New York Times*, October 16, 1959, p. 37; "Peering through Ivy," *New York Times*, May 3, 1961, p. 47; "A Novel Idea," *New York Times*, May 24, 1962, p. 43; letter from J. W. Blackwell to Jack Fullen, December 4, 1961, "Rose Bowl, 1962," 3/i/28, NGF.

39. The McCarthy quote can be found in David Halberstam, *The Fifties* (New York: Fawcett Columbine Books, 1993), 54; on the relationship between the Cold War and hostility towards homosexuals, see John D'Emilio, *Sexual Politics, Sexual Communities: The Making of a Homosexual Community in the United States, 1940–1970* (Chicago: University of Chicago Press, 1983) and David K. Johnson, *The Lavender Scare: The Cold War Persecution of Gays and Lesbians in the Federal Government* (Chicago: University of Chicago Press, 2004); see also Robert Dean, *Imperial Brotherhood: Gender and the Making of Cold War Foreign Policy* (Boston: University of Massachusetts Press, 2001).

40. William F. Buckley Jr., *God and Man at Yale: The Superstitions of Academic Freedom* (Chicago: Regnery Press, 1951); "To Fight Corruption," *New York Times*, January 5, 1952, p. 10.

41. "But It Goes beyond Four Sport Seasons," *Mobile Press Register*, December 14, 1959, p. 4A.

42. Thelin, *Games Colleges Play*, p. 200.

43. Stanley Cohen, *The Game They Played* (New York: Farrar, Strauss, & Giroux, 1977); Charles S. Rosen, *The Scandals of '51: How Gamblers Almost Killed College Basketball* (New York: Seven Stories Press, 1999); Sperber, *Onward to Victory*, 285–343. The Daley quote is found in Sperber, *Onward to Victory*, 302.

44. Joan Gosnell, "Kickoffs and Kickbacks: The 1951 Football Scandal at William and Mary" (MA thesis, College of William and Mary, 1990), 55–60; Watterson, *College Football*, 219–27.

45. Blackwell, *On Brave Old Army Team*; Frank Deford, "Code Breakers," *Sports Illustrated* (November 13, 2000): 82–98; Sperber, *Onward to Victory*, 344–57.

46. Blackwell, *On Brave Old Army Team*, 361; "West Point Lapse Is Linked to Trend," *New York Times*, January 15, 1952, p. 16.

47. Deford, "Code Breakers." Deford's article gives this individual the pseudonym Ned Braun. However, Blackwell, who came to press two years before Deford, openly identifies the individual as Jim Pfautz.

48. "Sports of the Times," *New York Times*, October 31, 1952, p. 35.

49. Edward Pessen, *Losing Our Souls: The American Experience in the Cold War* (Chicago: Ivan R. Dee, 1993), 196. The abuses of the Cold War are well documented; for a sampling, in addition to Pessen, see David Caute, *The Great Fear: The Anticommunist Purge under Truman and Eisenhower* (New York: Simon & Schuster, 1979); Whitfield, *The Culture of the Cold War;* Engelhardt, *The End of Victory Culture;* and Navasky, *Naming Names*.

50. Leo Cherne, "How to Spot a Communist," *Look* (March 4, 1947): 21–25; Pessen, *Losing Our Souls*, 130.

51. Anthony W. James, "Defenders of Tradition: College Social Fraternities, Race and Gender, 1945–1980" (PhD diss., University of Mississippi, 1998), 82.

52. "Fraternities Help Curb Reds, Goldwater Says," *New York Times*, November 27, 1960, p. 85.

53. Testimony of Reed Harris, March 4, 1953, Hearings before the Permanent Subcommittee on Investigations of the Committee on Government Operations (Washington, DC: U.S. Government Printing Office, 1953), 365, 446; David Oshinsky, *A Conspiracy So Immense: The World of Joe McCarthy* (New York: Free Press), 1983, 274–76.

54. Kaplan, "The Case for Big-Time Football," 111–18.

55. "The Foundation and the Hall of Fame," folder 15, Box #79, UASI.

56. Kaplan, "The Case for Big-Time Football."

57. Joseph Kaplan, "Clean House or Else," *Look* (December 9, 1958): 33–38.

58. Kaplan, "The Case for Big-Time Football." Though Conant stressed the value of competition, he was no friend of commercialized football. Chester LaRoche identified him as one of the game's—and by extension, the Republic's—enemies. As president of Harvard, he was one of the original signatories of the Ivy Group Agreement, forever restraining the influence of commercialized football among the Ivy League schools. See Sperber, *Onward to Victory*, 455–56, and Watterson, *College Football*, 203–4, 250–51.

59. Kaplan, "Clean House or Else."

60. Godfrey Hodgson, *America in Our Time: From World War II to Nixon, What Happened and Why* (New York: Knopf, 1978), 65–98, remains the definitive source on the liberal consensus. The term itself was coined by John Higham, "The Cult of 'American Consensus': Homogenizing Our History," *Commentary*, 27 (January 1959): 93–100. See also Robert M. Collins, "Growth Liberalism in the Sixties: Great Societies at Home and Grand Designs Abroad," in *The Sixties: From Memory to History*, ed. David Farber, 11–44 (Chapel Hill: University of North Carolina Press, 1994).

61. C. Wright Mills, *White Collar: The American Middle Classes* (New York: Oxford University Press), 1951; C. Wright Mills, *The Power Elite* (New York: Oxford University Press), 1956; Arthur Miller, *Death of a Salesman* (New York: Viking Press), 1949; David Riesman, with Reuel Denney and Nathan Glazer, *The Lonely Crowd: A Study of the Changing American Character* (New Haven, CT: Yale University Press), 1950; William H. Whyte, *The Organization Man* (New York: Simon & Schuster), 1956. The significance of Mills's and Miller's work is authoritatively discussed in Halberstam's *The Fifties*, and Riesman is thoroughly examined in Gilbert, *Men in the Middle*.

62. John Morton Blum, *V Was for Victory: Politics and American Culture during World War II* (New York: Harcourt, 1976), 132; for a broader discussion of the economic effects of the war and its legacy to Cold War industry and education, see pp. 117–46; William H. Chafe, *The Unfinished Journey: America since World War II*, 4th ed. (New York: Oxford University Press, 1999), 8, 112–17; Norman L. Rosenberg and Emily S. Rosenberg, *In Our Times: America since World War II*, 5th ed. (Englewood Cliffs, NJ: Prentice Hall, 1995), 65–69, 75–77.

63. David Riesman and Reuel Denney, "Football in America: A Study in Culture Diffusion," *American Quarterly* 3 (1951): 309–25.

64. Smith and Oulahan, "Football Is Pricing Itself Out of Business."

65. Watterson, *College Football*, 242; "33 Drop Football Teams," *New York Times*, August 31, 1951, p. 27; Thelin, *Games Colleges Play*, 169; Smith and Oulahan, "Football Is Pricing Itself Out of Business." See also Kristine Setting Clark, *Undefeated, Untied, and Uninvited: A Documentary of the 1951 University of San Francisco Dons Football Team* (Irvine, CA: Griffin, 2002) for a collection of documents addressing USF's decision to drop football.

66. Riesman and Denney, "Football in America."

67. Marshall Smith, "Sad News from the Campus: Nobody Loves the Football Hero Now," *Life* (November 11, 1957): 149–60.

68. Russell E. Crawford, "Consensus All-American," 58–65.

69. Ronald A. Smith, *Play-by-Play: Radio, Television, and Big-Time College Sport* (Baltimore, MD: Johns Hopkins University Press, 2001), 99.

70. Smith, "Sad News from the Campus."

71. Fred Russell, "Pigskin Preview," *Saturday Evening Post* (September 17, 1949): 30–31, 127–32.

72. Gerald R. Gems, *For Pride, Patriarchy, and Profit: Football and the Incorporation of American Cultural Values* (Lanham, MD: Scarecrow Press, 2000), 100.

73. Frank, "Saturday Afternoon Meat Grinders."

74. Russell, "Pigskin Preview."

75. Smith, "Sad News from the Campus."

76. Roger Kahn, "Halfbacks Carry the Mortgage," *Nation* (December 22, 1956): 539–41; Smith, "Sad News from the Campus." Roberts and Olson, *Winning Is the Only Thing*, 54, claim that football "def[ied] the major organizational trends in corporate America," explicitly rejecting "the control of anonymous corporate managers—'organization men' in gray flannel suits." However, their analysis only concerns professional football and focuses only on management, ignoring the effects on players. By arguing that the setting for professional sports during this period "more closely resembled the Robber Baron mold of the late 1800s than the corporate management 1950s," Roberts and Olson imply that the professional model existed outside the prevailing contemporary cultural trends.

77. Watterson, *College Football*, 153–76, 185–86; see also Gruensfelder, "A History of the Origin and Development of the Southeastern Conference," 65–67; Christopher J. Walsh, *Where Football Is King: A History of the SEC* (Lanham, MD: Taylor Trade, 2006), 10–14; and Bert Randolph Sugar, ed., *The SEC: A Pictorial History of Southeastern Conference Football* (Indianapolis: Bobbs-Merrill, 1979), unpaginated preface. Murray Sperber contends that both the Southern and Southeastern con-

ferences engaged in subsidization to address their status as "two of the weakest conferences . . . to gain a recruiting advantage over the other big-time football powers"; Sperber, *Onward to Victory*, 93–94. The remaining members of the Southern Conference continued to grapple with the question of subsidization after the breakaway of the SEC. In 1935, the conference tepidly embraced the reforms of Frank Porter Graham, president of the University of North Carolina, which advocated an outright ban on player compensation and proselytizing. The resulting furor not only almost cost Graham his job but ultimately caused the conference to repudiate the entire attempt at reform in December 1937; see Richard Stone, "The Graham Plan of 1935: An Aborted Crusade to De-emphasize College Athletics," *North Carolina Historical Review* 64, no. 3 (1987): 274–93.

78. The Carnegie Report is discussed in Watterson, *College Football*, 158–76; and Thelin, *Games Colleges Play*, 13–34; the Tunis Report data is found as an appendix in Watterson, *College Football*, 403–5; the SEC's embrace of such practices is discussed uncritically in Walsh, *Where Football Is King*, 11–15.

79. On the rising costs and facilities of the time, see "Colleges Concede Evils in Athletics," *New York Times*, March 23, 1951, p. 23; Smith and Oulahan, "Football Is Pricing Itself Out of Business"; on the role of nonprofit foundations at the University of Kentucky, see *Thelin, Games Colleges Play*, 116–24; and at Michigan State University, see Beth J. Shapiro, "John Hannah and the Growth of Big-Time Intercollegiate Athletics at Michigan State University," *Journal of Sport History*, 10 (1983): 26–40.

80. Kahn, "Halfbacks Carry the Mortgage."

81. Stanley, "Saturday Afternoon Meat Grinders," 54–59.

82. Sperber, *Onward to Victory*, 172. The SEC openly acknowledged that it provided inducements but fairly accurately claimed that such practices were the only way to compete with the jobs programs of the Big Ten and the PCC. With most SEC schools located in rural areas of the already impoverished South, local economies simply could not provide enough jobs on a comparable level of western and midwestern towns and cities; Gruensfelder, "A History of the . . . SEC," 97–98.

83. Watterson, *College Football*, 403–5.

84. On the organization of the two conferences, see Thelin, *Games Colleges Play*, 128–54, and Powell, "The Development and Influence of Faculty Representation"; on the jobs programs, see Watterson, *College Football*, 186–87; Sperber, *Onward to Victory*, 181–83; Mervin D. Hyman and Gordon S. White Jr., *Big Ten Football: Its Life and Times, Great Coaches, Players, and Games* (New York: Macmillan, 1977), 35–44. Other conferences, such as the Big Eight and the SEC, also claimed faculty control, but in those conferences, it implied merely a voting majority for the faculty on committees that included administrators, alumni, and students; Gruensfelder, "A History of the Origin and Development," 22, 46–47.

85. "Big Nine-Coast Rose Bowl Tie-Up Results in Widespread Criticism," *New York Times*, November 21, 1946, p. 52; Sperber, *Onward to Victory*, 172–73; Samuelson, *The Rose Bowl Game*, 211; "Illinois Now Hopes to Play Bowl Game," and "Thorns among Roses," *New York Times*, November 21, 1946, p. 52; Samuelson also noted that southern schools "were probably using Rose Bowl profits to promote

practices inconsistent with the lofty 'principles' of 'purists,'" Samuelson, *The Rose Bowl Game*, 210–11.

86. Samuelson, *The Rose Bowl Game*, pp. 213–14.

87. "Sports Editors Comment on Big 9–Rose Bowl Tie," *Pasadena Star News*, November 21, 1946, p. 20; Samuelson, *The Rose Bowl Game*, 213–14.

Chapter 2. Columbus: Struggling for the Soul of the Cold War University

Quoted in Rick Hamlin, *Tournament of Roses: A One Hundred Year Celebration* (New York: McGraw-Hill, 1988), 220.

1. "The White Resolution: A Legislative Check," Intercollegiate Conference Newsletter, October 26, 1961, Intercollegiate Conference, 1960–61 (3/i/18) NGF; Powell, "The Development and Influence of Faculty Representation," 33.

2. Powell, "The Development and Influence of Faculty Representation," 29; Hyman and White, *Big Ten Football*, 24–27.

3. Sperber, *Onward to Victory*, 172–73; "Rose Bowl 'Freeze-Out' of Army Causes Wave of Protest on Coast," *New York Times*, November 22, 1946, p. 22.

4. Powell, "The Development and Influence of Faculty Representation," 53, 114–15.

5. "Big Nine Signs Rose Bowl Pact," *Pasadena Star News*, November 20, 1947, p. 1; Powell, "The Development and Influence of Faculty Representation," 59–60; Memo from K. L. Wilson and W. R. Reed to Rose Bowl Interim and Negotiating Committees, October 29, 1958, "Rose Bowl 1958–60," file 10, Box #4, FCIA.

6. "Rose Bowl 'Freeze-Out' of Army Causes Wave of Protest on Coast," *New York Times*, November 22, 1946, p. 37; "Missing in Action," *Los Angeles Times*, December 16, 2003, online edition; Samuelson, *The Rose Bowl Game*, 212.

7. Powell, "The Development and Influence of Faculty Representation," 63, 68, 72–76; "Bucks Could Get Rose Bowl Shot, If . . .," *The Lantern*, November 17, 1961; Memo from K. L. Wilson and W. R. Reed to Rose Bowl Interim and Negotiating Committees, October 29, 1958, "Rose Bowl 1958–60," file 10, Box #4, FCIA. The terms of the contract also evolved during this period, by 1956 including a prohibition of back-to-back appearances and striking the possibility that the Big Ten might designate a team from outside their conference to participate; Memo from Bill Reed to Conference Joint Group, with Rose Bowl Contract attached, March, 20, 1956, "Commissioner's Office—Correspondence 1940–41, 1955–58," file 14, Box #2, FCIA.

8. John Scanlon, "The Scent of Roses: Ohio State Takes a Fresh Look at Big-Time Sports," *Saturday Review* (April 21, 1962): 56–78; letter from Tug Wilson to Bernie Moore, June 25, 1958, "Southeastern Conference," Box "SEC Files, 1960–1974," BAD; "Rose Bowl," *The Lantern*, November 28, 1961, p. 2.

9. Scanlon, "The Scent of Roses"; Hyman and White, *Big Ten Football*, 35–40.

10. "Background of Football Grants Told" and "Scholarship Reality," *The Lantern*, October 3, 1961, pp. 1, 2; Scanlon, "The Scent of Roses"; Hyman and White, *Big Ten Football*, 35–44.

11. Interview with William R. Reed, July 18, 1963, in Powell, "The Development and Influence of Faculty Representation," 301–2; "Report on the Faculty Council Committee on Intercollegiate Athletics at the Ohio State University," May 1957, found in "Intercollegiate Athletics: Report of the Faculty Council," (9/e/1), OAD; Scanlon, "The Scent of Roses."

12. "Report on the Faculty Council Committee on Intercollegiate Athletics at the Ohio State University," May 1957, found in "Intercollegiate Athletics: Report of the Faculty Council," (9/e/1), OAD; Scanlon, "The Scent of Roses"; "Minutes of the Intercollegiate Conference Joint Group," March 6–7, 1958, "Joint Group Minutes, 1956–61," file 2, Box #6, FCIA; Athletic Board Minutes, January 16, 1958, MAB; letter from Payson S. Wild to President John A. Hannah, Michigan State University, January 23, 1957, "Correspondence 1958–59," file 8, Box #1, FCIA; letter from Wendell Postle, Dean, College of Dentistry to Dr. T. Leroy Martin, Northwestern University, November 1956, covering "The 1956 'Blue' Paper," of the Athletic Board of the Ohio State University, "Correspondence 1958–59," file 8, Box #1, FCIA.

13. "Fullen Speaks on Scholarship Proposal," *The Lantern*, November 6, 1961, p. 2.

14. "Background of Football Grants Told," *The Lantern*, October 3, 1961, p. 1; "Scholarship Reality," *The Lantern*, October 3, 1961, p. 2.

15. "Football Crisis at Ohio State," *Pasadena Star News*, November 7, 1961, p. 17; "Hayes Defends Scholarship Rule Change," *The Lantern*, October 2, 1961, p. 1.

16. Athletic Board Minutes, September 20, 1961, MAB.

17. Thelin, *Games Colleges Play*, 128–54; Watterson, *College Football*, 277–86.

18. The group purposefully omitted the word "alumni" from its name so as to include former students who did not complete a degree. Texas A&M's alumni-oriented group, the Association of Former Students, similarly avoids the word. Woody Hayes's biographer claims that the *Columbus Dispatch*, a critic of Fullen, alleged that the group's name had nefarious purposes, allowing for an artificially high membership base, thus allowing the group a disproportionate influence in university affairs; John Lombardo, *A Fire to Win: The Life and Times of Woody Hayes* (New York: St. Martin's Press, 2005), 130.

19. Letter from John B. Fullen to Dr. T. Leroy Martin, March 2, 1959, "Correspondence 1959–60," file 9, Box #1, FCIA.

20. Kaplan, "The Case for Big-Time Football"; Tim Cohane, "Inside the West Coast Football Scandal," *Look* (October 7, 1956); Jack Starr and Clark Mollenhoff, "Football Scandal Hits the Big 10," *Look* (August 21, 1956); Jack Starr and Clark Mollenhoff, "The Big 10's Secret Report," *Look* (October 30, 1956); Jack Starr, "The Big New Battle in the Big 10," *Look* (June 25, 1957).

21. Thelin, *A History of American Higher Education*, 260–90; oral interview with Dr. Richard Armitage, May 28, 2002, OSUOHP; on the English Department, see Eric Solomon, "Free Speech at Ohio State University," *Atlantic Monthly* 21, no. 5 (November 1965): 119–32. For one campus's concern with funding and reputation, particularly the role of graduate students, see also Lowen, *Creating the Cold War University*; for general anxiety in higher education at the time regarding the role

of athletics, see Frank N. Gardner, "The Place of Athletics in Higher Education," *Journal of Higher Education* 31, no. 7 (October 1960): 364–68.

22. Steven P. Gietschier, "The 1951 Speaker's Rule at Ohio State," *Ohio History* 87, no. 3 (1978): 294–309; Solomon, "Free Speech at Ohio State"; Armitage interview, OSUOHP.

23. Scanlon, "Scent of Roses."

24. Armitage interview, OSUOHP.

25. Letter from Moody E. Prior, Dean, to Professor T. Leroy Martin, School of Business, March 14, 1960, "Rose Bowl—1958–1960," file 10, Box #4, FCIA; Thelin also discusses faculty anxiety regarding prestige during this period, *A History of Higher Education*, 279.

26. Lombardo, *A Fire to Win*, 47, 64.

27. William G. Robbins, "William Appleman Williams: 'Doing History Is Best of All. No Regrets,'" in *Redefining the Past: Essays in Diplomatic History in Honor of William Appleman Williams*, ed. Lloyd C. Gardner (Corvallis: Oregon State University Press, 1986), 8. Williams's allegation, contained in a letter to a colleague in 1985, seems out of character for Hayes. If the incident did occur, Williams apparently did not pursue the matter as no reference to it exists in his personnel file at Ohio State University. Williams's most recent biography repeats the episode with slight modification without citation; Paul M. Buhle and Edward Rice-Maximin, *Williams Appleman Williams: The Tragedy of Empire* (New York: Routledge, 1995), 67.

28. Lombardo, *A Fire to Win*, 53–54, 152–53; Armitage interview, OSUOHP; Paul Hornung, *Woody Hayes: A Reflection* (Champaign, IL: Sagamore, 1991), 159; Harry V. Jaffa, "L'Envoi to Woody Hayes," January 3, 2003, www.claremont.org/writings/precepts/030101jaffa.html (accessed October 18, 2008). Fourteen years after the faculty voted against sending the Buckeyes to the Rose Bowl, Hayes provided a copy of his book, *You Win with People*, to Armitage with the inscription, "To my friend Dick Armitage, even though you didn't let us go to the Rose Bowl."

29. "Fullen Cites Complex Campus Issues," *Columbus Star*, April 9, 1960, p. 3A; "Alumni Association," OVF; "Who Is Jack Fullen? Here Is His Biography," found in Fullen, John (Jack) Beck, BF; "Fullen-Hayes Feud Hits High Note over Rose Bowl," *Columbus Dispatch*, December 3, 1961, p. 2B. What really animated much of the animosity toward Fullen was the popular assumption that it was Fullen who had provided the Big Ten with the revelations that put Ohio State on probation in 1956; "Alumni Vote; Jack Fullen Stays Here," *The Lantern*, May 7, 1956, p. 3; Lombardo, *A Fire to Win*, 129–30.

30. "Hayes and Fullen Resume Long-Standing Feud," and "Columnist Views Fullen Issues," *The Lantern*, December 4, 1961, pp. 1, 4; "Fullen-Hayes Feud Hits High Note over Rose Bowl," *Columbus Dispatch*, December 3, 1961, p. 2B.

31. "'De-emphasis'—Wha-a-a-t?" *Ohio State University Monthly* (March 1960): 1–3. For a thorough review of Fullen's post-Sputnik links to higher education priorities and funding in Ohio, see "Sputnik Is Up There Still," *Ohio State University Monthly* (October 1958): 1–2; "Meagre—That's the Word for Ohio's Support of Higher Ed," *Ohio State University Monthly* (February 1959): 1–2; "Now Is the Time for All Good Alumni," *Ohio State University Monthly* (February 1959): 1–2; "What Comrade Big

SHOULD See," *Ohio State University Monthly* (September 1959): 1; "Khru and the View" *Ohio State University Monthly* (October 1959): 1–2; "Professors Should Drive Trucks," *Ohio State University Monthly* (September 1961): 1–2.

32. "Fullen Replies . . .," *The Lantern*, November 15, 1961, p. 3.

33. "Beautiful Ohio—So Proud—So Penurious," *Ohio State University Monthly* (March 1959): 1–2.

34. "The Free Ride," *Ohio State University Monthly* (July 1961): 1–2.

35. "Rose Bowl Comments," *Ohio State University Monthly* (April 1960): 2.

36. Perkins, *Plain Talk from a Campus*, vi–vii, 3, 192–93. Ironically, Perkins offered the undergraduate career of William Rainey Harper as an example of the studiousness to which Cold War era students should aspire. It was Harper who, as president of the newly formed University of Chicago, would do so much to elevate and emphasize football on that campus; see Robin Lester, *Stagg's University: The Rise and Fall of Big-Time Football at the University of Chicago* (Urbana: University of Illinois Press, 1998).

37. "The Cover," *Saturday Evening Post* (October 17, 1959): 1; "Sad News from the Campus, Nobody Loves the Football Hero Anymore," *Life* (November 11, 1957): 149–60.

38. "Ohio State Votes NO on Rose Bowl," *Ohio State University Monthly* (April 1959): 8.

39. "Fullen Speaks on Scholarship Proposal," *The Lantern*, November 6, 1961, p. 2; "The Free Ride," *Ohio State University Monthly* (July 1961): 1–2.

40. Letter from Moody E. Prior, Dean, to Professor T. Leroy Martin, School of Business, March 14, 1960, "Rose Bowl—1958–1960," file 10, Box #4, FCIA.

41. Oral interview with Novice G. Fawcett, June 17, 1985, OSUOHP.

42. Memo from K. L. Wilson and W. R. Reed to The Rose Bowl Interim and Negotiating Committees, October 29, 1958, "Rose Bowl 1958–1960," file 10, Box #4, FCIA.

43. Letter from Robert F. Ray, Faculty Representative, University of Iowa, to All Faculty Representatives, February 15, 1960, "Correspondence 1959–60," file 9, Box #1, FCIA; Preliminary Report of Conference Rose Bowl Committee, February 14–15, 1959, "Rose Bowl Statement of Policy, 1959," (9/3/1), OAD.

44. "Report of Special Joint Group Committee on Rose Bowl Participation," Appendix 2, Joint Group Minutes, March 5–6, 1959, "Joint Group Minutes 1956–1961," file 2, Box #6, FCIA; Rose Bowl Statement of Policy, "Rose Bowl Statement of Policy: 1959," (9/e/1), OAD.

45. Memo from K. L. Wilson and W. R. Reed to The Rose Bowl Interim and Negotiating Committees, October 29, 1958, "Rose Bowl 1958–1960," file 10, Box #4, Faculty Council on Intercollegiate Athletics 1906–71, NUA.

46. Memo from K. L. Wilson and W. R. Reed to The Rose Bowl Interim and Negotiating Committees, October 29, 1958, "Rose Bowl 1958–1960," file 10, Box #4, FCIA. For the Goldwater quote, see Rick Perlstein, *Before the Storm: Barry Goldwater and the Unmaking of the American Consensus* (New York: Hill & Wang, 2001), 390–92. Coincidentally, OSU political science professor Harry Jaffa, later Goldwater's speechwriter, was the architect of the candidate's famous assertion at the 1964 Republican National Convention.

47. Preliminary Report of Conference Rose Bowl Committee, February 14–15, 1959; and The Rose Bowl Statement of Policy, both located in "Rose Bowl Statement of Policy: 1959," (9/e/1), OAD; memo from K. L. Wilson and W. R. Reed to The Rose Bowl Interim and Negotiating Committees, October 29, 1958, "Rose Bowl 1958–1960," file 10, Box #4, FCIA.

48. Meeting Minutes, January 20, 1959, and February 20, 1959, MAB; "Brief Statement of the Discussion on the Rose Bowl at the Faculty Council Meeting of March 10, 1959," marked CONFIDENTIAL, "Rose Bowl 1958–59," (3/i/27), NGF.

49. Letter from Richard Armitage, Assistant Dean, to W. J. McKeachie, University of Michigan, June 16, 1959, "Athletics—Pro & Con 1952, 1959–63, 1969," (9/e/1), OAD; "Writer Discusses Bowl Bid," *The Lantern*, December 1, 1961, p. 3.

50. Minutes of the Intercollegiate Conference Joint Group, January 24, 1960, "Joint Group Minutes 1956–1961," file 2, Box #6, FCIA; Meeting Minutes, January 27, 1960, "Athletic Board Minutes: October 1957–June 1962," Box #2 (9/e/1), RADO; letter from Marcus L. Plant, Secretary of the Faculty Representatives of the Intercollegiate Conference to Mr. Thomas J. Hamilton, Executive Director, Athletic Association of Western Universities, March 10, 1960, "Athletic Assn of Western Univs.," file 12, Box #7, FCIA.

51. Powell, "The Development and Influence of Faculty Representation," 41; The Rose Bowl Statement of Policy, "Rose Bowl Statement of Policy: 1959," Box 1 (9/e), OAD; "Bucks Could Get Rose Bowl Shot, If . . .," *The Lantern*, November 17, 1961, p. 3; Remarks from Professor Marcus L. Plant, University of Michigan, delivered June 1, 1959, "Rose Bowl 1958–1960," file 10, Box #4, FCIA.

52. Letter from Loyal Davis to Professor T. Leroy Martin, March 17, 1960, "Correspondence 1959–60," file 9, Box #1, FCIA.

53. Letter from J. Lyndon Shanley to Professor T. Leroy Martin, March 9, 1960, "Rose Bowl 1959–1960," file 10, Box #4, FCIA.

54. Letter from Frederic Heimberger, Vice President, to President Novice G. Fawcett, May 22, 1959, "Rose Bowl 1958–1959," (3/i/27), NGF; Meeting Minutes, June 15, 1960, and December 5, 1960, MAB.

55. Report of the Athletic Council to the Faculty Council, December 13, 1960, "Rose Bowl 1958–59," (3/i/27), NGF.

56. "Spirit Factor in Football Upsets," *Los Angeles Times*, November 13, 1961, part IV, p. 2; see also the sports section of the *Chicago Tribune*, November 11–24, 1961.

57. Meeting Minutes, November 15, 1961, MAB.

58. Minutes of the Athletic Council, November 27, 1961, "Athletic Board Minutes October 1957–June 1962," Box #2 (9/e-1/2), RADO.

59. Armitage interview, OSUOHP; Scanlon, "Scent of Roses."

60. Meeting Minutes, November 28, 1961, MFC. The only faculty member to speak in favor of the measure was Professor Mars Fontana of the Department of Metallurgical Engineering.

61. Interview with James McCoy in Powell, "The Development and Influence of Faculty Representation," 227; Meeting Minutes, November 28, 1961, MFC.

62. Meeting Minutes, November 28, 1961, MFC; Scanlon, "Scent of Roses."

63. Scanlon, "Scent of Roses."

64. Fawcett interview, OSUOHP; "OSU Students Parade in Bowl Ban Protest," *Columbus Dispatch*, November 29, 1961, p. 1; "Council Rejects Bowl Ban," *The Lantern*, November 29, 1961, p. 1; "Demonstrators, Petitions Gain Nothing From Efforts," *The Lantern*, November 30, 1961, p. 1; Francis P. Weisenburger, *History of the Ohio State University*, vol. 10: *The Fawcett Years, 1956–1972* (Columbus: Ohio State University Press, 1972), 212–13; Statement Issued by President Fawcett Relative to Participation in the Rose Bowl Game on January 1, 1962, November 29, 1961, "Rose Bowl 1961–62," (9/e/1), OAD; Scanlon, "Scent of Roses."

65. McCollum, *Pac-10 Football*, 185–86; Lombardo, *A Fire to Win*, 144; Scanlon, "Scent of Roses." McCollum has Hayes saying of the faculty, "I cannot question the faculty's sincerity or their right to act. But I do seriously question their judgment." Almost all secondary sources that discuss the Rose Bowl incident describe in glowing detail Hayes's stunned reaction, as if Hayes and the football team had been blindsided. The careful, and endless, retelling of Hayes's lonely walk through the rain-soaked streets of Cleveland help position Hayes as rational in his disciplined response and the faculty as engaging in some kind of unmeasured temper tantrum. Such a retelling conveniently ignores the growing sentiment of faculty opposition that developed well before the November 1961 vote and was well known to everyone who followed the situation. The notion that Hayes simply walked out of a packed-house alumni function for an hour simply to get his thoughts in order seems incredulous.

66. "Horvath Has Choice Words," *Columbus Dispatch*, November 29, 1961, p. 6B; telegram from [19 signatories] to Board of Trustees; telegram from George Baker to Faculty Council; telegram from Margaret Guiler to Faculty Council; telegram from Darwin Wilkoff to Faculty Council; letter from Dorothy Melick to Richard Armitage, November 30, 1961; telegram from Byron E. Scribner to Board of Trustees, December 5, 1961; letter from Glen H. and Claire Thomas to John H. Bricker, Chair Board of Trustees, November 30, 1961, all found in "Rose Bowl 1962" (3/i/28), NGF; Fawcett interview, OSUOHP; Armitage interview, OSUOHP; "Public Speaks Its Mind on Rose Bowl Trip Ban," *Columbus Dispatch*, December 1, 1961, p. 5B.

67. Letter from James R. Kidd to Novice G. Fawcett, March 13, 1960; letter from W. E. Slabaugh to Novice G. Fawcett, March 13, 1960; letter from Paul G. Korn to Novice G. Fawcett, July 8, 1960, all found in "Athletics Issue 1960," (3/i/5), NGF.

68. Newspaper sentiments from around the state, both pro and con, were surveyed exhaustively in "Editorial Comment," *Ohio State University Monthly* (January 1962): 30; "Fullen Firm on Decisions," *The Lantern*, November 30, 1961, p. 1.

69. Letter from W. S. Judy to Professor Richard Armitage, April 12, 1959, "Rose Bowl 1962," NGF; "Open Letter to the Faculty," *The Lantern*, June 9, 1962, p. 2; "John Carroll Roots for OSU Faculty," undated clipping found in "Rose Bowl 1962," (3/i/28), NGF.

70. "Beneath the Bowl: Some Facts You Must Know," *Ohio State University Monthly* (February 1962): 1–2.

71. Lombardo, *A Fire to Win*, 134–35; on Hornung's attire and behavior at Buckeye games, see Sperber, *Onward to Victory*, 463. Hornung's understandings, and misunderstandings, of the episode had not diminished after thirty years. In his

recollections of Hayes, he claimed "the administration lateraled [*sic*] the decision to the Faculty Council," implying the administration abrogated its legitimate authority on the matter. Having ignored the issue of faculty control and suggesting that the faculty were usurpers, Hornung proceeded to then suggest they were dupes as well. Hornung renewed Hayes's allegations that Fullen, not an independent faculty, lay behind the faculty's vote; Hornung, *Woody Hayes*, 175–76, 158–59. Lombardo, too, is smitten with the idea that Fullen lay at the heart of the crisis. "The majority of the Council was convinced, with a push by Fullen, that too many financial resources were being allocated to the athletic department, especially to the football team." Contrary to Lombardo's assertions, no evidence exists to suggest that faculty opposition came from financial imbalance toward the athletic department. Additionally, Lombardo ignores the fact that Fullen was not at the faculty meeting or even in town throughout the entire crisis. Finally, Lombardo also erroneously places culpability on OSU president Novice Fawcett for "let[ting] the decision stand," ignoring that any action by Fawcett that countermanded faculty council actions on athletics would violate Big Ten rules and mean Ohio State's possible dismissal from the conference; *A Fire to Win*, 142–45.

72. "Ohio State and the Rose Bowl," *Columbus Dispatch*, November 28, 1961, p. 2B; "In the Press Box," *Columbus Dispatch*, December 1, 1961, p. 26B; "Dictation by Faculty Perils Big 10 Sports," *Columbus Dispatch*, March 7, 1960, p. 2B; "Rose Bowl Disappointment," *Columbus Dispatch*, November 29, 1961, p. 2B.

73. "Faculty Council Votes No to Rose Bowl," *Columbus Citizen-Journal*, November 29, 1961, p. 1.

74. "Scarlet 'n' Gray," *The Lantern*, November 30, 1961, p. 5; "Columnist Views Fullen Issues," *The Lantern*, December 4, 1961, p. 4.

75. "An Editorial," *The Lantern*, November 30, 1961, p. 1.; "Rose Bowl," *The Lantern*, November 28, 1961, p. 2; "Scarlet 'n' Gray," *The Lantern*, November 30, 1961, p. 5; "Columnist Views Fullen Issues," *The Lantern*, December 4, 1961, p. 4. Media complicity in sports-related student disturbances was not invented in Columbus. When Georgia governor Marvin Harris threatened to force Georgia Tech to refuse a 1955 Sugar Bowl bid because Tech's opponent included a black player, student unrest was fomented by a media that, disappointed at students' early lack of agitation, prodded students by asking, "Aren't you gonna do something?" Robert W. Dubay, Politics, Pigmentation, and Pigskin: The Georgia Tech Sugar Bowl Controversy of 1955, *Atlanta History* 39, no. 1 (1995): 21–35.

76. "Letter Sent Out Warning Students of Spring Riots," *The Lantern*, March 29, 1956, p. 1; Letter from Richard Armitage, Assistant Dean, to Dr. Sol Maggied, January 26, 1962, "Rose Bowl 1962," NGF; "OSU Students Parade in Bowl Ban Protest," *Columbus Dispatch*, November 29, 1961, p. 1; "Demonstration Includes Hike to Downtown," *The Lantern*, November 29, 1961, p. 1.

77. "Faculty Bowl Opponents Shield Identity, Proponents Speak Out," *Columbus Dispatch*, November 30, 1961, p.2A; "OSU Faculty Spends about $100,000 Yearly on Trips," *Columbus Dispatch*, December 1, 1962, p. 27A; "State University Faculties' Travel Rapped," *Columbus Dispatch*, December 1, 1961. p. 1; "Fullen-Hayes Feud Hits High Note over Rose Bowl," *Columbus Dispatch*, December 3, 1962, p.

2B; Letter from Andrew Wright to Miss Mary McGarey, December 3, 1961, "Rose Bowl 1962," (3/i/28), NGF.

78. Lewontin, "The Cold War and the Transformation of the Academy," 30–31.

79. Scanlon, "Scent of Roses"; Solomon, "Free Speech at Ohio State;" Jaffa, "L'Envoi to Woody Hayes." Jaffa saw humanities opposition not from any concern for the Cold War political economy but because of their frustration over seeing their own scholarly work outshone by the outsized reputation of Hayes and OSU football and their snobbish assumptions of Columbus as a cultural backwater, a point Solomon does little to dispel. See also Lowen, *Creating the Cold War University*, 147–63, for the origins of "imbalance" within the research university and the slighting of the humanities.

Chapter 3. Baton Rouge: Postwar Football and a Fate Worse Than Integration

The comment appears in a letter from Peter B. Young to the editor of the LSU *Daily Reveille*, July 20, 1956, p. 4.

1. "LSU Sports Policy," *Baton Rouge State-Times*, November 20, 1961, p. 2A; "It's Still Just a Game (Isn't It, Folks?)," *Baton Rouge Morning Advocate*, November 14, 1961, p. 2A; "To Bowl or Not to Bowl," *Baton Rouge Morning Advocate*, November 18, 1961, p. 8A; "Don't Bar L.S.U. from Any Bowl," *Shreveport Times*, November 17, 1961, p. 4.

2. "Georgia Tech Being Considered for Rose," *New Orleans Times-Picayune*, November 9, 1961, sec. 6, p. 2; "Rose Bowl Considering Georgia Tech," *Montgomery Advertiser*, November 9, 1961, p. 4D; "Rose Bowl Screening Boss Confirms Tech Candidacy," *Atlanta Constitution*, November 9, 1961, p. 33.

3. Samuelson, *The Rose Bowl Game*, 213–14; as late as November 1961, at least one southern sports writer declared that since the 1946 agreement, "the Rose Bowl has been just another bowl as far as prestige is concerned." Once the Rose Bowl was willing to consider the South again, however, it was safe once again to declare it a "glamour bowl," "Random Shots," *Baton Rouge Morning Advocate*, November 10, 1961, p. 26; "Rose Bowl Screening Boss Confirms Tech's Candidacy," *Atlanta Constitution*, November 9, 1961, p. 33.

4. "Mississippi to Play in Cotton Bowl Jan. 1," *Atlanta Constitution*, November 10, 1961, p. 41; "Rose Bowl Considering Georgia Tech," *Montgomery Advertiser*, November 9, 1961, p. 4D.

5. "Rose Bowl Screening Boss Confirms Tech Candidacy," *Atlanta Constitution*, November 9, 1961, p. 33.

6. Adam Fairclough, *Race and Democracy: The Civil Rights Struggle in Louisiana, 1915–1972* (Athens: University of Georgia Press, 1995), chapters 4, 5, and 7; Greta de Jong, *A Different Say: African American Struggles for Justice in Rural Louisiana, 1900–1970* (Chapel Hill: University of North Carolina Press, 2002), 144–74. De Jong correctly points out that scholars are divided on the effects of the war on black gains.

7. "Bill to Prohibit White-Negro Play Introduced Here," *Baton Rouge Morning*

Advocate, June 3, 1952, p. 4B; "'Segregation' Sports Bill Taken Favorably by Louisiana Senate," *Baton Rouge Morning Advocate*, June 13, 1952, p. 5B; "Segregation Bill Killed by Senate," *Baton Rouge Morning Advocate*, June 17, 1952, p. 4B.

8. Bruce Adelson, *Brushing Back Jim Crow: The Integration of Minor League Baseball in the American South* (Charlottesville: University of Virginia Press, 1999), 109, 154–55.

9. "Maryland, Navy Series May be Renewed Soon," *Washington Post*, December 17, 1955, p. 14.

10. "Louisiana," *Southern School News*, November 4, 1954, p. 3.

11. Charles Martin, "Jim Crow in the Gymnasium: The Integration of College Basketball in the American South," *International Journal of the History of Sport* 10, no. 1 (1993): 68–86; "Louisiana," *Southern School News*, January 6, 1955, p. 3.

12. Robert W. Dubay, "Pigmentation and Pigskin: A Jones County Junior College Dilemma," *Journal of Mississippi History* 46, no. 1 (1984): 43–50. Interestingly, Coleman raised no public objection when the Cotton States League team in Meridian signed a black player in 1954, although the incident was short-lived as the league folded following the season.

13. Robert W. Dubay, "Politics, Pigmentation and Pigskin: The Georgia Tech Sugar Bowl Controversy of 1955," *Atlanta History* 39, no. 1 (1995): 21–35; Charles Martin, "Racial Change and 'Big-Time' College Football in Georgia: The Age of Segregation, 1892–1957," *Georgia Historical Quarterly* 80, no. 3 (1996): 532–62; FBI file 100–15769.

14. "Georgia Acts to Ban Negroes in Baseball," *New York Times*," February 15, 1957, p. 1; "Sports Ban in Key Test," *New York Times*, February 22, 1957, p. 22; "Mixed-Sports Ban Blocked in Georgia," *New York Times*, February 23, 1957, p. 1.

15. Adelson, *Brushing Back Jim Crow*, 204.

16. Adelson, *Brushing Back Jim Crow*, 177–81; "Louisiana," *Southern School News*, May 1956, p. 12.

17. "Cancel Tech, AF Go," *Shreveport Times*, March 17, 1956, p. 1B; letter from W. M. Rainach to Dr. R. L. Ropp, April 4, 1956, file #131 "Correspondence—Louisiana Polytechnic Institute," Box 13; and letter from R. L. Ropp to Senator W. M. Rainach, April 9, 1956, both found in WMR.

18. Neil McMillen, *The Citizens' Council: Organized Resistance to the Second Reconstruction, 1954–1964* (Champaign: University of Illinois Press, 1971), 59–72; Fairclough, *Race and Democracy*, 191–94;

19. "Synopsis of Facts—Southern Gentlemen file," FBI file 105–385673; Numan Bartley, *Race and Politics in the South during the 1950s* (Baton Rouge: Louisiana State University Press, 1969), 90–92. On Rainach, see William McFerrin Stowe, "Willie Rainach and the Defense of Segregation in Louisiana, 1954–1959" (PhD diss., Rice University, 1989).

20. Articles of Incorporation attached to Memorandum from SAC, New Orleans to Director, FBI, July 6, 1955, FBI file 100–15769.

21. "Senate Adopts Integration Ban," *New Orleans Times-Picayune*, July 6, 1956, p. 6; "Senate OK's Interracial Activities Bill," *Daily Reveille*, July 10, 1956, p. 1.

22. "Senate Adopts Integration Ban," *New Orleans Times-Picayune*, July 6, 1956,

p. 6; "Ban on Mixed Athletic Events Finally Passed," *Baton Rouge Morning Advocate*, July 6, 1956, p. 1.

23. "Long Undecided about Bill to Bar Interracial Events," *New Orleans Times-Picayune*, July 15, 1956, p. 1; "Mixed Sports Ban Is Signed," *New Orleans Times-Picayune*, July 17, 1956, p. 1; Stowe, "Willie Rainach," 59–61; "Louisiana," *Southern School News*, October 1956, p. 5; "Long Signs Bill to Ban Mixed Athletic Contests in State," *Baton Rouge Morning Advocate*, July 17, 1956, p. 1; "Louisiana," *Southern School News*, August 1956, p. 11.

24. Howard Zinn, "A Fate Worse Than Integration," *Harper's Magazine* (August 1959): 53–56.

25. Editorial, *Baton Rouge Morning Advocate*, May 29, 1956, p. 2A; Editorial, *Baton Rouge Morning Advocate*, May 3, 1956, p. 2A.

26. Adelson, *Brushing Back Jim Crow*, 179–80.

27. "Sports of the World," *Birmingham World*, December 18, 1956, p. 4.

28. Adelson, *Brushing Back Jim Crow*, 180–81, 207–8.

29. "Negroes Allocated 75 Seats for Sugar Bowl Classic," *Louisiana Weekly*, December 20, 1958, p. 2; "This Morning . . .," *Washington Post*, July 30, 1956, p. 9.

30. "Bowl Group Urges 'Serious Consideration' of Race Bar," *New Orleans Times-Picayune*, July 14, 1956, p. 1. What is perhaps most amazing about the sports ban and its effect on the Sugar Bowl is the relative apathy over the negative impact on urban tourism, boosterism, and general economic development from the economic and social elite that made up the game's organizers. In discussing the general attitude among the New Orleans business elite, historian Adam Fairclough declared, "Crescent City businessmen were not necessarily more racist, merely less progressive." They were "a closed elite . . . [a] stagnant, inward-looking group that lacked civic consciousness and displayed more interest in prestige, tradition, and family than in economic development." In 1961, the city faced a catastrophic failure in leadership during its attempt to integrate the public schools, which included violence and enough legislative buffoonery that federal judges were ruling state segregation laws unconstitutional as fast as couriers could take them from the capitol to the courthouse. Having allowed their humiliation to become a national spectacle, they were more than willing to allow sportswriters to deride the Sugar Bowl as nothing more than the "White Supremacy Bowl," Fairclough, *Race and Democracy*, 253–54.

31. "Long Undecided about Bill to Bar Interracial Events," *New Orleans Times-Picayune*, July 15, 1956, p. 1.

32. "Army Shifts Tulane Game over Segregated Seating," *Washington Post*, September 17, 1957, p. A1; "Legislative Action," *Southern School News*, November 1956, p. 15; "Sports of the World," *Birmingham World*, December 18, 1957, p. 4. Navy was also denied permission to play the University of Georgia in the 1956 Oyster Bowl, held in Norfolk, Virginia, due to a segregated seating arrangement.

33. "Random Shots," *Baton Rouge Morning Advocate*, July 20, 1956, p. 2D.

34. "Wisconsin to Call Off LSU Contests," *New Orleans Times-Picayune*, July 20, 1956, p. 24; "Colorado Bars All Sports Competition in Louisiana," *Birmingham World*, December 18, 1857, p. 4.

35. "Random Shots," *Baton Rouge Morning Advocate*, June 16, 1956, p. 2B, see also, "Sports of the World," *Birmingham World*, December 18, 1957, p. 4.

36. Bartley, *The Rise of Massive Resistance*, 228–29.

37. Stowe, "Willie Rainach," 218–27; Fairclough, *Race and Democracy*, 154–55, 205–6; Mary Jacqueline Hebert, "Beyond Black and White: The Civil Rights Movement in Baton Rouge, Louisiana, 1945–1972" (PhD diss., Louisiana State University, 1999), 130–40. The Rainach quote is found in Stowe, "Willie Rainach," 226.

38. Letter from Troy H. Middleton to Senator W. M. Rainach, December 28, 1956; letter from Troy H. Middleton to Congressman Overton Brooks, December 28, 1956; letter from Troy H. Middleton to Hobart Corning, December 28, 1956, all found in file 130, "Correspondence—Louisiana State University," Box #13, WMR. See also Stowe, "Willie Rainach," 235–37; Fairclough, *Race and Democracy*, 205–6; Hebert, "Beyond Black and White," 130–40.

39. The raw data on letter winners can be found in the appendix to Peter Finney, *Fighting Tigers, 1893–1993: One Hundred Years of LSU Football* (Baton Rouge: Louisiana State University Press, 1993), 482–93.

40. Frank James Price, *Troy H. Middleton: A Biography* (Baton Rouge: Louisiana State University Press, 1974), 334–35.

41. Letter from Troy H. Middleton to Senator W. M. Rainach, April 15, 1958, and letter from W. M. Rainach to the Honorable Troy H. Middleton, April 21, 1958, both in file 91, "Correspondence Me–Mir," Box #9, WMR.

42. Price, *Troy Middleton*, 13, 20.

43. On the hiring of Dietzel and Corbett, see Finney, *Fighting Tigers*, 193–203; *New Orleans Times-Picayune*; the response to Middleton's reorganization is found in "Meeting Minutes of Athletic & Student Affairs Committee," March 24, 1955, file 19, Athletic and Student Affairs Committee; and telegram from Cullen Schouest to Buck Sterling Gladd, February 11, 1955, file 17, Joint Athletic Committee and Athletic Council Meeting, both in Box #12, RBS; and Minutes of Joint Board of Athletic and Student Affairs Committee and Committee of Athletics, February 16, 1955, file 12, Joint Athletic Committee and Athletic Council Meeting, Box #17, RBS. Middleton was less deferential in responding to student opposition to the new policy, sternly rebuking them and reminded them that henceforth, athletics were no different than any other aspect of university policy: "student participation is not expected nor permitted."

44. "Random Shots," *Baton Rouge Morning Advocate*, July 20, 1956, p. 2D; "Random Shots," *Baton Rouge Morning Advocate*, November 19, 1961, p. 2C; "LSU Board Resignations Demanded," *Shreveport Times*, February 21, 1956, p. 1. Charles Martin has unearthed no known Gentlemen's Agreements in existence after 1956 and none in the North after 1946.

45. Meeting Minutes of Board of Supervisors, February 18, 1956, file 4, Statement Re: Segregation and Intercollegiate Athletics, Box #4; Meeting Minutes of the Athletics and Student Affairs Committee, May 27, 1956, file 120, Athletics and Student Affairs Committee Meetings, Box #12, both in RBS.

46. Stowe, "Willie Rainach," 223–24.

47. Press Release from Southern Gentlemen's Organization, February 19, 1956,

file 13 Correspondence Southern Gentlemen's Organization, Box #1, NTP; "LSU Board Resignations Demanded," *Shreveport Times*, February 21, 1956, p. 1.

48. Statement by President Troy H. Middleton to Board of Supervisors. LSU April 7, 1956, file 4, Statement Re: Segregation and Intercollegiate Athletics, Box # 28, RBS.

49. Meeting Minutes of Board of Supervisors, April 7, 1956; and Statement by President Troy H. Middleton to Board of Supervisors. LSU April 7, 1956, both found in file 4, Statement Re: Segregation and Intercollegiate Athletics, Box # 28, RBS.

50. Meeting Minutes of Board of Supervisors, April 7, 1956; and Meeting Minutes of Board of Supervisors, May 28, 1956, both found in file 4, Statement Re: Segregation and Intercollegiate Athletics, Box # 28, RBS; "Move to Revive Color Ban in Athletics at LSU Killed by Board," *Baton Rouge Morning Advocate*, April 8, 1956, p. 1; Resolution, hand dated May 28, 1956, file 130, Box #13,WMR; "Color Ban Defeated Again," *Daily Reveille*, June 14, 1956, p. 6. The symbolism of the service academies in scheduling LSU football, however, was more imagined than real: LSU has never played any of the three service academies.

51. Meeting Minutes of Board of Supervisors, May 28, 1956, file 4, Statement Re: Segregation and Intercollegiate Athletics, Box # 28, RBS; "Move to Revive Color Ban in Athletics at LSU Killed by Board," *Baton Rouge Morning Advocate*, April 8, 1956, p. 1.

52. Stowe, "Willie Rainach," 226–27, 230–34; FBI file 100–15769.

53. Stowe, "Willie Rainach," 237–39; Fairclough, *Race and Democracy*, 205, 219; Hebert, "Beyond Black and White," 130–40.

54. Meeting Minutes of Board of Supervisors, September 1, 1956, file 4, Statements Re: Segregation and Intercollegiate Athletics, Box #28, RBS; Doyle, *An American Insurrection*, 74.

55. "Segregation Is Still Major Issue," *Daily Reveille*, April 17, 1956, p. 8; "Song of the South: Discord," *Daily Reveille*, June 19, 1956, p. 4.

56. "How to Win Battles and Lose Wars," *Daily Reveille*, July 30, 1956, p. 4; "The Rich, the Happy—And the Dumb!" *Daily Reveille*, July 19, 1956, p. 4.

57. Stowe, "Willie Rainach," 227–28; "Louisiana's Public Schools 'Solidly Segregated' as School Year Begins," *Southern School News* (September 1956): 14; Price, *Middleton*, 366–67.

58. Stowe, "Willie Rainach," 218, 228–30; "Louisiana's Public Schools 'Solidly Segregated' as School Year Begins," *Southern School News* (September 1956): 14; Hebert, "Beyond Black and White," 143–44; Price, *Middleton*, 366–67.

59. Stowe, "Willie Rainach," 241–54, Hebert, "Beyond Black and White," 162–67; Bartley, *Massive Resistance*, 228–29.

60. Stowe, "Willie Rainach," 241–54; Hebert, "Black and White," 162–67; letter from Dr. N. L. Moncrief to Dr. Troy H Middleton, June 19, 1958, file 91, "Correspondence Me–Mir," Box #9, WMR. Middleton so firmly believed in law and order and abiding by regulations that, contrary to most of his colleagues in the officer corps during World War II, he refused to keep a diary. "It was against regulations. I believe in obeying them," Price, *Troy H. Middleton*, xiii.

61. The entire investigative findings and transcripts of the hearings in the Bail-

lio affair are found in the Rainach papers, as first discovered by Stowe, "Willie Rainach," 254–57.

62. Letter from W. M. Rainach to Troy H. Middleton, August 16, 1957; letter from W. M. Rainach to Troy H. Middleton, August 17, 1957; letter from Troy H. Middleton to W. M. Rainach, August 19, 1957; and letter from Troy H. Middleton to W. M. Rainach, August 21, 1957, all found in file 130, "Correspondence—Louisiana State University," Box #13, WMR.

63. Letter from Troy H. Middleton to W. M. Rainach August 19, 1957; and letter from Troy H. Middleton to W. M. Rainach, August 21, 1957, both found in file 130, "Correspondence—Louisiana State University," Box #13, WMR; letter from Sterling Gladden to Carl Heck, December 20, 1957, file 21 Athletic and Student Affairs Committee Meeting, Box #12, RBS; "Inside Corner," *Shreveport Times*, July 28, 1957, p. 1D. An example of the deference the board gave to Middleton on his handling of athletic affairs occurred in December 1958 when it retroactively confirmed both Middleton's decision to give to Corbett full authority to accept or reject bowl invitations, and Corbett's decision to accept the 1959 Sugar Bowl bid; see Meeting Minutes from Board of Supervisors, December 6, 1958, file 4, Statements Re: Segregation and Intercollegiate Athletics, Box #28, RBS.

64. "Court Voids Louisiana Ban on Racially Mixed Sports," *New York Times*, November 29, 1958, p.1; "Mixed Sports Ban Held Void," *New Orleans Times-Picayune*, May 26, 1959, p. 1; "Sports Color Line Voided in Louisiana by High Court," *New York Times*, May 26, 1959, p. 1; "Sugar Bowl May Land Air Force," *Washington Post*, November 29, 1958, p. A10; "Service Football Draws Criticism," *New York Times*, February 13, 1959, p. 34; "Service Football Teams Are Free to Play in Southern Bowl Games," *Washington Post*, May 29, 1959, p. D3.

65. Bartley, *Massive Resistance*, 329.

66. Stowe, "Willie Rainach," 262, 269.

67. McMillen, *Citizens' Council*, 267, 286; Fairclough, *Race and Democracy*, 231–33

68. "Bengal Hopes of NCAA Berth Doubtful; Amedee to Start," and "Can Tigs Go to NCAA? Who Knows," both in *Baton Rouge Morning Advocate*, May 12, 1961, p. 2C; "LSU to Stay Home; SEC without Entry," *Baton Rouge Morning Advocate*, May 14, 1961, p. 1C.

69. "LSUNO Cancels Play in Which Negro Has Role," *Baton Rouge Morning Advocate*, November 17, 1961, p. 1A; "LSUNO Drops Drama with Negro Player," *Louisiana Weekly*, November 25, 1961, p. 1; letter from Homer Hitt to Troy Middleton, November 13, 1961, file 1, Committee of the Whole Board, Box #33, RBS.

70. "Sugar Bowl to Bid for LSU-Alabama Match," *New Orleans Times-Picayune*, November 14, 1961, p. 8, sec. 2; "Random Shots," *Baton Rouge Morning Advocate*, November 15, 1961, p. 2B; "From the Bench," *New Orleans Times-Picayune*, November 16, 1961, p. 9; "Mississippi to Play in Cotton Bowl Jan. 1," *Atlanta Constitution*, November 10, 1961, p. 41.

71. "Tigers, Tech Eyed by RB," *Baton Rouge Morning Advocate*, November 9, 1961, p. 2D.

72. "Time Out," *Daily Reveille*, November 16, 1961, p. 9.

73. "Sugar Bowl Seeks Tide & LSU," *Birmingham Post-Herald*, November 14, 1961,

p. 14; "From the Bench," *New Orleans Times-Picayune*, November 16, 1961, p. 9; "Random Shots," *Baton Rouge Morning Advocate*, November 14, 1961, p. 2C.

74. "'Irrevocably No,' Say Tigs, Sugar Bowl," *Baton Rouge Morning Advocate*, November 16, 1961, p. 2E; Marty Mulé, *Eye of the Tiger: 100 Years of LSU Football* (Collingdale, PA: Diane, 1993), 152.

75. "SEC Champs," *Daily Reveille*, May 16, 1961, p. 7.

76. "Random Shots," *Baton Rouge Morning Advocate*, November 15, 1961, p. 2B; "Random Shots," *Baton Rouge Morning Advocate*, November 14, 1961, p. 2C.

77. "Sports from the Press Box," *Baton Rouge State-Times*, November 16, 1961, p. 2E; "LSU Officials Delay Bowl Talk until End of Season," *Baton Rouge Morning Advocate*, November 12, 1961, p. 1C; "The Bowls in Review," *Baton Rouge State-Times*, November 20, 1961, p. 2C.

78. "LSU & the Rose Bowl," *New Orleans Times-Picayune*, November 16, 1961, p. 8, sec. 2; "LSU Tells Coast It Can Clear Way," *Pasadena Star-News*, November 16, 1961, p. 26.

79. "Is LSU Thinking Roses," *New Orleans Times-Picayune*, November 15, 1961, p. 7 sec. 2; "No Race Problem for Tigs?" and "Tigers Hold Second Pick for Rose Bowl," *Baton Rouge Morning Advocate*, November 16, 1961, p. 2E; "LSU Tells Coast It Can Clear Way," *Pasadena Star-News*, November 16, 1961, p. 26.

80. "Bowl Game May Be Topic of LSU Board Meet," *Baton Rouge Morning Advocate*, November 17, 1961, p. 1; "Bowl Ban May Be Topic at Meet of LSU Board," *Baton Rouge Morning Advocate*, November 18, 1961, p. 1.

81. "A Day of Decision," *Baton Rouge State-Times*, November 18, 1961, p. 1B.

82. "Bowl Game May Be Topic of LSU Board Meet," *Baton Rouge Morning Advocate*, November 17, 1961, p. 1.

83. "Sports from the Press Box," *Baton Rouge State-Times*, November 16, 1961, p. 2E.

84. "Don't Bar L.S.U. from Any Bowl," *Shreveport Times*, November 17, 1961, p. 6A.

85. "State Sentiment May Favor Playing in Rose," *Baton Rouge State-Times*, November 18, 1961, p. 2E.

86. "A Day of Decision," *Baton Rouge State-Times*, November 18, 1961, p. 1B; "Citizen's Group Shocked by LSU," *New Orleans Times-Picayune*, November 16, 1961, p. 1, sec. 2.

87. Letter from Mr. and Mrs. William J. Wright to President of LSU, November 16, 1961, file 1, Committee of the Whole Board, Box #33, RBS; "Time Out," *Daily Reveille*, November 16, 1961, p. 9; "Time Out," *Louisiana Weekly*, November 25, 1961, p. 9.

88. Telegram from E. Otis Edgerton Jr., Don Moorhead, T. M. Eskew, Elbert Ryder, O. W. Lovell, J. B. Franks, Floyd Swank, Albert L. Stokes, Donald R. Stokes, L. O. Ferguson, Mrs. T. M. Eskew, Homer Allen, George Blankenship, Fred Edgerton, L. O. Deville, Clarice R. Andrews, T. Wynn Holloman, Charlise Deville, A. B. Andrews, Albert Ryder, Herbert Paul, Marvin Tyder, Titter Couvillon Edgerton, William Parish, and Phyllis Parish to John J. Doles, November 17, 1961, file 1, Committee of the Whole Board, Box #33, RBS.

89. "Statement by LSU Board Clears Path for Any Bowl Game," *Baton Rouge*

State-Times, November 18, 1961, p. 1; "LSU Clears Way for Play with Mixed Teams, *Baton Rouge Morning Advocate*, November 19, 1961, p. 1; "Okay for LSU to Play Bowl Appears Open," *New Orleans Times-Picayune*, November 19, 1961, p. 1; Meeting Minutes of the Board of Supervisors, November 18, 1961, file 1, "Minutes of Board Meeting of Committee of the Whole," Box #33, RBS.

90. Meeting Minutes of the Board of Supervisors, November 18, 1961, file 1, "Minutes of Board Meeting of Committee of the Whole," Box #33, RBS.

91. Letter from W. M. Shaw to John Doles, November 27, 1961, file 4, "Statements Re: Segregation and Intercollegiate Athletics," Box #28, RBS.

92. "About the Sugar Bowl," *Daily Reveille*, November 21, 1961, p. 8; "To Bowl or Not to Bowl," *Baton Rouge Morning Advocate*, November 18, 1961, p. 8A.

93. Letter from W. M. Shaw to John Doles, November 27, 1961, file 4, "Statements Re: Segregation and Intercollegiate Athletics," Box #28, RBS.

94. Letter from W. M. Shaw to John Doles, November 27, 1961, file 4, "Statements Re: Segregation and Intercollegiate Athletics," Box #28, RBS.

Chapter 4. Tuscaloosa: The Pariah of Postwar Football

Opening quote by Jim Murray from "Bedsheets and 'Bama," *Los Angeles Times*, November 20, 1961, part 4, p. 1.

1. Dennis McDougal, *Privileged Son: Otis Chandler and the Rise and Fall of the "Los Angeles Times Dynasty"* (Cambridge, MD: Perseus, 2001), 231; Marshall Berges, *Life and "Times" of Los Angeles: A Newspaper, a Family, and City* (New York: Simon & Schuster, 1984), 280.

2. Pete Daniel, *Lost Revolutions: The South in the 1950s* (Chapel Hill: University of North Carolina Press, 2000), 8–9; Numan Bartley, *The New South, 1945–1980* (Baton Rouge: Louisiana State University Press, 1995), 132.

3. Mary Dudziak, *Cold War Civil Rights and the Image of American Democracy* (Princeton, NJ: Princeton University Press, 2000); Thomas Borstelmann, *The Cold War and the Color Line: American Race Relations in the Global Arena* (Cambridge, MA: Harvard University Press, 2001).

4. The definitive treatment of desegregation at the University of Alabama is E. Culpepper Clark's *The Schoolhouse Door: Segregation's Last Stand at the University of Alabama.*

5. "Fear and Hatred Grip Birmingham," *New York Times*, April 12, 1960, p. 1; "Race Issue Shakes Alabama Structure," *New York Times*, April 13, 1960, p. 1; Diane McWhorter, *Carry Me Home: Birmingham, Alabama and the Climactic Battle of the Civil Rights Revolution* (New York: Simon & Schuster, 2001), 157–59, 163–65.

6. On the Freedom Rides, see Raymond Arsenault, *Freedom Rides: 1961 and the Struggle for Racial Justice* (New York: Oxford University Press, 2006); Glenn T. Eskew, *But for Birmingham: The Local and National Movements in the Civil Rights Struggle* (Chapel Hill: University of North Carolina Press, 1997), 153–65; McWhorter, *Carry Me Home*, 194–235.

7. John Temple Graves, *The Fighting South* (Tuscaloosa: University of Alabama Press, 1985; reprint of the original work, 1943), 90–91. Citations are to the 1985 edition. Graves linked the Lost Cause and football, among other things, in ex-

plaining southern response to World War II. "Shouting baptismals, the moan of Negro spirituals, . . . the 88-year-old tradition of a Lost Cause, the 15-year-old tradition of Rose Bowls . . . all made their contribution to the Southern mind about the war" (70–71).

8. Andrew Doyle, "Turning the Tide: College Football and Southern Progressivism," *Southern Cultures* 3, no. 3 (1997): 28–51.

9. On antebellum white stereotypes of black males, see John W. Blassingame, *The Slave Community: Plantation Life in the Antebellum South* (New York: Oxford University Press, 1972), 223–48; on black females, see Deborah Gray White, *Ar'n't I a Woman?: Female Slaves in the Plantation South* (New York: W. W. Norton, 1985), 27–61.

10. Jean Butts Jones, "Father Is a Football Coach," *Saturday Evening Post* (November 20, 1954): 37, 170–72; "Dogs Can Be Taught Some Amazing Things," *Online Athens*, October 6, 1996, online posting.

11. Anthony James, "Paternalism's Demise: Blind Jim Ivy and Ole Miss, 1896–1955," *Mississippi Folklife* 28, no. 1 (Spring 1995): 17–24; David G. Sansing, *The University of Mississippi: A Sesquicentennial History* (Jackson: University of Mississippi Press, 1999), 275–76.

12. Stoddard, *Turnaround*, 97–99; "Merrill Collins," People, VF; letter from Paul W. Bryant to Frank Rose, April 2, 1958, "Athletic Department," Box #1, FR1.

13. Doyle, *An American Insurrection*, 100, 112–13.

14. Taylor Branch, *Parting the Waters: America in the King Years, 1954–1963* (New York: Simon & Schuster, 1988), 659; Willie Morris, *Terrains of the Heart and Other Essays on Home* (Oxford, MS: Yoknopatawpha Press, 1981), 253.

15. On the decline of Alabama football and Whitworth's tearful goodbye, see Stoddard, *Turnaround*, 26; on Lucy, see Clark, *The Schoolhouse Door*, 53–113.

16. Clark, *Schoolhouse Door*, 24–26, 80–82, 128–32.

17. "Goodbye to 'Bama," *Time* (November 19, 1956): 58.

18. Morris, *The Courting of Marcus Dupree*, 115. Technically, Carmichael was not fired but had clearly worn out his welcome and relieved everyone with his departure.

19. Clark, *Schoolhouse Door*, 138–39.

20. Letter from Ehney [no last name] to Ernest Williams, October 31, 1957; letter from R. R. Dansby to Board of Trustees, October 24, 1957; letter from R. R. Miree to Ernest Williams, November 4, 1957, all found in "Correspondence—Special Committee for Football Head Coach 1957," Box #1, AAD.

21. Clark, *Schoolhouse Door*, 142.

22. E-mail from Timothy Bryant to the author, November 30, 2006, in the author's possession.

23. Thomas D. Clark, *The Emerging South*, 2nd ed. (New York: Oxford University Press, 1968), 162–63.

24. "Where Bama Plays," originally published in the *Tuscaloosa News*, reprinted in *Montgomery Advertiser*, December 25, 1961, p. 4A. Ole Miss also played their games away from the on-campus Hemingway Stadium in favor of Memorial Stadium in Jackson, and sometimes Memphis's stadium for the same reason, but with nowhere near the regularity of Alabama's scheduling.

25. Letter from Frank Rose to Raiford Ellis, December 27, 1959, "Athletic Department" file, Box #1, FR1.

26. Letter from Paul W. Bryant to Dr. Frank Rose, May 6, 1959,and letter from Paul W. Bryant to Dr. Frank Rose, September 16, 1960, both in "Athletics Department" file, Box #1, FR1.

27. "Where Bama Plays," originally published in the *Tuscaloosa News*, reprinted in *Montgomery Advertiser*, December 25, 1961, p. 4A.

28. McWhorter, *Carry Me Home*, 306; Keith Dunnavant, *The Fifty-Year Seduction: How Television Manipulated College Football, from the Birth of the Modern NCAA to the Creation of the BCS* (New York: St. Martin's Press, 2004), 41–42; Dunnavant, *Coach*, 329, 94–95. Bryant was not alone in using the media to cultivate college football's faithful. Robert Kerr has demonstrated how, prior to the rise of coaches' shows, Bud Wilkinson at Oklahoma used his weekly *Bud Wilkinson's Football Letter* as a means to espouse the values of teamwork, discipline, and community cohesion that allowed Oklahomans to identify with Sooner football; Robert L. Kerr, "The Great White Father and the Antichrist: *Bud Wilkinson's Football Letter* as Cultural History," *American Journalism* 18, no. 3 (2001): 35–60.

29. On Gentleman's Agreements, see Charles Martin, "Racial Exclusion and Intersectional Rivalries: The Rise and Fall of the Gentlemen's Agreement in Big-Time College Football," paper given at the 1995 annual meeting of the Southern Historical Association, New Orleans, LA; see also James R. Coates, "Gentlemen's Agreement: The 1937 Maryland-Syracuse Football Game" (MA thesis, University of Maryland, 1982), and Patrick B. Miller, "Slouching towards a New Expediency: College Football and the Color Line during the Depression Decade," *American Studies* 40, no. 3 (Fall 1999): 5–30; the Gallalee incident is found in Clark, *Schoolhouse Door*, 21.

30. Untitled editorial note, *Southern Presbyterian Journal* (December 28, 1955): 2.

31. Letter from W. A. Gamble to H. B Dendy and L. Nelson Bell, February 10, 1956, and letter from L. Nelson Bell to W. A. Gamble, February 18, 1956, both found in folder 15, Box #26, LNB. For background in Bell, see David L. Chappell, *A Stone of Hope: Prophetic Religion and the Death of Jim Crow* (Chapel Hill: University of North Carolina Press, 2004), 117–21, 140–43.

32. Letter from John Graves to Tom [Waring], February 10, 1960, file 6 "John Temple Graves, 1952–1961," Box #401, TRW.

33. Letter from T. R. Waring to John Temple Graves, February 8, 1960, file 9, Box #1, JTG.

34. Ever careful of diction and any misconstrued meaning, Waring and Graves took to using "endure" with regards to integration rather than "accept"; see T. R. Waring to John Temple Graves, February 8, 1960, and T. R. Waring to John Temple Graves, February 16, 1960, file 9, Box #1, JTG; and John Graves to Tom [Waring], February 10, 1960, file 6 "John Temple Graves, 1952–1961," Box #401, TRW.

35. William Rogers, Robert Ward, Leah Rawls Atkins, and Wayne Flint, *Alabama: The History of a Deep South State* (Tuscaloosa: University of Alabama Press, 1994), 583–84, 618–19.

36. Letter from T. R. Waring to John Temple Graves, February 16, 1960, file 9, Box #1, JTG.

37. Letter from Walter C. Langsam to Frank A. Rose, November 5, 1958, and letter from Frank A. Rose to Walter C. Langsam, November 17, 1958, both found in "Athletic Department," Box #1, FR1.

38. "Random Shots," *Baton Rouge Sunday Advocate*, November 19, 1961, p. 2C.

39. "Benny Marshall Says," *Birmingham News*, December 2, 1959, p. 2, and "'Bama to a Bowl," *Birmingham News*, December 6, 1959, p. 10. For representative coverage from around the state, see, "Alabama Will Play Penn State in Liberty Bowl," *Alabama Journal*, December 1, 1959, p. 1; "'Bama Is Due to Accept Liberty Bowl Bid Today," *Birmingham Post-Herald*, December 1, 1959, p. 1; "Recognition for Crimson Tide," *Mobile Press-Register*, December 2, 1959, p. 4A; and "Alabama Improved Slowly," *Mobile Press-Register*, December 10, 1959, p. 5F, "The Tide's In," *Thomasville Times*, December 6, 1970, p. 2B; "Tide Makes Itself Heard," *Gadsden Times*, December 6, 1959, p. 4.

40. "'Bama Acceptance Pleasing to Little," *Birmingham Post-Herald*," December 2, 1959, p. 18, and "Clettus Atkinson," *Birmingham Post-Herald*, December 4, 1959, p. 7; "Benny Marshall Says," *Birmingham News*, December 11, 1959, p. 22; "Alabama Will Play Penn State in Liberty Bowl," *Alabama Journal*, December 1, 1959, p. 1.

41. Dan T. Carter, *The Politics of Rage: George Wallace, the Origins of the New Conservatism, and the Transformation of American Politics* (New York: Simon & Schuster, 1995), 90–96.

42. Leo Andrew Doyle, "'Causes Won, Not Lost': Football and Southern Culture, 1892–1983" (PhD diss., Emory University, 1998), 315; "Tide Congratulated," *Tuscaloosa News*, December 1, 1959, p. 1; Barra, *Last Coach*, 227.

43. Clark, *Schoolhouse Door*, 27–31, 142; letter from Hill Ferguson to J. Y. Brame, December 23, 1959, "Liberty Bowl Game," Box #5, FR2.

44. Clark, *Schoolhouse Door*, 46–47.

45. Letter from Gessner T. McCorvey to Dr. Frank Rose, December 12, 1959, "Liberty Bowl Game," Box #5, FR2.

46. Letter from Brewer Dixon to Frank Rose, December 1, 1959, and letter from Thomas S. Lawson to Frank A. Rose, December 16, 1959, both in "Board of Trustees, 1958–1959," Box #9, FR3.

47. Clippings file from Citizens Councils of Alabama to Jeff Bennett, undated (postmarked October 25, 1956), "Segregation, 1956–1982," Box #4, JJB.

48. Telegram from James B. Laseter to Coach Bear Bryant, December 7, 1959, "Liberty Bowl Game," Box #5, FR2; Dunnavant, *Coach*, 251–52.

49. Resolution from Dallas County Citizens Council, December 7, 1959, and letter from Frank A. Rose to M. Alston Keith, December 16, 1959, both in "Liberty Bowl Game," Box #5, FR2.

50. "New High Tide near Gettysburg," *Birmingham Post-Herald*, December 7, 1959, p. 10. For a more thorough examination of Graves's segregationist views, see Chappell, *A Stone of Hope*, 156–64.

51. Letter from B. G. Robinson Jr. to Frank A. Rose, December 7, 1959; letter from William H. Kilgore to Dr. [Frank] Rose, December 2, 1959; letter to John M.

Gallalee from Harry J. Greene and Charles A. Shorter, December 14, 1959, with attached resolution dated December 8, 1959, all found in "Liberty Bowl Game," Box #5, FR2.

52. Letter from J. Y. Brame to Walter P. Jones, December 15, 1959, "Liberty Bowl Game," Box #5, FR2.

53. "Betraying the Cause," *Tuscaloosa News*, December 14, 1959, p. 4.

54. "As I See It," *Montgomery Advertiser*, December 13, 1959, p. 1B.

55. Memo from J. Jefferson Bennett to Frank A. Rose, undated, "1959, Dr. Frank A. Rose," Box #1, JJB; letter from Jeff Coleman to Paul W. Bryant, December 30, 1959, and letter from J. Allen Reynolds Jr. to Paul "Bear" Bryant, December 2, 1959, both found in "Athletic Department," Box #1, FR1.

56. "The Silent Protest," *Montgomery Advertiser*, December 3, 1959, p. 4A.

57. "Liberty Bowl and Race," *Anniston Star*, reprinted in *Tuscaloosa News*, December 9, 1959, p. 4.

58. "The Tide Goes Bowling Again," *Tuscaloosa News*, December 3, 1959, p. 4, and "A Victory Would Help," *Tuscaloosa News*, December 18, 1959, p. 4.

59. Barra, *Last Coach*, 228–29.

60. "Big 10 Doubtful for Rose," *Los Angeles Times*, November 7, 1961, part 4, p. 1; "'Bama Anxious, Big 10 Doubtful," *Pasadena Star News*, December 7, 1961, p. 16; "'Bama Smelling Roses," *Pasadena Star News*, November 8, 1961, p. 22.

61. Barra, *Last Coach*, 4; "A Rose by Any Other Name," *Atlanta Journal*, November 15, 1961, p. 54; "Rose Bowl Out?" *Birmingham Post-Herald*, November 13, 1961, p. 6; "Dusting 'em off," *Birmingham News*, December 14, 1961, p. 13; "Bama Has Choice of Rose, Cotton," *Tuscaloosa News*, November 20, 1961, p. 8.

62. "Yes, the Rose Bowl Is Watching Alabama," *Birmingham News*, November 9, 1961, p. 75; "Alabama Is Bowl Conscious," *New York Times*, November 9, 1961, p. 47; "Alabama Seen for Rose Bowl Bid," *Pasadena Star News*, November 13, 1961, p. 20; "Sugar Bowl Seeks Tide & LSU," *Birmingham Post-Herald*, November 14, 1961, p. 14; "Sugar Says 'Bama to Rose," *Montgomery Advertiser*, November 14, 1961, p. 4B; "From Pasadena to Miami—It's Bowl Bidding Time," *Atlanta Journal*, November 25, 1961, p. 11.

63. "'Bama Choice of Writers for Bowl," *Los Angeles Times*, November 14, 1961, part 4, p. 1.; "One Vote for South," *Los Angeles Times*, November 12, 1961, sec. H, p. 2.; "Alabama Rose Bowl Express Picks Up Steam," *Pasadena Star News*, November 14, 1961, p. 22; "Rotarians Cool on Big 10 for Rose Bowl Bid," *Los Angeles Times*, November 25, 1961, part 4, page 3; "A Scent of the Roses," *Atlanta Journal*, November 9, 1961, p. 65; letter from Hugh William Rose to Frank A. Rose, November 26, 1961, "General Correspondence, Q-R 1961," Box #3, FR4.

64. "Big Ten Stays in Bowl Focus," *Los Angeles Examiner*, November 10, 1961, sec. 4, page 1; "Rose Bowl Still Most Popular," *Los Angeles Times*, November 17, 1961, part 4, p. 4; "Selection Group Is Favoring Tide," *Tuscaloosa News*, November 20, 1961, p. 9; "UCLA Seen Backing Bama for Rose Shot," *Tuscaloosa News*, November 8, 1961, p. 9.

65. Letter from Daniel J. Haughton to Frank Rose, November 20, 1961, and letter from Frank A Rose to Daniel J. Haughton, November 29, 1961, both found in "General Correspondence H-J," Box #2, FR4; letter from Frank Rose to John E.

Canaday 23, 1961, and letter from Frank A. Rose to John Canaday, November 29, 1961, "General Correspondence C," Box #1, FR4; letter from Daniel J. Haughton to Frank Rose, December 4, 1961, "Sugar Bowl Game," Box #8, FR2.

66. "Negro Groups Nixes Alabama," *Daily Bruin*, November 15, 1961, p. 2.

67. "Alabama an Insult to Bowl," *Los Angeles Examiner*, November 15, 1961, sec. 4, p. 1.

68. "Case for a Mutual Welcome," *Los Angeles Examiner*, November 21, 1961, section 4, p. 1.

69. "'Bama and Ol' Bear," *Los Angeles Times*, November 19, 1961, part 4, p. 1.

70. "Bedsheets and 'Bama," *Los Angeles Times*, November 20, 1961, part 4, p. 1.

71. "'Bama and Ol' Bear," *Los Angeles Times*, November 19, 1961, part 4, p. 1.

72. "Hesh My Mouf," *Los Angeles Times*, November 22, 1961, part 4, p. 1.

73. "Living Color," *Los Angeles Times*, November 29, 1961, part 4, p. 1.

74. "Alabama Gets Rose Bowl Bid," *Chicago Tribune*, November 20, 1961, part 4, p. 7; "Coast News Media Viewing Bama for Bowl," *Montgomery Advertiser*, November 16, 1961, p. 11A.

75. "Negro Boycott Proposed if Rose Bowl Calls Bama," *Montgomery Advertiser*, November 19, 1961, 1A.

76. From *Birmingham News*, November 20, 1961, p. 40, found in RB 1961.

77. "Racial Opposition to 'Bama Mounts," *Montgomery Advertiser*, November 20, 1961, p. 4B; "Which Bowl for Bama? Sugar's Sweet," *Tuscaloosa News*, November 19, 1961, p. 1; "Rose Bowl Out?" *Birmingham Post-Herald*, November 13, 1961, p. 6; "Rose Bowl, in a New Light," *Atlanta Journal*, November 17, 1961, p. 20.

78. "Rose Can Do without 'Bama, Says Writer," *Birmingham Post-Herald*, November 16, 1961, p. 10; "Blood-Colored White Supremacists," *Montgomery Advertiser*, November 26, 1961, p. 4A; "Western Nitwit Discovers Dixie," *Montgomery Advertiser*, December 10, 1961, p. 3B.

79. For an extensive survey of all in-state media comment, see RB 1961; "Looking with Land," *Tuscaloosa News*, November 27, 1961, p. 8.

80. "Who's on First—Besides Alabama, Ohio State?" *Atlanta Journal*, November 20, 1961, p. 9; "Rose Bowl Foe Still Undecided," *Daily Bruin*, November 21, 1961, p. 6.

81. Interview with anonymous, November 13, 2002, notes in the author's possession.

82. Bryant and Underwood, *Bear*, p. 197; "No Rosey Glow over Alabama," *Atlanta Journal*, November 29, 1961, p. 33; Doyle, "'Causes Won, Not Lost,'" 323.

83. "'Bama Expected to Meet Arkansas in Sugar Bowl" and "'Bama, Arkansas in Sugar," both in *Birmingham Post-Herald*, November 20, 1961, pp. 1, 24; "From the Bench," *Mobile Press-Register*, November 19, 1961, p. 2B.

84. Letter from Frank A. Rose to Robert S. Johnston, November 22, 1961, "General Correspondence, J&K," Box #2, FR4.

85. Donald R. Noble, introduction, in William Bradford Huie, *Mud on the Stars*, (Tuscaloosa: University of Alabama Press, 1996), x–xi.

86. "Betraying the Cause," *Tuscaloosa News*, December 14, 1959, p. 4.

87. On the role of the *Crimson-White* in student politics, see Phillip Weiss, "The Most Powerful Fraternity in America," *Esquire* (April 1992): 102–10; on segrega-

tionist anxieties over Jewish students and the paper, see Clark, *Schoolhouse Door*, 160–62.

88. Letter from Heinz Pfeifer to the author, no date (postmarked December 5, 2005), in the author's possession. Pfeiffer was a graduate student of Pauling's and later a colleague at Caltech.

89. Clark, *Schoolhouse Door*, 130.

90. The literature on Caltech's pranks and obsession with the Rose Bowl is ample, see Neil Sternberg, *If at All Possible, Involve a Cow: The Book of College Pranks* (New York: St. Martin's Press, 1992), 60–67; William Dodge Jr., Reuben B. Moulton, Harrison W. Sigworth, and Adrian C. Smith Jr., *Legends of Caltech* (Pasadena: California Institute of Technology Alumni Association, 1983), 35–38; William Dodge Jr., Reuben B. Moulton, Harrison W. Sigworth, and Adrian C. Smith Jr., *More Legends of Caltech* (Pasadena: California Institute of Technology Alumni Association, 1989), 60–63.

91. Letter from Heinz Pfeiffer to the author, December 5, 2005, in the author's possession.

92. "A 'Bear' at 'Bama," *Time* (November 17, 1961): 72; letter from J. Jefferson Bennett to Editor, Time Magazine, November 16, 1961, folder 10, "General Correspondence, 1960–1962," Box # 23, JJB; "UA Charges 'Time' Article about Bryant Misleading," *Tuscaloosa News*, November 18, 1961, p. 1; Andrew Doyle, "Bear Bryant: Symbol for an Embattled South," *Colby Quarterly* 32 (March 1996): 72–86.

93. Eskew, *But for Birmingham*, 178–79, 279; McWhorter, *Carry Me Home*, 403; Carter, *Politics of Rage*, 116.

94. Letter from Daniel J. Haughton to Frank Rose, November 20, 1961, "General Correspondence, H&I," Box #2, FR4.

95. Letter from W. R. Rivers to Norman Chandler, December 5, 1961, "General Correspondence, Q&R," Box #3, FR4.

96. Letter from D. J. Haughton to Frank Rose, December 4, 1961, "Sugar Bowl Game," Box #8, FR2.

97. Letter from Frank A. Rose to Robert S. Johnston, November 22, 1961, "General Correspondence, J&K," Box #2, FR4.

98. Letter from Frank A. Rose to John Canaday, November 29, 1961, "General Correspondence, C," Box #1, FR4.

99. Letter from Frank A. Rose to W. R. Rivers, December 19, 1961, "General Correspondence, Q&R," Box #3, FR4.

100. Letter from Frank A. Rose to Daniel J. Haughton, November 29, 1961, "General Correspondence, H&J," Box #2, FR4.

101. Letter from Frank Rose to Winton Blount, November 22, 1961, "Board of Trustees, 1961," Box #4, FR4.

102. Clark, *Schoolhouse Door*, 256; "Race Issue Where Bryant, Gov. Wallace Split," unattributed clipping found in "Paul Bryant Commentary," People, VF; Carter, *Politics of Rage*, 111–12.

103. Paul W. Bryant and John Underwood, *Bear: The Good Life and Hard Times of Alabama's Coach Bryant*, 4th ed. (New York: Little, Brown, 1975), 201; Barra, *Last Coach*, 182. Barra has pointed out that Bryant's autobiography contains

numerous errors in terms of exact names, dates, and places, generally reflecting Bryant's *desired* memories rather than factual re-creations.

104. Bryant and Underwood, *Bear*, 317; letter from Jim Owens to author, July 7, 1997, in the author's possession.

105. "Tide Takes Sugar," *Crimson-White*, November 30, 1961, p. 4.

Chapter 5. Westwood: College Football and Cold War Dissent

Opening comment from the inaugural Address of Franklin D. Murphy, Chancellor, September 23, 1960, file 10, Box #57, FDMP.

1. Thelin, *Games Colleges Play*, 130.

2. Minutes of the Executive Committee Meeting, April 19, 1961, folder 15, Box #79, UASI.

3. On the PCC scandal, see Thelin, *Games Colleges Play*, 128–54; Watterson, *College Football*, 277–86; a more partisan discussion of the scandal, including the Hollis anecdote, as well as the lingering animosity that it engendered, can be found in Hendrik Van Leuven, *Touchdown UCLA! The Complete Account of Bruin Football* (Tomball, TX: Strode, 1982), 110–14. The comments between UCLA and Stanford are found in a letter from Bradford A. Booth to Chancellor Raymond Allen, February 11, 1958, "Athletics, 1953–1972," Box #5, Administrative Files, 1935–1982, ASEO.

4. Smith, *Play-by-Play*, 65–66. On Oklahoma's football finances, see Frank, "Saturday Afternoon Meat Grinders," 54–59; and Dent, *The Undefeated*, 47–52.

5. E-mail from Tom Hansen, Commissioner, Pacific-10 Conference, to the author, dated November 15, 2002, in the author's possession; "Hamilton's Move West May Be Good for College Grid," clippings file, TJH.

6. Dunnavant, *The 50 Year Seduction*, 40–41; clippings file, Hamilton Papers, Confidential Memo from Bradford A. Booth to Chancellor Raymond Allen, October 30, 1957, "Athletics, 1953–1972," Box #5, Administrative Files, 1935–1982, ASEO; Starr, "The Big New Battle in the Big 10," 147–54; letter from Eddie Schultz Jr. to Captain Thomas Hamilton, dated July 22, 1959, and letter from Murray Chass to Thomas J. Hamilton, dated June 30, 1959, both found in TJH. John Thelin notes the attempt by Penn to align with the group in *Games Colleges Play*, 149.

7. "Pitt's Tom Hamilton Becoming Top Man in College Football," clippings file, TJH; "West Point Lapse Is Linked to Trend," *New York Times*, January 15, 1952; "Navy Out to Make Money on Grid Team," *Los Angeles Times*, November 12, 1958, part 4, p. 3.

8. Letter from Harry A. Stuhldreher to Mr. and Mrs. T. J. Hamilton, dated June 30, 1959; letter from Lt. Col. Charles E. Henise to Tom [Hamilton], dated July 17, 1959, all found in TJH.

9. Dunnavant, *The Fifty-Year Seduction*, 40–41; "Rube-Barbs," dated October 5, 1958, clippings file, TJH; "Hits and Bits," *Birmingham World*, December 6, 1961, p. 7.

10. Letter from Frank L. Kidner to Thomas J. Cunningham, March 2, 1960 and

letter from Thomas J. Cunningham to Frank L. Kidner, March 11, 1960, "246-S Intercollegiate Athletic Advisory Council, 1959–1960," Box #123, FDM.

11. Dunnavant, *The 50-Year Seduction*, 41.

12. "Conform or Else," folder 1950, Box #6, SAC. On the loyalty oath controversy, see Caute, *The Great Fear*, 422–27.

13. On Kerr's understanding of the Cold War function of the multiversity, see his Godkin lectures, *The Uses of the University*, on his Master Plan for Higher Education, see his memoir, *The Gold and The Blue: A Personal Memoir of the University of California, 1949-1967*, vol. 1 (Berkeley: University of California Press, 2001).

14. "Is Democracy Un-American?" *Daily Bruin*, September 28, 1955, p. 3.

15. "Sense of Purpose," *Daily Bruin*, May 5, 1961, p. 4.

16. "Cold War Myths," *Daily Bruin*, April 15, 1966, p. 5.

17. "The Border, Where?" *Daily Bruin*, March 24, 1952, p. 2.

18. "Mandate for Action," *Daily Bruin*, March 26, 1952, p. 2; "FEPC beyond Scope of SEC, Says Rosen," *Daily Bruin*, April 10, 1953, p. 1.

19. "SLC Attacks Police Action in Nashville," *Daily Bruin*, March 3, 1960, p. 1. On the university's historic policies banning such discussion, see C. Michael Otten, *University Authority and the Student: The Berkeley Experience* (Berkeley: University of California Press, 1970); on the West Adams bombing, see Josh Sides, *L.A. City Limits: African American Los Angeles from the Great Depression to the Present* (Berkeley: University of California Press, 2003), 101–3.

20. Otten, *University Authority and the Student*, 170–78; "University Rule 17 Liberalized, *Daily Bruin*, October 7, 1958, p. 1; "Rule 17 Divided into Two Parts," *Daily Bruin*, October 26, 1959, p. 1; "Kerr Clarifies Directive," *Daily Bruin*, November 25, 1959, p. 1; "Kerr Limits Group Recognition," *Daily Bruin*, September 18, 1961, p. 1; "Kerr Keynotes Controversy," *Daily Bruin*, November 7, 1961, p. 1. For a lengthy discussion of the evolution of the Kerr Directives at UCLA, see Kurt Edward Kemper, "Reformers in the Marketplace of Ideas: Student Activism and American Democracy in Cold War Los Angeles" (PhD diss., Louisiana State University, 2000), 96–99, 106–25.

21. "Kerr Modifies 'Facilities Use' Regulation," *Daily Bruin*, February 15, 1961, p. 1.

22. "The New Fight," *Daily Bruin*, October 26, 1959, p. 4, "On Campi," *Daily Bruin*, September 27, 1960, p. 2.

23. On black migration to and circumstances in Los Angeles, see Douglas Flamming, *Bound for Freedom: Black Los Angeles in Jim Crow America* (Berkeley: University of California Press, 2005); Sides, *L.A. City Limits*; Lawrence Brooks de Graaf, "Negro Migration to Los Angeles, 1930 to 1950" (PhD diss., UCLA, 1962); Lawrence B. de Graaf, "The City of Black Angels: Emergence of the Los Angeles Ghetto, 1890–1930," *Pacific Historical Review* 39 (August 1970): 323–52; Sally Jane Sandoval, "Ghetto Growing Pains: The Impact of Negro Migration on the City of Los Angeles, 1940–1960" (MA thesis, California State University, Fullerton, 1974).

24. UCLA Office of the Registrar, Statistics, October 1935–August 1940, University Archives, UCLA. For a general discussion of the founding of UCLA, see Edward A. Dickson, *The University of California at Los Angeles: Its Origins and Forma-*

tive Years (Los Angeles: Friends of the UCLA Library, 1955); on the university's first half century, see Andrew Hamilton and John B. Jackson, *UCLA on the Move during Fifty Golden Years, 1919–1969* (Los Angeles, CA: Ward Ritchie Press, 1969); for a critical discussion of the role of UCLA students during this period, see Kemper, "Reformers in the Marketplace of Ideas."

25. Quintard Taylor, *In Search of the Racial Frontier: African Americans in the American West, 1528–1990* (New York: W. W. Norton, 1998), 280.

26. Carey McWilliams, *Southern California Country: An Island on the Land* (New York: Duell, Sloan & Pearce, 1946), 325. Scholars too, at the time, saw the postwar West as facing a crossroads. Historian L. D. Reddick posited the West either as "a land of human democracy or else in letters large enough for the world's passing planes to read should be written the words 'Keep Out, For Whites Only'"; L. D. Reddick, "The New Race Relations Frontier," *Journal of Educational Sociology* 19, no. 3 (1945): 129–45. Notions of California exceptionalism in the postwar period were not limited solely to race. Historians have ascribed a cultural exceptionalism, too; see Timothy White, *The Nearest Faraway Place: Brian Wilson, the Beach Boys, and the Southern California Experience* (New York: Henry Holt, 1994).

27. "Opportunity Knocks," *California Bruin*, July 12, 1944, p. 4.

28. Sara Boynoff, "Los Angeles: A Race Relations Success Story," *Look* (March 19, 1957): 25–29.

29. Carey McWilliams, *California: The Great Exception* (New York: Current Books, 1949), 76, 23; Boynoff, "Los Angeles: A Race Relations Success Story"; see also Flamming, *Bound for Freedom*, 55–58.

30. "Required Reading," *California Bruin*, March 3, 1945, p. 4.

31. "Move to Reconsider," *Daily Bruin*, November 11, 1948, p. 4. Students at UCLA were not the only ones sure of the school's future eminence. Provost Earle Hedrick declared shortly before his death in 1943, "I was convinced that this institution was destined to be one of the greatest universities in the world"; Karen Mack, "Our Peerless Leaders," *UCLA Magazine* (Fall 1994): 38–39.

32. "Johnson Commends Lack of Racial Discrimination," *California Daily Bruin*, November 29, 1945, p. 3.

33. "Tolerance Convocation Held Today," *Daily Bruin*, May 5, 1947, p. 1; "6 California Girls Here to Study Bias," *New York Times*, February 24, 1947; "Panel Urges Racial Unity," *Daily Bruin*, May 6, 1947, p. 1.

34. Boynoff, "Los Angeles: A Race Relations Success Story."

35. Kevin Allen Leonard, "'In the Interest of All Races': African Americans and Interracial Cooperation in Los Angeles during World War II," in *Seeking El Dorado: African Americans in California*, ed. Lawrence B. de Graaf, Kevin Mulroy, and Quintard Taylor, 309–42 (Seattle: University of Washington Press, 2001); Flamming, *Bound for Freedom*, also discusses the shifting, and by the 1950s, declining opportunities for blacks in Los Angeles.

36. "Racial Positivism," *Daily Bruin*, September 16, 1958, p. 2.

37. "Liberal Attitude," *Daily Bruin*, April 27, 1961, p. 5.

38. On UCLA's rivalry with USC and the Victory Bell tradition, see *UCLA Traditions: A Collection of UCLA Stories, Customs, and Rituals* (Los Angeles: UCLAlumni Association, n.d.), 22–25, in the author's possession; and Steve Springer and Mi-

chael Arkush, *60 Years of USC-UCLA Football* (Stamford, CT: Longmeadow Press, 1991), 72–73.

39. "Jackie Robinson Urges UCLA to Promote Human Relations," *Daily Bruin*, February 16, 1954, p. 1.

40. Boynoff, "Los Angeles: A Race Relations Success Story."

41. "Campus Goal," *Daily Bruin*, May 20, 1955, p. 4.

42. "An Open Letter," *Daily Bruin*, October 3, 1962, p. 4.

43. Thomas G. Smith, "Outside the Pale: The Exclusion of Blacks from the National Football League, 1934–1946," *Journal of Sport History* 15, no. 3 (1988): 225–81.

44. "Negro Stars Left Off East, West Rosters," *Daily Bruin*, December 28, 1945, p. 4; "No Missouri Compromise," October 29, 1940, *Daily Bruin*, p. 4.

45. Flamming, *Bound for Freedom*, 266–67.

46. Amy Bass, *Not the Triumph, but the Struggle: The 1968 Olympics and the Making of the Blacks Athlete* (Minneapolis: University of Minnesota Press, 2002), 74–79, provides an authoritative discussion of Cromwell's racialist convictions.

47. Woody Strode and Sam Young, *Goal Dust: The Warm and Candid Memoir of a Pioneer Black Athlete and Actor* (Lanham, MD: Madison Books, 1990), 27–30.

48. David Falkner, *Great Time Coming: The Life of Jackie Robinson from Baseball to Birmingham* (New York: Simon & Schuster, 1995), 49.

49. Springer and Arkush, *60 Years of USC-UCLA Football*, 101. Fifteen years after the publication of Springer and Arkush's book, Roberts again addressed the issue of race during his playing days and told a far more complimentary tale of both his teammates and his coaches. Traveling to play the University of Texas in 1956, an Austin hotel refused to allow Roberts and two other black teammates to stay with the rest of the Trojans. Head coach Jess Hill immediately pulled the whole team from the hotel and found alternate lodgings, with Arnett claiming that the hotel's actions "kind of ticked us off"; "Civil Wrong Turned Right," *Los Angeles Times*, January 2, 2006, online edition.

50. Miller, "Slouching towards a New Expediency," 7.

51. "The Narrow Mind," *Daily Bruin*, November 9, 1945, p. 8; Jack Olson, "The Black Athlete, Part II: Pride and Prejudice," *Sports Illustrated* (July 7, 1968): 20. Michigan State University also earned a reputation as a "good place" for black athletes by the late 1950s and early 1960s. There too the university benefited from the positive public image of providing opportunities to blacks but did little to address the off-campus housing and social discrimination and was particularly anxious about the prospect of black athletes engaging in interracial dating; see Beth J. Shapiro, "Intercollegiate Athletics and Big-Time Sport at Michigan State University: Or 'The Difference between Good and Great Is a Little Extra Effort'" (PhD diss., Michigan State University, 1982), 141, 156; and Mike Celizic, *The Biggest Game of Them All: Notre Dame, Michigan State, and the Fall of '66* (New York: Simon & Schuster, 1992), 112–24.

52. "NAACP on R.P.," *Daily Bruin*, October 8, 1958, p. 2.

53. "Mythology," *Daily Bruin*, February 8, 1960, p. 4; for a general discussion of campus restrictions on black students during this period, see Kemper, "Reformers in the Marketplace of Ideas," 37–92.

54. "Look to the West," *Daily Bruin*, March 21, 1960, p. 4.

55. "Discrimination," *Daily Bruin*, October 30, 1962, p. 4.

56. "Bloody Victory," *Daily Bruin*, May 15, 1963, p. 4.

57. Singleton's background is found in Raymond Arsenault's *Freedom Riders: 1961 and the Struggle for Racial Justice*, 384–85, 423; see also Willy Siegel Leventhal, "Rick Tuttle and the Ghosts of Mississippi," *UCLAlumni Magazine* 13, no. 1 (September 2000): 10–13; on the UCLA NAACP, see "UCLA Chapter NAACP Activity Report, Spring 1958," file "1958–1959," Box #18, NAACP; "NAACP Gains Campus Status," *Daily Bruin*, September 23, 1960, p. 1; "Campus Issues," April 4, 1962, file "1962," Box #6, SAC; on the sit-ins, see "CORE boycotts, flyers, etc.," file 11, Box #12, CRM, "Students to Picket Local Stores," *Daily Bruin*, March 14, 1960, p. 1; "Pickets Begin Third Day," *Daily Bruin*, March 17, 1960, p. 1; "Picketers Agin' Dixie Policy," *Daily Bruin*, April 7, 1960, p. 1. The number of UCLA students who participated in the Freedom Rides remains unclear. Sources at the time put the number at fourteen, a figure agreed upon by Arsenault's exhaustive research, though another recent account by a participant puts it at fifteen; neither figure agrees with CORE records from the period, which list sixteen. These figures all apparently dealt with those who went to Mississippi, excluding those who went to Houston; "Freedom Riders Tell Saga," *Daily Bruin*, February 15, 1962, p. 3; Arsenault, *Freedom Riders*, 384–85; Leventhal, "Rick Tuttle and the Ghosts of Mississippi"; "Freedom Rider Cases on Appeal," microfilm series 1:38, roll #3, Papers of CORE.

58. Steven McNichols, "The Last Freedom Ride," UCLAOHP.

59. Arsenault, *Freedom Riders*, 384–85, 423; Leventhal, "Rick Tuttle and the Ghosts of Mississippi"; "Freedom Riders Tell Saga," *Daily Bruin*, February 15, 1962, p. 3.

60. Both Singleton and James Stiven, ASUCLA president that year, commented on the role of Barouh's death; oral interview with James Stiven, January 5, 1997, San Diego, California; oral interview with Robert Singleton, Los Angeles, California, January 8, 1997, transcripts of both in the author's possession.

61. CORE's chutzpah on the issue was not insignificant because in 1952, the university threatened with suspension students from the Young Republican Club who insisted on naming their group Uclans for Eisenhower. The university also prohibited the group from meeting in a sorority house as planned, even though the Greek houses were not owned by the university or on university property; "GOP Group Asked to Change Name," *Daily Bruin*, October 10, 1952, p. 1.

62. "On Campi," *Daily Bruin*, September 27, 1960, p. 2; "Can't We Hope?" *Daily Bruin*, September 20, 1960, p. 4.

63. "Apathy," *Daily Bruin*, November 30, 1961, p. 4.

64. "Jackson Jail: Freedom Rider Tells Experience," *Daily Bruin*, October 3, 1961, p. 1; "An Open Letter," *Daily Bruin*, September 20, 1961.

65. Letter from George Houser to Cornelius Steelink, March 17, 1950, microfilm series 3:57, reel #13, CORE. On CORE's membership issues in Los Angeles throughout the period, see August Meier and Elliot Rudwick, *CORE: A Study in the Modern Civil Rights Movement* (Urbana: University of Illinois Press, 1975), 60–61, 74, 95, 110.

66. Letter from Joann Love Allen to National Office, undated, 5:15, reel #18, CORE.

67. Sides, *L.A. City Limits*, 150–51; "Report on Los Angeles CORE," by Everett M. Mackinen, September 7, 1961, 5:15, reel #18, CORE.

68. "Los Angeles CORE Annual Report, June 1961–June 1962," file 41, Carton #3, SPC. It is perhaps indicative of the limits of CORE's resources in the Budweiser campaign that in Josh Sides's examination of the events, he labels it an NAACP initiative, not even mentioning CORE participation; Sides, *L.A. City Limits*, 150–51.

69. Kevin Allen Leonard, "'I Am Sure You Can Read between the Lines': Cold War Anti-Communism and the NAACP in Los Angeles," *Journal of the West* 44 (Spring 2005): 16–23.

70. Josh Sides, "'You Understand My Condition': The Civil Rights Congress in the Los Angeles African-American Community, 1946–1952," *Pacific Historical Review* 67 (May 1998): 233–57; Sides, *L.A. City Limits*, 139–51; see also Flamming, *Bound for Freedom*, 365–72; and Shana Beth Bernstein, "Building Bridges at Home in a Time of Global Conflict: Interracial Cooperation and the Fight For Civil Rights in Los Angeles, 1933–1954" (PhD diss., Stanford University, 2003), 181–218. For anticommunist rhetoric at UCLA during the period, see Kemper, "Reformers in the Marketplace of Ideas," 35–92.

71. Byron Atkinson, "Creating the Office of Student Affairs," UCLAOHP.

72. Letter from Milton E. Hahn to Chancellor Raymond B. Allen, dated November 3, 1954, obtained and reprinted in *The Observer*, an underground student paper, March 30, 1955, found in folder "1954," Box #6, SAC.

73. Kemper, "Reformers in the Marketplace," 82–82, 88–91; George Garrigues, "Loud Bark and Curious Eyes: A History of the UCLA *Daily Bruin*, 1919–1955" (MA thesis, University of California, Los Angeles, 1970), 198–99.

74. Letter from Milton E. Hahn to Miriam Fisher, undated, reprinted as "An Open Letter," *Daily Bruin*, October 31, 1955, "NAACP Controversy," *Daily Bruin*, October 31, 1955, p. 4.

75. William Coit Ackerman, *My Fifty Year Love-in at UCLA* (Los Angeles: Fashion Press, 1969), 87–88.

76. The circumstances of Hahn's departure have never been satisfactorily explained. Even his official university obituary, which was extremely complimentary, noted that his departure came "after a round of particularly difficult infighting"; University of California Academic Senate, University of California: In Memoriam, 1980 (Berkeley, CA: University of California), 1980, pp. 107–8; see also, "Will Our Dean of Students Return?" *Daily Bruin*, October 28, 1959, p. 1.

77. Singleton interview; Mack, "Our Peerless Leaders"; Eugene Lee, *The Origins of the Chancellorship: The Buried Report of 1948* (Berkeley, CA: Center for the Studies in Higher Education and Institute of Governmental Studies, 1995); "Murphy Says DB Editorial Answered Hillings Amply," *Daily Bruin*, October 24, 1960, p. 1.

78. Franklin D. Murphy, "My Chancellorship: An Utterly Candid View," UCLAOHP.

79. "University Must Challenge, Test," *Daily Bruin*, March 19, 1961, p. 1.

80. Oral interview with Dr. Charles E. Young, August 3 and 11, 1999, Los Angeles, California.

81. Singleton interview; "FDM's Comm Begins Anti-Discrim Work," *Daily Bruin*, April 18, 1961, p. 1; letter from Scott Van Leuven to Fellow Students, May 1, 1964, "Calif. Social Action-Housing & Prop. 14," Box #2, CRM. For Murphy's public stance on the Kerr Directives, see letter from Franklin D. Murphy to Harry Shearer, November 17, 1961, "246–BV Student Govt., Kerr Directives, 1958–1964," Box #122, FDM.

82. "A Nation Takes a Ride," *Daily Bruin*, October 4, 1961, p. 8.

83. Minutes of the Student Legislative Council, May 1961–May 1962, October 13, 1961, SLC; "Petitions Sent to AG," *Daily Bruin*, October 16, 1961, p. 1.

84. "Our Unfinished Business," *Daily Bruin*, October 18, 1961, p. 8.

85. CORE housing notice, "1962," Box #6, SAC.

86. Most of the items appeared in the "On Other Campi" section of the *Daily Bruin*, see September 19, 1961, p. 3; September 21, 1961, p. 2; October 5, 1961, p. 5; October 10, 1961, p. 8; October 16, 1961, p. 1; October 18, 1961, p. 4; November 6, 1961, p. 7; November 13, 1961, p. 3.

87. "Petition Requests $5000 Assistance," *Daily Bruin*, November 28, 1961, p. 1.

88. "Endorsement the Real Issue," *Daily Bruin*, December 11, 1961, p. 4.

89. "Loan Vote Begins Today" and "Yes on the Riders," both found in *Daily Bruin*, February 14, 1962, p. 1.

90. "BOC Refuses $5000 Freedom Rider Loan" and "A Sham," both in *Daily Bruin*, March 9, 1962, p. 1.

91. "Negro Group Nixes Alabama," *Daily Bruin*, November 15, 1961, p. 2; "Students to Boycott Alabama," *California Eagle*, November 23, 1961, p. 1; Van Leuven, *Touchdown UCLA!*, 132–33. I am deeply indebted to Hendrik for providing copies to me of his interview notes from his book.

92. "Blitherings," *Daily Trojan*, November 16, 1961, p. 4.

93. "Race and the Rose Bowl," *Pasadena Star-News*, November 24, 1961, p. 14.

94. "Case for a Mutual Welcome," *Los Angeles Examiner*, November 21, 1961, sec. 4, p. 1; "Bedsheets and 'Bama," *Los Angeles Times*, November 20, 1961, sec. 4, p. 1.

95. "Race and the Rose Bowl," *Pasadena Star-News*, November 24, 1961, p. 14.

96. See as examples "No Missouri Compromise," *California Bruin*, October 29, 1940, p. 2, and "Bigots in Washington," November 21, 1958, p. 4, both in *Daily Bruin*; "Tread Softly," November 29, 1960, *Daily Bruin*, p. 4; "We Do Tread Softly, November 30, 1960, *Daily Bruin*, p. 4; "South Westwood," December 8, 1960, *Daily Bruin*, p. 4; "Moderates, Arise," *Daily Bruin*, November 22, 1961, p. 4.

97. "Bully for Boycott," *Daily Bruin*, November 22, 1961, p. 5.

98. "Keep Alabama Out of the Rose Bowl," *California Eagle*, November 16, 1961, p. 1.

99. "Don't Bring Dixiecrats to Rose Bowl," *Los Angeles Sentinel*, November 23, 1961, p. 10B; "Brock Says," *Los Angeles Sentinel*, November 16, 1961, p. 14B.

100. "Alabama an Insult to Bowl," *Los Angeles Examiner*, November 15, 1961, sec. 4, p. 1; "Case for a Mutual Welcome," *Los Angeles Examiner*, November 21, 1961, sec. 4, p. 1; "'Bama and Ol' Bear," *Los Angeles Times*, November 19, 1961, part 4, p. 1; "Bedsheets and 'Bama," *Los Angeles Times*, November 20, 1961, part 4, p. 1; "Living Color," *Los Angeles Times*, November 29, 1961, part 4, p. 1; "Student Paper Reports," *New York Times*, November 18, 1961, p. 17.

101. John R. Wooden, as told to Jack Tobin, *They Call Me Coach* (Waco, TX: Word Books, 1972), 77; Wooden noted that had he known that he "was not working for the University but rather for the Associated Students," he "would never have considered [UCLA] in the first place."

102. Garrigues, "Loud Bark and Curious Eyes," 50–53.

103. Ackerman, *My Fifty Year Love-In at UCLA*, 79, 289–90.

104. "Platform: New UCLA Campus Political Party," 1959 folder, Box #6, SAC.

105. "Council for Mexican-American Education," 1954 folder, Box #6, SAC.

106. "The Right Man at the Right Time: J. D. Morgan," Franklin Murphy to David Rose, UCLAOHP; Minutes, October 12, 1960, SLC.

107. Report on Examination of Statement of distributive share of football game with the University of Minnesota played at the Rose Bowl on January 1, 1962, "14 Rose Bowl 1961–1966," Box #27, FDM; oral interview with Robert Fischer, Los Angeles, California, March 28, 1997.

108. Student activists' displeasure with administrative control of their finances as well as football's favored position on campus appeared again in 1965 when Murphy proposed using student funds to help build an on-campus football stadium for the Bruins. The students overwhelmingly rejected the proposal in a campus referendum, drawing more votes even than student opposition to the war in Vietnam, which was on the same referendum. As a prelude to the referendum, activists held a protest touch-football game in Murphy's spacious office, with one activist quipping, "He wants football on campus? We'll give him football on campus," "Vote Says No to Stadium on Campus," *Daily Bruin*, December 15, 1965, p. 1; Joel Siegel, "A Sixties Scrapbook," *UCLA Magazine* (75th anniversary issue, Fall 1994): 40.

109. Robert Cohen, *When the Old Left Was Young: Student Radicals and America's First Student Movement, 1929–1941* (New York: Oxford University Press, 1993), 118–29; Ralph Brax, *The First Student Movement: Student Activism in the United States during the 1930s* (Port Washington, NY: Kennikat Press, 1981), 38–40; "What Is the Situation on Our Campus?" "What's It All About???" and "The U.C.L.A. Americans," newspaper clipping hand dated 11/2/34, all found in 1934 folder, Box #1, SAC.

110. "Drama Group Offers 'Uncle Tom's Cabin,'" *Daily Bruin*, December 3, 1940, p. 1;"Poor Uncle Tom," *Daily Bruin*, December 5, 1940, p. 4; "To Straighten Out a Mess," *Daily Bruin*, December 9, 1940, p. 2.

111. Ackerman, *My Fifty Year Love-in at UCLA*, 152–53.

112. Letter from Earl J. Miller to Robert Gordon Sproul, December 12, 1940, "ASUCLA 40–2," Box #90, and Confidential Memo, undated [in 1936 file], file 105, Box #24, both found in CO.

113. Letter from Andrew Hamilton to Raymond Allen, September 16, 1953, file 228 "Loyalty Oath and Subversive Activities," Box # 266, CO.

114. "NAACP May Walk on UCLA Games in Houston," *Daily Bruin*, December 8, 1961, p. 14; "SLC Asks Chancellor for Athletic Segregation Policy," *Daily Bruin*, January 4, 1962, p. 1; "Wires Sent Brown, Kerr on Athletics Segregation," *Daily Bruin*, January 5, 1962, p. 1; "FDM to Set Athletic Policy on Segregation," *Daily*

Bruin, January 6, 1962, p. 1. Rather than separate the team, head coach John Wooden had the team stay in campus dorms, initiating a long-standing refusal during his tenure to bow to segregation. Oddly enough, the issue arose most often not in the South but in Utah, because of long-standing racial assumptions, since repudiated, of the Mormon faith.

115. "SLC Commentary," *Daily Bruin*, January 5, 1962, p. 4.

116. The discussion of such a policy began at least as early as March 1960; letter from Thomas J. Cunningham to Chancellor Glenn T. Seaborg, April 1, 1960; letter from Thomas J. Cunningham to Members of the Executive Committee of the IAAC, May 10, 1960; letter from Clark Kerr to Chancellor Franklin D. Murphy, September 7, 1960; and letter from Franklin D. Murphy to Wilbur Johns, January 24, 1962, all found in file 246–S, "Intercollegiate Athletics Advisory Council 1959–60," Box #123, FDM; letter from Bradford A. Booth to Thomas J. Cunningham, April 29, 1964 and memo from Bradford A. Booth to Vice Chancellor Charles E. Young, June 10, 1964, both found in "General Counsel 1960–77," Box #66, RAF.

117. Letter from Brad Pye Jr. to Vic Kelley, October 10, 1961, "Dept. of Intercollegiate Athletics, 1962–64," Box #27, FDM; Press Box Discrimination," *Los Angeles Sentinel*, October 5, 1961, p. 10B; "Tan Press Excluded," *California Eagle*, November 23, 1961, p. 6; "UCLA & USC Give Negro Writers Shabby Deal," *Los Angeles Sentinel*, November 9, 1961, p. 10B (the article mentioned the same treatment afforded USC, who also played their home games at the Coliseum and also excluded the black media from the press box); letter from Andrew Hamilton to Charles Young, October 13, 1961; letter from Charles E. Young to Brad Pye Jr., June 4, 1962; and letter from Franklin D. Murphy to Wilbur Johns, June 19, 1962, all found in "Dept. of Intercollegiate Athletics, 1962–64," Box #27, FDM. In conjunction with UCLA's actions, USC also allowed full access to the press box.

Conclusion

1. "Is Rose Eyeing Navy?" *New Orleans Times Picayune*, November 30, 1961, sec. 2, p. 10.

2. "Rose Bowl Still Undecided," *Pasadena Star News*, November 21, 1961, p. 14.

3. "Aggies Rate Roses, King Wires Coast," *Salt Lake Tribune*, November 25, 1961, p. 1C; "King Sends Telegrams to Brown, Others," *Los Angeles Times*, November 25, 1961, part 4, p. 5; "Rep. Wants Utah State in Rose," *Pasadena Star News*, November 25, 1961, p. 9.

4. "Biography," finding aid and document inventory, DSK.

5. "Aggie Coach Eyes Bowls," *Salt Lake Tribune*, November 26, 1961, p. 2D.

6. "Sports Mirror," *Salt Lake Tribune*, November 27, 1961, p. 21.

7. Letter from Pete Newell to the author, undated (postmarked July 12, 1997), in the author's possession.

8. Letter from Milton Gordon to Wilbur C. Johns, July 2, 1962, "General Counsel, 1960–1977," Box #66, RAF.

9. Letter from Pete Newell to the author, undated [postmarked July 12, 1997], in the author's possession.

10. "Coast Teams Agree to Negotiate with Big Ten on Rose Bowl Pact," *New York Times*, December 15, 1961, p. 50; "Big Ten and Big Five Discuss Bowl Pact Today," *New York Times*, January 2, 1962, p. 34; "Rose Bowl Pact Nears Approval," *New York Times*, January 3, 1962, p. 28.

11. Telephone conversation with the author, June 18, 2007.

12. Speech given to the first annual Vince Lombardi Award Dinner, January 21, 1971, Houston, Texas, full text found in John R. Coyne, *The Impudent Snobs: Agnew vs. the Intellectual Establishment* (New Rochelle, NY: Arlington House, 1972), 444–47.

13. "League May Never Be the Same after Donohue," *Los Angeles Times*, May 30, 1972, part 3, p. 1.

14. "The Front Runners," *New York Times*, October 30, 1969, p. 63.

Selected Bibliography

Archival Material

Birmingham Public Library, Birmingham, Alabama
  Papers of John Temple Graves II (JTG)
Louisiana State University, Baton Rouge
  University Archives, Hill Memorial Library
    Records of the Board of Supervisors (RBS)
  Microform Collections, Middleton Library
    Papers of the Congress on Racial Equality (CORE)
Louisiana State University, Shreveport, Shreveport
  Archives and Special Collections, Noel Library
    Papers of William M. Rainach (WMR)
    Papers of Ned Touchstone (NP)
Northwestern University, Evanston, Illinois
  University Archives, Deering Library
    Records of the Faculty Council on Intercollegiate Athletics (FCIA)
The Ohio State University, Columbus
  University Archives
    Biographical Files (BF)
    Minutes of the Athletic Board (MAB)
    Minutes of the Faculty Council (MFC)
    Ohio State University Oral History Project (OSUOHP)
    Records of the Athletic Department (OAD)
    Records of the Athletic Department, Director's Office (RADO)
    Papers of Novice G. Fawcett (NGF)
Pasadena Museum of History, Pasadena, California
  Tournament of Roses Collection (TRC)
South Carolina Historical Center, Charleston
  Papers of Thomas R. Waring Jr. (TRW)
University of Alabama, Tuscaloosa
  University Archives, Mary Harmon Bryant Hall
    Papers of Frank Rose RG 837680 (FR1)
    Papers of Frank Rose RG 832848 (FR2)
    Papers of Frank Rose RG 831456 (FR3)
    Papers of Frank Rose RG 835552 (FR4)

Papers of J. Jefferson Bennett (JJB)
Records of the Athletic Department (AAD)

Paul W. Bryant Museum
Records of the Athletic Department (BAD)
Red Books (RB)
Vertical Files (VF)

University of California, Berkeley
Special Collections, Bancroft Library
Papers of the NAACP (NAACP)
Social Protest Collection (SPC)

University of California, Los Angeles, Los Angeles
University Archives, Powell Library
Administrative Files of the Chancellor's Office (CO)
Administrative Files of Chancellor Franklin D. Murphy (FDM)
Administrative Files of Robert A. Fischer (RAF)
Office of the Registrar, Statistics (ORS)
Records of the Academic Senate, Executive Office (ASEO)
Student Activism Collection (SAC)

Department of Special Collections, Young Research Library
Papers of Franklin D. Murphy (FDMP)
Civil Rights Movement in America Collection (CRM)
UCLA Oral History Project (UCLAOHP)

Offices of the ASUCLA, Kerchoff Hall
Minutes of the Student Legislative Council (SLC)

University of Notre Dame, South Bend, Indiana
Archives of University of Notre Dame, Hesburgh Library
Records of the National Football Foundation and Hall of Fame (UASI)
Football Programs, 1958–1960 (PATH)

University of Utah, Salt Lake City, Utah
Special Collections, Manuscript Division, J. Willard Marriot Library
Papers of David S. King (DSK)

Wheaton College, Wheaton, Illinois
Billy Graham Center Archives
Papers of Lemuel Nelson Bell (LNB)

Private Collections
Courtesy of Thomas J. Hamilton Jr.
Papers of Thomas J. Hamilton (TJH)

Government Documents

Hearings before the Permanent Subcommittee on Investigations of the Committee on Government Operations (Washington, DC: U.S. Government Printing Office, 1953)

Congressional Record
Federal Bureau of Investigation Case File #100–15769
Federal Bureau of Investigation Case File #105–385673

Newspapers and Periodicals

Alabama Journal
Atlanta Constitution
Baton Rouge Morning Advocate
Baton Rouge State-Times
Birmingham News
Birmingham Post-Herald
Birmingham World
California Eagle
Chicago Tribune
Columbus Citizen-Journal
Columbus Dispatch
Columbus Star
Lexington Herald-Leader
Louisiana State University *Daily Reveille*
Louisiana Weekly
Los Angeles Herald
Los Angeles Sentinel
Los Angeles Times
Mobile Press-Register
Montgomery Advertiser
New Orleans Times-Picayune
New York Times
Ohio State University *Lantern*
Ohio State University Monthly
Pasadena Star News
Salt Lake Tribune
Shreveport Times
Southern School News
Tuscaloosa News
University of Alabama *Crimson-White*
UCLA *Daily Bruin*
USC *Daily Trojan*
Washington Post

Secondary Sources

"A 'Bear' at 'Bama.'" *Time* (November 17, 1961): 72.
Abbott, Carl. "College Athletic Conferences and American Regions." *Journal of American Studies* 24, no. 2 (1990): 211–48.

Ackerman, William Coit. *My Fifty Year Love-In at UCLA*. Los Angeles: Fashion Press, 1969.

Adelson, Bruce. *Brushing Back Jim Crow: The Integration of Minor League Baseball in the American South*. Charlottesville: University of Virginia Press, 1999.

Anderson, Lars. *The All Americans*. New York: St. Martins' Press, 2004.

Andrews, Donald S. "The GI Bill and College Football." *Journal of Physical Education, Recreation, and Dance* 55 (September 1984): 23–26.

Arsenault, Raymond. *Freedom Riders: 1961 and the Struggle for Racial Justice*. New York: Oxford University Press, 2006.

Austin, Brad. "Protecting Athletics and the American War Defenses at Ohio State and across the Big Ten during the Great Depression." *Journal of Sport History* 27 (Summer 2000): 247–70.

Barra, Allen. *The Last Coach: A Life of Paul "Bear" Bryant*. New York: W. W. Norton, 2005.

Bartley, Numan. *The Rise of Massive Resistance: Race and Politics in the South during the 1950s*. Baton Rouge: Louisiana State University Press, 1969.

———. *The New South, 1945–1980*. Baton Rouge: Louisiana State University Press, 1995.

Bass, Amy. *Not the Triumph, but the Struggle: The 1968 Olympics and the Making of the Black Athlete*. Minneapolis: University of Minnesota Press, 2002.

Berges, Marshall. *Life and* Times *of Los Angeles: A Newspaper, a Family, and a City*. New York: Simon & Schuster, 1984.

Bernstein, Mark F. *Football: The Ivy League Origins of an American Obsession*. Philadelphia: University of Pennsylvania Press, 2001.

Bernstein, Shana Beth. "Building Bridges at Home in a Time of Global Conflict: Interracial Cooperation and the Fight for Civil Rights in Los Angeles, 1933–1954." PhD diss., Stanford University, 2003.

Blackwell, James. *On Brave Army Team: The Cheating Scandal that Rocked the Nation: West Point, 1951*. New York: Ballantine Books, 1996.

Blum, John Morton. *V Was for Victory: Politics and American Culture during World War II*. New York: Harcourt, 1976.

Borstelmann, Thomas. *The Cold War and the Color Line: American Race Relations in the Global Arena*. Cambridge, MA: Harvard University Press, 2001.

Boynoff, Sara. "Los Angeles: A Race Relations Success Story." *Look* (March 19, 1957): 25–29.

Branch, Taylor. *Parting the Waters: America in the King Years, 1954–1963*. New York: Simon & Schuster, 1988.

Brax, Ralph. *The First Student Movement: Student Activism in the United States during the 1930s*. Port Washington, NY: Kennikat Press, 1981.

Bryant, Paul W., and John Underwood. *Bear: The Good Life and Hard Times of Alabama's Coach Bryant*, 4th ed. New York: Little, Brown, 1975.

Butler, Mike. "Confederate Flags, Class Conflict, a Golden Egg and Castrated Bulls: A Historical Examination of the Ole-Miss-Mississippi State Football Rivalry." *Journal of Mississippi History* 59 (Summer 1997): 123–39.

Carter, Dan T. *The Politics of Rage: George Wallace, the Origins of the New Conservatism, and the Transformation of American Politics*. New York: Simon & Schuster, 1995.

Caute, David. *The Great Fear: The Anticommunist Purge under Truman and Eisenhower*. New York: Simon & Schuster, 1979.

Celizic, Mike. *The Biggest Game of Them All: Notre Dame, Michigan State, and the Fall of '66*. New York: Simon & Schuster, 1992.

Chafe, William H. *The Unfinished Journey: America since World War II*, 4th ed. New York: Oxford University Press, 1999.

Chappell, David L. *Inside Agitators: White Southerners in the Civil Rights Movement*. Baltimore: Johns Hopkins University Press, 1994.

———. *A Stone of Hope: Prophetic Religion and the Death of Jim Crow*. Chapel Hill: University of North Carolina Press, 2004.

Cherne, Leo. "How to Spot a Communist." *Look* (March 4, 1947): 21–25.

Clark, Daniel A. "'The Two Joes Meet—Joe College, Joe Veteran': The G.I. Bill, College Education, and Postwar American Culture." *History of Education Quarterly* 38 (Summer 1998): 165–89.

Clark, E. Culpepper. *The Schoolhouse Door: Segregation's Last Stand at the University of Alabama*. New York: Oxford University Press, 1993.

Clark, Kristine Setting. *Undefeated, Untied, and Uninvited: A Documentary of the 1951 University of San Francisco Dons Football Team*. Irvine, CA: Griffin, 2002.

Clark, Thomas D. *The Emerging South*, 2nd ed. New York: Oxford University Press, 1968.

Coates, James R. "Gentlemen's Agreement: The 1937 Maryland-Syracuse Football Game." MA thesis, University of Maryland, 1982.

Cohane, Tim. "Inside the West Coast Football Scandal." *Look* (August 7, 1956): 36–41.

Cohen, Robert. *When the Old Left Was Young: Student Radicals and America's First Student Movement, 1929–1941*. New York: Oxford University Press, 1993.

Cohen, Stanley. *The Game They Played*. New York: Farrar, Strauss & Giroux, 1977.

Cohodas, Nadine. *The Band Played Dixie: Race and the Liberal Conscience at Ole Miss*. New York: Free Press, 1997.

Collins, Robert M. "Growth Liberalism in the Sixties: Great Societies at Home and Grand Designs Abroad." In *The Sixties: From Memory to History*, edited by David Farber, 11–44. Chapel Hill: University of North Carolina Press, 1994.

Crawford, Russell E. "Consensus All-American: Sport and the Promotion of the American Way of Life during the Cold War, 1946–1965." PhD diss., University of Nebraska, 2004.

Daniel, Pete. *Lost Revolutions: The South in the 1950s*. Chapel Hill: University of North Carolina Press, 2000.

Davies, Richard O. *America's Obsession: Sports and Society since 1945*. Fort Worth, TX: Harcourt Brace, 1994.

de Graaf, Lawrence Brooks. "Negro Migration to Los Angeles, 1930 to 1950." PhD diss., University of California, Los Angeles, 1962.

———. "The City of Black Angels: Emergence of the Los Angeles Ghetto, 1890–1930." *Pacific Historical Review* 39 (August 1970): 323–52.

de Jong, Greta. *A Different Day: African American Struggles for Justice in Rural Louisiana, 1900–1970*. Chapel Hill: University of North Carolina Press, 2002.

Deford, Frank. "Code Breakers." *Sports Illustrated* (November 13, 2000): 82–98.

Dennis, Lawrence E., and Joseph F. Kauffman, eds. *The College and the Student: An Assessment of Relationships and Responsibilities in Undergraduate Education by Administrators, Faculty, and Public Officials*. Washington, DC: American Council on Education, 1966.

Dent, Jim. *Junction Boys: How Ten Days in Hell with Bear Bryant Forged a Championship Team*. New York: St. Martin's Press, 2000.

———. *The Undefeated: The Oklahoma Sooners and the Greatest Winning Streak in College Football History*. New York: St. Martin's Press, 2001.

Dickson, Edward A. *The University of California at Los Angeles: Its Origins and Formative Years*. Los Angeles: Friends of the UCLA Library, 1955.

Diez, Fermin. "The Popularity of Sports in America: An Analysis of the Values of Sports and the Role of Media." In *Researching American Culture: A Guide for Student Anthropologists*, edited by Conrad Phillip Kottak, 259–65. Ann Arbor: University of Michigan Press, 1982.

Dodge, William, Jr., Reuben B. Moulton, Harrison W. Sigworth, and Adrian C. Smith Jr. *Legends of Caltech*. Pasadena: California Institute of Technology Alumni Association, 1983.

———. *More Legends of Caltech*. Pasadena: California Institute of Technology Alumni Association, 1989.

Domer, Thomas Michael. "Sport in Cold War America, 1953–1963: The Diplomatic and Political Use of Sport in the Eisenhower and Kennedy Administrations." PhD diss., University of Wisconsin–Milwaukee, 1976.

Doyle, Andrew. "'Causes Won, Not Lost': College Football and the Modernization of the American South." *International Journal of the History of Sport* 11 (August 1994): 231–51.

———. "Bear Bryant: Symbol for an Embattled South." *Colby Quarterly* 32 (March 1996): 72–86.

———. "Turning the Tide: College Football and Southern Progressivism." *Southern Cultures* 3, no. 3 (1997): 28–51.

———. "Foolish and Useless Sport: The Southern Evangelical Crusade against Intercollegiate Football." *Journal of Sport History* 3 (Fall 1997): 317–40.

Doyle, Leo Andrew. "Causes Won, Not Lost: Football and Southern Culture, 1892–1983." PhD diss., Emory University, 1998.

Doyle, William. *An American Insurrection: James Meredith and the Battle of Oxford, Mississippi, 1962*. New York: Dell, 2003.

Dubay, Robert W. "Pigmentation and Pigskin: A Jones County Junior College Dilemma." *Journal of Mississippi History* 46, no. 1 (1984): 43–50.

———. "Politics, Pigmentation and Pigskin: The Georgia Tech Sugar Bowl Controversy of 1955." *Atlanta History* 39, no. 1 (1995): 21–35.

Dudziak, Mary. *Cold War Civil Rights and the Image of American Democracy*. Princeton, NJ: Princeton University Press, 2000.

Dunnavant, Keith. *Coach: The Life of Paul Bear Bryant*. New York: Simon & Schuster, 1996.

———. *The Fifty-Year Seduction: How Television Manipulated College Football, from the Birth of the Modern NCAA to the Creation of the BCS*. New York: St. Martin's Press, 2004.

Dyreson, Mark. "The Emergence of Consumer Culture and the Transformation of Physical Culture: American Sport in the 1920s." *Journal of Sport History* 16 (Winter 1989): 261–81.

———. "Regulating the Body and the Body Politic: American Sport, Bourgeois Culture, and the Language of Progress, 1880–1920." In *The New American Sports History: Recent Approaches and Perspectives*, edited by S. W. Pope, 121–44. Urbana: University of Illinois Press, 1997.

Efron, Edith. "The Two Joes Meet—Joe College, Joe Veteran." *New York Times Magazine* (June 16, 1946): 21, 55.

Engelhardt, Tom. *The End of Victory Culture: Cold War America and the Disillusioning of a Generation*. New York: Basic Books, 1995.

Epling, Robert Thomas. "Seasons of Change: Football Desegregation at Tennessee and the Transformation of the SEC, 1963–1967." PhD diss., University of Tennessee, 1997.

Eskew, Glenn T. *But for Birmingham: The Local and National Movements in the Civil Rights Struggle*. Chapel Hill: University of North Carolina Press, 1997.

Fairclough, Adam. *Race and Democracy: The Civil Rights Struggle in Louisiana, 1915–1972*. Athens: University of Georgia Press, 1995.

Falkner, David. *Great Time Coming: The Life of Jackie Robinson from Baseball to Birmingham*. New York: Simon & Schuster, 1995.

Finney, Peter. *Fighting Tigers, 1893–1993: One Hundred Years of LSU Football*. Baton Rouge: Louisiana State University Press, 1993.

Flamming, Douglas. *Bound for Freedom: Black Los Angeles in Jim Crow America*. Berkeley: University of California Press, 2005.

Frank, Stanley. "Saturday Afternoon Meat Grinders." *Collier's* (October 1, 1949): 54–59.

Gardner, Frank N. "The Place of Athletics in Higher Education: Hold That Tiger!" *Journal of Higher Education* 31 (October 1960): 364–68.

Garrigues, George. "Loud Bark and Curious Eyes: A History of the UCLA *Daily Bruin*, 1919–1955." MA thesis, University of California, Los Angeles, 1970.

———. "The Great Conspiracy against the UCLA *Daily Bruin*." *Southern California Quarterly* 59, no. 2 (1977): 217–30.

Gems, Gerald D. *For Pride, Patriarchy, and Profit: Football and the Incorporation of American Cultural Values*. Lanham, MD: Scarecrow Press, 2000.

Gietschier, Stephen P. "The 1951 Speaker's Rule at Ohio State." *Ohio History* 87, no. 3 (1978): 294–309.

Gilbert, James. *Men in the Middle: Searching for Masculinity in the 1950s*. Chicago: University of Chicago Press, 2005.

"Goodbye to 'Bama." *Time* (November 19, 1956): 58.

Gosnell, Joan. "Kickoffs and Kickbacks: The 1951 Football Scandal at William and Mary." MA thesis, College of William and Mary, 1990.

Gottlieb, Robert, and Irene Wolt. *Thinking Big: The Story of the* Los Angeles Times, *Its Publishers and their Influence on Southern California*. New York: G. P. Putnam's Sons, 1977.

Goulden, Marc Edward. "From Country Club to Rat Race: A Social History of College Students, 1920–1960." PhD diss., University of Wisconsin, 1995.

Graves, John Temple. *The Fighting South*. Reprint, Tuscaloosa: University of Alabama Press, 1985. Originally published 1943.

Greenberg, Milton. *The GI Bill: The Law That Changed America*. New York: Lickle, 1997.

———. "How the GI Bill Changed Higher Education." *Chronicle for Higher Education*, June 18, 2004: B9–B11.

Griswold, Robert L. "The 'Flabby American,' the Body, and the Cold War." In *A Shared Experience: Men, Women, and the History of Gender*, edited by Laura McCall and Donald Yacavone, 323–48. New York: New York University Press, 1998.

Gruensfelder, Melvin Henry. "A History of the Origin and Development of the Southeastern Conference." MS thesis, University of Illinois, 1964.

Halberstam, David. *The Fifties*. New York: Fawcett Columbine Books, 1993.

Hamilton, Andrew, and John B. Jackson. *UCLA on the Move during Fifty Golden Years, 1919–1969*. Los Angeles, CA: Ward Ritchie Press, 1969.

Hamlin, Rick. *Tournament of Roses: A One Hundred Year Celebration*. New York: McGraw-Hill, 1988.

Hebert, Mary Jacqueline. "Beyond Black and White: The Civil Rights Movement in Baton Rouge, Louisiana, 1945–1972." PhD diss., Louisiana State University, 1999.

Hodgson, Godfrey. *America in Our Time: From World War II to Nixon, What Happened and Why*. New York: Knopf, 1978.

Hornung, Paul. *Woody Hayes: A Reflection*. Champaign, IL: Sagamore, 1991.

Horowitz, Helen Lefkowitz. *Campus Life: Undergraduate Cultures from the End of the Eighteenth Century to the Present*. Chicago: University of Chicago Press, 1987.

Humphrey, Hubert H. "A Five-Point Fitness Program." *Journal of Health, Physical Education, and Recreation* 33 (October 1962): 21–22, 72–74.

Hurley, Andrew. *Diners, Bowling Alleys, and Trailer Parks: Chasing the American Dream in the Postwar Consumer Culture*. New York: Basic Books, 2001.

Hyman, Mervin D., and Gordon S. White Jr. *Big Ten Football: Its Life and Times, Great Coaches, Players, and Games*. New York: Macmillan, 1977.

Jaffa, Harry V. "L'Envoi to Woody Hayes." www.claremont.org/writings/precepts/030101jaffa.html.

James, Anthony W. "Paternalism's Demise: Blind Jim Ivy and Ole Miss, 1896–1955." *Mississippi Folklife* 28 (Spring 1995): 17–24.

———. "Defenders of Tradition: College Fraternities, Race and Gender, 1945–1980." PhD diss., University of Mississippi, 1998.

Jones, Jean Butts. "Father Is a Football Coach." *Saturday Evening Post* (November 20, 1954): 37, 170–72.

Kahn, Roger. "Halfbacks Carry the Mortgage." *Nation* (December 22, 1956): 539–41.

Kaplan, Joseph. "The Case for Big-Time Football." *Look* (December 12, 1956): 111–18.

———. "Clean House or Else." *Look* (December 9, 1958): 33–38.

Kemper, Kurt Edward. "Reformers in the Marketplace of Ideas: Student Activism and American Democracy in Cold War Los Angeles." PhD diss., Louisiana State University, 2000.

Kennedy, John F. "The Soft American." *Sports Illustrated* (December 26, 1960): 15–17.

Kerr, Robert L. "The Great White Father and the Antichrist: *Bud Wilkinson's Football Letter* as Cultural History." *American Journalism* 18, no. 3 (2001): 35–60.

Kuznick, Peter J., and James Gilbert, eds. *Rethinking Cold War Culture*. Washington, DC: Smithsonian Institution Press, 2001.

Lasch, Christopher. *The Culture of Narcissism: American Life in an Age of Diminishing Expectations*. New York: Norton, 1978.

Lee, Eugene. *The Origins of the Chancellorship: The Buried Report of 1948*. Berkeley, CA: Center for the Studies in Higher Education and Institute of Governmental Studies, 1995.

Leonard, Kevin Allen. "'In the Interest of All Races': African Americans and Interracial Cooperation in Los Angeles during World War II." In *Seeking El Dorado: African Americans in California*, edited by Lawrence B. de Graaf, Kevin Mulroy, and Quintard Taylor, 309–39. Seattle: University of Washington Press, 2001.

———. "'I Am Sure You Can Read between the Lines': Cold War Anti-Communism and the NAACP in Los Angeles." *Journal of the West* 44 (Spring 2005): 16–23.

Lester, Robin. *Stagg's University: The Rise and Decline of Big-Time Football at the University of Chicago*. Chicago: University of Illinois Press, 1995.

Leventhal, Willy Siegel. "Rick Tuttle and the Ghosts of Mississippi." *UCLAlumni Magazine* 13 (September 2000): 10–13.

Lewontin, R. C. "The Cold War and the Transformation of the Academy." In *The Cold War and the University: Toward an Intellectual History of the Postwar Years*, edited by Noam Chomsky, 1–34. New York: New Press, 1998.

Lombardo, John. *A Fire to Win: The Life and Times of Woody Hayes*. New York: St. Martin's Press, 2005.

Lowen, Rebecca. *Creating the Cold War University: The Transformation of Stanford*. Berkeley: University of California Press, 1997.

MacCambridge, Michael. *America's Game: The Epic Story of How Pro Football Captured a Nation*. New York: Random House. 2004.

Mack, Karen. "Our Peerless Leaders: The Men Who Shaped UCLA." *UCLA Magazine*, 75th anniversary issue (Fall 1994): 38–39.

Mandelbaum, Michael. *The Meaning of Sports: Why Americans Watch Baseball, Football, and Basketball and What They See When They Do*. New York: Perseus, 2004.

Martin, Charles. "Jim Crow in the Gymnasium: The Integration of College Basketball in the American South." *International Journal of the History of Sport* 10, no. 1 (1993): 68–86.

———. "Racial Exclusion and Intersectional Rivalries: The Rise and Fall of the Gentlemen's Agreement in Big-Time College Football." Paper given at the annual meeting of the Southern Historical Association, New Orleans, LA, 1995.

———. "Racial Change and 'Big-Time' College Football in Georgia: The Age of Segregation, 1892–1957." *Georgia Historical Quarterly* 80, no. 3 (1996): 532–62.

———. "Integrating New Year's Day: The Racial Politics of College Bowl Games in the American South." *Journal of Sport History* 24 (Fall 1997): 358–77.

May, Elaine Tyler. *Homeward Bound: American Families in the Cold War Era*. New York: Basic Books, 1988.

McCollum, John D. *Pac-10 Football: The Rose Bowl Conference*. Seattle: Writing Works, 1982.

McDougal, Dennis. *Privileged Son: Otis Chandler and the Rise and Fall of the "L.A. Times" Dynasty*. Cambridge, MA: Perseus Publishing, 2001.

McMillen, Neil. *The Citizens' Council: Organized Resistance to the Second Reconstruction, 1954–1964*. Champaign: University of Illinois Press, 1971.

McWilliams, Carey. *Southern California Country: An Island on the Land*. New York: Duell, Sloan & Pearce, 1946.

———. *California: The Great Exception*. New York: Current Books, 1949.

McWhorter, Diane. *Carry Me Home: Birmingham, Alabama, and the Climactic Battle of the Civil Rights Revolution*. New York: Simon & Schuster, 2001.

Meier, August, and Elliot Rudwick, *CORE: A Study in the Civil Rights Movement*. Champaign: University of Illinois Press, 1975.

Meikle, Jeffrey L. *American Plastic: A Cultural History*. New Brunswick, NJ: Rutgers University Press, 1995.

Mennell, James. "The Service Football Program of World War I: Its Impact on the Popularity of the Game." *Journal of Sport History* 16 (Winter 1989): 248–60.

Michelson, Herb, and Dave Newhouse. *Rose Bowl Football since 1902*. New York: Stein & Day, 1977.

Miller, Patrick B. "Athletes in Academe: College Sports and American Culture, 1850–1920." PhD diss., University of California, 1987.

———. "Harvard and the Color Line: The Case of Lucien Alexis." In *Sports in Massachusetts: Historical Essays*, edited by Ronald Story, 1–31. Westfield: Institute for Massachusetts Studies, 1991.

———. "The Manly, the Moral, and the Proficient: College Sport in the New South." *Journal of Sport History* 24 (Fall 1997): 285–316.

———. "Slouching towards a New Expediency: College Football and the Color Line during the Depression Decade." *American Studies* 40 (Fall 1999): 5–30.

Morris, Bonnie. *The High School Scene in the Fifties: Voices from West Los Angeles*. Westport, CT: Bergin & Garvey, 1997.

Morris, Willie. *The Courting of Marcus Dupree*. New York: Dell Books, 1983.

———. *Terrains of the Heart and Other Essays on Home*. Oxford, MS: Yoknopatawpha Press, 1981.

Mrozek, Donald J. "The Cult and Ritual of Toughness in Cold War America." *In Rituals and Ceremonies in Pop Culture*, edited by Ray B. Browne, 178–91. Bowling Green, OH: Bowling Green State University Popular Press, 1980.

———. *Sport and American Mentality, 1880–1910*. Knoxville: University of Tennessee Press, 1983.

———. "The Interplay of Metaphor and Practice in the U.S. Defense Establishment's Use of Sport, 1940–1950." *Journal of American Culture* 7, no.1–2 (1984): 54–59.

———. "The Habit of Victory: The American Military and the Cult of Manliness." *In Manliness and Morality: Middle Class Masculinity in Britain and America, 1800–1940*, edited by J. A. Mangan and James Walvin, 220–39. New York: St. Martin's Press, 1987.

———. "Sport in American Life: From National Health to Personal Fulfillment,

1890–1940." In *Fitness in American Culture: Images of Health, Sport, and the Body, 1830–1940*, edited by Kathryn Grover, 18–45. Amherst: University of Massachusetts Press, 1989.

Mulé, Marty. *Eye of the Tiger: 100 Years of LSU Football*. Collingdale, PA: Diane, 1993.

Navasky, Victor. *Naming Names: The Social Costs of McCarthyism*. New York: Viking Press, 1980.

Noble, Donald R. Introduction to *Mud on the Stars*, by William Bradford Huie. Tuscaloosa: University of Alabama Press, 1996.

Olson, Jack. "The Black Athlete, Part II: Pride and Prejudice." *Sports Illustrated* (July 7, 1968): 20–31.

Oriard, Michael. *Reading Football: How the Popular Press Created an American Spectacle*. Chapel Hill: University of North Carolina Press, 1993.

———. *King Football: Sport and Spectacle in the Golden Age of Radio and Newsreels, Movies and Magazines and the Popular Press*. Chapel Hill: University of North Carolina Press, 2001.

Oshinsky, David. *A Conspiracy So Immense: The World of Joe McCarthy*. New York: Free Press, 1983.

Otten, C. Michael. *University Authority and the Student: The Berkeley Experience*. Berkeley: University of California Press, 1970.

Ownby, Ted. "Manhood, Memory, and White Men's Sports in the Recent American South." *International Journal of the History of Sport* 2 (August 1998): 103–18.

Perkins, John A. *Plain Talk from a Campus*. Newark, NJ: University of Delaware, 1959.

Perlstein, Rick. *Before the Storm: Barry Goldwater and the Unmaking of the American Consensus*. New York: Hill & Wang, 2001.

Pessen, Edward. *Losing Our Souls: The American Experience in the Cold War*. Chicago: Ivan R. Dee, 1993.

Peterson, Robert W. *Pigskin: The Early Years of Pro Football*. New York: Oxford University Press, 1997.

Pierce, Charles P. "Black Sunday." *Sports Illustrated* (November 24, 2003): 56–62.

Plant, Marcus L. "The Place of Intercollegiate Athletics in Higher Education: Faculty Control." *Journal of Higher Education* 32 (January 1961): 1–8.

Pollard, James E. *Ohio State Athletics, 1875–1959*. Columbus: Ohio State University Athletic Department, 1959.

Pont, Sally. *Fields of Honor: The Golden Age of College Football and the Men Who Created It*. New York: Harcourt, 2001.

Pope, Steven W. "An Army of Athletes: Playing Fields, Battlefields, and the American Military Sporting Experience, 1890–1920." *Journal of Military History* 59 (July 1995): 435–56.

Powell, John Talbott. "The Development and Influence of Faculty Representation in the Control of Intercollegiate Sport within the Intercollegiate Conference of Faculty Representatives from Its Inception in January 1895 to July 1963." PhD diss., University of Illinois, 1965.

Price, Frank James. *Troy H. Middleton: A Biography*. Baton Rouge: Louisiana State University Press, 1974.

Reddick, L. D. "The New Race Relations Frontier." *Journal of Educational Sociology* 19, no. 3 (1945): 129–45.

Riesman, David, and Reuel Denney. "Football in America: A Study in Culture Diffusion." *American Quarterly* 3, no. 4 (1951): 309–25.

Riesman, David, Reuel Denney, and Nathan Glazer. *The Lonely Crowd: A Study of the Changing American Character*. New Haven, CT: Yale University Press, 1950.

Roberts, Randy, and James Olson. *Winning Is the Only Thing: Sports in America since 1945*. Baltimore: Johns Hopkins University Press, 1989.

Rogers, William, Robert Ward, Leah Rawls Atkins, and Wayne Flint. *Alabama: The History of a Deep South State*. Tuscaloosa: University of Alabama Press, 1994.

Rominger, Donald W. Jr., "From Playing Field to Battleground: The United States Navy V-5 Preflight Program in World War II." *Journal of Sport History* 12 (Winter 1985): 252–64.

Rosen, Charles S. *The Scandals of '51: How Gamblers Almost Killed College Basketball*. New York: Seven Stories Press, 1999.

Rosenberg, Norman L., and Emily S. Rosenberg. *In Our Times: America since World War II*, 5th ed. Englewood Cliffs, NJ: Prentice Hall, 1995.

Russell, Fred. "Pigskin Preview." *Saturday Evening Post* (September 17, 1949): 30–31, 127–32.

Samuelson, Rube. *The Rose Bowl Game*. Garden City, NY: Doubleday, 1951.

Sandoval, Sally Jane. "Ghetto Growing Pains: The Impact of Negro Migration on the City of Los Angeles, 1940–1960." MA thesis, California State University, Fullerton, 1974.

Scanlon, John. "The Scent of Roses: Ohio State Takes a Fresh Look at Big-Time Sports." *Saturday Review* (April 21, 1962): 56–78.

Schoor, Gene. *100 Years of Army-Navy Football*. New York: Henry Holt, 1989.

Scott, Harry Alexander. *Competitive Sports in Schools and Colleges*. New York: Harper & Bros., 1951.

Shapiro, Beth J. "Intercollegiate Athletics and Big-Time Sport at Michigan State University: Or 'The Difference between Good and Great Is a Little Extra Effort.'" PhD diss., Michigan State University, 1982.

———. "John Hannah and the Growth of Big-Time Intercollegiate Athletics at Michigan State University." *Journal of Sport History* 10 (Fall 1983): 26–40.

Sides, Josh. "'You Understand My Condition': The Civil Rights Congress in the Los Angeles African-American Community, 1946–1952." *Pacific Historical Review* 67 (May 1998): 233–57.

———. *L.A. City Limits: African American Los Angeles from the Great Depression to the Present*. Berkeley: University of California Press, 2003.

Smith, Marshall. "Sad News from the Campus: Nobody Loves the Football Hero Now." *Life* (November 11, 1957): 149–60.

Smith, Marshall, and Richard Oulahan Jr. "Football Is Pricing Itself out of Business." *Life* (October 16, 1960): 60–65.

Smith, Ronald A. *Sports and Freedom: The Rise of Big-Time College Athletics*. New York: Oxford University Press, 1988.

———. *Play-by-Play: Radio, Television, and Big-Time College Sport*. Baltimore: Johns Hopkins University Press, 2001.

Smith, Thomas G. "Outside the Pale: The Exclusion of Blacks from the National Football League, 1934–1946." *Journal of Sport History* 15 (Winter 1988): 225–81.

Solomon, Eric. "Free Speech at Ohio State." *Atlantic Monthly* 65 (November 1965): 119–23.

Sperber, Murray. *Onward to Victory: The Crises That Shaped College Sports*. New York: Henry Holt, 1998.

Spivey, Donald. "'End Jim Crow in Sports': The Protest at New York University, 1940–1941." *Journal of Sport History* 15 (Winter 1988): 282–303.

Springer, Steve, and Michael Arkush. *60 Years of USC-UCLA Football*. Stamford, CT: Longmeadow Press, 1991.

Starr, Jack. "The Big New Battle in the Big 10." *Look* (June 25, 1957): 147–53.

Starr, Jack, and Clark Mollenhoff. "Football Scandal Hits the Big 10." *Look* (August 21, 1956): 19–25.

———. "The Big 10's Secret Report." *Look* (October 30, 1956): 34–42.

"Stern's Law." *Nation* (November 15, 1958): 350–51.

Sternberg, Neil. *If at All Possible, Involve a Cow: The Book of College Pranks*. New York: St. Martin's Press, 1992.

"Still Ivied Autumn?" *Newsweek* (October 15, 1956): 75–78.

Stoddard, Tom. *Turnaround: The Untold Story of Bear Bryant's First Year at Alabama*. Birmingham, AL: Black Belt Press, 1996.

Stone, Richard. "The Graham Plan of 1935: An Aborted Crusade to De-emphasize College Athletics." *North Carolina Historical Review* 64, no. 3 (1987): 274–93.

Stout, Glenn. "Jim Crow, Halfback." *Boston Magazine* (December 1987): 124–34.

Stowe, William McFerrin. "Willie Rainach and the Defense of Segregation in Louisiana, 1954–1959." PhD diss., Rice University, 1989.

Strode, Woody, and Sam Young. *Goal Dust: The Warm and Candid Memoir of a Pioneer Black Athlete and Actor*. Lanham, MD: Madison Books, 1990.

Susman, Warren. *Culture as History: The Transformation of American Society in the Twentieth Century*. New York: Pantheon Books, 1984.

Taylor, Quintard. *In Search of the Racial Frontier: African Americans in the American West, 1528–1990*. New York: W. W. Norton, 1998.

Thelin, John R. *The Cultivation of Ivy: A Saga of the College in America*. Cambridge, MA: Schenkman, 1976.

———. *Games Colleges Play: Scandal and Reform in Intercollegiate Athletics*. Baltimore: Johns Hopkins University, 1994.

———. *A History of American Higher Education*. Baltimore: Johns Hopkins University Press, 2004.

Thompson, Wade. "My Crusade against Football." *Nation* (April 11, 1959): 313–16.

Tindall, George Brown. "The Benighted South: Origins of a Modern Image." *Virginia Quarterly Review* 40 (Spring 1964): 281–94.

———. *The Emergence of the New South, 1913–1945*. Baton Rouge: Louisiana State University Press, 1967.

Van Leuven, Hendrik. *Touchdown UCLA! The Complete Account of Bruin Football*. Tomball, TX: Strode, 1982.

Wakefield, Wanda Ellen. *Playing to Win: Sports and the American Military, 1898–1945*. New York: SUNY Press, 1997.

Wallace, Francis. "Football's Black Market." *Saturday Evening Post* (November 9, 1946): 20–21, 145.

Walsh, Christopher J. *Where Football Is King: A History of the SEC*. Lanham, MD: Taylor Trade, 2006.

Watterson, John Sayle. *College Football: History, Spectacle, Controversy*. Baltimore: John Hopkins University Press, 2000.

Weisenburger, Francis P. *History of the Ohio State University*, vol. 10: *The Fawcett Years, 1956–1972*. Columbus: Ohio State University Press, 1972.

Weiss, Lawrence G. "Goldwater and Colorado U." *Nation* (December 8, 1962): 402–4.

Weiss, Philip. "The Most Powerful Fraternity in America." *Esquire* (April 1992): 102–10.

Whitfield, Stephen J. *The Culture of the Cold War*. Baltimore: Johns Hopkins University Press, 1991.

———. "The Road to Rapprochement: Khrushchev's 1959 Visit to America." In *The Other Fifties: Interrogations of Midcentury American Icons*, edited by Joel Foreman, 307–32. Champaign: University of Illinois Press, 1997.

Whittingham, Richard. *Rites of Autumn: The Story of College Football*. New York: Free Press, 2001.

Wills, Garry. *John Wayne's America*. New York: Touchstone Books, 1997.

Wilson, Charles Reagan. *Judgment and Grace in Dixie: Southern Faiths from Faulkner to Elvis*. Athens: University of Georgia Press, 1995.

Wooden, John R., as told to Jack Tobin. *They Call Me Coach*. Waco, TX: Word Books, 1972.

Zang, David W. "Winning and Losing in the Vietnam Era at the University of Pennsylvania." PhD diss., University of Maryland, 1984.

Zinn, Howard. "A Fate Worse Than Integration." *Harper's Magazine* (August 1959): 53–56.

Zweiback, Adam J. "The 21 Turncoat GIs: Nonrepatriates and the Political Culture of the Korean War." *Historian* 60 (Winter 1988): 345–62.

Index

KURT EDWARD KEMPER is an associate professor of history at Dakota State University in Madison, South Dakota.

Sport and Society

A Sporting Time: New York City and the Rise of Modern Athletics, 1820–70 *Melvin L. Adelman*

Sandlot Seasons: Sport in Black Pittsburgh *Rob Ruck*

West Ham United: The Making of a Football Club *Charles Korr*

Beyond the Ring: The Role of Boxing in American Society *Jeffrey T. Sammons*

John L. Sullivan and His America *Michael T. Isenberg*

Television and National Sport: The United States and Britain *Joan M. Chandler*

The Creation of American Team Sports: Baseball and Cricket, 1838–72 *George B. Kirsch*

City Games: The Evolution of American Urban Society and the Rise of Sports *Steven A. Riess*

The Brawn Drain: Foreign Student-Athletes in American Universities *John Bale*

The Business of Professional Sports *Edited by Paul D. Staudohar and James A. Mangan*

Fritz Pollard: Pioneer in Racial Advancement *John M. Carroll*

A View from the Bench: The Story of an Ordinary Player on a Big-Time Football Team (*formerly* Go Big Red! The Story of a Nebraska Football Player) *George Mills*

Sport and Exercise Science: Essays in the History of Sports Medicine *Edited by Jack W. Berryman and Roberta J. Park*

Minor League Baseball and Local Economic Development *Arthur T. Johnson*

Harry Hooper: An American Baseball Life *Paul J. Zingg*

Cowgirls of the Rodeo: Pioneer Professional Athletes *Mary Lou LeCompte*

Sandow the Magnificent: Eugen Sandow and the Beginnings of Bodybuilding *David Chapman*

Big-Time Football at Harvard, 1905: The Diary of Coach Bill Reid *Edited by Ronald A. Smith*

Leftist Theories of Sport: A Critique and Reconstruction *William J. Morgan*

Babe: The Life and Legend of Babe Didrikson Zaharias *Susan E. Cayleff*

Stagg's University: The Rise, Decline, and Fall of Big-Time Football at Chicago *Robin Lester*

Muhammad Ali, the People's Champ *Edited by Elliott J. Gorn*

People of Prowess: Sport, Leisure, and Labor in Early Anglo-America *Nancy L. Struna*

The New American Sport History: Recent Approaches and Perspectives *Edited by S. W. Pope*

Making the Team: The Cultural Work of Baseball Fiction *Timothy Morris*

Making the American Team: Sport, Culture, and the Olympic Experience *Mark Dyreson*

Viva Baseball! Latin Major Leaguers and Their Special Hunger *Samuel O. Regalado*

Touching Base: Professional Baseball and American Culture in the Progressive Era (rev. ed.) *Steven A. Riess*

Red Grange and the Rise of Modern Football *John M. Carroll*

Golf and the American Country Club *Richard J. Moss*

Extra Innings: Writing on Baseball *Richard Peterson*

Global Games *Maarten Van Bottenburg*

The Sporting World of the Modern South *Edited by Patrick B. Miller*

The End of Baseball As We Knew It: The Players Union, 1960–81 *Charles P. Korr*

Rocky Marciano: The Rock of His Times *Russell Sullivan*

Saying It's So: A Cultural History of the Black Sox Scandal *Daniel A. Nathan*

The Nazi Olympics: Sport, Politics, and Appeasement in the 1930s *Edited by Arnd Krüger and William Murray*

The Unlevel Playing Field: A Documentary History of the African American Experience in Sport *David K. Wiggins and Patrick B. Miller*

Sports in Zion: Mormon Recreation, 1890–1940 *Richard Ian Kimball*

Sweet William: The Life of Billy Conn *Andrew O'Toole*

Sports in Chicago *Edited by Elliot J. Gorn*

The Chicago Sports Reader *Edited by Steven A. Riess and Gerald R. Gems*

College Football and American Culture in the Cold War Era *Kurt Edward Kemper*

REPRINT EDITIONS

The Nazi Olympics *Richard D. Mandell*

Sports in the Western World (2d ed.) *William J. Baker*

Jesse Owens: An American Life *William J. Baker*

The University of Illinois Press
is a founding member of the
Association of American University Presses.

Composed in 9/13 ITC Stone Serif
with ITC Stone Sans display
by Jim Proefrock
at the University of Illinois Press

University of Illinois Press
1325 South Oak Street
Champaign, IL 61820-6903
www.press.uillinois.edu